Medieval Arms & Armour: A Sourcebook

Armour and Weapons

ISSN 1746-9449

Series Editors

Kelly DeVries
Robert W. Jones
Robert C. Woosnam-Savage

Throughout history armour and weapons have been not merely the preserve of the warrior in battles and warfare, but potent symbols in their own right (the sword of chivalry, the heraldic shield) representing the hunt and hall as well as the battlefield. This series aims to provide a forum for critical studies of all aspects of arms and armour and their technologies, from the end of the Roman Empire to the dawn of the modern world; both new research and works of synthesis are encouraged.

New proposals for the series are welcomed; they should be sent to the publisher at the address below.

Boydell & Brewer Limited
PO Box 9
Woodbridge, Suffolk, IP12 3DF
editorial@boydell.co.uk

Medieval Arms & Armour: A Sourcebook

Volume I: The Fourteenth Century

Ralph Moffat

THE BOYDELL PRESS

The right of Ralph Moffat to be identified as
the author of this work has been asserted in accordance with
sections 77 and 78 of the Copyright, Designs and Patents Act 1988

First published 2022
Paperback edition 2025
The Boydell Press, Woodbridge

ISBN 978 1 83765 252 5 Paperback
ISBN 978 1 78327 676 9 Hardback

The Boydell Press is an imprint of Boydell & Brewer Ltd
PO Box 9, Woodbridge, Suffolk IP12 3DF, UK
and of Boydell & Brewer Inc.
668 Mt Hope Avenue, Rochester, NY 14620–2731, USA
website: www.boydellandbrewer.com

A CIP catalogue record for this book is available
from the British Library

The publisher has no responsibility for the continued existence or accuracy of URLs for
external or third-party internet websites referred to in this book, and does not guarantee
that any content on such websites is, or will remain, accurate or appropriate

For Karen Watts – an apprentice could not have wished for a better sorcerer.

Contents

List of Illustrations

All the illustrations are reproduced with the generous assistance of the Friends of Glasgow Museums.

List of Documents

Preface

And well did he (my scholar Galeas of Mantua) say that without books, one can be neither a good master nor scholar of this art (of combat). And I, Fiore, confirm it, for this art is so vast that there is not a man in the world with such a good memory that he can hold in his mind even a quarter part of this art without books. For one *cannot* be a master knowing but the quarter part of this art.

Ben chello diseua che sença libri non sara çamay nissuno bon magistro ne scolaro in questa arte E io fior lo confermo pero che quest arte e si longa che lo non e al mondo homo de si granda memoria che podesse tenere a mente sença libri la quarta parte di quest arte Adoncha cum la quarta parte di quest arte non sapiando piu non saria magistro.

—Fiore dei Liberi, *Il Fior di battaglia*, c. 1400.[1]

This sourcebook is born of a lifelong passion for medieval arms and armour. Through it, I aim to share this passion with others. When handling real weapons or pieces of armour at a table, peering at them through the glass of a display case, or admiring artistic depictions such as tomb effigies, burning questions push themselves to the forefront of my mind: how can we animate these static objects? What if the (mainly) men who made, fixed, and bore them could talk to us? What would they say? What tales would they tell? And, most importantly of all, *how* can we make these things happen?

There are numerous approaches to this field of study. Three of the main ones are: the practice of living history, crafting, and the detailed examination of objects and documentary evidence. I am far too fragile of body and pusillanimous of mind for living history, suffering from that weakness of combative will shared with those the master jouster King Duarte I classifies as failing 'de segurança du suas voontades'.[2] As to a life dedicated to craft, I proved too scrawny of limb – the beating of hammer on anvil causing 'apprentice elbow' – and too delicate of eardrum. The chronicler Froissart, with his fingers in his ears, tells us of one battle that:

---

[1]   Los Angeles, J. P. Getty Museum, MS Ludvig XV 13, fol. 1r–fol. 1v.
[2]   Duarte, *Livro da ensinança de bem cavalgar*, n. ed. (Lisbon, 1843), p. 598; S. Anglo, *The Martial Arts of Renaissance Europe* (New Haven, CT, 2000), p. 232.

even if all the heaumers (plate armourers) of Paris *and* Brussels were working together practising their craft, they couldn't make such a din as that made by the fighters and the blows on basinets!

se tous les heaulmiers de Paris et de Bruxelles feussent ensemble leur mestier faisant ilz neussent pas mene ne fait greigneur noise comme les combatans et les ferans sur ces bacinetz faisoient.[3]

So not for me then the raging battlefield or roaring forge but the quiet sanctuary of the museum store, library, and archive. Although not the physical one of the knight errant, mine is a quest all the same. My gauntlets are cotton gloves, my sword a magnifying glass, my lance a sharp pencil, my shield a pad of paper, the windmills at which I tilt obscure script on ragged parchment and replacement rivets on a medieval helmet. Yet by undertaking this quest, timid though it may be, I hope in this volume the reader will discover not one Holy Grail but many.

The study of arms and armour faces a perennial problem: lack of material culture. A canny veteran advised Edward II to arrange a long truce with the warlike Scots so that 'thair armyng sall worth ald / And be rottyn, distroyit, or sald'.[4] It is for this reason that the number of objects that *do* survive can be considered the mere tip of an enormous iceberg. Below the waterline lurks the vast amount of arms and armour that was once in use but is now lost. Some fantastic pieces have come down to us: the accrued collection of a noble family in Churburg Castle Armoury in the South Tyrol,[5] chance finds from the wars between Christian forces and the Ottomans,[6] to name but a few. Detailed examination of excavated material has greatly added to our knowledge.[7] It is necessary to highlight that the vast majority of these survivals are from the second half of the century. The Braidwood Gill helm crown-plate, found in 1820 in South Lanarkshire (see Figure 28) reflects the fragmentary nature of the finds from the first half.[8] And there is always the tantalizing prospect that many, many more artefacts are yet to see the light of day. It is because of this paucity that my chosen approach to the study will prove to be of great benefit for our better understanding and engagement.

---

3   Rouen, Bibliothèque municipale, MS U28 (1147), fol. 158r–fol. 158v. MS images reproduced in HRI *Online Froissart*, ed. P. Ainsworth and G. Croenen (Sheffield, 2013).

4   Barbour's *Bruce*, ed. A. A. M. Duncan (Edinburgh, 1997), p. 347.

5   O. Trapp, *The Armoury of the Castle of Churburg*, trans. J. G. Mann, 2 vols (London, 1929); M. Scalini, *The Armoury of the Castle of Churburg* (Udine, 1996).

6   C. J. ffoulkes, 'Italian Armour from Chalcis in the Ethnological Museum, Athens', *Archaeologia* 62 (1911), pp. 381–90; S. W. Pyhrr, 'Armor from the Imperial Ottoman Arsenal', *Metropolitan Museum Journal* 24 (1989), pp. 85–116.

7   One of the most extensive excavations is published in B. Thordeman, *Armour from the Battle of Wisby, 1361*, 2 vols (Copenhagen, 1939). Other chance finds include: a basinet found in 1881 during the rebuilding of Schloss Braunfels, Hesse (see Figure 8) and J. G. Mann, 'The Visor of a 14th-Century Bascinet found at Pevensey Castle', *Antiquaries Journal* 16 (1936), pp. 412–19. M. Rijkelijkhuizen and M. Volken, 'A poor man's armour? Late-medieval leather armour from excavations in the Netherlands', *Leather in Warfare: Attack, Defence and the Unexpected*, ed. Q. Mould (Leeds, 2017), pp. 57–77 is one of many studies that reveals the wealth of material yet to be investigated.

8   J. G. Scott, 'Two 14th-Century Helms found in Scotland', *Journal of the Arms & Armour Society* 4 (1962), pp. 68–71.

Acknowledgements

I would like to thank Profs Peter Ainsworth, Sydney Anglo, Ros Brown-Grant, Wendy Childs, Kelly DeVries, Noel Fallows, Kouky Fianu, Richard Firth Green, J. R. S. Phillips, Nigel Ramsay, Clifford J. Rogers, Greame Small, Matthew Strickland, Jane H. M. Taylor, David Trotter, Drs Adrian Ailes, Bruce Barker-Benfield, Claude Blair, Steve Boardman, Dirk Breiding, David Caldwell, Toby Capwell, John Cox, Mario Damen, Geert De Wilde, Paul Dryburgh, Nickolas Dupras, Bill Flynn, Robert W. Jones, Andy King, Sarah Lynch, Alastair Macdonald, Martin MacGregor, Elizabeth McDonald, Ralph McLean, Malcolm Mercer, Lauren Moreau, Alan V. Murray, Bernard Nurse, Marianne O'Doherty, Zsuzsa Papp, Tony Pollard, Alasdair Raffe, Christopher Retsch, Thom Richardson, David Scott-Macnab, Debra Strickland, Mary Swan, Pierre Terjanian, Mark Tizzoni, Alex Woolf, Messrs Arthur Credland, Ian Bottomley, Harry Campbell, Clive Cheeseman (Richmond Herald), Keith Dowen, Andrew Gray, Mark Hall, Tony Hirst, Stuart Ivinson, Arne Koets, John Lambert, Philip Lankester, Jean-Marie Lebeurier, Matthew Payne, Frédéric Petot, Graeme Rimer, Jim Spriggs, Nathan Williams, Tony Willis, R. C. Woosnam-Savage, Henry Yallop, Ms Anne-Marie Arnaud Ibres, Marion Bernard, Barbara Canepa, Emily Champion, Julia Cook, Sophie Ellis, Kate Husband, Vida Milovanovic, Caroline Palmer, Nicola Pink, Dorina Salim, Stephanie Taylor, Barbara Wright, my colleagues at Glasgow Museums, the Royal Armouries, Leeds, and the universities of Edinburgh and Leeds, the team at Boydell, and my family Frank and Norah Mayo, Scott and Caroline Moffat, and Dr Jennie Morgan.

Using the Sourcebook

This study can be used simply as a glossary to quickly check meanings. The documents are printed in chronological order. Each is numbered. When referred to in the introduction to the source-types and illustrated glossary the document number is in bold font in parentheses, e.g. (**134**). The sourcebook can, however, be used at a more advanced level in order for the reader to build up their own better understanding of the subject. In this section I provide two examples of how our sources – textual and material – work hand in glove to increase our knowledge. The first is development and the second relates to living history.

1. Development

This sourcebook does not seek to provide a detailed study of the development and evolution of arms and armour. What it does do, however, is furnish researchers with solid evidence – evidence that is essential to any future study in the field.[1] Here are two examples:

First, take schynbalds: a type of shin defence. No physical specimens have yet been positively identified. In our sources they are described as being 'of plate' and pieces of iron for their making are listed in Scarborough Castle (**39**); thus we can conclude that they were a solid metal defence. Their form is nowhere described. They are recorded most frequently in the earlier part of the century. There *is* reference to them in an inventory of 1397 (**144**). This could well, however, be interpreted as their forming part of much old harness piled up in Pleshey Castle. Such appearance – then disappearance – is telling. This might hint at the fact that they did not offer such good protection to the lower leg as did the fully-enclosing greave and were therefore superseded. We can draw the conclusion that they were a defence for the front of the

---

[1] The rude health of the discipline is evidenced by a flourishing of studies. Just a few examples from Anglophone scholarship alone are: T. Capwell, *Armour of the English Knight, 1400–1450* (London, 2015); T. Richardson, *The Tower Armoury in the Fourteenth Century* (Leeds, 2016); K. Dowen, 'The Introduction and Development of Plate Armour in Western Europe, c. 1250–1350', *Fasciculi Archaeologiae Historicae* 30 (2017), pp. 19–28.

leg only. This type of evidence can be employed, for example, by scholars working in such fields as medieval literature.[2]

Second, an arming doublet is recorded amongst the possessions of an English knight in 1387 (**131**). There are no extant medieval arming doublets. We know from medieval artwork and two arming treatises of the mid-fifteenth century that they were the padded fabric foundation to which the metal plates of a harness are laced.[3] This is a small, yet significant, contribution to our knowledge of the development of plate armour. This manner of affixing the harness is currently understood to have come into use at the beginning of the fifteenth century.[4] Furthermore, although this arming doublet is listed in an inventory of 1387, its owner – Sir Simon Burley (born c. 1336) – had been soldiering since the 1350s.

As well as the attachment of plates, the arming doublet and matching hose (padded legwear) have pieces of mail affixed to them. These sections – known as voiders – fill the gaps (voids) that go unprotected by the plates: the armpit, crook of the elbow, groin, rump, back of the thigh and knee, and the gap at the ankle between greave and sabaton. A payment is made for complete legharness with voiders in 1378 (**105**) and 30 small pieces of mail 'in the form of voiders' are inventoried in 1397 (**143**). Thus these three fleeting references to schynbalds, the arming doublet, and voiders in our sources serve to necessitate a reassessment of the accepted chronology of the design and use of plate armour.

2. Living History

There is much practical information for practitioners of living history – the fighters, crafters, and artists: people who devote time, effort, and expertise bringing the past to life to draw new audiences into the weird and wonderful world of the Middle Ages. To give just one example: fabric and leather lining of harness. Don Luis Zapata de Chaves (1526–95), an authority on jousting, instructs his reader that a suitable harness must be:

> tight fitting, and arranged in such a way that one piece fits with another, so that they do not clatter or catch on each other, padded on the reverse side with thin pieces of leather.

[2] A recent case study is R. Firth Green and R. Moffat, 'Schynbalds in The Awntyrs off Arthure (l. 395): Two Notes', *Notes & Queries*, unnumbered (2020), pp. 1–6.

[3] New York, Pierpont Morgan Library, MS M775, fol. 122v–fol. 123r, printed and examined in Viscount Dillon, 'On a Ms. Collection of Ordinances of Chivalry of the 15th Century belonging to Lord Hastings', *Archaeologia* 57 (1900), pp. 29–70 (at pp. 43–6). An edition and analysis of Oxford, Bodleian Library, MS Ashmole 856, pp. 376–83 is to be found in R. Moffat, '"Armed & redy to come to the felde": Arming for the Judicial Duel in 15th-Century England', *Courts of Chivalry and Admiralty in Late Medieval Europe*, ed. A. Musson and N. Ramsay (Woodbridge, 2018), pp. 121–33.

[4] C. Blair, *European Armour, circa 1066 to circa 1700* (London, 1958), pp. 77–8; T. Capwell, 'A Depiction of an Italian Arming Doublet, c. 1435–45', *Waffen- und Kostümkunde* 44 (2002), pp. 177–95; Capwell, *Armour of the English Knight*, pp. 155–7. An 'armyngdoublett" and 'armyngpointes' (laces) were purchased for the Earl Marshal between 1414 and 1415: Berkeley Castle Archives, Muniment D1/1/30. I am grateful to Drs Claude Blair and Toby Capwell for their encouragement to further investigate this feature.

For it tarnishes a jouster's image if his armour clangs like kettles each time he moves, or if it makes him stand as stiff as a statue.

justas a la persona, y ellas entre sí que unas y otras ajusten, y donde una con otra junta, por que no suenen ni chapeen, con cuero delgado del enbés estofadas. Porque es gran deslustre a un justador yrle las armas como calderas sonando, o como un armado de monumento.[5]

Lining in this manner is well understood from existing harnesses crafted in Don Luis' day. In our sources we find a French duke making payment to have his legharness lined with satin (136). This would not only look dashing, it would also prevent the clanging so despised by Don Luis and, crucially, allow the plates of the harness to slide effortlessly over the arming doublet beneath, greatly improving manoeuvrability.

As well as evidence for lining plate, we also find it for mail armour – a phenomenon little noted in the fourteenth century and certainly lacking in surviving pieces. One jouster at the Royal Armouries informed this author, on experimenting with a rudimentary fabric lining for his mail skirt, that a lance strike to the groin was 'far less painful' than those inflicted in previous encounters! It is hoped that those consulting this sourcebook will find evidence to improve the protection afforded by their harness, thus reducing the chance of injury – or worse.

[5] L. Zapata de Chaves, *Del Justador*, Madrid, Biblioteca Nacional MS 2790, ed. and trans. N. Fallows, *Jousting in Medieval & Renaissance Iberia* (Woodbridge, 2010), p. 388.

English Pronunciation

The fourteenth century witnessed the English language come into its own. Indeed, in his work of 1354 Henry, duke of Lancaster, entreats his reader: 'if the French be no good I must be excused, for I am English and don't use French much' ('si le franceis ne soit pas bon, jeo doie estre escusee, pur ceo qe jeo sui engleis et n'ai pas moelt hauntee le franceis').[1] It is at this time that arms and armour spelling and pronunciation branched out from their French roots. The post-medieval infiltration of 'Gallicisms', being the use of a French name such as *solerette* when the contemporary English 'sabaton' was in use, is a problem that greatly exercised scholars past[2]. Orally presenting research is key to widening the appeal of our area of study. I have faith that this list will offer its user some protection from petty, nit-picking pedants of the worst sort (this author included).

Here I offer a simple guide by the use of rhyme and homophones:

- basinet as *bass* (fish) *in it*
- bevor with *Trevor*
- chapel de fer as *chapel* (church) *di fur* – also, the words all run together
- coif as *koi* (carp) + terminal *f*
- couter as *cow ter* (the *ter* in *terror*)
- cuir bouilli as *queer bully*
- cuisse with *quiche* but the initial *qu* sound as in *quack*
- gorget as *gorge it*
- grapper with *trapper*
- pallet as in *colour palette*
- pauldron as *(a)ppalled Ron*
- pisan as *peas Anne*
- poleyn as *Paul ain* (the *ain* in *pain*)
- pollaxe with *doll axe*

[1] *Le Livre de Seyntz Medicines: The Devotional Treatise of Henry of Lancaster*, ed. E. J. Arnould (Oxford, 1940), p. 239.
[2] A. R. Wagner and J. G. Mann, 'A 15th-Century Description of the Brass of Sir Hugh Hastings at Elsing, Norfolk', *Antiquaries Journal* 19 (1939), pp. 421–8. See also the articles cited in the section on a working vocabulary below.

Towards a Working Vocabulary

Alonso, Bishop of Burgos (d. 1456) was highly critical of those who revelled in

> having many arms or in changing the conformation of them and devoting one's energy
> to discovering new pieces of armour and giving them new names so that if our ancestors
> arose from the dead they would not understand them.

> en tener muchas armas ni en mudar el tajo de ellas y poner su trabajo en hallar nuevas
> formas de armaduras y poner nombres nuevos, que si nuestros antecesores se levantasen
> no los entenderían.[1]

Descendants, as well as ancestors, find themselves in this same predicament. With obsolescence comes obscurity. An anonymous Scottish Lowlander's account of 1678 is telling. A large force of Highland soldiers, he relates, have equipment 'of the most odde and anticque forme'. He definitely recognizes the names found in the national arming acts of the fourteenth and fifteenth centuries, but is uncertain of their meaning.

> And truely I doubt not but a man, curious in our antiquities, might in this host
> finde explications of the strange pieces of armour mentioned in our old lawes, such
> as bosnet, iron hat, gorget, pesane, wambrassers and reerbrassers, panns, legsplents,
> and the like, above what any occasion in the lowlands would have afforded for several
> hundereds of yeers.[2]

As a young novice setting out on a journey to understand the bewildering world of medieval arms and armour, I wrestled with a great deal of vocabulary. On approaching my generous and kind masters with a difficult or obscure term, this apprentice was often met with a 'Don't know', 'Absolutely no idea', and – most frequently – 'Why don't *you* find out for *yourself*.' A gauntlet thrown down in this manner had to be taken up.

Nomenclature and esoteric specialized vocabulary is a constant hindrance to the understanding of arms and armour. There is not space in this volume for a detailed

---

[1]   A. de Cartagena, *Tratados militares*, ed. N. Fallows (Madrid, 2006), pp. 265–6; ed. and trans. N. Fallows, *Jousting in Medieval & Renaissance Iberia* (Woodbridge, 2010), pp. 70–1.
[2]   Edinburgh, National Library of Scotland, Adv. MS Wodrow xcix.29, fol. 206r. I extend my thanks to Dr Ralph McLean for his kind assistance locating this document.

analysis of etymological origins and development, including such phenomena as loanwords, nicknames, puns, homophones, and zoomorphisms. It is clearly a period of rapidly evolving terminology – there are fossil words from Classical Latin (*galea, lorica, cirotheca*), new vernaculars in French and English, and a peppering of words from further afield, for instance aketon, jazerant,[3] and sparth.[4] A brief explanation is given if it is beneficial to understanding – e.g. basinet comes from the French for 'small basin'. Such a tricky, tongue-twisting task must be passed to expert linguists and lexicographers. It is hoped that there may be something of interest amongst the sources and some mystery words still in need of concrete definition. There are, for example, earlier references – such as brigandine – and linguistic oddities – such as musekins.

Wherever and whenever possible I endeavour to keep to the language and terminology as used by the men themselves – be they knights, men-at-arms, chroniclers, or craftsmen – as instructed (a touch too sternly) by such twentieth-century authorities as Charles Beard, Sir James Mann, and Claude Blair.[5] I am steadfastly unapologetic that this volume seeks to establish a working vocabulary in English. For the master archer Roger Ascham, writing in 1545, clear translation into, and use of, his own language was key. He accuses 'manye Englishe writers', who by 'usinge straunge wordes, as Latine, Frenche, and Italian, do make all thinges darke and harde'.[6] Linguistically limited to sources in Latin, French, English, (some) Italian, and Scots, there is clearly much work to be undertaken on similar sources in our wealth of dialects and languages used in Europe and beyond. It is for both new and established colleagues in the field to take up this gauntlet.

A valiant attempt has been made by a team of a dozen experts from across Europe: the *Glossarium armorum: Arma defensiva*.[7] Its multilingual format sought to ensure the consistency of arms and armour terminology: a *lingua franca*. The languages are Czech, Danish, English, French, German, and Italian. The team included museum professionals and academics such as Claude Blair, A. V. B. Norman, Ortwin Gamber, and archaeologist Ada Bruhn de Hoffmeyer. It is very accessible and benefits greatly from its having clear line drawings. However, the *Glossarium* relies a great deal on *de facto* usage from various historical periods, an accumulation of collectors' appellations and museum curators' categorizations – these are often based on nomenclature employed in succeeding centuries, what Sir James Mann calls the school of 'practical

---

3   See their entries in *The Encyclopedia of Medieval Dress and Textiles of the British Isles, c. 450–1450*, ed. G. Owen-Crocker, E. Coatsworth and M. Hayward (Leiden, 2012).

4   R. Moffat, 'A Sign of Victory?: "Scottish Swords" and Other Weapons in the Possession of the "Auld Innemie"', *Arms & Armour* 15 (2018), pp. 122–43.

5   C. R. Beard, 'Armour and the "New English Dictionary"', *The Connoisseur: An Illustrated Magazine for Collectors*, vol. 81, no. 324 (August 1928), pp. 235–7; J. G. Mann, 'Armour and the "New English Dictionary"', *The Connoisseur: An Illustrated Magazine for Collectors*, vol. 82, no. 326 (October 1928), pp. 121–2; J. G. Mann, Preface to O. Trapp, *The Armoury of the Castle of Churburg*, I, pp. v–xviii (at pp. xiii–xvii); J. G. Mann, 'The Nomenclature of Armour', *Transactions of the Monumental Brass Society* 9 (1961), pp. 414–28; Blair, *European Armour*, pp. 9–10; C. Blair, 'Armour and the Study of Brasses', *Monumental Brasses as Art and History*, ed. J. Bertram (Stroud, 1996), pp. 37–40.

6   R. Ascham, *Toxophilus, the Schole, or Partitions, of Shooting* (London, 1545), pp. xv–p. xvi.

7   O. Gamber and others, *Glossarium armorum: Arma defensiva* (Graz, 1972).

students of armour' that has contributed 'its own quota of words, generally in the form of descriptive or slang terms such as *pig-faced bascinet*'.[8]

It is the established practice in Anglophone scholarship to follow the spellings and nomenclature set out by Claude Blair in his seminal *European Armour, c. 1066–c. 1700* (1958). In this sourcebook I respectfully diverge from the following:

1. The components of the arm harness: vambrace, couter, and rerebrace (see Figure 18). I do not 'follow the modern practice, based partly on 16th- and 17th-century usage, of referring to the parts above and below the couter as the upper and lower cannons of the vambrace respectively',[9] but rather I return to the original use of vambrace and rerebrace for the forearm and upper arm.

2. Basinet rather than bascinet. The reason is twofold. First, it preserves the etymological origins from the French for 'small basin': the diminutive suffix being *-ette*. Second, it remains true to its form in sources from England from the second half of the century. I replace the *y* sometimes used as an internal vowel in Middle English *basynet* with *i*.

3. *Cervelière*. By this century it means helmet lining rather than a metal skullcap.[10]

4. From its non-appearance in the sources we can reject entirely 'coat of plates', replacing it with 'plates' or 'pair of plates'.

5. Jupon or jupel – as shown in the glossary – is not an over-garment for heraldic display but a fabric foundation for metal torso defences such as the haubergeon.

6. Staples. The English word replaces the French *vervelles* – a component used to attach the aventail to the basinet (see the illustrated glossary).

7. The erroneous 'surcoat' is correctly 'coat armour'.[11]

I do not make a claim to have provided concrete definitions for all weapons and armour parts. I hope, though, that by consulting this sourcebook you will be able to know your jazerant from your jack, pisan from poleyn, and even your paunce-seat from your couter!

---

8   Mann, 'Armour and the "New English Dictionary"', pp. 121–2.
9   Blair, *European Armour*, pp. 44–5.
10 Blair, *European Armour*, pp. 29–30 and p. 51.
11 See the entry in *The Encyclopedia of Medieval Dress and Textiles of the British Isles, c. 450–1450*, ed. G. Owen-Crocker, E. Coatsworth and M. Hayward (Leiden, 2012).

Part I

Introduction to the Source-Types

I

Textual Source-Types

It must be stated from the outset that the two source-types – textual and material – always work in tandem to deepen our understanding. It is only out of necessity to the format of a sourcebook that they are introduced in this manner. There are many instances in which the documentary evidence is all that survives. For instance, there are no surviving aketons from the fourteenth century – or indeed any century. These fabric defences were required by law to be borne by fighting men across Christendom.

Confessio Amantis armorum

In an ancient ballad, two peckish ravens (*The Twa Corbies*) happen upon a 'new slain knight'. One caws to his fellow: 'ye'll sit on his white hause-bane [collar-bone], and I'll pike oot his bonny blue een.' So have I, carrion-like, gorged on the fat generated by the hard graft of others: chasing down footnotes, endnotes, quotations, and bibliographies in the writings of the eminent scholars who have gone before. From the researches of the likes of Meyrick, De Cosson, and Dillon to ffoulkes, Laking, Mann, Norman, and Blair, a feast has been served up for the curious. Many references appear multiple times in succeeding works, and thus the strands of the web spread and entwine into a near-impossible tangle. Most can often ultimately be traced to the Herculean labours of such glossarists and lexicographers as Du Cange in the 1600s and Godefroy and Gay in the nineteenth century.[1] These scholars sometimes drew directly from original manuscripts or, for many entries, from printed editions. It is of paramount importance that due respect is shown to this valuable research – especially as it was undertaken in a pre-digital age. The maxim attributed to Bernard of Chartres – 'nos esse quasi nanos gigantium humeris insidentes' – reminds us of our own diminutive stature when compared to the gigantic form built on centuries of accrued knowledge. Furthermore, this author has benefited greatly from having been granted privileged access to unpublished material such as the J. G. Mann Papers in the Royal Armouries Library and the C. R. Beard Card Index of Costume in the Library of the Society of Antiquaries.[2]

---

[1]   *Glossarium mediæ et infimæ latinatis*, ed. C. du Fresne, sieur Du Cange and others (Niort, 1883–87); F. Godefroy, *Dictionnaire de l'ancienne langue française*, 10 vols (Paris, 1881–1902); V. Gay, *Glossaire archéologique du Moyen Âge et de la Renaissance*, 2 vols (Paris, 1887–1928).

[2]   I am extremely grateful to Messrs Philip Lankester and Stuart Ivinson, Drs Claude Blair and Bernard Nurse, and Ms Barbara Canepa.

Whenever feasibly possible, I have endeavoured to source the original document. Loss, damage, or difficulty of access have, at times, hampered progress. By providing detailed references it is hoped that many originals might yet be tracked down. Indeed, this writer actively encourages his readers to do so.

Note on Transcription and Translation

Transcription

> Ye reverend redaris
> My copeis [of documents are] auld mankit and mutillait
> Gif ye get crymis correct thame to your micht
> And curse na clark that cunnyngly thame wrait
> Bot blame me [who] badly brocht this buik till licht.

—George Bannatyne, c. 1565.[3]

Bannatyne was a passionate collector of poems. By scouring ancient manuscripts he mined a rich seam of literary culture and preserved it for us. His assessment of his sources as 'auld mankit and mutillait' is very pertinent. Quite a few of our documents have only just endured the ravages of time. In many cases the parchment or paper is in very poor condition, sometimes little but damaged fragments, the ink faded and only visible under ultraviolet light. Some transcriptions have been made from old photographs or microfilms (or even photocopies of these) of lost originals. Others are transcribed from early scholars' copies of manuscripts which have subsequently been lost to us. By including detailed references I hope that doubters will check my transcriptions for themselves.

As instructed by Bannatyne, I will not curse any skilled clerk. Such charges as scribal error or inaccuracy due to a lack of familiarity should not be levelled when it is *we* who have failed to comprehend. Wherever possible, I have endeavoured to provide my own interpretation of the most probable meaning. There is no standardized spelling, capitalization, or punctuation in any of these documents. I only include the bracketed corrective [*sic*] if the spelling, proper noun, or word order drastically affects the meaning. Therefore the scribe scribbling down the contents of the armoury of Mons Castle (**74**) will not be picked up on his (twice) confusing the gender of a definite article ('le viese maniere').

In order to be true to the original script, where recognizable contemporary scribes' signs (*notae communes*) are used they are expanded in square brackets: e.g. p[ro], p[ar], q[ue], p[re]d[ic]to[rum]. For word endings, abbreviations, and contractions that do not have specific scribal signs – an example being a single macron penned over a word – I use a single inverted comma: thus cu' for *cum* (Lat. with), London' (Lat. *Londinensis, -dinium*), Reg' R' (Lat. king's reign). Thankfully, this neatly avoids

---

3   Edinburgh, National Library of Scotland, Adv. MS 1.1.6.

the need to provide what might be considered 'correct' declensions in Latin. It should be strongly argued that, as many of these words are neologisms and originate in vernacular tongues (e.g. breastplate, hauberk), they cannot be declined at all. I share the sentiment of a Scottish nobleman corresponding with his kinsman Richard II. Do not be surprised ('mervaile yhe nocht'), he entreats, 'that I write my lettres in englis fore that ys mare clere to myne vnderstandyng than latyne ore Fraunche'.[4]

A great many of the documents are written in the form of lists with only one entry per line. In this sourcebook they have been condensed into single paragraphs to reduce their length without compromising their meaning. I have expunged such terms as 'item' and *eidem* (Lat. 'to the same' person) commonly employed by the compilers of inventories, household accounts, and legally-binding documents. Superfluous elaborate honorary titles such as mon dit seigneur (Fr. my said lord) have also, wherever possible, been removed. So numerous are the lacunae in the paper and vellum that these gaps are represented by bracketed ellipses: [...] only if the meaning is drastically affected.

Translation

> What a wonder! For there are in the Sacred Scriptures certain – indeed several – Latin words that pierce the reader's heart with great devotion but when translated into French are found to be vulgar and lacking in edification and delectation.

> Quel merveille! car il y a en la sainte escripture certains et plusiers motz en latin qui du lisant percent le cuer en grant devocion, lesquex translatez en francois se treuvent en vulgal sans saveur et sans delectacion.

> —Sir Philippe de Mézières.[5]

So a wise knight eloquently frames the issue. To best allow the reader to engage with these primary sources I have presented the original text in as clear a form as possible. Therefore it is not necessary to be completely reliant on my translation. It is highly likely that, by looking again, better interpretations will be suggested and more useful insight gained. For example: a lower-case *u* read as an *n*, or a capital *D* as a *C*, can radically change the meaning of a word or phrase. Contractions and abbreviations frequently prove themselves devious pitfalls to even the most wary.[6] When it comes to prose sources I have sometimes broken up long sentences constructed of multiple sub clauses. Rearrangement of syntax has also been considered necessary in some instances. This allows for a smoother-flowing and more readable text. I fully admit to having selected a few different words, for example 'barked' instead of 'said', in the narrative of chroniclers' accounts. When it comes to the nuts and bolts of the arms

---

4   London, British Library, MS Cotton Vespasian F. VII.
5   De Mézières, *Le Songe du Vieil Pelerin*, II, pp. 223–4.
6   An amusing example is to be found in C. Blair, 'Hedgehog-Quill Fletchings: A Warning for Future Researchers', *Journal of the Society of Archer-Antiquaries* 46 (2003), p. 36.

and armour, however, I have been very fastidious. The section on the establishment of a working vocabulary above lays out the framework in more detail.

A fifteenth-century writer explains his motivation for putting pen to parchment. This he has done

> so that those who wish to joust in the future can use this (text) as an exemplar yet may correct or amend it as necessary so they may read and understand it better.

> [...] affin que pour lauenir ceulx qui vouldront Jouster y preignent exemple Soit de y adJouster ou de y oster co[m]me mieulx verro[n]t et congnoistront y estre necessaire.[7]

Despite the extent of his efforts, he accepts the inevitability that 'there will always be those who know better and will want to dispute this' ('Sauf et Reserue en tout et par tout la correct[i]on de ceulx qui y vouldront dire po[ur] le mieulx').[8] In such a spirit do I encourage the reader to question and interrogate the sources and translations thereof. And so, *pace* Bannatyne, it is *this* author who must shoulder the blame if he has 'badly brocht this buik till licht'.

Types of Documents

The textual sources can be divided into two general categories: official documents and prose. By 'official' I mean those of a legally-binding type such as wills, inventories, acts of parliament, legal complaints and inquisitions, craft statutes, official and mercantile correspondence, and challenges to judicial duels. Those categorized as 'prose' are religious works, chroniclers' accounts, expert advice, travellers' accounts, and letters of challenge to take part in such chivalric combats as celebratory jousts.

Official Documents

Wills

These, along with inventories, are the most numerous source-type in this work. Superficially, they appear to be rather cursory and somewhat dully pragmatic – 'I bequeath *this* to him', 'let *them* have the choice of ...', etc. A closer look, however, reveals more. It is important to keep in mind the active role of the testator. We hear their own words and last wishes, as opposed to a post-mortem inventory of their goods – usually compiled by impartial functionaries. By listening to their voices we can make out a faint echo: that these objects held more value than simply the prosaic material worth. The beneficiaries had myriad connections. We find individual family members: sons, cousins, even bastards (**121** and **137**). Faithful servants and comrades-in-arms from hard-fought campaigns are rewarded. One protective knight insists his son reach the age of 18 before receiving his war harness (**114**), an armourer passes on the tools of his craft (**140**), and a duchess leaves to her son the haubergeon

---

7   Paris, Bibliothèque nationale de France, MS fr. 1997, fol. 69r.
8   Paris, Bibliothèque nationale de France, MS fr. 1997, fol. 73r.

of his murdered father (**151**). The atavistic nature of medieval identities is apparent. Ancient heirlooms proclaim the (self) importance of noble families. We find Godfrey of Bouillon's haubergeon – the armour of the conqueror of Jerusalem from whom the De Bohun family claimed descent (**32**). For the earls of Warwick theirs is the sword belonging to their eponymous ancestor Guy of Warwick – the giant-slaying hero of a popular romance (**89**). There is evidence of the influence of chivalric ideals on the funeral ceremonies of certain warriors. The arms, armour, and horses of the deceased are bidden to play a central role (**65**, **100**, and **139**). Testators patently express pride in the quality of treasured possessions such as an axe decorated with silver bequeathed by a goldsmith (**108**). Practical matters are also addressed. Men of various social standing often have a number of harnesses and weapons. A rector in war-torn Cumberland gives his bow, arrows, and sword (**117**). The residue of military equipment is retained for the defence of Dalkeith Castle (**137**). There are bequests of armour and arms already in the possession of, or returned to, the beneficiary (**114**, **134**, and **137**).

A final, and very significant, point: these documents were (and are) legally binding. Precision of vocabulary and meaning are essential to their proper execution. Indeed, what could possibly be worse than ending up with a bog-standard sword whilst your kinsman received the one with the silver-gilt hilt you had been certain was to be yours?!

Inventories and Household Payments

As the most numerous source-type in this book, I provide here a much lengthier introduction in five subsections.

1. Armourers and Keepers of Armour

These source-types are, essentially, just lists. It is the identities of the men who compiled and are recorded in these lists, however, that elevate them to the status of an invaluable source for study. They are professional armourers and keepers of armour. Men such as Hugh Bungay, Keeper of Edward of Caernarfon's Armour; John Dounton, who served Henry, earl of Derby (soon to be King Henry IV); and Stephen atte Fryth – a London armourer entrusted to record the forfeited goods of rebellious noblemen.[9] They had hands-on understanding of the production, purchase, and care of the goods in their charge.

We know little about the way in which inventories of forfeited goods were compiled. They may well have been quickly scribbled to meet tight delivery deadlines. Were the specialists – armourers – dictating to scribes? Are the surviving rolls of parchment good copies made from these hastily-scrawled rough versions:

---

[9] More on London armourers can be found in R. Moffat, 'Armourers and Armour: Textual Evidence', *The Encyclopedia of Medieval Dress and Textiles of the British Isles, c. 450–1450*, ed. G. Owen-Crocker, E. Coatsworth, and M. Hayward (Leiden, 2012), pp. 49–52; R. Moffat, '"A hard harnest man": The Armour of George Dunbar, 9th Earl of March', *Transactions of the East Lothian Antiquarian and Field Naturalists' Society* 30 (2015), pp. 21–37; and R. Moffat, '*Alle myne harneys for the justes*: Documents as a Source for Medieval Jousting Armour', *The Medieval Tournament as Spectacle: Tourneys, Jousts and Pas d'Armes*, 1100–1600, ed. A. V. Murray and K. Watts (Woodbridge, 2020), pp. 77–97.

copies of copies? What *is* clear is that they are practical, working documents compiled by one individual at a certain location (such as a castle) and the contents ticked off by another upon delivery to a final destination. Exactitude of vocabulary was key to the proper functioning of this process.[10]

Detailed household accounts chart the relationships of trust formed between the keepers and craftsmen, the one purchasing from the other equipment on which their patrons' lives depended. Here there is no room for error and substandard work. As with the wills, by quietly listening we hear the voices of these men, be it discussing the products, arguing over the quality and temper of the steel, debating the benefits of new-fangled designs, or haggling over prices. Although often just fleeting references, certain individual craftsmen can be identified and their progress traced. Gilot the hauberger (Wee Willie the mail-maker) was amongst those who confirmed the articles of the London Armourers in 1322 (**28**). He is almost certainly the William the hauberger who received mail defences from Caerphilly Castle in 1326 (**35**). In 1331 he held the title King's Armourer (**42**). Another example is Stephen atte Fryth's career progression. He is classed as an armourer of London and had the likes of Henry, earl of Derby, among his clientele. By 1397 he had attained the same rank as Wee Willie in the royal household (**104**, **138**, and **144**).

In addition to the sound of voices, we can hear the striking of hammer on anvil, smell the blood and sweat, and feel the (no doubt many) tears. This is an aspect that jumps out of these sources again and again: the skill, care, and sheer hard work put into the upkeep of armour and weapons. There are many instances of repair and refurbishment. A constant battle is waged against rust as attested by numerous payments for oil and bran: by rolling mail defences in a scouring barrel the bran acts as an effective abrasive. Elbow grease was often the most effective (and cost effective) 'substance'. For every piece of plate armour referred to as 'burnished' or 'white', a man (or boy) would be required to diligently polish it to a mirror finish. Emery from Alexandria was used on Edward of Caernarfon's harness and one pound of the stuff on Henry, earl of Derby's (**9** and **138**). There are white shammies for polishing hauberks and many bespoke trunks, coffers, and bags constructed for the carriage of weapons and armour.

Vegetius was a Roman military writer much read in the Middle Ages. For him, upkeep of kit was essential for both practical and psychological reasons:

> þe glittering of cleir geir & harneis giffis allwayis terror to þair Innemies bot þe rowst & filth of þe harnes schawis al way[s] þe sweirnes [laziness] & inabilitie of þaim þat beris it.
>
> —Vegetius, as translated by the herald Adam Loutfut, c. 1490.[11]

---

[10] See, for example, Moffat, 'A Sign of Victory?', pp. 122–43, and Moffat, *'Alle myne harneys for the justes'*, pp. 77–97.

[11] Edinburgh, National Library of Scotland, Adv. MS 31.3.20, fol. 81r.

By 1446, an anonymous writer informs us, the most common arm defences borne in France were made in Milan ('les plus co[m]muns qui se font a milan'). But, he continues:

> if you were to ask me from what pieces they are made, I would reply that it is unnecessary for me to go into detail – for everyone knows. Thus it would be remiss of me to waste words *and* time.

> si vous me demandez de quantes pieces Ilz sont faiz Je vous Respons quil nest Ja besoing que Je le declare plus particulierement Car tout le monde le scet et est si en vsaige que ce ne seroit a moy que perdre p[ar]olles et temps.[12]

In this vein, the familiarity these professionals show to the products of their craft can be considered a double-edged sword. On the one edge, we benefit from their expertise for such details as nomenclature, cost, care, and upkeep. On the other, there is no need for their providing any explanation or detailed description to third parties, ourselves included. What are, for instance, the arm defences 'of the new type' purchased for Edward III (**52**)? Or similarly-categorized basinets purchased for the soldiers of a French invasion fleet (**125**)? We must not lose heart. There is a great deal of information contained in these sources. By working equally as hard as our craftsmen we can tease it out – as the four following subsections will demonstrate.

2. 'I can find no harness of the fleur de lis in any part of Brabant': Making and Marking.
So Richard Thyrkyll (or Threlkeld), a ship's captain, despondently reported to Henry VIII from Antwerp in 1513.[13] In his oft-quoted letter, he refers to the practice of marking products by means of a punch or incised or inlaid design – this often in latten (copper-alloy). Two categories of mark are relevant to the discussion: the 'view mark' of the place of production and that of an individual craftsman or his workshop: the 'maker's mark'. A third category – the proof mark – is dealt with in the section on mercantile correspondence and in the illustrated glossary.

Marks in the first category are most commonly made by punches. The indentation is usually a version of a town or city's heraldic coat of arms – Augsburg's pinecone and the party-per-pale chevrons with spread-eagle of Nuremberg are instantly recognizable. A goldsmith at Tours received payment in 1470 for having 'engraved two iron punches with the town's arms for marking the harnesses [i.e. plate armours] and brigandines' ('gravé les armes de la ville en deux poinssons de fer pour marquer les harnois and brigandines').[14] Marking them thus is proof of their quality before export or sale as they have been 'viewed' by senior members of the craft confraternity. This practice is also discussed in the section on craft statutes below. It serves to explain

---

12 Paris, Bibliothèque nationale de France, MS fr. 1997, fol. 65r.
13 London, British Library, MS Galba B. III, fol. 75r, printed in *Letters and Papers, Foreign and Domestic, Henry VIII, vol. 1, 1509–1514*, ed. J. S. Brewer (London, 1920), p. 847.
14 J. B. Giraud, *Documents pour servir à l'histoire de l'armement au Moyen Âge et à la Renaissance*, 2 vols (Lyon, 1895–1904), I, pp. 186–7, citing original documents in the Archives municipales de Tours.

such terms as 'of London', 'of Flanders', etc. in our sources. The increasing frequency of the designation 'Lombardy make' and 'of Milan' is of note. The rise to prominence of Milan and its environs as a European centre of armour production is well established in the scholarship.[15] Nevertheless, there is a significant chronological gap in our understanding of this rise from the chronicler Galvaneo Flamma's celebration of the city's 'wondrous number' of craftsmen in 1288 to the surviving detailed armourers' accounts of the fifteenth century.[16] Our sources go some way to filling it.

These sources attest to quality manufacture in other parts of Europe. There are two instances of swords recorded as 'of Passau' (**131** and **138**). This Bavarian town was renowned as a centre of excellence for the manufacture of steel blades by the sixteenth century. Schmid[17] has identified the names of individual craftsmen working in the fourteenth century from the town's archives but has records of marks from only as early as the 1460s.

There are numerous occurrences of armour and weapons from specific locations of, as yet, unidentified type. Bordeaux is a good example. The compiler of one particularly long inventory only once uses an adjective – this London armourer, Stephen atte Fryth, lists a 'fine' Bordeaux sword (**144**). Narrative accounts frequently laud Bordeaux-made weapons. Jehan Froissart, a worldly-wise chronicler from Valenciennes, speaks in glowing terms of:

> slicing and needle-sharp iron lanceheads [...] swords forged in Bordeaux are so sharp and hard that none can match them [...] axes and daggers so strong and so well tempered there can be none better.

> glaiues de feer de bordeaulx agur mordans et trenche[n]s [...] espees estoie[n]t forgees a bourdeaulx dont le tailla[n]t estoit si aspre et si dur que plus ne pouoit [...] haches et de dagues si tres fortes et si bon trempees que on ne pouoit mieulx.[18]

We should be wary of falling into the trap of dismissing Froissart's comments as patriotic hyperbole, for the assessment of a professional armourer chimes with that of the man of letters. The heraldic arms of Bordeaux then comprised the three lions (or leopards) of the Plantagenets above a castle set upon water with a crescent thereon. No weapons with this mark have been found, yet.

Another example: mail of Chambly is alluded to several times (**24**, **31**, and **121**). This small town lies 25 miles north of Paris. Although appearing only in French documents in this sourcebook, the products made by the town's craftsmen were

---

15   For example Blair, *European Armour*, p. 79; J. G. Mann, 'The Sanctuary of the Madonna delle Grazie [...] Italian Armour during the 15th Century', *Archaeologia* 80 (1930), pp. 29–54. See also the discussion of the Datini archives below.

16   Galvaneo Flamma, *Chronicon extravagans de antiquitatibus Mediolani*, ed. A. Ceruti (Turin, 1869), pp. 448–9: 'armorum fabricatores in mirabili copia'. For more detail see W. Boeheim, 'Werke Mailänder Waffenschmiede in den Kaiserlichen Sammlungen', *Jahrbuch der Kunsthistorischen Sammlungen des Allerhöchsten Kaiserhauses* 9 (1889), pp. 375–418 (at pp. 375–6).

17   W. M. Schmid, 'Passauer Waffenwesen', *Zeitschrift für Historische Waffenkunde* 8 (1918–20), pp. 317–42 (at p. 336).

18   Besançon, Bibliothèque municipale, MS 865, fol. 352r. MS images reproduced in HRI *Online Froissart*, ed. P. Ainsworth and G. Croenen (Sheffield, 2013).

evidently cherished across the Channel. It was the theft of a mail horse cover (*coopertorium*) of 'Chaumbliz' that smarted most for an armour dealer at Saint Pancras in 1276.[19] There is no extant Chambly-made mail. But that is not to say that artefacts might not yet come to light, for makers' marks *have* been identified on mail crafted by German masters.[20] Even very well-known pieces still have secrets to reveal – as shown by Dupras. After close inspection, he has identified a maker's mark on three links of the aventail of the Lyle basinet in the Royal Armouries.[21] Armed with this knowledge, we would easily recognize the haubergeon recorded as having been purchased in Turin, which had every single link marked by its maker (**97**), should its ilk come to light.

This brings us on to the secondary category of mark: the maker's mark. This was of the individual craftsman or his workshop. The authorities of Paris in 1415 instituted an ingenious system to avoid any complications or misunderstandings. Each craftsman was required to imprint their mark on a lead sheet securely stored in the Châtelet ('et seront tenus lesdits heaumiers dapporter chacun endroit soy lemprainte de son seing en un plonc en la Chambre du procureur du roy au Chastelet de Paris').[22]

There is a rare reference: a sword of Lombardy work among the possessions of a French churchman bears the dramatic-sounding 'mark of the scorpion' (**80**). There are several extant sixteenth-century Milanese blades with this mark – for example, five staff weapons in the Royal Armouries' collection.[23] The phenomenon of marks of this kind also features in the discussion of craft statutes, legal complaints, and mercantile correspondence below. As more European material culture comes to light, let us hope that Lady Luck will smile on us more favourably than she did on Henry VIII's despairing Captain Thyrkyll.

3. Animal, Vegetable, and Mineral: Natural Resources

The extent to which natural resources are utilized is well documented. We find a veritable menagerie of animal parts, with mammals providing the lion's share. Baleen plates from enormous filter-feeding whales are used in the construction of gauntlets, reinforced sleeves, and crossbows.[24] The hides of a range of ruminants are purchased: cows, calves, bucks, roes, goats, and sheep. The differentiation of 'white' and 'red' from the norm relates to the plant-matter used in the leather-tanning process: oak

---

[19] *The London Eyre of 1276*, ed. M. Weinbaum (London, 1976), p. 122.

[20] Trapp, *The Armoury of the Castle of Churburg*, I, pp. 3–6; W. Reid and E. M. Burgess, 'A Habergeon of Westwale', *Antiquaries Journal* 40 (1960), pp. 46–57; Scalini, *The Armoury of the Castle of Churburg*, pp. 193–7.

[21] N. Dupras, 'Medieval Armourers and their Workshops' (Ph.D. thesis, University of Leeds, 2012), p. 171.

[22] Paris, Archives de la Préfecture de Police, cote AD 4, Collection Lamoignon, vol. II, fol. 48r.

[23] C. J. ffoulkes, *Inventory and Survey of the Armouries of the Tower of London*, 2 vols (London, 1916), II, pp. 241–3: four bills (Inv. IX.10, IX.28, IX.29, and IX.30) and one glaive (Inv. IX.48). Mr R. C. Woosnam-Savage kindly assisted with these details. Marks on sword blades of the same era are illustrated in J. Gelli and G. Moretti, *Gli armaroli Milanese: i Missaglia e la loro casa* (Milan, 1903), p. 4, pl. II, but no detailed information is provided.

[24] R. Moffat and J. Spriggs, 'The Use of Baleen for Arms, Armour and Heraldic Crests in Medieval Britain', *Antiquaries Journal* 88 (2008), pp. 207–15.

and birch bark for bog standard whilst more exotic plants produce fine colours – an example being the sumac shrub for a vivid red.[25] Parisian armourers in 1296 are prohibited from covering gauntlets with cheap black-tanned sheepskin or *mégis*: a thin, alum-tanned, sheep or goatskin ('basaine noire ne de mesgueiz') (**1**). The 1312 regulations of the same city (**16**) continue the prohibition of 'cuir de mouto' noir'. Hungarian leather (**92**) is singled out at the Tower of London – presumably for its superior quality. Twisted horsehair is formed into tough ropes for the torsion-powered springald, and sinew is used to construct the composite crossbow. From the avian species, the flight feathers of the goose and peacock are prepared for arrow fletchings. The striking feathers of the peacock's train serve as crest ornaments.[26]

Wood is an essential component for the construction of a range of weapons, especially missile and staff weapons. Various species are used – ash, birch, elm, yew (both Irish and Spanish), as well as willow faggots for gunpowder. Charles VI even goes so far as to have trees from his hunting forest felled for crossbow quarrel-shafts for his invasion force (**125**).

One of our sources provides evidence for one of the main ingredients for making varnish. Gauntlet plates must be 'linseed varnished' ('v[er]nices linees') before being stitched into the leather or fabric in the 1312 Parisian armourers' regulations (**16**). From other medieval sources we can find the rest of the recipe. The miscellany of a physician at the monastery of Saint Gall of around 1455 recommends 1lb of solid resin, 3lb of linseed oil, and 3lb of Greek pitch (a heat-treated pine resin), stating that 'it shall be good to varnish crossbows' ('vernixe salda lb. 1., olio de semente de lino lb. 3., pece grega lb. 3.; e sarà bona da Ivernicare balestre').[27] A half-pound was bought for the repair of crossbows at Beaumaris Castle in 1307 and Master Ralph received payment for varnishing one large shield for the Tower in 1372 (**13** and **92**). 'Black-varnished' armour ('verniciato nero') is referred to (**81**). A Venetian manuscript dated to before 1513 describes 'the best varnish for varnishing arquebuses, crossbows, and iron armour' ('vernice ottima per invernichare archibusi et balestre et armadure di ferro'). The recipe comprises 2lb of linseed oil, 1lb of granulated resin, and 2oz of white Greek pitch ('olio seme de lino 2. vernice in grani libre 1. pece grecha chiara oz 2.'). A subsequent recipe suggests a ratio of 10oz of oil to one of pitch: this being common pitch, thus the varnish 'will be black and good for sword pommels, spurs, and suchlike' ('x oncie d' olio et una di pece. Et se la togli nera sara buona per pomi de spade et sproni, et similia').[28] This might well be the same type as that used to take the shine off the blades of 4,000 axes prepared for planned massacre in Paris in 1415,

---

25 J. Cherry, 'Leather', *English Medieval Industries: Craftsmen, Techniques, Products*, ed. J. Blair and N. Ramsay (London, 1991), pp. 295–318.

26 For details see the relevant entries in the illustrated glossary.

27 London, British Library, Sloane MS 416, fol. 139r, printed in C. L. Eastlake, *Materials for a History of Oil Painting* (London, 1847), p. 252.

28 Venice, Biblioteca Nazionale Marciana, MS It. IV, 48, printed in M. P. Merrifield, *Original Treatises [...] on the Arts of Painting [...]*, 2 vols (London, 1849), II, 605 for dating; II, 637 for text.

so they could not be seen in the darkness ('quatre mille haches, les fer vernissés, afin qu'on ne les cognust de nuict, et quatre mille jaques noires').[29]

As well as the vegetable tanning-matter described above, plants prove invaluable. There is cotton (both wool and cloth), linen (made from flax), and canvas for padded defences and linings. Satins, silks, and velvets are used by the ell for fine coverings – even for helmet straps and linings.

Bran and oil is effective for scouring mail. The specific type of oil is not recorded. Armourers at the Greenwich workshop bought one 'gallon of neites oille' in 1536–37.[30] This refers to neatsfoot oil. Most vegetable matter produces oil. For instance, the by-product of the production of flax thread is linseed, a name that has been in use (according to the editors of the *Oxford English Dictionary*) in English from c. 1000, and 'linseed-oil' from 1548.

There are materials for constructing plate armour such as good-quality osmund iron smelted from the bog ores of Scandinavia and the Baltic, whilst charcoal and sea coal fuel forges (for example **104**). Emery serves as an abrasive for the care of armour. The vast quantities of latten in use must have required an immense army of miners and metalworkers to provide enough copper, tin, lead, and zinc for the production of this alloy.[31] Pure tin also proves itself to be a good protective coating to prevent corrosion (**1**, **16**, **76**, and **86**). It goes without saying that precious metals were used in abundance to decorate arms for those with ample means. Exotic substances such as amber and pearls adorned lace-tips and decorative heraldic crests and ailettes (for example **35**).

4. The Good, the Bad, and the Ugly

As in wills, there are items listed that are held to be physical links to the past, objects that must have had special meaning to their owners. That they are recorded by detached individuals is of significance. Here it is not only the conviction of the owner but also a wider acceptance of an object's origin. Thomas, duke of Gloucester, had a pair of plates that had belonged to his father Edward III (**144**). King Louis X had the knife of his great grandfather, Saint Louis the crusader king (**24**). Weapons called 'Saracen' or 'Turkish', as well as the exotic jazerant body defence, might well have been brought back from such campaigns. Trophies from expeditions within Christendom such as Scottish axes, Irish sparths,[32] and lancegays would have been the subject of many a veteran's tale. Intriguingly, there is a weapon that serves as a symbol of legal entitlement: the falchion described as the 'Charter of the Lands of Wigmore' (**27**). Its existence lends some credence to a chronicler's account of an incident in 1279. When questioned as to the validity of his right to hold certain lands, John, earl Warenne,

---

[29] Jean Juvénal des Ursins, *Histoire de Charles VI, roy de France, Mémoires pour servir à l'Histoire de France*, ed. J. F. Michaud and J. J. F. Poujoulat (Paris, 1836), pp. 524–5.

[30] London, British Library, Royal MS 7 F.XIV, fol. 68r, printed in F. H. Cripps-Day, *Fragmenta armamentaria* [...] *Greenwich Armour* (Frome, 1944), p. 50.

[31] C. Blair and J. Blair, 'Copper Alloys', *English Medieval Industries: Craftsmen, Techniques, Products*, ed. J. Blair and N. Ramsay (London, 1991), pp. 81–106.

[32] Moffat, 'A Sign of Victory?', pp. 129–36.

we are told, flourished an old and rusty sword ('gladium antiquum et eruginatum') with which his ancestors had taken the said lands by right of conquest.[33] It would be pleasing to imagine these rare and exotic artefacts placed on display accompanied by an explanatory label (please indulge the author here, being a museum professional).

In these source-types we have reference to contemporary villains as well as heroes of ages past. Despised by many of their contemporaries as upstarts, Sir Piers Gaveston and Roger Mortimer, earl of March, had a great deal of lavishly-decorated equipment in their possession (**18**, **27**, and **43**). This was, no doubt, by the gift of their royal benefactors. The much-hated criminal duo, father and son Sirs Hugh Despenser, had their retinue of thugs in aketons emblazoned with the family's coat of arms (**35**).

5. From Adorned with Gold to 'rottyn, distroyit, or sald'

There is great detail on arms and armour at the beginning and end of its working life. Purchases of gleaming new equipment for wealthy noblemen are starkly juxtaposed with the sorry state of state-funded military hardware: the *matériel* of the sinews of war. We are given a flavour of the culture of *largesse*, that being: extravagant generosity as an overt demonstration of material wealth and noble or royal status. For Louis, duke of Orléans, it was essential that his team of household knights and squires were suitably equipped for a feat of arms against challengers come from Aragon, he himself footing the bill (**147**). We can imagine Edward III's joy on receiving a basinet of Lombardy make from a visiting foreign knight (**52**). His son the Black Prince showered gifts of arms and armour on his brothers-in-arms as well as foreigners – armour covered with cloth of gold for jousts being a particularly fine present. The prince's indignation when informed that the recipient of some armour he had lent did not want to return it is almost palpable (**70**). We are also privy to the extraordinary fact that this prince was just seven years old when a full harness of mail and plate was purchased for him (**50**). His training therein would dramatically affect the development of his skeleton and musculature. When fighting his first battle at 16 he would have felt his armour as a second skin. Thomas Beaufort, half-brother of Henry, earl of Derby, was a mature 15 or 16 years old when he was gifted jousting harness (**138**). Are there many more records containing such boyhood treasures? Let us hope so.

As time passes, fashions and technologies change. Worn-out tourneying gear borne in the glittering festive occasions of yesteryear is piled up and left to rot in castle armouries or flogged off to be cannibalized.

Given the popularity of hunting among the elite of medieval Europe, there are disappointingly few hunting weapons described as such.[34] Edward of Caernarfon was a devotee. He commissioned his Master of the Hunt, William Twiti, to put pen to paper (or parchment) to compose an expert treatise. We find Edward's hunting horns, knives, and a chain for a greyhound in Caerphilly Castle (**35**). In other inventories there are listed a couple of hand-spanned bows (i.e. longbows) for hunting, as well as

---

[33] *The Chronicle of Walter of Guisborough*, ed. H. Rothwell (London, 1957), p. 216.
[34] H. L. Blackmore, *Hunting Weapons: From the Middle Ages to the Twentieth Century* (London, 1971), pp. 2–3.

a boar spear (**92** and **144**). A white greyhound with a golden collar is the prize to be awarded the best jouster at Smithfield in 1390 (**135**).

In stark contrast to the trappings of wealth, many of these sources give us a glimpse of the experiences of common soldiers in rotten aketons and rusted kettlehats in rain-soaked castles. There is upcycling, repair, and re-use. Much is categorized as old or in poor condition (helmet linings have even been eaten by rats! (**101**)), some have meagre value, some none at all: *nullius valoris*. A variety of tools and raw materials for the purposes of production and upkeep are recorded. Pieces of iron are ready to be formed into shin defences in Scarborough Castle, ribs of whale baleen are kept in store to repair crossbows. Whether the royal funds applied for were actually spent on new equipment or disappeared to line unscrupulous pockets (or purses) will never be known. Might there have been a temptation to artificially inflate the cost of replacements and repairs for nefarious purposes?

A wealth of data for crunching is to be found here. Wilde's fictional Lord Darlington defines the cynic as one who 'knows the price of everything, and the value of nothing'. The century witnessed erratic fluctuations in the value of currencies – the value of human life, however, remained constant. An investment in the best quality weapons and harness available was essential to survival. There can be little surprise at the vast range of prices – from *haute couture* to low-budget ranges. Henry, earl of Derby, was the son of one of the richest men in Europe. A single element of the elaborate jousting kit purchased for his teenaged half-brother cost a great deal more than the total combined elements of armour and weapons for a footsoldier.

A key point to conclude this whole section: like wills, these source-types are legally-binding documents. Inventories of forfeited goods were confirmed by royal indenture. Documentation relating to budgets (then as now) would be subject to detailed scrutiny through thorough audits of such penny-pinching bean-counters as stewards and masters of households. One keeper of armour even went to the extent of commissioning an armoire to serve as a filing cabinet for his records (**138**).

Professor Sydney Anglo in his magisterial *Martial Arts of Renaissance Europe* is adamant:

> The information contained in such records may enable us to resolve many problems of chronology, nomenclature, etymology and comparative costs and values: but they are also dangerously seductive and reductive because scholars working too closely with inventories (glossing an entry in one document by reference to similar entries in others) may tend, like the legendary Ooslum Bird, to fly round in ever-diminishing circles. The process can generate footnotes of imposing bulk but uncertain utility.[35]

I suggest an alternative ornithological analogy. The pelican in her piety will peck so hard at her breast that the blood gushes forth to nourish her brood. Despite all the dangers (in particular the prospect of sharing the Ooslum Bird's final destination), our interrogation of these primary source-types will work to slake our own thirst for knowledge and enable us to share this knowledge, thus whetting the appetite of others.

---

[35] Anglo, *The Martial Arts of Renaissance Europe*, p. 203.

Craft Statutes and Related Documents

As in so many of these sources, we can hear the voices of the men themselves. By banding together the craftsmen, as recognized freemen of a city, express their common concerns, fears, and status consciousness. Officially recording their 'articles' or statutes stakes a strong claim for the superiority of their work (**1**, **16**, **28**, **66**, and **79**). Thus we are told that certain men were importing and selling cheap, unregulated, substandard products leading to the injury – even death – of the customer. This consequence being to the 'villainous slander' of the members (**28**). The public burning of products that did not meet their exacting standards at the corner of the Rue de la Heaumerie in Paris sent out a clear message as to how seriously these craftsmen took their regulations (**1**, **16**, and **79**). The use of poor-quality materials is firmly addressed. It is through their self-regulation that we gain a great deal of insight into the types of materials and the manner of the construction of defences. Quality control is enforced through the use of individual makers' marks and elected wardens' inspection marks. This will, in the future, aid in the process of the identification of newly-discovered armour as discussed in the section on making and marking above. Moreover, we are also introduced to elements of the structure of these organizations, such as the length of apprenticeships and the cost of ingress (enrolment). That sons of Parisian masters were exempt from this payment sheds light on familial rights and relationships. The regulation of the lengths of apprenticeship demonstrates the level of skill these men had gained by the time they had risen to the rank of journeymen and master.

It is clear that many stories are yet to be told about the men who made, and traded in, arms and armour. Why, for instance, did London craftsmen have such a stranglehold on the loan of equipment for tournaments by the 1330s that a royal statute was necessary to cap the prices (**40**)?

Acts of Parliament and Muster Rolls

Much of medieval society was highly militarized at this time. Robert I (the Bruce), following years of warfare, seeks to remedy a serious problem: the men of the kingdom are very poorly harnessed (**26**). Kings of Scots did not command a professional army but a Royal Host drawn from the able-bodied male populace. These men and boys were obliged to provide 40 days' service a year for the defence of the realm. Each had to be armed according to their rank – be it only a bow. It should be borne in mind that acts such as these stipulate the bare minimum required by law. Those who could afford additional and superior equipment would certainly have invested in it. In 1389 some of the Scottish common folk ('communi vulgo') were extremely disgruntled – an English chronicler informs us – when a truce was concluded with their southern enemy, as they had invested in a great deal of equipment ('abundantiori militia') for a planned invasion.[36]

---

[36] Thomas Walsingham, *Historia Anglicana*, ed. H. T. Riley, 2 vols (London, 1864), II, pp. 182–3.

Another act (**107**) introduces the fascinating phenomenon of local churches laying claim to the equipment of the men defending the periphery of the English realm after their decease. There is evidence that these claims were successful. In 1404 the Sacristan of Durham Priory recorded arms and armour once in the possession of local men 'in the hands of the Prior'.[37] Might it have been by way of backlash that one knight from Cumberland insists in his will (**114**) that 'no armour be offered nor given to the church'?

Muster rolls serve to demonstrate how effectively arming acts were enforced. Depending on the number of men under their command, we find those enrolled as fully-armoured and half-armoured. Knives rather than swords are slung from archers' belts, indicating their place in the social order. An impression is formed as to the military might of a kingdom such as England. The fertile and industrious county of Norfolk could support a large force of well-equipped soldiers (**71** and **75**). These source-types serve to highlight the enormous level of demand for arms and armour of varying quality and cost.

Royal Decrees

Matters arise from time to time that require royal intervention. This can produce surprising results. Two examples (**105** and **102**) are provided to show the level of detail contained in such sources and so prove their great benefit to our study. The first is a royal grant of arms and armour to a knight. The man in question, Sir Robert Salle, had risen to this station from humble origins, being a stonemason's son. Here King Richard II bestows fine weapons and armour embellished with cloth of gold – we can see that he has even been granted his own coat of arms.

The document is in Latin and French. This is very useful in furthering our understanding of specialized vocabulary: features such as the increasing dominance of the vernacular and the divergence of the French of England from that of France.

The second document highlights the strengths of the international bonds of knighthood and the honour of nobility. Edward III spent his formative years battling against the Scots. As an ally of France, the troublesome northern kingdom would prove itself a thorn in his side for much of his reign. Here, we discover the servants of Scotsmen purchasing arms and armour in London. Some is for a judicial duel but some, however, has been made for the use of George, earl of March, and is for war – this at exactly the same time as he was waging a successful campaign against the English! The document is signed by Earl George's implacable foe Harry Hotspur – do we see here some degree of respect shown to a fellow fighter? Also, is there a suggestion that London craftsmanship was held in high esteem by these Scots?[38]

Legal Complaints and Inquisitions

The dazzling reflection of sunlight off polished steel can readily blind us to the mundane and brutal reality of the use, and misuse, of armour and weapons. All

---

37 Durham Cathedral Archives, GB-0033-DCD.
38 These sources are examined in more detail in Moffat, '"A hard harnest man"', pp. 21–37.

fighting weapons are specially-designed tools for killing and maiming humans.[39] In these source-types we come across the plight of some of those at the sharp end. There is, for instance, a widow's plea for justice for her husband's atrocious murder, the legal inquest recording in gruesome detail the horrific nature of his injuries such as the depth of wounds (**19**). An upstanding Londoner has her solid oak door smashed in by pollaxe-wielding robbers (**21**). There is plunder from the dead and captives after battle (**29**) and losses suffered on surrendering a castle (**12**).

We are presented with detailed records of social and personal discord. Those living next to an armourer complain of their walls shaking with the blows of hammers and the choking smoke from the forge: 'there goes the neighbourhood' once craftsmen have set up shop (**104**). Masters and their apprentices fail to get on, allowing us a peep into the everyday life of the medieval armourer (**77** and **98**). One is made to swear that he will not mark basinets with false marks (**122**). This is an added complication to the prospect of identifying future finds as discussed above. The legal wrangling over makers' marks by the armourers of fifteenth-century Milan is well known.[40] Here we find it going on in fourteenth-century London.

Armour can be used as collateral. There is a whiff of desperation in the tone of a soldier's supplication. He simply must redeem the harness he had pawned with Italian bankers for hard cash (**8**). In a plea to the Court of the Count of Hainaut (**48**) whingeing lords complain of the extent of the armour they are expected to provide.

Official Correspondence

Two examples (**47** and **55**) are included to confirm the value of this source-type. In the alarmed tone of a spy's report of a French invasion force we are informed of the number of men and the makeup and extent of their military equipment. From such sources as royal payments we find this not to be some hysterical exaggeration on the part of the informant.

Wars can be long, dull, and uneventful. In the second document a small triumph is celebrated: an anonymous soldier serving in English-occupied Scotland brags that one of his men slew an enemy. Not only does he break the news of the killing but he also relates the details of the manner of death – the lance piercing both material and metal defences.

Mercantile Correspondence

Wherever there is demand – for in Europe (and beyond) in this century there certainly was – it is inevitable that there will be supply. Despite their coming from published documents, these excerpts are included to indicate how much useful information such sources contain.

---

[39] A recent detailed study is R. C. Woosnam-Savage and K. DeVries, 'Battle Trauma in Medieval Warfare', *Wounds and Wound Repair in Medieval Culture*, ed. L. Tracy and K. DeVries (Leiden, 2015), pp. 27–56.

[40] C. A. De Cosson, 'Milanese Armourers' Marks', *Burlington Magazine*, vol. 36 (February 1920), pp. 150–3.

Orders placed by merchants from Montauban (north of Toulouse) provide early evidence for the proofing of armour (**60**). The process involves shooting at it at close range with bow or crossbow. A phenomenon usually associated with the fifteenth century,[41] here it takes place in the 1340s.

Francesco di Marco Datini (1335–1410) was an Avignon-based arms dealer. The remarkable archive of his commercial activities is preserved in his native city of Prato. The extracts presented (**81** and **123**) are totally reliant on snippets from Brun[42] and, to a much greater extent, Frangioni's extensive research.[43] I do not stake any claim to be an Italianist. These extracts have been included for three reasons:

Firstly, to highlight the vast potential for the study of arms and armour such resources present. These excerpts deal with head defences only. There is much more to be revealed when it comes to body armour and weapons.

Secondly, to help us better appreciate the vast web of commerce that had been spun across Europe by this time. From Milan and Avignon to Lyon, Barcelona, and Valencia, Datini's suppliers and agents are under great pressure to meet the enormous demand for their products. We find substantial variety in the quality and cost of their wares. A basinet made by a Paris master has its latten decoration applied in Avignon and many a rusted item is fixed up for resale. Such dubious practices confirm the validity of the charges levelled against those importing substandard work made by the confraternities of armour-makers in London and Paris.

The third reason is to demonstrate their value to our understanding of construction techniques and production levels. There are intriguing details. Roughed out helmets and visors are shipped to Avignon. 'Rough' refers to a piece sheared from a metal sheet and hammered into its basic shape. In fact, 'rough from the hammer' is a term still in use by makers of plate armour today. The helmets recorded as 'black-beaten' ('nigr' verbat") in 1335 were undoubtedly the same (**45**). After it has been 'roughed out' the piece must then be shaped and planished using purpose-designed hammers on anvils called stakes. It is then filed, ground, and finally, polished – or, alternatively, coated with varnish, latten, or tin. The basinet 'to be used as a template' would ensure the Avignon-based craftsmen construct and assemble a finished piece to the required standard.[44]

As shown in the inventories and household payments above, the dominance of Milan is confirmed. Will we ever know exactly in what quantities, and how speedily, armour was knocked out by Daniello Coco and his workers? Are there mail defences somewhere out there with Simone Corrente's mark on the links? Might we yet find basinets stamped with the mark of Giacomuollo da Villa's workshop? Let us hope so.

---

41   R. Moffat, 'The Importance of Being Harnest: Armour, Heraldry and Recognition in the Mêlée', *Battle & Bloodshed: The Medieval World at War*, ed. L. Bleach and K. Borrill (Newcastle, 2013), pp. 5–24 (at pp. 10–12).

42   R. Brun, 'Notes sur le commerce des armes à Avignon au XIVe siècle', *Bibliothèque de l'École des chartes* 109 (1951), pp. 209–31.

43   L. Frangioni, 'Bacinetti e altre difese della testa nella documentazione di una azienda mercantile, 1366–1410', *Archaeologia medievale* 11 (1984), pp. 507–22.

44   See Dupras, 'Medieval Armourers and their Workshops', pp. 89–97, for technical details.

An important concluding point: the Datini archive is a fluke survival. He was just one of many merchants who profited from prolonged conflicts as well as the rage for jousting and tournaments. Who is to say that there are not many, many, more documents of this kind unknowingly secreted away in archives, libraries, museums, and private collections? A good example: in their study of 1903, Gelli and Moretti located amongst the *Lettere ducali* of Galeazzo, duke of Milan, letters of immunity and friendship issued to 'Simone de Currentibus, *fabbricatore di armature*' in 1371, which were renewed in 1395.[45] This can only be the Simone Corrente referred to in our sources.

It is hoped that by presenting these excerpts this might act to spur on fellow researchers to bury themselves in such vast archives as the Datini, scour others for more, and strive to share their findings.

Challenges to Single Combat in a Judicial Duel

Making recourse to exercise the right to trial by battle – also known as the judicial duel – was well established by the fourteenth century. God would be on the side of the victor. If the defeated was not killed in the course of the fighting he would subsequently be executed.

The reasons for the word-length of these challenges (**14**, **54**, **93**, and **128**) and the level of precision given are not entirely clear. The appellant (challenger) does not inform us exactly *why* he has decided to provide such minutiae as the materials to be used in the fabrication of linings, straps, and buckles. Yet by doing so, we are presented with a wealth of detail. Layer by layer and piece by piece, each constituent part is described and prescribed.

We gain insight into the medieval mindset. In addition to earthly defences we are introduced to the sacred – such as the *Chemise de Chartres* – and the profane, if not outright damnable: eldritch advantage from black magic and evil spells. There is clear evidence that thorough inspections were carried out. The Count of Hainaut's Council ordered that a lance be shortened and sharpened horse defences be removed prior to one combat.

Prose Sources

Religious Works

Most of our sources are the products of secular society. Engaging with clerical views is also worthwhile. For the Dominican preacher John Bromyard the age is one of sin and folly (**3**). The knight is cowardly in battle. His reproachful conduct is only compounded by his penchant for frivolous decoration of arms with precious metals and fabrics. Worse, the prospect of plundering such booty only emboldens his foe. This austere churchman patently perceives vanity as an expression of the cardinal sin of pride. We hear echoing from the pulpit: 'et omnia vanitas' (Ecclesiastes 1:2).

---

[45]   J. Gelli and G. Moretti, *Gli armaroli Milanese: i Missaglia e la loro casa* (Milan, 1903), p. 2, citing Milan, Archivio Storico Civico, Lettere ducali.

Nonetheless he is not averse to employing the hauberk as an analogy – its virtuous links protecting the soul as the physical do the body. He holds up King Arthur and the heroes of old as paragons: righteous warriors devoting their martial skills to crusading and the defence of the realm.

The anonymous treatise from early-fourteenth-century England is an altogether different beast (**2**). Appearing in the middle of a hodgepodge manuscript of sermons, poems, and treatises, nowhere are we informed what it is actually *for*. One interpretation is that this short text serves as a working glossary, perhaps to help preachers understand the baffling array of equipment available to the knight for war, tourney, and joust – such activities appearing with great frequency in the popular romances of the day. Armed with this information they would have been able to tailor their sermons to the interests of their lay congregation.[46]

Chroniclers' Accounts

Men of letters were not always men of arms. Nevertheless their writings are a valuable source for our study. The unknown compiler of a chronicle in English (**38**) conveys the sense of mortal danger faced by Queen Isabella during her fly-by-night escape from the forces of Henry, earl of Lancaster. The account contains an extremely rare, if not unique, instance from this century of a woman bearing armour.

Jehan Froissart (**112**, **120**, and **146**) was a man who was as well connected as he was travelled. His informants of events included heralds, nobles captured in battle, and a great many knights such as the grizzled veteran Sir Richard Stury. These are first-hand accounts. As a historian and poet, his prose is clearly heavily influenced by the dramatic events of romance and histories of glories past. When it comes to arms and armour, however, much can be taken to be accurate. An example: Froissart tells us Sir Robert Salle drew his fine Bordeaux sword when attacked by a mob of revolting peasants. We find a sword, dagger, axe, and lancehead of Bordeaux listed amongst this knight's royal gifts (**105**).

Thomas Walsingham, as a monk of Saint Albans, might be considered to be a contemplative cleric cosseted in the cloister. This, though, would be a misconception. He is clearly in the know about the tumultuous goings-on in his native Norfolk and reliably informed of the destruction of John of Gaunt's palatial lodgings on the Thames (**118** and **119**). Such men of the cloth might well have acquaintances among, and also be kin of, fighting men.

Although writing in the fifteenth century, the unnamed chronicler at Pluscarden Abbey in Moray (**73**) draws on earlier authorities such as John of Fordun (d. c. 1363) for his account of an incident following the Battle of Poitiers.[47] The Douglas family, whose ancestor is the subject, were a powerful force in the kingdom by this time and their role as the great 'war wall' against English invasion was well established. The wily

---

[46] An in-depth examination of this source is R. Moffat, '*The Manner of Arming Knights for the Tourney*: A Re-Interpretation of an Important Early-14th Century Arming Treatise', *Arms & Armour* 7 (2010), pp. 5–29.

[47] Dr Steve Boardman kindly drew my attention to this episode. I am most grateful to Drs Zsuzsa Papp and Mark Tizzoni for their generous assistance with my translation of this passage and (**69**).

Sir William Ramsay of Colluthie, who helps the young Archibald Douglas escape their captors, was 'weil kent' as a battle-hardened warrior and crusader.

The type of language clerical chroniclers employ can prove difficult to interpret. They draw on a lexicon of vocabulary from the classical texts in which the learned were versed – thus we find, for instance, a bellicose bishop compared to a warrior of Mars, the Roman god of war (**118**). What these writers do best is breathe life into the people and events they describe. A sense of movement animates static iron and steel. We feel ourselves plunged into the midst of the action – be it a bishop grinding his teeth like a wild boar (**118**), a nobleman preparing for single combat (**146**), a punch in the face with a spiked gauntlet (**69**), a love-struck squire jumping over the barriers before a besieged castle to issue a challenge (**112**), a canny knight outsmarting his boastful captors after defeat in battle (**73**), a queen armed as a knight stealing away into the night (**38**), or a 'shower of shite': a motley mob of revolting peasants loosing their arrows to inflict a brutal death (**120**).

Biographies and Travellers' Accounts

I have included one of each in order to demonstrate their usefulness to our study (**110** and **141**). First is the oft-quoted description of the intense training regime of a French war leader in his formative years. Known by his nickname Boucicaut, his anonymous biographer's account seems somewhat far-fetched. However, in the light of the evidence that full mail and plate armour was purchased for the seven-year-old Black Prince, it cannot be dismissed as exaggerated nonsense. The surviving portions of an armour made for the twelve-year-old Dauphin (later Charles VI) and dedicated to Chartres Cathedral are fully functional.[48] An Iberian fightmaster writing in Milan in the fifteenth century thought it necessary to devote six chapters to various vaulting techniques.[49] Such gruelling training was – indeed, still is – essential for any warrior to fight effectively in harness.

Second, a Catalan knight expresses his wonder at the exotic – the strange attire and weapons of an Irish chieftain's retainers.[50] Sir Ramón paints a vivid portrait of warriors from, what must have seemed to him, another world. Surviving artefacts and artwork (e.g. the exquisite miniature in London, British Library, MS Harley 1319, fol. 9r) prove his observations to be very accurate.

Expert Advice

As an experienced jouster, Henry, duke of Lancaster, weighed into a debate between two bands of knights:

> if *I* were involved in (feats of) arms with knights, I would ensure my helm was fastened as securely as possible. For, of a hundred chipping in their two-pence-worth, you would find that four score shared *my* view.

---

[48] F. H. Cripps-Day, 'The Armour at Chartres', *The Connoisseur: An Illustrated Magazine for Collectors*, vol. 110, no. 146 (December 1942), pp. 91–5.

[49] Pietro Monte, *Exercitiorum atque artis militaris collectanea in tris libros distincta* (Milan, 1509), Lib. II, Caps 141–6.

[50] I am extremely grateful to Prof. Noel Fallows for locating this work and his generous assistance with translation.

si ie estoie ens es armes ou les ch[iua]l[e]rs sont Je feroye mon heaulme tenir du plus fort que Je pourroye Et de cent qui seroient qui seroie[n]t en ce party vous en trouuerez iiijxx de mo[n] oppinion.[51]

Our writers too are keen to impart their wisdom. We can picture the warrior-monk Sir Roger Stanegrave plotting against his 'infidel' captors whilst fettered in fetid Egyptian prisons for over thirty years (**41**). He demonstrates his understanding of the technicalities of war: the efficacy of crossbowmen, the skills of the enemy, the best breed of warhorse, the importance of discipline, and the psychology of defeat. Sir Philippe de Mézières was a knight who spent as much time away from his native France travelling as Sir Roger did in captivity (**133**). He advises a young king to lead by example. Give up jousting and tournaments: use a lifetime of martial training to fight for faith. Both knights share the dream of a united Christian reconquest of the Holy Land and both understand the crucial role of arms and armour.

Written Challenges to Combat:
The Love of a Lady or Throwing Down the Gauntlet

For a wise knight, it was imperative that an impressionable monarch must:

> especially avoid books and romances replete with tall tales – such as the tales of Lancelot and the like – that so often encourage the reader to futile undertakings, folly, vanity, and lust.

> et par espical des livres et des romans qui sont rempliz de bourdes et qui attrayent le lysant souvent a impossibilite, a folie, vanite et pechie, comme les livres des bourdes de Lancelot et semblables.[52]

His counsel evidently fell on deaf ears. These 'tall tales' inflamed the imaginations of many people in the century, for even such a curmudgeon as the Dominican preacher John Bromyard (**3**) lauds the feats of King Arthur and the heroes of old. These challenges to combat (**67**) are quite a challenging source-type to take on.[53] They are expressions of an elaborate literary courtly culture. The fantastical and pseudo-historical are intertwined. A letter is addressed to the Queen of King Arthur's Realm of Great Britain. The chivalrous fighting men of England, we are told in another, are descended from valiant Trojan warriors, their capital rebranded as New Troy. Knights errant are bound with garter chains that cannot be unlocked until the defeat of a sworn number of opponents – all for the unattainable love of a lady. Despite their florid prose, the authors of these texts *do* properly address the practicalities of combat: the types of weapons and saddles, the number of lance courses to be run on horseback, the number of axe blows and dagger thrusts. Thus they pass from the realm of pure

---

[51] As related by Froissart. Besançon, Bibliothèque municipale, MS 865, fol. 325v. MS images reproduced in HRI *Online Froissart*, ed. P. Ainsworth and G. Croenen (Sheffield, 2013).

[52] Philippe de Mézières, *Le Songe du Vieil Pelerin*, ed. G. W. Coopland, 2 vols (Cambridge, 1969), II, 221.

[53] Thanks are due to Prof. Nigel Ramsay for bringing my attention to the documents in Edinburgh University Library.

literature to the sweat-drenched and blood-soaked reality of the hard-fought contest. Sir John Cornwall – a man very well versed in feats of arms – picks up on some of the inconsistencies in a letter of challenge he has received (**148**). In his reply he requests clarification of the use of arm defences and if the basinets are to be fitted with visors.

By reading these texts we are drawn into the glittering circle of the international chivalric elite – combatants from the warring kingdoms of Christendom. These were tough fighting men who, within a few weeks, might be feasting together after a joust on London Bridge, killing and enslaving 'pagans' in the Baltic, then glowering at each other across a waterlogged battlefield.

My liberal use of 'possibly', 'probably', 'perhaps', 'might be', 'maybe', and 'as yet, unknown' throughout is a clear indication of how much more there remains to be discovered. It is very likely that sources yet to be brought to light will make much of that which is unknown known. Well might we yet find baleen genulers, cuir bouilli mustilers, and detailed instructions for the manufacture of gaignepains.

2

Material Source-Types

Armour and Weapons

To have the privilege to hold a real medieval object in one's hand is to experience a tangible link to the past. To grip the hilt of a sword or the shaft of a pollaxe, to hold a helmet or gauntlet is quite remarkable. Close examination trains the eye to recognize such details as the manner of manufacture and application of decoration. To compare the size, weight, and 'feel' of various pieces gives an incredible insight into how they have been borne and wielded. To a greater extent, museums are facilitating this cotton-gloved 'hands-on' approach. Indeed, readers are encouraged to take advantage of this opportunity whenever it arises. Second to this invaluable experience is the provision of images: these must suffice for the purposes of our study. Wherever possible, images of objects from the pertinent era have been chosen to illustrate the glossary. Where this is more difficult, earlier or later examples are used.

As outlined in the preface, the surviving artefacts from our century represent a miniscule fraction of those that had been in use. Metals and fabrics were (and are) valuable commodities. After the Battle of Bannockburn the slain were completely stripped and left 'nakyt'.[1] Such rich pickings could be reused in multifarious ways. In the British Museum is a fourteenth-century kettlehat that has been converted into a kettle for domestic use. In 1423 ingenious London brewers found that mail links of an old haubergeon made ideal curtain rings for a wall hanging in their meeting hall.[2]

Another good case of re-use has been revealed in the excavated remains of a sixteenth-century body defence known as a jack of plate. The small metal plates sewn into its fabric were cut-down pieces from a defence much in use in the previous century – the brigandine. This flexible torso defence could, itself, be constructed from sections cut from plate armour.[3]

Unknown or murky provenance (i.e. 'said to have come from', 'attributed to') bedevils the study of many an artefact. When presented with such unreliable

[1] Barbour's *Bruce*, ed. A. A. M. Duncan (Edinburgh, 1997), p. 505.
[2] London Guildhall Library, CLC/L/BF/A/021/MS05440, fol. 101v. Ms Hannah Dunmow was most helpful in locating this document.
[3] I. Eaves, 'On the Remains of a Jack of Plate excavated from Beeston Castle in Cheshire', *Journal of the Arms & Armour Society* 13 (1989), pp. 81–154.

information, we are often forced to rely on stylistic grounds such as comparison with artworks and similar pieces with better-known provenance for the purposes of dating and place of origin, production, and use. Even objects with an impeccable provenance are not always cut-and-dried cases. A good example is the past life of the 'Avant' armour in Glasgow Museums' collection. One of the oldest near-complete plate armours in existence, it was generously bequeathed to the people of the City by R. L. Scott in 1939. It comes from the Armoury of Churburg Castle in the South Tyrol. The majority of the harness (the contemporary term for a complete armour) was made in the Corio brothers' workshop in Milan between 1438 and 1440. In the Castle Armoury it was mounted with a right-hand gauntlet and a helmet. Both of these are of a slightly-later date and of much larger size. They are also the products of different workshops. The Avant harness, along with its associated helmet and gauntlet, was purchased by William Randolph Hearst in 1934. Hearst employed a craftsman to polish the steel plates, replace some straps, and fashion a replica left-hand gauntlet at some point before its sale to R. L. Scott in 1938.[4] The helmet retains a lining that was, most probably, fitted during its working life. There is a small section of the original leather tab on the right cuisse (thigh defence). This tab would have served to lace the cuisse to an arming doublet. In the 1970s much of the leather was replaced by specialists in the Armoury at the Tower of London. In the following decade the whole harness was completely re-leathered by the Tower's craftsmen. This involved the replacement of almost all the straps, internal articulating leathers, and many rivets. Furthermore, the polished steel surfaces were dulled to match the dove grey of the armours remaining at Churburg Castle.[5]

Telling the story of this harness serves as a firm reminder that we must tread *very* cautiously when investigating any medieval object. What may superficially appear complete might well be a composite. Damage and repair can take place at any point on its journey from the past. Parts can be replaced – especially with swords, whose cross-guards and pommels can be removed. Very few staff weapons retain their original wooden shafts; the bow-stave of a crossbow may be original but the tiller could be a later addition (see Figure 20).

We should not dwell too much on the negative. Each object speaks to us, not in an audible language, but in its very form. Every single indentation on the inside of a plate or helmet is a hammer-blow struck by its maker. The chiselling and filing of visors, rolled edges, and roughly-sheared lames speak of the level of skill and the speed of production. Hand clipping rivets and washers is the tedious task of tired young apprentices; grooves in mail links are from the wire-maker's drawplate. A series of small nicks on the edge of each plate aid the man leathering and riveting together a full harness when a large shipment of components lies strewn across his workshop.

---

4   J. G. Mann, 'Three Armours in the Scott Collection', *Scottish Art Review* 6 (1956), pp. 2–17 (at pp. 5–6); R. C. Woosnam-Savage, 'Robert Lyons Scott 1871–1939: A Biographical Note', F. Joubert, *Catalogue of the Collection of European Arms & Armour formed at Greenock by R. L. Scott*, ed. R. C. Woosnam-Savage and T. Capwell, 2nd edn (Huntingdon, 2006), p. i–p. ix (at p. vi–p. vii).

5   Glasgow Museums Object File E.1939.65.e.

Artworks

Depictions of arms and armour are a key source-type. We have the great privilege to be the inheritors of so much precious material culture: stained glass, carvings, sculpture, ivories, tomb effigies, manuscript illustrations – to name but a few. Such works depict much of what is now lost: the dyed-leather straps, gilded buckles, fine linings, and luxurious fabric coverings – a sumptuous palette of vivid colours splashed across the blank canvas that is the bare steel and iron. They are the product of artists who had observed their subjects in life and in great detail. Many depict men of high status and considerable means, these being very lucrative patrons' commissions.

A key fact must be kept to the forefront of our minds when investigating this material culture as a source-type: such artwork was not produced for our eyes to furnish information to trace a line of development.

Tomb Sculpture: Effigies and Brasses

In 1408 a witness to the Court of Chivalry provided a description of a tomb brass in the church at Elsing in Norfolk. It depicts a knight, Sir Hugh Hastings, who died in 1347. Although the evidence he gave was principally for the purposes of describing a heraldic coat of arms, the level of detail in his description is remarkable. It is, he states, 'a great and large marble stone on which is made a great image and of fine stature of a knight' ('une grande et large peere de marbille sur quelle est fait une ymage grande et de belle estature dun Ch[iuale]r'). He proceeds to name the various defences, even noting that 'his plate vambrace and rerebrace gilded, with round couters and besagews of the ancient type' ('ses vaunbraces et rerebraces de plate dorrez ouec les couters et basagues roundes de la ancien entaile').[6] When casting our eye over a tomb brass, or any such artwork, we too are seeking evidence.

From the earliest beginnings of the study of arms and armour the importance of tomb sculpture as a key source has been well understood. These artworks have inspired many a lavishly-illustrated monograph and even a journal devoted to their interpretation. In this section I will address two issues only: an argument and a problem.

First the argument – one that has been put forward numerous times – that men are often depicted in death as warriors when in life they had never once brandished a weapon in anger or strapped on a breastplate. One example will suffice to demonstrate this to be the mootest of points. In response to a royal demand for five hundred well-armed men to serve in Scotland in 1318, the Commonalty of the City of London agreed to send two hundred. This was only on the condition that citizens of the more powerful and better sort might provide another to serve in their stead ('potencioribus

---

6   London, College of Arms, MS entitled 'Processus in Curia Marescalli', 2 vols, II, pp. 345–54. Richmond Herald graciously allowed access to this manuscript. An excerpt has been printed in A. R. Wagner and J. G. Mann, 'A 15th-Century Description of the Brass of Sir Hugh Hastings at Elsing, Norfolk', *Antiquaries Journal* 19 (1939), pp. 421–8.

& melioribus Ciuitatis inueniat p[ro] se vnu' homi[n]em armatum').[7] The Common Clerk of this same city, John Carpenter, writing in 1419, informs us that

> Now it was said that in times of old aldermen were named with the same honour as barons. To make clear, it is known that from around the year of our Lord 1350 that in the interment of aldermen they were honourably served in this ancient manner, viz. that in the church in which the alderman was to be interred, one (man) astride a trappered horse, armed in his (the deceased's) arms, bearing aloft in his hand the banner, the shield, helm, and suchlike of his (the deceased's) arms with the banner – in the same manner as the interment of barons.

> [...] Aldermanni tam no[m]i[n]e q[u]am honore Barones antiquitus diceba[n]tur vt p[atet]

> Exp[er]tu' est e[ni]m circa annu' d[omi]ni millesimu' CCCiii quinqua gesimu' q[uo] d in Sepulturis Aldermannor[um] Seruabat[u]r honorificus ille modus antiqus [sic] videl[ice]t ut in eccl[es]ia qua Sepeliendus esset Aldermannus vnus [sic] armatus in eius armis Sup[er] equm phalaratu' vexillum ferens in manu Sursum asserret Scutu' geleam & arma sua cet[er]a cu' vexillo sicut ad huc modus est diu[ers]is Baronibus Sepeliri.[8]

Carpenter was correct in his assertion. This was, indeed, an 'ancient' custom. A contemporary document relating to a funeral at Broomhill Priory, Norfolk, in 1245 describes the event. Armour worth 20 marks ('armatu' p[re]cij xx marc'') was borne before the body ('ante corpus') of the deceased. Furthermore, in the procession 'there rode a certain nobly-armoured squire' ('equitauit quida' armig' nobil' armatura'') clad in armour worth 100s. ('p[re]c' armatur' C solid''). An attendee enquired of the Prior if the said horse with armour might be sold to him ('dictu' equ' cu' armatura' venditio'').[9]

Status, not battle experience, is the motive behind both this dramatic equestrian performance and the commissioning of funerary sculpture. This is solid proof that even the most battle-shy individual of some means might well be portrayed as a warrior in death, either through their own volition or that of their kin. Thus the circumlocutory situation: to be represented as a warrior one needs be shown in harness – such harness is that borne by a warrior and is thus rendered as such. Yes, brasses and effigies were crafted in schools and workshops: so too were arms and armour.

The second issue I will address is a problem, one that is particularly pertinent to the earlier part of the fourteenth century. Experts such as Norman and Blair have drawn attention to the stark time lag between documentary evidence and the depiction of arms and armour.[10] Such documents as castle inventories clearly reveal that even common soldiers had access to solid limb and torso defences. Yet we find nobles, knights,

---

7   London, London Metropolitan Archives, London Letter-Book E, fol. 79r.
8   London, London Metropolitan Archives, COL/CS/01/012, Liber Albus, fol. 8r. I am grateful to Ms Louisa Macdonald and Mr Francisco Castanon for arranging photography of this document.
9   London, Society of Antiquaries of London Library, MS SAL/MS/778/32. I am grateful to Ms Barbara Canepa for providing an image of this document.
10 C. Blair, 'The Conington Effigy: 14th-Century Knights at Conington, Dodford and Tollard Royal', *Church Monuments* 6 (1991), pp. 3–20 (at pp. 10–14); C. Blair, 'Armour and the Study of Brasses', *Monumental Brasses as Art and History*, ed. J. Bertram (Stroud, 1996), pp. 37–40 (at p. 194, endnote 3); A. V. B. Norman, 'Two Early-14th-Century Military Effigies', *Church Monuments* 1 (1985), pp. 10–19 (at p. 10).

squires, and gentry arrayed in the mail armour their grandfathers – even great grandfathers – would have donned, with plate armour only making its appearance in the 1330s. For Blair this is 'deliberate conservatism in funerary representations of knights, perhaps with the idea of showing them as idealised chivalric figures'.[11] Well worthy of a detailed study in its own right, this author would lean towards a more nuanced interpretation. Are these artworks an expression of a self-conscious atavism? Is there an underlying fear that one's dynasty might appear too *arriviste*? Whatever the case, both issues discussed above bring us back to the key point: artists simply *did not* craft these objects for the benefit of scholars in centuries to come to enable them to trace a straightforward linear development. No, the purpose was to demonstrate the status of the deceased. Thus we find ourselves, yet again, in the circumlocutory situation described above.

Capwell offers a robust defence of tomb effigies as a key primary source for better understanding the development of armour.[12] He convincingly demonstrates how details on carvings match those of the existing material culture. This approach certainly rings true for the latter part of the fourteenth, and throughout the fifteenth, century. However, given the complications discussed in this section, it may not be fully applicable to the period here.

Artworks in Other Media

Artwork in two dimensions or in bas relief will always be subject to one major limitation. An artist seeks to portray in their chosen medium three-dimensional objects: harness and weapons. We must be willing, therefore, to accept the limitations of our interpretation. The different materials employed – wood, ivory, copper-alloy, stained glass – permit an artist to achieve different levels of detail. Through their chosen medium one craftsman (e.g. a painter) is recreating the craft of another: the armourer or weapon-maker.

The work of an artist (and his workshop of assistants) must be carefully 'read'. Does he have an eye for detail? Are certain decisions made for aesthetic reasons? For instance, one artisan might decide to include such details as straps, buckles, and hinges, and another the main plates only – the gilt-latten effigy of the Black Prince at Canterbury Cathedral being a case in point (Figure 5). Some media, such as brasses, do not use colour whilst others may well have lost their painted decoration. We must exercise the same degree of caution when investigating these sources as with pieces of arms and armour. Sections of stained glass and tomb brasses might be replaced, effigies repaired and repainted, and original polychrome lost – such interventions include:

- the stained glass depictions of members of the De Clare and Despenser families in Tewkesbury Abbey
- the partly-restored brass of Sir John Northwode in the Abbey Church at Minster on Sea, Kent
- the repainted effigies of a lord and lady of the Beauchamp family in Worcester Cathedral
- the heavily-restored tomb of the Earl and Countess of Devon in Exeter Cathedral.

---

[11]   Blair, 'The Conington Effigy', p. 14.
[12]   Capwell, *Armour of the English Knight*, pp. 30–52.

The documentary evidence presented in this sourcebook must act, to some extent, to shake our confidence in making definitive pronouncements. For example, in the century of our study we are faced with the problem of there being a great many artworks where the fabric of the heraldic coat armour conceals much of the armour borne beneath. Separate mail defences such as paunces (skirts) and sleeves are abundant in our documents. Therefore we cannot say with certainty that a complete hauberk or haubergeon is borne beneath the rest of the defences depicted, say, in a tomb brass (see Figure 10).[13] Similarly, a series of dots might be interpreted as a representation of the external rivet-heads of a pair of plates. On the other hand, they might equally be interpreted as a decorative pattern for the luxurious facing of a jazerant (Figure 31). The mail is fitted inside this body defence so it cannot be differentiated from any other textile facing in an artistic rendering. There are a variety of leg-defence types recorded – schynbalds, mustilers, genulers, jambers – but their forms are nowhere described. We cannot ascribe these to an artwork with any certainty until more detailed information comes to light.

We must also be encouraged. Plate sabatons to protect the feet are in use from 1303–4, and breastplates (at least for jousting) from the late 1330s (**9** and **52**). We observe that decorative heraldic ailettes have fallen out of favour by the 1330s. The accepted period of the dominance of plate harness can be pushed back with the introduction of the arming doublet and its mail voiders, as argued in the 'Using the Sourcebook' section.

Central to the importance of artistic sources is the fact that each was produced by a man who had seen their subject at first hand – be it a carver of a tomb effigy, a maker of a tomb brass (Figure 10) or a stained glass panel (Figure 10 and Figure 43), or even an idler doodling in the margin of a prayer book (Figure 46). Such a man had actually heard the creaking of a springald (Figure 49), the clanking of sword on buckler (Figure 13 and Figure 14), and the shattering of lances in a joust (Figure 17 and Figure 19).

The work of artists after the Middle Ages is also of great value. We must be extremely grateful for every single image of that which is now lost – be it an etching made in the 1870s of a painted tomb-niche showing huntsmen preparing their bows (Figure 11) or a line drawing of a helm and reinforce unearthed in the late-eighteenth century that has subsequently disappeared (Figure 28). Such sources are, nevertheless, at one more remove from the original. They must be accepted to be an artist's attempt to replicate an artist's attempt to depict men or objects. Despite this, their value vastly outweighs the prospect of us having nothing whatsoever.

For an anonymous Frenchman writing in 1446, the intrinsic effectiveness of artwork as an aid to his readers' understanding was self-evident. 'Thus I shall say no more, for you may better comprehend by viewing the painting than if I should put it in writing' ('Si me en tays atant Car par la painture le pourrez aussi bien comprendre

---

[13]   One of the few scholars to have pointed out this difficulty is A. V. B. Norman. Norman, 'Two Early-14th-Century Military Effigies', p. 5.

co[m]me si Je le bailloye p[ar] escript').[14] For us, too, text and image work smoothly in tandem to serve to greatly increase our understanding.

By engaging with all our sources, voices from the past *can* be heard, and many insights gained, and dramas enacted, and thus, as the English playwright Thomas Nashe states with *élan*:

> Our forefathers' valiant acts (that have lain long buried in rusty [tomb] brass and worm-eaten books) are revived, and they themselves raised from the grave of oblivion.[15]

---

14 Paris, Bibliothèque nationale de France, MS fr. 1997, fol. 69r. It is most disappointing that the paintings to which he alludes were never copied into the surviving manuscript.

15 T. Nashe, *Pierce Penniless His Supplication to the Devil* (London, 1592), chap. II.

Part II

The Documents

Paris, Bibliothèque nationale de France, MS fr. 24069, fol. 115r–fol. 115v

Statutes of the Armourers of Paris, 1296

Cest ce que li armeurier de p[ar]is eut ordene & accorde pour le profit de lour mestier et pour eschiuer les frauds les faussetes et les mauesties qui en dit mestier estoient fetes & ont este en temps passe que nus ne puisse f[et]e cote ne gamboison de tele dont lenu[er]s et lendroit ne soit de tele noeue et dedenz de coton et de plois de toiles et Se enisq[ue]s est q[u]il soeint dedenz decroes que p[ar] lour s[er]emenz que il ni metent escroe de tele dont laune nait contre viij d au meins Se len fait cote ne gamboison dont lendroit soit de cendal et lenu[er]s soit de tele Si Soeule[men]t il que ele soit noeue et Se il ia ploit dedenz de tele ne de cendal que le plus cort ploit soit de demie aune et demi q[u]artier de lonc au meins deuant & autant derrieres et les autr[e]s plois lons ensiuans et Se il ia borre de soie que le leit de la borre Soit de demie aune et demy q[ua]rtier au meins deua[n]t et autant derrieres et Se il ia coton que le coton vienge tout [con]t[re]ual Jusques aus piez que nul ne Cueure bacin qui ne soit sainz puiz plain ponce puiz le p[ar]tus en amont et que nulles gorg[er]etes a bacin ne soient fetes que lendroit et lenu[er]s ne Soient neufz et couces de coton dedenz que nuls ne puisse fete couu[er]tures a cheual do[n]t lendroit & lenu[er]s ne soit neuf' et couces de coton de coton de len' que len ne puisse broch' Se il ne sont arriere poinc' ganteles de baleine fors sus teiles noueus et q[u]il seront de bone baleine q' nuls ne face ganteles de plates q' les plates ne soient estaimees ou v[er]nicees et que il ne soient pas couu[er]s de basaine noire ne de mesgueiz et q' desouz les testes de chescun clou ait vn Riuet dargent pel ou dor pel ou aut[re] Riuet q[ue]l que il soit et que touz cuissoz de plates & toutes Trumel[ie]rs de plates soient faites en ceste man[ier]e ou en meilleur q' len ne cueuir nulle Cuirie que lenu[er]s & lend[r]oit ne soit neuf' q' len ne mete nul viel Cuir en Oeure auecq[ue]s nuef' de ce nest en Cuirie q' len ne puisse desormes t[r]aire p[ar]mi col[er]etes de cotes ne p[ar]mi poignez de manches Se ce nest de coton que nul ne face Oeure faite a deux fois soit de toile ou de cendal q' les p[ar]ties ne soient enf[er]mes p[our]pointes et couchies et q' nul ne face Oeure emplie a v[er]ges en Oeure de guerre q' nul ne sent[r]emete ne ne tienge ouureour se il ne Soit dudit mest' q' nul ne puisse desormes [con]port' p[ar] la ville de la par' armeures q[ue]lles q' il soie[n]t se ce ne sont les pou[e]rs deu mest' q' demorent es Rues foraines q' ne les puent vendre en lour hostelx et que il Jurgent sur sainz q' il sont fetes en lour mesons p[ro]pres et fetes et app[ar]eillies de lour mains et app[ar]eillies de lour mains Et q[ui]conques sera oeure q[ue]le que ele soit [con]t[re] lestablissem[en]t desus dit ele sera forfaite et arse et cil Sus qui ele S[er]a t[r]uuet en S[er]a en lam[an]de le Roi Ou quel mest' il aura q[ua]tre p[ro]udes ho[m]mes qui les choses desus dites s[er]ont gard' loiam[en]t par lour S[er]emez Les quelx le p[re]uost de par' met[r]a et ost[er]a a sa volente Q[u]iconques voudra leuer Ouureor En mest' desus dit il lachat[er]a deu Roy xij s' de par' des quelx li Rois aura viij s' et les proudes ho[m]mes qui gard[er]ont le mest' iiij s' Q[u]iconq[ue]s mesp[re]ndra en aucun des articles desus diz il paiera vij s' dam[an]de des quelx li Rois aura v s' et les gardes deu mestier ij solz

Ordained and agreed by the Armourers of Paris for the benefit of their craft and to avoid such fraud, falsity, and evil doings that this craft has been heretofore subjected. None may make linen coat or gambeson lest the inside and out be of new linen stuffed with tubes of linen. If it be lined with tubes they must swear that it be stuffed with strips of linen worth no less than eight *deniers*. The facings of coats or gambesons must be made of sendal (lightweight silk or very fine linen) and the linings of new linen. The lining tubes must be stuffed with linen or sendal. The shortest tube must be at least a half-ell and half-quarter ell in length both on the front and back and other tubes must be longer. If burrs of silk are used they must be at least a half-ell and half-quarter ell in length. If cotton is used it must come right down to the feet. None may cover any basinet if it cannot be smoothly polished above the (lining) perforations. No gorget for basinet may be made lest the outside and inside be of new cotton and completely lined within. None may make horse covers lest the outside and inside be of new cotton and completely lined within. None may sew baleen gauntlets lest they be lined inside like a pourpoint with new linen and they must use good baleen. None may make plate gauntlets lest the plates be tinned or varnished. They may be not covered with black-tanned sheepskin or *mégis* (a thin, alum-tanned, sheep or goatskin). Beneath each nail-head (wherever it may be) must be a rivet of silver or gold bar. All plate cuisses and *trumelières* [leg defences] must be made in this manner or better. None may cover or line any cuirie if the material be not new. None may replace any old leather with new in making the cuirie. None may sew drawstrings through collars of coats or through points of sleeves if the string be not of cotton. None may remake any work be it of linen or sendal lest all parts be reinforced, sewn like a pourpoint, and stuffed. No work for use in war may be stuffed with twigs. None may take into his employ any man that be not of this craft. Henceforth none should import armour of any sort into the City of Paris that has not been inspected by men of the craft. They who reside in the streets of the foreign (merchants) may not sell any armour in their lodgings lest they swear by the Saints that they be made in their own houses and made and equipped by their own hands. Whosoever makes work, wherever it may be, contrary to the statute aforesaid must pay the King's fine and it shall be forfeited and burnt. There shall be four worthy men of this craft who shall loyally ensure by their oath the aforesaid matters whom the *Prévôt* of Paris may appoint and remove at will. Whosoever wants to become a craftsman of this craft must purchase it (the right) from the King's dues for 12 Parisian *sous*. The King shall have eight *sous* of this and the worthy men who are Wardens of the Craft four *sous*. Whosoever contravenes in any way the articles aforesaid shall pay a fine of seven *sous*. The King shall have five *sous* of this and the Wardens of the Craft two *sous*.

2

London, British Library, Additional MS 46919, fol. 86v–fol. 87r
The Manner of Arming Knights for the Tournament, Joust, and War, England, Early-14th Century

Modus armandi milites ad torneamentum Primo fit ig[n]is et extendi' tapetu' & spoliatus ad camisia' Pectine p[ar]at capillos In pede calciat' de quyr Induit ocreas Gall' mustylers i[n] tibiis de ascer ou de quyr boily Deinde quysouns in femorib[u]s & genicularia gall' genulers Deind' aketoun & dein' ca[m]isia de chartres & coyfe de chartres & pelui[m] i[n] q[u]a e' cerueylere defendens cap' ne [con]tiguetur' peluis cu' capite deinde lorica' quyree cote armere in q[u]a fu[er]it sig[n]a milit' & gaynepayns ou gayns de baleyne sa espeye i. gladi' & flagellu' & galeam i. heaume Ad bellu' aketoun plates de alemayne ou autres cu' p[re]ceb[u]s aketon' vt supra [sic] & bone gorgieres gladi' haches a pik & cultell' scutu' raro p[or]tat' ad bellu' q[uam] impediret plus quam p[ro]moueret Ad hastiludia aketoun hauberc gambisoun q[ou]d f[uer]it de pa[n]no serico & [con]sim' si s[i]c p[re]c[i]osum neulers ke su[n]t plates de ascer scut' bacyn & galea

The Manner of arming knights for the tournament: first make a fire and roll out a carpet, then strip to the shirt and brush the hair, put leather boots on the feet, place greaves (in French mustilers) of steel or cuir bouilli on the shins, then cuisses on the thighs and knee defences (genulers in French), then aketon, and then camisia de Chartres and coif of Chartres,[1] and bacin (basinet) in which there will be a lining to prevent contact between the basinet and head, then hauberk, cuirie, coat armour on which is the knight's sign (heraldic arms), and gaignepains or baleen gauntlets, his espeye (i.e. sword), and flail, and helm (i.e. heaume). (Arming) for war: aketon, German pair of plates or others with the pièce (reinforcing plate), aketon above [sic], and a good gorget, sword, axe with (thrusting) spike, and knife. The shield is seldom carried in battle as it impedes more than it aids. (Arming) for the joust: aketon, hauberk, gambeson made of silk or suchlike precious cloth, (and) there should be nought (borne) but steel pair of plates, shield, basinet, and helm

3

J. Bromyard, *Summa Prædicantium*, 2 vols (Venice, 1586), II, p. 112 and p. 450

John Bromyard (d. c. 1352) was a Dominican friar and preacher at the Blackfriars, Hereford. Here he preaches on the nobility of his day as well as employing the hauberk as an analogy.

---

[1] Moffat, 'The Manner of Arming Knights for the Tourney', p. 10: 'a garment in the shape of, and that had come into contact with, the *sancta camisia* of Chartres cathedral'.

On the Nobility

vbi nobiles [...] contra Deum viuunt per guerras brigas & discordias [...] vnde arma sua emunt & deaura[n]t & superflue se ornant & vnde equos emunt & nutriunt & milites & stipendiarios conducunt [...] Et sicut ad vanitatem arma sua fecerunt & deaurauerunt ita de vanitate nuda & non de probitate gaudea[n]t & laude[n]tur [...] Nonne multi sic laudantur nobiles moderni temporis quis aliquem illoru' laudare audiuit vel laudare potuit de strenua inimicorum expugnatione & patriæ & ecclesiæ defensione sicut commendantur & laudantur Karolus magnus Rolandus & Oliuerius & alij antiqui milites sed hoc quod galeam habent deauratam precij 40 librarum & alas & alia insignia exteriora eiusde' formæ & maioris precij Et quod in hastiludio grossam & quadratam portauit lanceam qualem nullus alius portauit vel portare potuit & quod equum & asce[n]sorem poiecit in terram Et quod ita bene equitauit & lanceam illiam ita agiliter mouit ac si leuissima fuisset Et quod cum tot equis venit ad parleamentum vel torneamentum Et qualis est ista laus nisi laus impiorum & miserorum & timidorum [...]

Quid vale[n]t arma tunc deaurata quæ hostes audaciores faciunt [...] Et quæ fugie[n]do hostibus læti proijciunt vt vel ocius fugiant sicut nuper accidit Que laus est contra hominem pacis fortissimum portare lanceam & equum & ascensorem ad terram deiicere & hostem nec cum quacunque tangere lancea quia nec ei tantum appropinquare voluit quod cum longissima illum tangere potuissent Vel quæ laus est quod bene equitauit & faciliter lancea' mouit & agiliter se habuit co[n]tra amicum & vicinum & agiliter fugit inimicum regni Vel quæ laus est quod in factis armorum prohibitis sicut in torneamentis & huiusmodi [...] sint gloriosi & appetant laudari & in factis virtuosis sic in bellis iustis & in defensione patriæ [...]

On the Hauberk

In via nanque est lorica in patria gloria In via igitur lorica dicitur quia sicut lorica quodda' genus armoru' est corporis in quo omnes annuli co[n]catenantur & mutuo se tene[n]tur Ita iusticia quoddam genus armouru' est amimæ in quo omnes virtutes concatenatæ sunt & continentur [...] Et sicut ex fractura vnius annuli domini inuaso periculu' imminet toti corpori [...]

On the Nobility

[...] where nobles [...] live against (the will of) God by wars, fights, and discords [...] they buy arms and have them gilded and superfluously decorated, and they buy and feed horses, and employ soldiers and mercenaries [...]. And it is for vanity that they have their arms crafted and gilded – they take joy in, and praise, naked vanity *not* integrity. [...] Should such nobles at the present time be so greatly praised? Can any of them be praised now or in the past for the strenuous destruction of enemies and the defence of the Fatherland and Church in the way that Charlemagne, Roland, and Oliver, and other great knights of old are commended and praised? It has come to this: they have a gilded helm worth £40, and (decorative) ailettes, and other outward insignia (i.e. heraldic coat armours) of the same type and greater price. In the joust they wield large and heavy lances which no others wield – or are able to wield – so to knock horse and rider to the ground. And because he (the jouster) rides well and can wield his lance so agilely, thus it (seems to be) of the utmost lightness. He comes thus to gatherings or tournaments with many horses. And in what manner is this renown save the renown of damnation, worthlessness, and cowardliness?!

Of what value, then, are gilded arms that embolden (enemy) hosts? For those fleeing the hosts gladly cast them off so that they might flee all the faster – as befell of late. What renown is there in most forcefully wielding lance and (spurring on) horse and approaching to knock the man of peace to the ground, yet touching none of the (enemy) host whatsoever with the lance – wanting only to approach them if he be at such a distance that they cannot touch him? Or what renown is there in he who rides well and agilely wields his lance against friend and neighbour, yet agilely flees the King's enemies? Or what renown is there in taking part in prohibited feats of arms such as tournaments and the like [...] glory and enduring praise is to be found in such virtuous deeds as just wars and the defence of the Fatherland.

On the Hauberk

The hauberk is indeed the path to the glorious Fatherland. Therefore the path is called 'hauberk': just as the hauberk is a type of body armour in which all the rings are linked and affixed together, so justice is a type of armour for the soul in which all virtues are linked together. And, if one of the Lord's rings is broken the whole body is threatened by the peril of being penetrated (i.e. by a lethal weapon).

4

Lille, Archives départementales du Nord, B450/4401
Inventory of the Goods of Connétable Raoul de Nesle, Paris, Bailleul, Nesle, and Elsewhere, 1302

Inuentor' de lartiller' chest asauoir arbalestes ars maniers & Cor' Ne[r]us fraisnich' iiij arbalestes de cor' & iij de fust xvi lb' biaulieu Pluseurs glaiues & grant plance de q[u] atriaus pour le garniss' de le tour' ii arbalest' a tour & xii a pie toutes de cor' Paris xix arbalestes de cor' iiij xx l' xvij arbalestes de fust xiiij l' ij petites arbalest' de genes xl s' viij ars maniers xx s' i baston a iiij viroles dargent & aut' baston & vne mache xx s' vne hache & plusours coutiaus a taillier xl s' A Neele & a paris i ganboisson iiij vi l' vns cuissens ganboisies des arm' de neele xx s' vn auketons x l' iii couu[er]tures a cheual gamboisies C s' i hauberion & i camail xii l' i gazarant & i camail de maisme viij l' iiij piec' de flanchieres lx s' ii bras & vns gousses iiij l' ii gorgerete pisaines xxx s' vnes plates vermeilles vi l' vnes autres plates des armes de neele iiij l' iij bacines l s' iij pair' de cuirs a bras & vns ganteles xxx s' ij couu[er]tures de plates xl s' ij paires de gans des arm' de neele xxx s' viij q[ue] capiaus q[ue] hiaumes & i bacin xiij l' ii gorgeretes de plates xl s' ij harnas de jau[m]bes fourbis de coi les greues sont closes C s' vnes autres demie greues fourbies iiij l' vns bras de fer & i coutes xx s' xi q[ue] targes quescus C s' le tour xviij haubers xx l' vij hauberions q[ue] corses viij l' xlii pieche de causes xx l' xxxiiij piech' de test' q[ue] crupieres a cheual & iiii petit' piech' de fer x l' x espees sans argent C s' vne espee de gennes garnie dargent x l' vne autre espee a i fuerre vermeil garni dargent vi l' vne autre a fuerre vert de soie seme descuchons xx s' vne autre espee a i fuerre noire a Beug' v[er]t garni dargent vi l' vne aut' a pomel de cristal iiij l' vne mesericorde a fuerre de cuir bouli a i pomel dargent xx s' ii aut' misericordes a fuerre vermaus a bendez dargent xl s' vi coutiaus a pointe de coi li vns est garnis dargent iiij l' xxx fers a glaiue de diuerses fachons lx s' Neele iiij haubers vi fers a glaiue de nul pris Paris i ganboison C s' i aut' gambois' lx s' vnes espauliers de balaine a tournoier xxiiij s' vns cuirs a bras xvi s' vnes couu[er]tures a cheual poupoi[n]t' ij test' de soie a cheual iii chapiaus de montauben iiij hiaumes & i bachinet v[er]nicie viii l' xvi s' i autre bacinet v s' ij paire de plates C s' iii paires de plates toutes garnies pour son cors xii l' viii q[ue] hauberions q[ue] haubers & iij camaus xliii l' vne gorgiere xx s' vnes couu[er]tures de fer a cheval vi l' vne autres couu[er]tres de fer vii l' vne aut[re]s couu[er]tures viii l' [...] haubers a tournoier xl s' pluseurs menues piech' de hauberions iiij l' ij espees ij petites misericordes lx s' ix espees chascune vi s' & sont loiees dune long' Beuges liii s' xv espees loiees dune Beuge de soie chascune xij s' vne espee garnie a pell' C s' vne aut' espee garnie de brodur' des armes de neele vi l' vij coutiaus a poi[n]te xxx s' v aut' coutiaus x s' ij coutiaus garniz dargent vj s' i coutel a ymage a cristal v s' xiiii fers a glaiue lvi s' iiij aut' fers a glaiue plus petis viii s' ij pair' de ganteles couuers de Rouge cuir xx s' iij maces lx s'

Inventory of the artillery – that is to say: crossbows (of wood), of sinew, and hand-spanned bows: Fraisniches: three crossbows of horn and three of wood 16 (Parisian) *livres*. Bailleul: several old glaives and great quarterstaffs for equipping the tower of no value, two torsion crossbows and 12 foot-spanned of horn [no value provided]. Paris: 19 horn crossbows four score l., 17 wooden crossbows 14l., two little crossbows of Genoa 40s., eight hand-spanned bows 20s., one baton (club) with three silver ferrules, another baton, and one mace 20s., one axe and several cutting knives 40s. Armour, gambesons, and old hauberks at Bailleul, Nesle, and Paris – Bailleul: one gambeson 3l., one pair of gamboised cuisses (i.e. made in the manner of a padded gambeson) with the (heraldic) arms of Nesle 20s., one aketon 10l., three gamboised horse covers 100s., one haubergeon and one aventail 12l., one jazerant and one aventail the same 8l., four pieces of flanchers (horse's flank defences) 60s. two (mail) sleeves and one gusset 4l., three Pisan gorgets 30s., one pair of plates of vermilion (velvet) 6l., another pair of plates of the arms of Nesle 4l., three basinets 50s., three pairs of cuiries with sleeves and one pair of gauntlets 30s., two (horse) covers of plate 40s., two pairs of gauntlets of the arms of Nesle 30s., eight (helmets) both chapel de fers and helms and one basinet 13l., two plate gorgets 40s., two furbished (polished steel) pairs of legharness the greaves of which are closed (i.e. enclose the leg) 100s., another pair of furbished legharness with demi-greaves 4l., one pair of iron (mail) sleeves and one couter 20s., 11 (shields) both targes and shields 100s. The tower: 18 hauberks 20l., seven hauberks with corsets 8l., 42 pieces of chausses 20l., 34 pieces of horse testers and cruppers, and four little pieces of iron (mail) 10l., ten swords without silver (decoration) 100s., one sword of Genoa garnished with silver 10l., another sword with one scabbard of vermilion (velvet) garnished with silver 6l., another with green silk scabbard strewn (decorated) with escutcheons 20s., another sword with one black scabbard with green bag garnished with silver 6l., another with crystal pommel 4l., two misericords with scabbards of cuir bouilli one with a silver pommel 20s., two other misericords with velvet scabbards with silver (heraldic) bends 40s., six knives with points (for thrusting) one of which is garnished with silver 4l., 30 glaive-heads of divers types 60s. Nesle: four hauberks, six glaive-heads of no value. Paris: one gambeson 100s., another gambeson 60s., one pair of spaudlers of baleen for tourneying 24s., one cuirie with sleeves 16s., one pourpointed (i.e. made in the manner of a padded pourpoint) horse cover, two silk horse testers, three chapeaux de Montauban, four helms, and one varnished basinet 8l. 16s., another basinet 5s., two pairs of plates 100s., three pairs of plates completely equipped for his body 12l., eight (mail shirts) both haubergeons and hauberks, and three aventails 43l., one gorget 20s., one iron (mail) horse cover 6l., another iron (horse) cover 7l., another (horse) cover 8l., [...] hauberks for tourneying 40s., several little pieces of haubergeons 4l., two swords, two little misericords 60s., nine swords each worth 6s. and bound in a long bag 53s., 15 swords bound in a silk bag 12s. each, one sword garnished with leather 100s., another sword garnished with embroidery of the arms of Nesle 6l., seven knives with points 30s., five other knives 10s., two knives garnished with silver 6s., one knife with an image in crystal 5s., 14 glaive-heads 56s., four other smaller glaive-heads 8s., two pairs of gauntlets covered with red leather 20s., three maces 60s.

5

Now-Lost Document from the Archives de Pas-de-Calais, A 179, printed in J. M. Richard, *Une Petite-Nièce de Saint Louis: Mahaut, comtesse d'Artois et de Bourgogne, 1302–1329* (Paris, 1887), pp. 387–9
Household Payments of Robert, Count of Artois, Paris, 1302

I [...] samit, acheté pour couvrir unes plattes pour monsgr par Geoffroy Coquatris à Paris, XII lb., IIII aunes et demie de toile jaune achetée par Jehan le barbier pour fourrer les plattes VI s. IX d., IIC L clos dorés pour cloer les plattes VI s. VIII d., XV clos à boce dorés pour atachier les charnières des plattes et les espées III s., pour la façon de la couverture de ces plattes et pour cloer les et apparellier et une gorgiere de plattes XX s., X aunes de cendal vermeil achaté pour garnir IIII bacinés cest assavoir pour garnir les cervelieres et faire les paveillons des dis bacinés XXXVIII s., III aunes et demie de toile rouge achetée pour mettre dessous les cendaux des bacinés IIII s. I d., III aunes et demie de bougheran acheté pour fourrer les paveillons de ces bacinés VIII s., III aunes et demie de toile blanche pour mettre dessous le boukeran dessus dit IIII s. XVIII d., V quarterons de coton pour ces bacinés III s., demie once de soye à keudre ouvraiges de ces bacinés XXVI d., VIII las de soye pour ces bacinés XXXII d., IIII piaux de lievre [*sic*] blanches à couvrir ces bacinés XX d., une pel à faire coroiies à en armer les armeures monsgr XVIII d., une selle pour guerre broudée des armes monsgr li cuens, garnie d'un tartare d'outremer vermeil à treçons et florons et escuçons broudez sus la couverture tout entour, fourrée de cordouan vermeil, garnie de houces de toile et de cuir [...], une selle pour guerre de veluau et de loremerie des armes monsgr à une couverture verte, dyaprée d'un tartare d'outremer ouvré à treçons et florons et escuçons broudez sus la couverture tout entour, fourrée de cordouan vermel et garnie de houces de toile et de cuir [...], une sele à cheval pour guerre garnie toute d'un drap de soie jaune tout dyapré à treçons et florons et escuçons broudez sus la couverture tout entour à II escuçons broudez de tueaus et de pelles des armes le connestables de France la couverture fourrée de cordouan vermeil et garnie de houces de toile et de cuir, LX lb. par., une sele de fin azur dyaprée des armes monsgr pour guerre, garnie de cordouan vermeil, toute la couverture cousue de soie à IIII coustures, garnie de houces de toile et de cuir VI lb., I grant escu de fin azur dyapré des armes monsgr en guige et garni de houce de cuir, VI lb., I escu des armes monsgr Symon dyapré en guige et garni de houce de cuir, LX s., I escu des armes mestre Tyerri en guige dyapré et garni de houce de cuir LX s., XII granz seles pour guerre, pour les escuiers monsgr d'Artois, à granz escuçons des armes monsgr, garnis de cordouan vermeil XXXVI lb., VIII chapeaus de Montauban de fin or, en chascun II escuceaus des armes monsgr, garnis de corroies, et XIIII targes de fin or, en chascune I escu de fin azur des armes monsgr pour chascune XX s.

one (length of) samite (shimmering silk fabric) bought for covering a (pair of) plates for my Lord by Geoffroy Coquartis at Paris 12 (Parisian) *livres*, 4½ ells of yellow cloth bought by Jehan le Barbier to line the plates 6s. 9d., 250 gilt nails to nail the plates 6s. 8d., 15 nails with gilt bosses to attach the hinges of the plates and the swords 3s., for making a cover for these plates and for nailing and equipping one plate gorget 20s., ten ells of vermilion sendal (lightweight silk or very fine linen) bought to equip four basinets viz.: to fit the shaped helmet linings and the covers for these basinets 38s., 3½ ells of red cloth bought to cover the sendal of these basinets 4s. 1d., 3½ ells of buckram (cotton fabric) bought to line the covers of these basinets 8s., 3½ ells of white cloth to cover this buckram 4s. 18d., five quarters of cotton for these basinets 3s., a half-ounce of silk to sew the (face) openings of these basinets 26d., eight silk laces for these basinets 32d., four hare skins (prob. *chièvre*: goat/doeskin) for covering these basinets 20d., one hide to make leathers to arm my Lord's armour 18d., one war saddle embroidered with my Lord's (heraldic) comital arms garnished with vermilion Outremer tartaryn (silk fabric) and tresses and flowers and escutcheons embroidered all over the cover lined with vermilion cordwain (high-quality Spanish leather) fitted with covers of cloth and leather [...], one war saddle of velvet and horse brasses of my Lord's arms with a green cover diapered (decorated) with Outremer tartaryn worked with tresses and flowers and escutcheons embroidered all over the cover lined with vermilion cordwain and fitted with covers of cloth and leather [...], one war horse's saddle garnished all over with yellow silk cloth diapered all over with tresses and flowers and escutcheons embroidered all over the covers and two escutcheons embroidered with tiles and scrolls of the (heraldic) arms of the *Connétables* of France – the cover lined with vermilion cordwain and fitted with covers of cloth and leather 60 Parisian *livres*, one war saddle of diapered fine azure with my Lord's arms fitted with vermilion cordwain – the whole cover sewn with silk with four stitches fitted with covers of cloth and leather 6l., one large shield of diapered fine azure with my Lord's arms with guige (shield strap) and fitted with a leather cover 6l., one shield with the diapered arms of my Lord Symon with guige and fitted with a leather cover 60s., one shield with the diapered arms of Master Tyerri with guige and fitted with a leather cover 60s., 12 large war saddles for my Lord of Artois's squires with large escutcheons of my Lord's arms fitted with vermilion cordwain 36l., eight chapeaux de Montauban of fine gold each with one fine azure (heraldic) shield of my Lord's arms 20s. each

6

Kew, National Archives, E 101/11/5
Purchase of Armour for William, Earl of Ross, Dunfermline, Fife, 1302–3

pur j gambessoun achate dunt fu fet un aketun pur le cunte lx s. un autre gambessoun xl s. un pissane e un gorger xxx s. un chapel de fer xxx s. un bacinet viij s. un peyre jamberis oue les wampes e un peyr poleyns x s. viij d. un colret de fer v s. vj d. xx aunys de sendal vermayl xxiij s. iiij d. vj aunys e demy de sandal blaunk ix s. ix d. viij aunys e demy de tele vermayl ij s. x d. ix aunys de worstede iij s. saye ij s. viij d. fil xvj. d. iiij aunys de aylisham x d. un fer pur le corps au conte c s.

for one gambeson purchased from which an aketon was made for the Earl 60s., another gambeson 40s., a pisan and a gorget 30s., a chapel de fer 30s., a basinet 8s., a pair of jambers with the vamps (feet) and a pair of poleyns 10s. 8d., an iron collar 5s. 6d., 20 ells of vermilion sendal (lightweight silk or very fine linen) 23s. 4d, 6½ ells of white sendal 9s. 9d., 8½ ells of vermilion linen 2s. 10d., nine ells of worsted (woollen cloth) 3s., silk 2s. 8d., thread 16d., four ells of Aylsham (woollen cloth) 10d., a (piece of) iron for the Earl's body 100s.

7

London Metropolitan Archives, DL/A/J/001/MS25176
Account of the Executors of Richard, Bishop of London, 1303

vj sell' p[ro] armig[er]is x targ' v gladiis xv lanceis ij Capell de ferro j spryngold' & C q[u]arell' ad id[e]m xxviij balist' C quarell' j helmo[n]u' vij bacin' ferr' j tena ferr' xvij baudr' v p[ar]ibus genual' viij testar' xiij trapp' p[ro] equis j testar' nouo j par' de trapp' v Aketon' iiijor Gambes' & ij debilib[u]s ij testar' & ij coop[er]tor' de ferr' p[ro] equis v hauberk' iiijor Corsett' ij Gorger' iij tenis ferr' j par manicular' ferr' iiijor par' caligar[u]m ferr' j par' Quissar' j gladio

six saddles for squires, ten targes, five swords, 15 lances, two chapel de fers, one springald with 100 quarrels for it, 28 crossbows, 100 quarrels, one helm, seven iron basinets, one iron coif, 17 baldrics, five pairs of genulers, eight testers, 13 horse trappers, one new tester, one pair of trappers, five aketons, four gambesons and two worn-out (gambesons), two testers, and two iron (mail) horse covers, five hauberks, four corsets, two gorgets, three iron coifs, one pair of iron (mail) sleeves, one pair of iron (mail) chausse, one pair of cuisses, one sword

8

Kew, National Archives, SC 8/329/E905
Royal Petition of John Folborn' for the return of his armour, c. 1303

come il engagea ses armures a s' Labre chief de tote la Compaignie des Richards de Luk' au noef chastel sor Tyne por C souz dest[er]lings a paier a vn certain iour en engleterre ou en Irland' a quel iour dez C souz furent paies viij Jours auant le iour de la paye en Irland' a leur compaignie demorante a Diuelyne E por ce q[ue] leur l[ett] re ne poeit venir a lour compaignouns demorants a noef chastel sor Tyne le iour done de la decte de ceaux C souz il vendirent les dites armures a Guilliame de Haukeswell' E qua[n]t la l[ett]re leur q[ue] lez C souz furent paietz il firent tantost le dit Guilliame venir' & le distrent quil precist ses deners en manier quil ne turneyeit les armurers entierement Dont il ne rendist puis quil auoit son argent recue q[ue] vn akeyton' vn Gaumbeson' vnes trappes quisseaux & greues poinctes & retint deuers li vn aketon' ij Gaumbesons vnes trappes j Bacinet quisseaux & greues poinctes & vne sele a sum[n]er

Because he had pawned his armour to Sir Labre, head of the whole company of Riccardi de Lucca (bankers) at Newcastle-upon-Tyne for 100s. sterling to be paid on a certain day in England or in Ireland, as the 100s. was paid eight days before the day that payment was due in Ireland to their company at Dublin and their letter recording debt of 100s. had not yet come from their colleagues at Newcastle-upon-Tyne on the given day, they sold this armour to William Hawkswell. When the letter proving that the 100s. had been paid was produced, this William came immediately and said to them that he had placed such a value that he did not return all the armour. Thus he only returned that which he had received as payment: one aketon, one gambeson, one (pair of horse) trappers, pointed (i.e. made in the manner of a padded pourpoint) cuisses and greaves, and kept for himself: one aketon, two gambesons, one (horse) trapper, one basinet, pointed cuisses and greaves, and one sumpter saddle

9

Kew, National Archives, E 101/363/18
Account of Hugh Bungay, Armourer to Prince Edward of Caernarfon, August 1303–March 1304

Armatur' ferr' p[ro] corpore Principis Manekino Larmurer de London' p[ro] trib[us] bacinett' xx s ij par' Jamber' p[re]t' par' ij mar' vno capello ferri cu' cresta lx s vno alio capello ferri rotundo lx s vno casside cum visera liij s iiij d vno alio casside integro

p[ro] guerra scoc' empt' p[ar] Joh[ann]em Dengaigne & hugonem de Bungeye xv li
Bernardo de Deuon' Armurar' London' p[ro] duob[us] par' Jamber' p[re]t' par' xx
s vno pari de Quissotz plat' vj s viij d vna pari de Poleyns & duob[us] par' sabater'
pret' in toto xiij s iiij d & vno pari cirothecar[um] plat' x s e[m]pt' ab eod' p[ar] H'
de Bungeye p[ro] corp[or]e Princ' p[ro] guerra lxx s armature p[ro] Ingeniatore P[ri]
ncipis Hugoni de Bungeye pro vno bacinetto vj s vno aketon' xvj s & vno pari plat'
xx s empt' p[er] eunde' ap[u]d Breghyn & dat' p[er] P[ri]ncipe Rob[er]to de Glasham'
Ingeniatori suo q[ue] p[re]parauit ingenu' d[omi]ni P[ri]ncipis ibidem p[ro] castro
insultando per manus p[ro]prias xlij s Bungeye p[ro] f[ac]tura armor[um] p[ro]
guerra scoc' Hugoni de Bungeye Armurar' P[ri]nc' assignato ad faciend' diu[er]sas
armatur' p[ro] corpore P[ri]nc' & q[u]or[um] scutifer' suor[um] p[ro] guerra scoc'
videl[ice]t vj vnciis sericii diu[er]si coloris emp' p[ro] punctura duor[um] aketon'
P[ri]nc' vj s stip[end]u' viij vall[e]tor[um] facientiu' & pungentiu' eosdem apud
London' p[ro] xiij dies xxvj s vno pari bracer' de balen' p[ro] eod' xxiiij s f[ac]tura ij
par' de Quissotz broudat' de armis d[omi]ni s[er]ico & laqueis p[ro] eisde' xj s v par'
calcar' deaurat' v s emendac[i]o[n]e ij loricar[um] P[ri]nc' vt in filo ferr' emp' p[ro]
eisdem stipend' loricar' lapidib[us] amarill' de Alexandr' oleo furfure & al' munuit'
reb[us] empt' p[ro] eisdem mundand' & reparand' p[er] vices in guerra xxx s vj d j
pisan' p[ro] corpore P[ri]nc' vna lb di' Archall' p[ro] quaddam alia pisan' emendanda
xij s iiij d p[ro] ij gambison' p[ro] corpore Princip' videl[ice]t p[ro] iiij m[i]l' ccc peciis
aurifil' pret' m[i]l viij s iiij d vj vnciis s[er]ici p[ro] punctura eor[un]dem & laqueis de
s[er]ico magnis & paruis l s ij d stip[end]u' vj op[er]ar' brouddantiu' ij gambisones
de armis Principis p[ro] lxj dies & q[u]atuor vall[e]tor[um] pungentiu' eosdem p[ro]
xxiiij dies cxvj s iij d p[ro] apparatu & hernes' iij bacinettor[um] d[omi]ni xxxiij s iiij
cereuellar' pro ij capell' ferr' & vno bacinetto cu' visera & vno casside P[ri]nc' f[ac]
tis de sindone & s[er]ico laqueis & f[ac]tura' eor[un]de[m] xij s clauis anul' deaurat'
p[ro] capell' inde muniend' xvj s vij d ij crestis cupri deaurat' de armis P[ri]nc' depictis
xliiij s iiij ensib[us] de guerra p[ro] d[omi]no p[ro] sindone s[er]ico & filio auri emp'
ad zonara & vaginas inde faciend' vna cu' h[er]nes' arg' deaur' f[ac]tura & broudac[i]
o[n]e de armis Glouc' & Hereford' cxj s v d reparac[i]one & pictura vnu' scuti de
armis P[ri]nc' guigis de s[er]ico clauis & claspis deaurat' eodem scuto xxiiij s iiij d
vna cresta de cupro deaurata de armis p[er]gamen' penneis pauonu' & f[ac]tura vni'
creste p[er]licate Bungeye p[ro] f[ac]tura armor[um] Hugoni de Bungeye p[ro] iiij
pellib[us] cap[ri]nis rubeis p[ro] corigiis inde faciend' p[ro] diu[er]sis armatur' d[omi]
ni ix s vno coffino de corio bullito ferro ligato p[ro] bacinetto P[ri]nc' imponendo &
inf[r]a portando iij s iiij d vno casso de corio p[ro] crestis d[omi]ni imponend' iiij s ij
d vno par' long' coffr' p[ro] lineis armatur' d[omi]ni imponend' & cariand' in guerra
scoc' xxxij s iiij d ob' vno pari bulg' magnar[um] nouo p[ro] armatur' ferr' imponend'
& inf[r]a cariand' viij s iiij d fraer' de corio albo p[ro] loriciis inf[r]a imundand' iiij s ij
ciliciis empt' p[ro] h[er]nes' inde coop[er]iendo inter London' & Rokesburgh iij s x
d imundac[i]o[n]e t[ri]um capellor[um] ferri & vj capitu' lanc' p[er] vices in sc[oci]a
guerra vij s ij d pro expen[s]oris sui c[on]t[r]a f[ac]turam hernes' lxvij s x d ob

45

Iron armour for the Prince's body: Manekin the armourer of London for three basinets 20s., two pairs of jambers price of the pair two marks, one chapel de fer with a crest 60s., one other round chapel de fer 60s., a *casside* [an unknown helm type] with visor 53s. 4d., one other complete helm for the Scottish war bought by John Dengaigne and Hugh Bungay £25, Bernard of Devon, armourer of London for two pairs of jambers price of the pair 20s., one pair of plate cuisses 6s. 8d., one pair of poleyns and two pairs of sabatons total 13s. 4d., a pair of plate gauntlets 10s. bought by Hugh Bungay for the Prince's body for the war 70s. Armour for the Prince's engineer: Hugh Bungay for a basinet 6s., an aketon 16s., and a pair of plates 20s., bought by him at Brechin in August and given by the Prince's own hands to Robert Glasham his engineer there as he prepared the Prince's (siege) engines for the assault on the castle there 42s. Bungay for making armour for the Scottish war: Hugh Bungay, armourer to the Prince for making divers armour for the Prince's body and for his squires for the Scottish war viz.: 6oz of silk of divers colours bought for sewing two of the Prince's aketons 6s., wages of eight valets for making and sewing them at London for 13 days 26s., a pair of sleeves of baleen for them 24s., making two pairs of cuisses embroidered with the Lord's arms in silk and straps for them 11s., five pairs of gilt spurs bought 5s., mending two of the Prince's hauberks, for iron wire for them, haubergers' wages, emery stones of Alexandria, oil, bran, and other necessary things bought to mend and repair them for use in the war 30s. 6d., one pisan for the Prince's body, 1½lb of copper for mending another pisan 12s. 3d., for two gambesons for the Prince's body viz.: 4,300 pieces of gold thread, price of the thousand 8s. 4d., 6oz of silk for sewing them, large and small silk laces for them 50s. 2d., wages of six workmen embroidering the two gambesons with the Prince's (heraldic) arms for 61 days and four valets sewing them for 24 days 116s. 3d., equipping and harnessing three of the Lord's basinets 23s., four helmet linings for the Prince's two chapel de fers and one basinet with visor and one helmet made of sindon (linen), and silk laces, and for making them 12s., gilt nails for the chapel de fer and mending it 16s. 7d., crests of gilt copper painted with the Prince's arms 44s., four war swords bought by him for the Lord, sindon, silk, and gold thread for making belts and scabbards with silver-gilt harness for them, making and embroidering them with the arms of Gloucester and Hereford 111s. 5d., repairing and painting a shield with the Prince's arms, guiges (shield straps) of silk, gilt nails, and clasps for this shield 24s. 4d., a crest of gilt copper of the (Prince's) arms, parchment, peacock feathers, and making a pearled crest 44s. Bungay for the making of armour: Hugh Bungay for four red goatskins to be made into leathers for divers of the Lord's armour 9s., an iron-bound coffer of cuir bouilli to put in and carry the Prince's basinet 3s. 4d., a case of leather for the lord's crests to be put in 4s. 2d., one pair of long coffers for the Lord's linen armour to be put in and carried to the Scottish war 32s. 4½d., a pair of new large bags to put the iron (mail) armour in and carry to the war 8s., four polishers of white leather for cleaning hauberks for use 4s., two blankets to cover the harness between London and Roxburgh 3s. 10d., mending three chapel de fers and six lanceheads for use in the Scottish war 7s. 2d., for his expenses making the harness 67s. 10½d.

10

Kew, National Archives E 101/486/20
Inventory of Arms and Armour at Beaumaris Castle, Principality of
Wales, 9 June 1306

Armatur' vj Bacinett' deblies & parui valoris iiij accoto[u]n' iiij Hauberion' debiles
parui valoris ij Corcett' ferr' xxx Targ' vet[er]es & debiles & n[ou]o rep[ar]at' vna
balist' de Tour de Cornu j viz p[ro] eid[e]m tendend' j Balist' de cornu ij ped' j balist'
de cornu j ped' ij balist' de Ifo ij ped' de nouo rep[ar]at' j Balist' de Omello ij ped'
simul' de nouo rep[ar]at' p[ar] Const' xxviij balist' de Ifo vnius pedis de quib[us]
pred[ic]tus Const' fecit rep[ar]ar' xiiij & xiiij non rep[ar]at[u]r quia non possunt
tend' prop[t'] debilitatem xx balist' de Omell' vnius ped' s[u]nt debiles q[uo]d non
possunt tend' iiij Baldr' debiles & parui valoris p[ro] balist' vnius ped' tendend'
xj parui Cist' cum minutis quarell' vet[er]ibus xxix Arc' manuales de Omello vnu'
paruu' Ingen' stans sup[er] mur' q[uo]d vocat[u]r Trebuchet vij nuces ereas p[ro]
springaldis iiij Springald' vet[er]es iacentes & non rep[ar]at' cum ferremento debili
easd' p[er]tinent' v xx lj' Pilli equini pilati iiijxx & viij lj' canab' Pilati p[ro] d[ic]tis
Sp[ri]ngaldis vijC magn' quarell' cum ere pennati p[ro] Sp[ri]ngaldis pred[ic]tis due
forme eree p[ro] pilis plumbeys fundend' iiij forme eree rotunde p[ro] pil' p[re]d[ic]
tis tractandis ij rote eree polye pro eisd[e]m

Armour: six worn-out basinets of little value, four worn out aketons and four haubergeons of little value, two iron corsets, 30 old, and worn out, and newly-repaired targes,
one torsion horn crossbow, one vice for spanning it, one two-foot horn crossbow (i.e.
for two-foot-long bow-staves), one one-foot (i.e. for one-foot-long bow-staves) horn
crossbow, two two-foot yew crossbows – newly repaired, one two-foot elm crossbow
similarly newly repaired by the Constable, 28 one-foot yew crossbows of which the
Constable had 14 repaired and 14 could not be repaired as they were too worn out to
be spanned, 20 one-foot yew crossbows are worn out and cannot be spanned, four
worn out baldrics for (spanning) one-foot crossbows of little value, 11 small chests
with old small quarrels, 29 hand (spanned) bows of elm, one small engine set upon
the walls which is called a trebuchet, seven copper (trigger) nuts for springalds, four
old fixed springalds (i.e. set in position) not repaired with the appurtenant ironwork
worn out, five score lb. of woven horsehair, four score and eight lb. of woven canvas
for these springalds, 700 large quarrels fletched with copper for these springalds, two
copper formers for casting lead pellets, four round copper formers for forming these
pellets, two copper pulley wheels for them

11

Unlocated Original Document printed in C. H. Hartshorne, 'Caernarvon Castle', *Archaeologia Cambrensis* 1 (1855), pp. 242–6
Inventory of Caernarfon Castle, Principality of Wales, 9 August 1306

Armatur' P[ri]nc' invent' in Cast' de Carn' iij. Capell' f[er]ee cu' viser' iiij. Capell' fer' rotu[n]de' xiiij. Bacinett' vet[er]es & debil' iij. aketon' ij. par' cirotecar' de baleyne j. hauberc' vj. haubergon' iiij. corsett' .j. par' chauson' ix. Lanc' s[i]n' cap' Baleyne – vij. pec' integr' Baliste – .j. balist' de viz de ifo cu' vent' de baleyne & nuc' de er' iij. balist' de ifo ijor Pedu' vj. baliste de cornu un' ped' xxviij balist' di ifo bene rep[ar]at' q[u]or' iij. cu' vent' de baleyne xiij balist' q[u]or' xj. de ifo & ij. de holi deblies & vet[er]es .xv. arc' p[ro] balist' sine tel' un' x. p[rep]arat' ad ligand' et v. no' rep[er]ati .j. coste' ijor ped' de nouo rep[er]at' s[i]n' telar' Baldr' [...]

The Prince's Armour found in Caernarfon Castle: three chapel de fers with visors, four round chapel de fers, 14 old and worn out basinets, three aketons, two pairs of baleen gauntlets, one hauberk, six haubergeons, four corsets, one pair of chausses, nine lances without heads, seven whole pieces of baleen, one vice-spanned crossbow of yew with belly of baleen and copper (trigger) nut, three yew two-foot crossbows (i.e. for two-foot-long bow-staves), six horn one-foot crossbows (i.e. for one-foot-long bow-staves), 28 yew crossbows which might well be repaired three of which have baleen bellies, 13 crossbows 11 of which are of yew and two of holly old and worn out, 15 bows for crossbows without tillers (stocks) ten of which may be prepared with bindings and five cannot be repaired, one rib for a two-footer which may be repaired as new without tiller, baldrics [...]

12

Kew, National Archives, E 159/80, membr. 50
Losses of John Sampson when he surrendered Stirling Castle in 1299, Trinity Term [April–July] 1307

q[u]aunt William le Waleys vint pur coler nostre garnisture le iour sent Berthelmeu il perdist a son issir du chastel deux Aketons q[ue] lui custerent plus de xl s ij Gambesons plus de iiij li j hauberk & vn hauberion xl sol[i]d' j Pisane oue la Cape x s Jambers [et] quisoz plus de viij s vn chapel de feer xx s j chapel de Nerfs xl den' Gants de feer v s j peire de plates plus de vn marc' vn peire de Treppes ij marc' tres espeis vn misericord & deux Anlaces oue les maunches de Iuoir x s

when William Wallace came to take equipment from our [the King's] castle on Saint Bartholomew's day [24 August] he [John] lost at his departure from the castle: two aketons which cost him more than 40s., two gambesons more than £4, one hauberk and one habergeon 40s., one pisan with the cape 10s., jambers and cuisses more than

8s., one chapel de fer 20s., one chapel of sinew 40d., iron gauntlets 5s., one pair of plates more than one mark, one pair of trappers two marks, three swords, one misericord, and two anelaces with grips of ivory 10s.

13

Kew, National Archives E 101/486/2/4
Payments for Arms at Beaumaris Castle, Principality of Wales, 12 June–
7 August 1307

Joh' de medesend Const' ibid[e]m vid[elice]t xxij balist' de nouo rep[ar]ac' vij s' iiij d' in d[imid]j lj' vernic' v d' Et in d[imid]j lj' Cer' iiij d' ob' Et in filo pro d[ic]tis balist' ligand' iiij d' Ceclie de Kent op[er]anti pilu' p[ro] sp[ri]ngal' & aliis Ingeniis in eod[e] m Cast[r]o xviij d' Wil[he]l[m]o de Kyrkebi Cem[en]tar' facienti ix xx petras rotund' p[ro] Ingen' in Cast[r]o tasta' tap' p[ro] iiijto ad j d'

John Medesend, Constable of the same (castle) viz.: newly repairing 22 crossbows 7s. 4d., a half-pound of varnish 5d., a half-pound of wax a halfpence, thread for binding these crossbows 3d., Cecil Kent working on hair (i.e. weaving horsehair for the torsion ropes) for springalds and other (siege) engines in this castle 18d., William Kirkby, mason having made nine score round stones for (siege) engines in the castle one pence for four

14

Nantes, Bibliothèque municipale, Fonds Bizeul, MS 1701, p. 25
The Legal Agreement between the Vicomte de Rohan and the Seigneur de Beaumanoir for Single Combat, 14 August 1309

le viconte a laye de diex se deffandra par vn ho[m]me autre que luy & s[er]a a cheual le dit ho[m]me & atorne son cors en la men[ier]e q[ue] senseut il aura chemisse de chartres a braoyes a breoul garniz souffesaument pour ses chambes estiuellez de plates garniz de telles & de fer & dacier ou lun ou de lautr' & de boure de saye & de coton a souffere greues de fer & dacier garniz souffesaument esp[er]ons garniz souffesaument quessonz de fer & dacier a poullens de meymes a bragonieres de mailles garniz de telles de borre de saye & de cendieux ou de samit & de mailles a souffere hauqueton de cendieux & de telles & de borre de seye & de coton plates au cors de fer & de acier garnies de braz & de pans de mailles & de telles & de cendieux & de samit & de borre de saye & de coton a souffere goceons souffesanz de mailles bacim [sic] a visiere de fer & de acier garni de colerete de telles & de cendieux & de borre de saye & de coton & de colerete de fer & dacier souffesante & de cameill cope de mailles souffesante au bacim & sera garni le bacim de cerueliere souffesante gantelez de fer & dacier de plates garniz de teles & de cendieux & de samit & de borre de soye &

de coton & de cuer & de boucles a souffere escu de fuust & de cuers & de ners garni
souffesaument cheual enselle dune selle souffesante a doux estreix couerz de mailles &
de cendel & eslingoeres de cuer & de mailles garnies souffesaument & sera le cheual
couert de coureture de belutiau & de chanue & de telles & de cendieux & de fer &
dacier & de borre de saye & de coton & aura le cheual chamfrain bon & souffesant
garnie & a toutes cez chousses desus nomees tant pour le cors que pour le cheual aura
pieces de mailles la ou mestier sera & corde & correye fil & Aguille & poencons a
armer & laz & boucles & aguilletes ce que li souffera sanz ce que il pesse fere autre
malice couerte oultres la leste desus ditz fors tant soulement garnir de les chousses
desus dites & s[er]a son cheual ferre & le porra f[a]c' ferrer ov defferrer ou champ se
il veult ou estrendre ou lachier & le cheual & le cors de luy auant que la serent le sien
aller pour Eux ent[r]easaillir & aura vne espee a poente dou lonc de ceste v[ir]ge qui
a este a presant a croez & a Rondele dauant la mein & plom Ront & [...] a pointe
a plom Ront de la longour a ceste m[ar]che qui ci est enp[re]sant lalemele dou plus
lonc p[er]somet le bout & aura corde & correye laz pour lespee & pour les coutiaux li
souffera sans malice couerte y ajoster environ les cordes & les [...] naura le d' ho[m]
me environ son cors ne environ son cheual nulle [...] points qui pesse endoma[...]
fers celes qui sont en ceste lete

The Vicomte (with God's aid) shall defend himself against a man of his own standing
this man shall be mounted on horseback and shall protect his body in the following
manner: he shall have a chemise of Chartres[2] with breech and brayette suitably
equipped, plate long boots for his legs equipped with cloth and with iron and steel
(or with one or the other) with suitable padding of silk and cotton, suitably-equipped
greaves of iron and steel, suitably-equipped spurs, cuisses of iron and steel with
poleyns of the same, a brayer of mail garnished with silk and sendal (lightweight silk
or very fine linen) or with samite (shimmering silk fabric) and with suitable mail,
an aketon of sendal and linen and silk and cotton padding, a pair of plates on the
body of iron or steel equipped with mail sleeves and paunce and lined with linen and
sendal and samite and suitably padded with silk and cotton, suitable mail gussets, an
iron or steel basinet with visor equipped with a collar of linen and sendal and padded
with silk and cotton with a suitable iron or steel collar with a suitable mail aventail
pendant from the basinet (and the basinet shall be equipped with a suitable lining),
iron or steel plate gauntlets garnished with linen and sendal and samite and stuffed
with silk and cotton and leather with suitable buckles, a suitably-equipped shield of
wood, leather, and sinew, (he shall be mounted on) a horse saddled with a suitable
saddle with two reins covered with mail, sendal, and leather and suitably-equipped
mail, the horse shall have suitable bit and the saddle shall be equipped with suitable
surcingles and pooles, the horse shall have a cover of bolting-cloth and with canvas,
linen, and sendal and the (mail horse) cover of iron and steel and padded with silk
and cotton as shall be necessary, the horse shall have a good and suitably-equipped

[2]   Moffat, 'The Manner of Arming Knights for the Tourney', p. 10: 'a garment in the shape of, and that
      had come into contact with, the sancta camisia of Chartres cathedral'.

shaffron, and of all these defences aforesaid (both for the body and for the horse) shall have pieces of mail wherever shall be necessary and cord, leather-thread, arming points and laces, and buckles and straps of his choice without anything that might involve any hidden malice outwith the aforesaid list – save only equipping those things aforesaid, his horse shall be shoed and the farrier must shoe it in the field so it may be seen and accepted that the horse and his body be equal before they come to sally forth, this man shall have a sword with (thrusting) point the length of this rod here presented with a cross-guard and rondel before the hand, and round pommel, the end of the round pommel shall be the length of this mark here presented, the blade shall be as long as the top of the end of this mark and shall be corded with leather fretted for (the grip of) the sword and knife – he may choose without hidden malice to adjust the cords around his body. This man may not have any spikes or lanceheads anywhere on his body or his horse save for those which are devised in this legal agreement

15

Kew, National Archives, DURH 3/1, fol. 140v
Inventory of the Arms and Armour of Sir John Fitzmarmaduke, Raven-shelm (Ravensworth Castle), Palatinate of Durham, 1311

duo p[ar]ia de Trappes xl s ij galee xiij s iiij d j par de Waynpayns & ij brasers vj s viij d iiij frena cu' testar' xl d xvj sagitte ij d ij massuels xij d j arcus de Balayn vj s viij d ij capit' lancea & j soket' vj d iiij chapes p[ro] colers iij d iiij p[ar]ia de Chessys & j p[ar] calcar' xx s j tester vj s viij d cista co[n]tine[n]s p[re]missa xij d iiij scuta ij s j vet' galea ij d j Gaunbeson cu' allettys iij s iiij d j Aketon' rubeu' cu' manucis de Balayn xl s j Gaunbeson coop[er]tu' de panno cerico xl s

two pairs of (horse) trappers 40s., two helms 13s. 4d., one pair of gaignepains and two bracers 6s. 8d., three (horse) bits with tester 40d., 16 arrows 2d., two maces 12d., one bow of baleen 6s. 8d., two lanceheads and one socket 6d., three chapes for collars 3d., three pairs of chausses and one pair of spurs 20s., one tester 6s. 8d., the chest containing the above 12d., three shields 2s., one old helm 2d., one gambeson with (decorative heraldic) ailettes 3s. 4d., one red aketon with sleeves of baleen 40s., one gambeson covered with silk cloth 40s.

16

Paris, Bibliothèque nationale de France, MS fr. 24069, fol. 115r
Addition to the Statutes of the Armourers of Paris, April 1312

q' nul dores en aua[…] ne puist fete cote ganbosie[…] il nait iiij liures de coto' to' net se elles ne sunt fetes en f[…] mes & au desous soient […] ent' moins & q' il ait j pli viel linge enp[re]s lendroit de d[…] aune & demj q[ua]rt' deuant & au[…] derrieres que nul ne […] cote ou il ait bourre de soi escroes nulles ne de toiles ou de cendal se elles ne sunt f[…] enfremes & couchies que nul ne face gans […] plates q' les plates ne soient estamees ou v[er]nices linees & pourbatues b[ie]n & netem[en]t […]cune plate & ne soient cue[…] de nul cuir de mouto' noir & se len les cueuure de cuir rouges ou blans ou de soi ou daut' couu[er]ture q' il a toile desouz de la couleur to' au lonc & que il ait sous chascune teste de clou j riu[…] dor pel ou de […]ent pel q' le clou ne pourrisse lend' que len ne face cote ga[…]bosie espeese de la montra[…] de vj lb pesant que lenu' & lendroit ne soit neuf' se lenu[er]s ou lendroit est […] q' il soient forfetes & tel Euure doit est' fauce Et doit estre arse ces art' fur[…] Jeh' Ploiebaut p[re]uot de p[ar]is p[ar] le co[m]m[u]n' du mestr'

Henceforth none may make gamboised coat (i.e. gambeson) lest it be of three pounds of completely new cotton, be reinforced inside, and have a fold of old linen to the end of half an ell and half-quarter (ell) in front and on the back. None make a coat with burrs of silk, or strips, or linen, or sendal (lightweight silk) if they be not reinforced and stuffed. None make plate gauntlets lest the plates be tinned or linseed-varnished and each plate neat, well aligned, and well beaten, and not covered with any black sheep's leather. And, if they be covered in red or white leather or silk or any other covering, that it have linen of the same colour beneath throughout, and there should be a rivet of gold bar or silver bar upon every nail-head so that the nail beneath does not perish. None make gamboised coat heavier than six (demonstrable) pounds and that the inside and out be new and if the inside or outside be (of) old (material) it shall be forfeited and such work ought to be seized and burnt. These articles were made before Jehan Ploibaut *Prévôt* of Paris by the common (assent) of the craft.

17

Kew, National Archives E 101/468/20, fol. 1r–fol. 3r
Payments for the Construction of Five Springalds for the Tower of London, Eastertide 1312

Joh[ann]e de Crombwelle Constabular' Turr' London' q[uo]d fieri fac[er]et quinq[ue] sp[ri]ngald' p[ro] munic[i]one Garenestur' d[ic]ti Turr' London' cum o[mn]i festinac[i]o[n]e qua poet[ur]it Et memo[ran]d' q[uo]d tunc disp[ar]abat[u]r de pace int[er] Regem & Com' virente emis mandate Thome de H[er]tyngge Ingeniatori op[er]anti circa p[re]d[ic]tos sp[ri]ngald' ordinand' & fac' p[er] xij septim' xlij s' Joh[ann]i de Foresta & Rob[er]to de Folksto[u]n' carpentar' op[er]ant' p[er] xv dies circa eode' sp[ri]ngald' xvs' Thome de Sar[um] & socio suo & Simoni de Dereham' & soc[i]o suo Sarr' op[er]antib[us] circa grossu' maer' de magno ingenio p[ro] d[ic] tis springald' serrand' p[er] iiij dies viij s' Nich[ol]o de Dynes & Joh[ann]i le Rok carpentar' op[er]ant' p[er] xj dies circa d[ic]tos sp[ri]ngald' xj s' Thome de Salisbury Simoni de Derham sarr' op[er]antibus p[er] vij dies circa grossu' maer' sarrand' p[ro] d[ic]tis sp[ri]ngald' vij s' Joh[ann]i mariote & socio suo sarrat' op[er]antib[us] p[er] ij dies circa idem ij s' Henr' Garde' & socio suo sarr' op[er]ant' p[er] vj dies circa

idem vj s' Mag[ist]ro Jacobo de leuesham Fabro op[er]anti p[er] xij septim' circa Grap'
virol' guiones vertiuell' ligamenta & alios diu[er]s' app[ar]atus ferreos ad p[re]d[ic]tis
springald' ij s' vj d' Ade de Kelbourne cem' p[er] xvj dies in turrello vlt[r]a la Wat[er]
gate ad elargand' batillamenta p[ro] springald' in eisdem turrell' sictand' & p[er]
amsatib[us] & squach' eor[un]dem springald' melius h[ab]end' viij s'

John Cromwell, Constable of the Tower of London had five springalds made for
fortifying the defences of the said Tower of London with all possible speed; for it was
noted that at that time there was such a disturbance of the peace between the King
and the Commonalty (of the City) this command was caused to be sent. Thomas
Hertyngge, engineer working on designing and making the said springalds for 12
weeks 42s., John Forest and Robert Folkestone, carpenters working for 15 days on
these springalds 15s., Thomas Salisbury and his associate and Simon Durham and his
associate, sawyers working on sawing the large timbers of the great (siege) engine for
four days 8s., Nicholas Dynes and John Rok, carpenters working for 11 days on these
springalds 11s., Thomas Salisbury and Simon Durham, sawyers working for seven
days sawing large timbers for these springalds 7s., John Mariote and his associate,
sawyers working for two days on them 2s., Henry Gardener and his associate, sawyers
working for six days on them 6s., Master James Levesham, smith working for 12
weeks on grips, ferrules, gudgeons (pivots), hinge-straps, bindings and other divers
ironwork for these springalds 2s. 6d., Adam Kelbourne, mason for 16 days enlarging
the battlements on the tower over the Watergate to install springalds in this tower and
by affixing and reshaping them to better remain in place 8s.

18

Kew, National Archives, C 66/138
Possessions of Sir Piers Gaveston, Newcastle-upon-Tyne, Northumberland, and Elsewhere, 27 February 1313

vne cote armere des armes sire pieres vne autre ceinture de quir de Laonn en vn autre
coffre vne peire de plates eclouez & garniz dargent od quatre cheynes dargent cou[er]
z dun drap de veluet vermeil besaunte dor deux peires de Jambers de feer veutz &
noueaux autres diu[er]s garnementz des armes le dit pieres ouek lés alettes garniz &
frettez de p[er]les en vn sak' vn bacenet burny od surcils en vn autre sak' vne peire
de treppes des armes le dit piers deux cotes de veluet pur plates cou[er]ir vne veille
ban[ier]e des armes le dit Piers quarant vn destres e coursers & vn palefrei

one coat armour of Sir Piers' (heraldic) arms, one other belt of Leon leather, in
another coffer one pair of plates nailed and garnished with silver with four silver
chains covered with vermilion velvet cloth with gold (heraldic) bezants, other divers
garnishings of the said Sir Piers' arms with ailettes garnished and fretted with pearls,
in one sack one burnished (polished steel) basinet with 'surcils' (eyebrows), in one
other sack one pair of (horse) trappers of the said Piers' arms, two velvet coats for

covering (pairs of) plates, one old banner of the said Piers' arms, 41 destriers and coursers and one palfrey

19

Kew, National Archives, KB 27/220/105–7d
Plea to the Court of the King's Bench of Margaret, Wife of Robert Essington for justice for his murder by multiple assailants, Essington, Staffordshire, 3 July 1314

Joh[ann]es fil' Rog[er]i de Swynnerto[u]n cu' vno arcu facto de Taxu de Ispania quem tenuit in manu sua sinistra longitudo illius arcus de duab[us] vlnis Reg' grossitudo quatuor pollic[e]m h[omin]is qui quidem arcus tentus fuit de vna corda cuius corde longitudo fuit de duab[us] vlnis Regis & de vno quart' p[re]cij toti' arcus & corde decem & octo denar' sterlingor[um] et cu' vna sagitta barbata que vocat[u]r clotharewe q[u]am tenuit in manu sua dextra vnde caput illius sagitte fuit de ferro de longitudine quatuor pollic[e]m h[omin]is et de grossitudine in[te]gr[a]m duor[um] pollic[e]m h[omin]is prec' illius sagitte vnius denar' de quib[u]s arcu & sagitta d[ic] tus Jo[hann]es de illa sagitta p[er]cussit eu' en medio loco mamelli et fecit ei vnam plagam de longitudine tr[iu]m pollic[e]m h[omin]is et latitudine duor[um] pollic[e] m h[omin]is et de p[ro]funditate vsq[ue] ad cor vnde statim obijt int[er] brachia sua [another John] tene[n]s in manu sua dextra vnu' ensem de colonio tr[a]cto de ferro & acero facto de longitudine sex ped' h[omin]is & latitudine iux[t]a hultam q[u] atuor pollic[e]m h[omin]is p[re]c' ensis duor[um] solid' sterlingor[um] de quo ense d[ic]t[u]s Joh[ann]es p[er]cussit p[re]d[ic]t[u]m Robert[u]m quondam viru' suu' in medio loco iuncture int[er] ped' sinistr' & tibiam et amputauit ped' ip[s]ius Rob[er] ti de quo ictu d[ic]tus Rob[er]tus quondam vir' suis statim inter brachia sua obijt [Nicholas] cu' vno arcu tento de taxu hib[er]n' facto que' tenuit in manu sua sinistra et cu' vna sagitta barbata que vocat[u]r doggearwe et de illo arcu et de illa sagitta sagittauit p[re]d[ic]t[u]m Rob[er]t[u]m quonda' viru' suu' & de illa sagitta p[er]cussit ip[si]m Rob[er]t[u]m a duob[us] pollicib[us] h[omin]is subtus mamillam sinistr[a]m et fecit ei vnam plagam de latitudine duor[um] pollic[e]m h[omin]is & longitudine triu' pollic[e]m h[omin]is et de p[ro]funditate vsq[ue] ad cor [Thomas] cu' vno baculo vocat[u]r kentisshstaf' de Fraxino rotundo tene[n]s in ambab[us] manib[us] suis de longitudine duar[um] vlnarum Regis et grossitudine Octo pollic' h[omin] is p[re]c' vnius denar' et de baculo illo p[er]cussit Rob[er]t[u]m in medio loco g[r] aue capiti sui & fecit ei vnam plagam de longitudine sex pollic' et de latitudine duar[um] quatuor pollic[e]m h[omin]is et de p[ro]funditate vsq[ue] ad cerebru' vnde statim obijt int[er] brachia ip[s]ius Margarete [another assailant] tenuit de ambab[us] manib[us] suis p[er] spatulam sinistram vno cultello de Hib[er]n' in medio loco pectoris int[er] mamillas p[er]cussit & fecit ei vna plaga' de p[ro]funditate vsq[ue] ad cor [three more assailants each armed with 'vno cultello de Hib[er]n''] [another assailant] tenens vnu' arcu' qui vocat[u]r Turkeys de taxu de Ispania f[ac]to de vna

corda tento in manu' suam sinistram de longitudine vnius vlne Regis & dimid' et
de grossitudine in[te]gr[a]m quinq[ue] pollic[e]m h[omin]is longitudo corde septe'
pollic' h[omin]is [sic] p[re]c' arcus & corde viginti denar' sterlingor[um] et cu' vna
sagitta barbata que vocat[u]r Walsarewe q[u]am tenuit in manu sua dextra vnde
caput illius sagitte fuit de ferro de longitudine sex pollic[e]m h[omin]is et de grossitudine prop[r]e illam sagittam duor[um] pollic[e]m h[omin]is et sagitta illa facta fuit
de fraxino de longitudine triu' quart' vlne Reg' prec' eiusdem saggite vnius denar'
sterling' et de illo arcu & de illa sagitta sagittauit Rob[er]t[u]m suu' de sagitta illa
p[er]cussit et fecit ei vnam plagam a duob[us] pollicib[u]s h[omin]is de sub mamilla
dextra ascendendo de longitudine triu' pollic[e]m h[omin]is et latitudine duor[um]
pollic[e]m h[omin]is et de p[ro]funditate vsq[ue] ad cor [another assailant] cu' vno
arcu facto de ligno de hulmo tento de vna corda que' tenuit in manu sinistra de longitudine duar[um] vlnar[um] Regis et grossitudine septe' pollic[e]m h[omin]is prec'
arcus & corde duodecim denar' sterlingor[um] et cu' vna sagitta barbata que vocat[u]
r Scotische arewe q[u]am tenuit in manu sua dextra vnde caput illius sagitte factu'
fuit de ferro de longitudine q[ui]nq[ue] pollic[e]m h[omin]is et de latitudine p[ro]
p[r]e sagittam de dimid' pollic' h[omin]is et sagitta facta fuit de ligno quod vocat[u]r
in Romanis Boul de longitudine vnius vlne Regis et sagitta illa pennata fuit de pennis
pauonis Rubeis p[re]c' vnius denar' de quib[u]s arca & sagitta sagittauit Rob[er]t[u]
m et fecit ei vnam plagam in medio loco dorsi scilicet int[er] post[er]iore' p[ar]te
capitis & Braele [caused a wound three inches by one inch to the depth of the heart]
[another assailant] vno arcu facto de taxu Hib[er]' tenso de vna corda [worth 10d.]
vna sagitta barbata que vocat[u]r Scotisarewe [size as above] [another assailant] vn[a]
m arcu' tensum de vna corda [...] vnam sagittam vnde arcus fuit de Hulmo & sagitta
[space] et vocat[u]r Walfarewe

John son of Roger of Swynnerton with a bow made of Spanish yew which he held in
his left hand – the length of this bow two King's ells, the width four men's thumbs
(i.e. inches) – this bow was strung with a cord; this cord was 2¼ King's ells long –
the total value of the bow and cord 18d. Sterling – and with a barbed arrow which is
called a cloth arrow which he held in his right hand – the head of this arrow was of
iron four inches long and the total width two inches – the total value of this arrow
1d. – with which bow and arrow the said John shot (the victim) in the middle of the
breast leaving a wound three inches long and two wide and to the depth of the heart
from which he died in her (Margaret's) arms. (Another John) holding in his right
hand a drawn sword of Cologne made of iron and steel six men's feet in length and
four inches wide at the hilt – the value 2s. Sterling – with this sword the said John
struck the said Robert her husband in the middle of the joint between the left foot
and shin and cut off Robert's foot of which wound her husband Robert died in her
arms. (Nicholas) with a spanned bow of Irish yew which he held in his left hand and
with a barbed arrow called a dog arrow and with this bow and arrow shot the said
Robert her husband and with this arrow struck this Robert two inches beneath the
left breast and gave him a wound two inches long and three wide and to the depth of
the heart. (Thomas) with a round staff called a Kentish staff of ash two ells long and

eight inches thick worth 1d. – and with this staff he struck Robert in the middle of his head and gave him a wound six inches long and 2¼ inches wide and to the depth of his brain of which he died in this Margaret's arms. (Another assailant) held in both his hands from his left shoulder an Irish knife and struck him in the middle of the chest between the breasts and gave him a wound to the depth of the heart. [Three more assailants armed with Irish knives]. (Another assailant) holding a bow called Turkish made of Spanish yew strung with a cord in his left hand 1½ ells long and five inches wide in total; the length of the cord seven inches [sic] the bow and arrow worth 20d. Sterling – and with a Welsh arrow called a wolf arrow which he held in his right hand – the head of this arrow in all two inches wide and the arrow (shaft) made of ash three quarters of an ell long – the value of this arrow 1d. Sterling – and with this bow and arrow he shot Robert; the arrow giving him a wound two inches beneath the right breast extending to the length of three inches and two inches wide to the depth of the heart. (Another assailant) with a bow made of elm wood strung with a cord which he held in his left hand – two King's ells long and seven inches thick: value of the bow and cord 12d. Sterling – and with an arrow called a Scottish arrow which he held in his right hand – the head of this arrow was made of iron five inches long and the whole arrow half an inch wide; the arrow (shaft) was made of wood called birch in French one ell long and this arrow was fletched with red peacock (flight feathers) worth 1d. – with which bow and arrow he shot Robert and gave him a wound in the middle of the back, that being: between the back of the head and (waist) girdle [causing a wound three inches by one inch to the depth of the heart]. (Another) with a bow made of Irish yew strung with a cord worth 10d. with a barbed arrow called a Scottish arrow [size as above]. (Another) with a bow strung with a cord and an arrow; the bow was of elm and the arrow called a wolf arrow

20

London Metropolitan Archives, London Letter-Book D, fol. 165r
Request to the Mayor and Commonalty of the City of London from Edward II for 300 crossbowmen ('ho[m]i[n]es balistar"), 4 December 1314

[each provided with] singulis Aketonos bacinettos colerettos balistas & quarellos belts, aketons, basinets, collars, crossbows and quarrels

21

Oxford, Bodleian Library, MS Tanner 13, pp. 481–4
Alice Taylor's Appeal for Robbery, Parish of Saint Botolph, Aldgate, City of London, 1314

La vindrent ce' iij felonous[eme]nt oue iij haches q' lem appell' Boleaxes [sic] dount la teste de checune hach' fust de fer & dasser & la massue fust de coudr' la lungur' de chescune teste fust dun pie & la leeur' de d[em]j pie & la longur' de checune massue dune Aune & la g[r]ossur' de checune massue de x pouz & la porte q' fust deuant sa meson ouesq' les auantd' haches debruser' & vendrent al eus de sa chambre & les Bords del eus furent de Keyne ove les ditz hach' felonous[eme]nt debrus' & cele huch' oue les ditz haches debrus' & les bors de Keyne

These three (accused) feloniously came to her house with three axes called pollaxes. The head of each axe is of iron and steel being one foot long and a half-foot wide. Each haft is of hazel one ell long with a circumference of ten inches. They broke down the oak door with these axes and came into her chamber and broke open an oak-board chest.

22

Now-Lost Document from the Archives de Pas-de-Calais, A 342, printed in J. M. Richard, *Une Petite-Nièce de Saint Louis: Mahaut, comtesse d'Artois et de Bourgogne, 1302–1329* (Paris, 1887), pp. 394–6
Household Payments of Robert, Count of Artois, Paris, 1315

I auqueton de blanc cendal pour vestir plates, pour la façon, XX s., I auqueton de vermel cendal roiié d'or fait à II fois, LX s., II bachinés couvrir et garnir, XXX s., I bachinet fourbir et estoffer, XVI s., une haute gorgiere estoffer, X s., II paires de quiisseus [*sic*] vermaus roié d'or, XXX s., pour le pavillon d'une gorgerete, pour la façon, V s., I chapel d'achier estoffer, VIII s., I auqueton ralongier, et pour I autre atennier, VIII s., pour la façon d'unes couvertures de plates et pour les brachieres, VIII lb., le quevrechief d'une hyaume et livrer tout l'or et la soie, XII lb., II grenons et pour le lien du Hyaume Robert, pour ces II pieces de tout livrer or et soie et les pierres, XXV lb., uns gantelés brouder et estoffer, XX s., I auqueton fort à vestir de fer, pour la façon, XXVIII s., uns bras d'achier couvrir de brodure, L s., I hyaume de guerre, C s., I chapel de Montauban, et pour le haute gorgiere, VI lb., II bachinées couvers, XL s., le bachinet à visiere et à haute bretesque, LXX s., II paires de greves et II paires de poulains, IIII lb., [...] pour les plates et pour les gans, XII lb., pour l'épée, LXX s., I fer à glave, X s., une paire de gans, XX s., unes greves, XXX s., pour le harnais Robert refourbir, XXII s., II fers de glave, XX s. Donné à Estiene de Manricourt, pour lui aidier à armer, XXXII s., uns cauchons de haubreserie achatés par Petit pour Robert, XX s. Pour blanchir les hauberjons et les barbieres Robert, V s., II ceinturetes de cuir pour Robert, III s., II escuz pour jo[ust]er achatez à Paris, XX s., VII douzaines et demie d'aguillettes et pour laz de soie et pour drap de quoi on fist I fourrel d'espée pour Robert, XXIIII s., la garnison d'une espée pour Robert, II s., refaire les pans et les braz d'un hauberjon, IIII s., I hyaume et une espée burnir, VIII s., I braiel de cerf et pour I autre braiel pour assir les pans du haubrejon Robert, XII s., III couroies de cerf, III s., unes besaches de vache où l'en port le ha[r]nais Robert, XIIII s., VI aunes de drap de tarze pour les plates Robert, CVIII s., VI aunes de fort cendal pour claver les plates Robert, XXV s., III aunes de toile vermelle pour les plates, IIII s., VII bastons d'or, LXIII s., II bastons d'argent, XIIII s., II onces d'or de Chipre, XXIII s., pluseurs soies de couleurs, XLV s., vert cendal à la haute gorgiere, V s., toile vermelle pour claver les gantelés, X d., cendal vermel et pour soie as gantelés, II s. VI d., III esguilletes, VII d., pour laces, XII d., laces et boutons esmaillés, XXII d., pates et ataques II s. VI d., toile vermelle, II s. VI d., aguilletes d'argent, V s., ruben vermel, IIII d., II aunes de cendal vermel pour les gantelés garnir, VIII s., las et boutons d'or as brachieres, XL s., offrois à pelles et pour offrois des plates [...] XXIIII aunes et demie drap de soie de changant, XXVIII s., une chainture, LX s., las à boutons d'or, III s., las du braiel et pour autres las, V s., I las à or au coutel des plates, VIII s., camoscat, pour couvrir un gans, X s., veluet soussiet pour couvrir II paires de gans de plates, XXX s., les las et boutons de perles pris à Jacques de la Hale pour metre au coutel d'esmail Robert, XXXII s., V aunes de drap vermel de graine dont on fist I tunicle destaint pour Robert, IIII lb., bleu et gaune drap à armoier ladite tunicle, XVIII s., II paires d'esperons pour Robert, VI s., pour l'envers d'un auqueton pour Robert, V aunes et demie de toile XIII s. IX d., XII aunes et demie de toile, dont on fist III quemises de Chartres et I corset, XVI s. VI d.

for making: one aketon of white sendal (lightweight silk or very fine linen) for bearing (pairs of) plates 20s., one aketon of vermilion sendal striped with gold made twice over (i.e. inside and out) 60s., coverings and fittings for two basinets 30s., furbishing and stuffing one basinet (with a lining) 16s., stuffing one high (necked) gorget 10s., two pairs of cuisses of vermilion (cloth) striped with gold 30s., making the covering of one gorget 5s., stuffing one steel chapel (de fer) 8s., lengthening one aketon and shortening another 8s., making one cover of plate and for the bracers 8l., gilt and silk for the (heraldic) livery and coverchief (fabric headdress) of a helm 12l., two whiskers for the (heraldic) lion of Robert's helm – both pieces fully decorated with gold, silk, and pearls 25l., one pair of gauntlets embroidered and stuffed (with lining) 20s., making one strong aketon to bear iron (i.e. mail defences) 28s., one steel mail sleeve covered with embroidery 50s., one war helm 100s., one chapeau de Montauban and high (necked) gorget 6l., two covered basinets 40s., a basinet with visor and high 'bretesque' (i.e. in the shape of a castle's battlement) 70s., two pairs of greaves and two pairs of poleyns 4l., [...] for (pairs of) plates and gauntlets 12l., for a sword, 70s., one lancehead 10s., one pair of gauntlets 20s., one pair of greaves 30s., for refurbishing Robert's harness 22s., two lanceheads 20s., 32s. given to Etienne Manricourt to assist his purchase of arms, one pair of mail chausse bought by Small for Robert 20s., for scouring Robert's haubergeons and barbers (i.e. mail bevor: chin and throat defence) 5s., two leather belts for Robert 3s., two jousting shields bought at Paris 20s., 7½ dozen straps, silk laces, and cloth from which one sword-scabbard was made for Robert 24s., equipping one sword for Robert 2s., repairing the paunce and sleeves of a haubergeon 4s., one helm and burnishing one sword 8s., one buckskin and for another brayer for the seat of the paunce of Robert's haubergeon 12s., three buckskins 3s., one cowhide bag in which to carry Robert's harness 14s., six ells of Tarsus cloth for Robert's (pair of) plates 108s., six ells of strong sendal (lightweight silk or very fine linen) to nail Robert's plates 25s., three ells of vermilion cloth for the plates 4s., seven gold batons 63s., two silver batons 14s., two ounces of Cypriot gold (thread) 23s., several coloured silks 45s., green sendal for the high (necked) gorget 5s., vermilion cloth to nail the gauntlets 10d., vermilion sendal and silk for gauntlets 2s. 6d., three straps 7d., 12d. for laces, enamelled laces and buttons 22d., plaques and fittings 2s. 6d., vermilion cloth 2s. 6d., silver straps 5s., vermilion ribbon 4d., two ells of vermilion sendal for fitting gauntlets 8s., gold laces and buttons for bracers 40s., goldsmiths' work for scrolls and for goldsmiths' work for (pairs of) plates [...] 24½ ells of shimmering silk cloth 28s., one girdle 60s., laces with gold buttons 3s., brayer laces and for other laces 5s., one gilt lace for a knife (to mount on a pair of) plates 8s., camaca (silk fabric) to cover one (pair of) gauntlets 10s., thin velvet to cover two pairs of plate gauntlets 30s., laces and pearl buttons bought from Jacques de la Hale to affix to Robert's enamelled knife 32s., five ells of grain-textured vermilion cloth from which one dyed small tunic was made for Robert 4l., blue and yellow cloth for (heraldic) arms for this tunic 18s., two pairs of spurs for Robert 6s., 5½ ells of cloth for the inside of an aketon for Robert 13s. 9d., 12½ ells of cloth from which three chemises of Chartres[3] and one corset were made 16s. 6d.

23

Kew, National Archives, E 163/4/3
Forfeited Goods of Llywelyn Bren, Llandaff Cathedral Treasury, Principality of Wales, 1315

j Aketon j gaumbeyson j peyre des quisseus j coleret de linge teille j vel chapel de fer iij Haub[er]gons j couerture de fer j targe j peyre des gaunz de plat' j peyre de quisseus j cote darme' de bocram j gaunbeyson vermeil j Aketon nyent p[ar]fet j vele sele

one aketon, one gambeson, one pair of cuisses, one linen collar, one old chapel de fer, three haubergeons, one iron (mail horse) cover, one targe, one pair of plate gauntlets, one pair of cuisses, one buckram (cotton fabric) (heraldic) coat armour, one old gambeson, one unfinished aketon, one old saddle

24

Paris, Bibliothèque nationale de France, MS fr. 7855, pp. 163–73
Inventory of the Arms and Armour of King Louis X of France, Paris, 1316

This is a 17th- or 18th-century copy of a now-lost original

xxiii. hautes gorgieres doubles de chambli vns pans et vns bras de Jazeran d'acier vns pans et i. bras de roondez mailles de haute cloüeure vns pans et vns bras d'acier plus

---

3   Moffat, '*The Manner of Arming Knights for the Tourney*', p. 10: 'a garment in the shape of, and that had come into contact with, the *sancta camisia* of Chartres cathedral'.

fors de mailles roondes de haute cloüeure vns pans et vns bras d'acier plus fors de mailles roondes de haute cloüeure vns pans et vns bras de Jazeran d'acier et le camail de mesmes ii. coleretes pizaines de Jazeran d'acier vne barbiere de haute cloüeure de chambli i. Jazeran d'acier i. haubergon d'acier a manicles vne couuerture de Jazeran de fer vnes couuertures de mailles rondes demi cloée vne testiere de haute cloüeure de maille Ronde ii. camaus entiers de maille ronde i. haubert entier de Lombardie ii. autres haubergons de Lombardie iiii. paire de chauces de fer viii. paire de chaucons et i. chaucon par dessus vnes plates neuues couuertes de samit vermeil deus paires de plates autres couuertes de samit vermeil i. couteau a manche de fust et de fer qui fu saint Loys si comme l'en dit iii. paire de greues et iii. paire de pouloinz d'acier vi. autres paires de greues d'acier et ii. paire de pouloinz deus heaumes d'acier v. autres heaumes dont li vns est dorez et v. chapeaus roons dont les ii. sont dorez ii. cors d'acier ii. bacinez roonz iiii. espées garnies d'argent dont les ii. sont garnies de samit et les ii. de cuir vne espée garnie d'or et de cuir vne espée a parer garnie d'argent le poumel et le poing esmaillié viii. espées de Tholouse et ii. Misericordes xvii. espées de Bray vne espée de Jehan Dorgeret [recte Dorgelet] ii espées et vne misericorde de Verzi xv. espées de commun xv. coutiaus de commun et vii. fers de glaiue de Thoulouse ii. de commun et le bon fer de glaiue le Roy ii. chanfrains dorez et i de cuir vne flour de liz d'argent dorée pareure a mettre sur le heaume le Roy vns gantelez couuers de velueil vermeil vne cote gamboisiée de cendal blanc ii. houces i. gamboison de bordeure dez armes de France iii. paire de bracieres en cuir des armes de France iiii. paire d'esperons garnis de soye et ii. paire garnis de cuir vne testiere et vne croupiere broudée des armes de France ii. chapiaus de fer couuers iii. escus pains des armes le Roy et vnz d'acier xvi. paire de couuertures batuës et vne crouper des armes le Roy vnes couuertures de gamboisons broudées des armes le Roy iii. paires de couuertures gamboisees des armes le Roy et vnes indes jazeguenées ii. paire de couuertures batuës et vne coliere des armes le Roy vne quantité d'aguilletes et laz a armer vi. Bacinez vns cuissiaus gamboisiez et vns esquinebans de cuir bracieres houce d'escu et couuertures a cheual des armes le Roy lez fleurs d'or de Chipre broudées de pelles picieres et flanchieres de samit des armes le Roy les fleurs d'or de Chipre vns cuissiaus sans pouloins des armes de France vne cote gamboisiée a arbroissiaus d'or broudée a chardonnereus vnes couuertures gamboisiées de France et de Nauarre vnes couuertures de France et de Nauarre a fleurs de liz broudées flanciers et piciers de France et de Nauarre a fleurs de liz broudées i. escu et ii. targetes de France et de Nauarre et i. escu ynde a lettres d'or ii. Cotes gamboisiées de cendal blanc la couuerture d'vnes plates a fleurs de liz broudées vne houce de drap fenduë aus ii. Costés i. bacinet couuert de cendal blanc iiii. paire' de couuertures de Royz

23 high double gorgets of Chambly (i.e. high-necked, of double thickness of mail made at Chambly), one pair of paunce and one pair of steel (mail) sleeves of jazerant, one paunce and one pair of sleeves of round mail of high nailing (i.e. all the links are of round-sectioned wire and each riveted), one much stronger steel paunce and pair of sleeves of round mail of high nailing, one much stronger steel paunce and one pair of sleeves of round mail of high nailing, one steel paunce and one pair of sleeves

of jazerant and the aventail the same, two steel pisan collars of jazerant, a bevor of high nailing of Chambly (mail), one steel jazerant, one steel haubergeon with sleeves, one iron horse cover of jazerant, one horse cover of half-nailed round mail (i.e. fewer riveted links), one tester of round mail of high nailing, two complete aventails of round mail, one complete hauberk of Lombardy (make), two other haubergeons of Lombardy, four pairs of iron (mail) chausses, eight pairs of chausses and one pair of over-chausses, one new pair of plates covered with vermilion samite (shimmering silk fabric), two other pairs of plates covered with vermilion samite, one knife with a grip of wood and iron which once belonged to Saint Louis, three pairs of greaves and three pairs of steel poleyns, six other pairs of steel greaves and two pairs of poleyns, two steel helms, five other helms one of which is gilt, five round chapel de fers two of which are gilt, two steel corsets, two round basinets, four swords garnished with silver two of which are garnished with samite and two with leather, one sword garnished with gold and with leather, one adorned sword garnished with silver the pommel and the point enamelled, eight swords of Toulouse (make) and two misericords, 17 swords of Bray, one sword (that belonged to) Jehan (Baron) d'Orgelet, two swords and one misericord of Verzy, 15 common swords, 15 common knives and seven glaive-heads of Toulouse, two common glaive-heads and one of the King's good ones, two gilt shaffrons and one of leather, an adorned silver-gilt fleur-de-lys to place on the King's helm, one pair of gauntlets covered with vermilion velvet, one gamboised (i.e. made in the manner of a padded gambeson) coat of white sendal (lightweight silk or very fine linen), two huces (shield covers), one gambeson embroidered with the (heraldic) arms of France, three pairs of leather vambrace with the (heraldic) arms of France, four pairs of spurs garnished with silk and two pairs garnished with leather, a tester and a crupper embroidered with the arms of France, two covered chapel de fers, three shields painted with the King's arms and one of steel, 16 pairs of horse covers and a crupper decorated with the King's arms, one gamboised horse cover embroidered with the King's arms, three pairs of gamboised horse covers of the King's arms and one of jazerant of the Indies, two pairs of covers and one collar decorated with the King's arms, a quantity of laces and straps for arming, six basinets, one pair of gamboised cuisses and one pair of leather schynbalds, shield huce, and horse covers of the King's arms the flowers of Cypriot gold (thread) embroidered with pearls, peytral and flanchers (flank covers) of samite of the King's arms the flowers of Cypriot gold (thread), one pair of cuisses without poleyns of the arms of France, one gamboised coat embroidered with gold bushes with goldfinches, one horse cover decorated with the arms of France and of Navarre, one gamboised cover with the arms of France and of Navarre, one cover with the arms of France and of Navarre with embroidered fleur-de-lys, flanchers and peytrals with the arms of France and of Navarre with embroidered fleur-de-lys, one shield and two targes with the arms of France and of Navarre and one shield of the Indies with gilt letters, two gamboised coats of white sendal, the cover of a pair of plates with embroidered fleur-de-lys, one cloth huce torn in two halves, one basinet covered with white sendal, four pairs of horse covers of the King's arms

25

Unlocated Original Document printed in C. H. Hartshorne, 'Caernarvon Castle', *Archaeologia Cambrensis* 1 (1855), pp. 242–6
Inventory of Caernarfon Castle, Principality of Wales, 1316

vij pec' ferri Wallens' et D. vii. pec' ferri Ispann' [in] stauro Castri de Kaern' iiij. q[u] intell' [et] iiij. pec' ferri Ispann' Armatur' ij. p[ar]ib[us] platear[um] x. vet[er]ib[us] aketonib[us] ix. aketonib[us] vj. bacinettis vj. p[ar]ib[us] de gaumbers ij p[ar]ib[us] de genulers xij. capit' lancear[um] iiij. p[ar]ib[us] de gaumbers ij. p[ar]ib[us] de geinelers

seven pieces of Welsh iron and 507 pieces of Spanish iron in the store of Caernarfon Castle, four quintals (and) four pieces of Spanish iron. Armour: two pairs of plates, ten old aketons, nine aketons, six basinets, six pairs of jambers, two pairs of genulers, 12 lanceheads, four pairs of jambers, two pairs of genulers

26

Edinburgh, National Library of Scotland, Adv. MS 34.4.2, fol. 119v–fol. 120r
Act of Parliament for the Arming of the Scottish Host enacted by King Robert I, December 1318

quilib[et] hom' de regn' laicu' habens decem libr' in bonis habeat p[ro] corp[or]e suo in defension' regni vna' sufficiente' aketonam vnu' Bacinetu' & cyrotecas de guerra cu' lancea & gladio Et qui no' h[ab]uerit aketon' & Bacinetu' h[ab]eat vnu' bonu' hobirgellu' vel vnu' bonu' ferru' pro corp[or]e suo vnu' Capellu' de ferro & cyrotecas de guerra quicunq[ue] habens valore' uniu' vacce in bonis habeat vna' bona' lanceam v[e]l vnu' bonu' arcu' cu' vno schapho sagittar[um] videlic' viginti qu[a]tuor sag[it]tis cu' p[er]tinenciis

every layman of the realm owning £10 in goods have for his body for the defence of the kingdom: one sufficient aketon, one basinet and gauntlets for war with lance and sword. And who has not an aketon and basinet have one good haubergeon or a good iron (defence) for his body, one chapel de fer, and gauntlets for war. Whoever owns the value in goods of one cow have one good lance or one good bow with one sheaf of arrows viz.: 24 arrows with the appurtenances

27

Kew, National Archives, E 154/1/11B
Inventory of the Goods of Roger Mortimer, Earl of March, Wigmore Castle and Abbey, Herefordshire, 1322

Castro de Wygemore iij Sp[ri]ngaus cu' app[ar]atu iij Sp[ri]ngaus s[i]n' app[ar]atu xiiija balist' de cornu ad viz cu' tri' costis de cornu S[i]n' talar' vij balistis de ligno

ad viz cu' C & xxx q[u]arell' quor[um] lxx pennate de pe[n]nis eneis & lx de pe[n]
nis ligneis iij ingeniis p[ro] balistris tendend' xviij balistis de ligno ad vnu' pedem &
vna costa de ligno s[i]n' talar' cu' C q[u]arell' ij p[ar]ib[u]s de plates j quirre iij galee
p[ro] iustis iiij p[ar]ib[u]s brac[er]s j g[r]ate iij vaumplates iij p[ar]ib[u]s de besescus
viij Scutis iiij targ' j galea p[ro] guerra ij capell' cu' visur' vj galeis p[ro] torniame[n]
t' vn' capell' de ferro j capell de neruis ij p[ar]ib[u]s de gaumb[e]rs xij lanc' vij hastis
Lancear[um] iiij ferr' p[ro] frenis ad torniame[n]tu' ij arcub[u]s saracen' cu' iij Sagittis
saraceniis j macea de ferr' j panerio pleno de diu[er]sis instrame[n]t' p[ro] co[n]fec[ti]
one balistar[um] xiij capitib[u]s ferr' p[ro] lanceis j coronali p[ro] iustis ix capitib[u]
s magnis p[ro] sagittis ij rectis p[ro] ferris capiend' j Sp[ar]th de Hib[er]n' x cistis ij
coffr' trussator' Lib' j galeam p[ro] guerra ij capell' cu visur' v capell' de ferro ij p[ar]ia
de gaumb[e]rs iiij Sp[ri]ngaus cu' app[ar]atu j Sp[ri]gal' s[i]n' app[ar]atu xlij q[u]arell'
pe[n]nat' de pe[n]nis eneis lx q[u]arell' pe[n]nat' de pe[n]nis ligneis rem' ij Sp[ri]
ngaus s[i]n' app[ar]atu xiiij baliste de cornu ad viz cu' iij costis de cornu sine talar'
vij baliste de ligno ad viz xxviij q[u]arell' pennat' de pe[n]nis ereis iij ingenis p[ro]
balistis te[n]de[n]d' xviij baliste de ligno ad vnu' pedem j costa de ligno s[i]n' talar' C
& lx q[u]arell' ij p[ar]ia de plates j quire iij galee p[ro] iustis ij p[ar]ia brac[er]s j grate
iij vaumplates iij p[ar]ia de besescus viij Scuta iiij target' vj galee p[ro] torniament' j
capell de Neruis xij lancee vij haste Lancear[um] iiij ferr' p[ro] frenis ad torniame[n]
t' ij arci saracen' iij sagittis j macea de ferr' j paneriu' plenu' de p[ar]u' instrame[n]t'
p[ro] confect[i]one balistar[um] xiij capiti ferr' p[ro] lanc' j coronale p[ro] iustis ix
capita magna p[ro] sagittis j Sp[ar]th' de Hib[er]n' x ciste ij coffr' trussator' abbathia de
wygemore xj sagittis cu' magnis capitib[us] ferr' vno conu eneo q[uo]d vna cu' q[ua]
d' fauchone est vt d[icit]ur Carta terre de wygem' viij loricis j Corset de ferr' j pari de
gussettis j gorger' dup' vn p[ar]ib[us] de chaucons v coifes loricar[um] ij capell' ferr'
cu' viser' j galea cu' guichet j capell' ferreu' Rotu[n]d' j aketon coop[er]to de pa[n]no
de taffata taneto cu' vna Camisia de chartres v p[ar]ib[us] de chanfreins p[ro] equis
ad arma cu' q[ui]nq[ue] p[ar]ib[us] coop[er]torior[um] de frett' cu' flauncheris &
piceris de corio ij p[ar]ib[us] de treppes xj p[ar]ib[u]s coop[er]torior[um] ferr' p[ro]
equis & ij mantell' ferr' j p[ar]i cirothecar[um] de plate ij brac[er]s de plate j p[ar]i
de gaumb[e]rs j p[ar]i sot[u]lar' de plate j colar' de ferr' j scuto iiij lanc' p[ro] guerra
iij lanc' p[ro] iustis j p[ar]i de botes plumetez de ferr' ij glad' cu' h[ar]nes' argenteo
totu' lib' d[oim]no Regi ex[cep]t' j gorger' dupplici ij p[ar]ib[us] de treppres j scuto
iiij lanc' p[ro] guerra & iij lanceis p[ro] iustis que remanent in abb[at]ia

Castle of Wigmore: three springalds with apparatus, three springalds without
apparatus, 14 vice-spanned horn crossbows with three horn bows without tillers
(stocks), seven wooden vice-spanned crossbows with 130 quarrels 70 of which are
fletched with copper and 60 with wood fletchings, three engines for spanning
crossbows, 18 wooden one-foot crossbows (i.e. for one-foot-long bow-staves) and one
wooden bow without tiller, with 100 quarrels, two pairs of plates, one cuirie, three
helms for jousts, three pairs of bracers, one grapper, three vamplates, three pairs of
besagews, eight shields, four targes, one helm for war, two chapel de fers with visors,
six helms for tourneying, two Saracen bows with three Saracen arrows, one iron mace,

one pannier full of divers tools for constructing crossbows, 13 iron lanceheads, one coronal for jousts, nine large arrowheads, two rules for heading lances, one Irish sparth (axe), ten chests, two trussing coffers. Sold: one helm for war, two chapel de fers with visors, five chapel de fers, two pairs of jambers, three springalds with apparatus, one springald without apparatus, 42 quarrels fletched with copper fletchings, 60 quarrels fletched with wooden fletchings. Remains: two springalds without apparatus, 14 horn vice-spanned crossbows, with three horn bows without tillers (stocks), seven wooden vice-spanned crossbows, 28 quarrels fletched with copper fletchings, three engines for spanning these crossbows, 18 wooden one-foot crossbows, one wooden bow without tiller, with 160 quarrels, two pairs of plates, one cuirie, three helms for jousts, two pairs of bracers, one grapper, three vamplates, three pairs of besagews, eight shields, four targes, six helms for tourneying, one chapel of sinew, 12 lance-staves, seven lance shafts, three iron (horse) bits for tourneying, two Saracen bows, three Saracen arrows, one iron mace, one pannier full of little tools for constructing crossbows, 13 lanceheads, one coronal for jousts, nine large arrowheads, one Irish sparth, ten chests, two trussing coffers. Wigmore Abbey: 11 arrows with large iron heads, one copper horn which – along with a certain falchion – is called the 'Charter of the Lands of Wigmore', eight hauberks, one iron corset, one pair of gussets, one double gorget (i.e. two layers of mail), one pair of chausses, five mail coifs, two chapel de fers with visors, one helm with 'guichet' (small aperture), one round chapel de fer, one aketon covered in tawny taffeta cloth with one chemise of Chartres,[4] five pairs of shaffrons for arming horses with five pairs of fretted (horse) covers with flanchers (flank defences) and peytrals of leather, two pairs of (horse) trappers, 11 pairs of iron (mail) covers for horses, and two iron mantles, one pair of plate gauntlets, two plate sleeves, one pair of jambers, one pair of plate shoes, one iron collar, one shield, four war lances, three jousting lances, one pair of boots feathered with iron, two swords with silvered harness. All sold by order of the King except one double gorget, two pairs of (horse) trappers, one shield, four war lances, and three jousting lances which remain in the abbey

28

London Metropolitan Archives, London Letter-Book E, fol. 133r–fol. 133v
Articles of the Linen Armourers of London, 26 January 1322

[At the Hustings of the Common Pleas in the Guildhall before the Mayor, Aldermen, and Sheriffs] p[ar] assent Hugh' de Bungeye Will' de segraue Rog' Santige thom' de Copham Will[ia]m de lanshull' Rich' de kent Gilot' le Heauberg' Hugh' le Heam' mestre Rich' le Heaum' Simon le Heaum' Rob[er]t de Skelton' Joh' tauy Henr' Horpol Elys de Wodebergh' Will' le Heaum' Oliuer le Heaum' Will' de Stamford Will' de Lyndeseie Joh' de kesteuene Rob[er]t le Proude Rob[er]t seymer Reynaud le heauberg'

---

4   Moffat, '*The Manner of Arming Knights for the Tourney*', p. 10: 'a garment in the shape of, and that had come into contact with, the *sancta camisia* of Chartres cathedral'.

Rog' le salt[er]e & Ric' de Alakenhale arm[ur]ers fust ordine pur commun p[ro]fit
& assentu qe desoremes arm[ur]e faite en la Cite a uendre soit bone & couuenable
solom la forme q[ue] sensuyt q[ue] Aketoun e Gambezoun couertz de sendal' ou de
drap de seye & soient estoffez de noueille teille de Cotoun & de Cadaz e de veils
sendal' & nyent ou autre manere les blaunches Aketouns soient estoffes de veille
teille & de Cotoun & de Nouele teille dedenz & dehors pur ceo sire q[ue] ho[m]me
ad troue veils bacenetz debruses & fauses ore nouelement couers p[er] gentz q[ue]
riens ne seyuent del mestier q[e]ux sount mys en musseats & aportes en pais hors de
la Cite a uendre en la Cite meismes des qu[eu]x ho[m]me ne puet auoir coinscance
le queil il soient bons ou mauueises de queu chose graunt p[er]il porient a cheir au
Roi & a son people & vileyn esclaundre a les arm[u]rers & a tote la Cite Ordene est
& assentu q[ue] nul Feure ne nul ho[m]me q[ue] fait les fers des bacynetz desormes
face couerer nul bacynet il meismes a uendre mes le vende hors de sa mayn tut' new
& desgarnee ausi come leur soloit faire deuant ces houres & les qu[eu]x demoergent
desgarnices tanque eux soient vewes p[ar] le quatre q[ue] serront iurrez ou p[ar] deus
de eux le queil il soient couenables a garnit' ou noun Et se troue soit en nully meson
des arm[u]rers ou aillours en qi meson q[ue] ceo soit arm[u]re a uendre queile q[ue]
le soit qe ne su[n]t p[ro]fitable ou autre q[ue] nest ordine q[ue] ceo soit tantost pris
& aporte deuant meire & andermans & p[ar] eux soit aiuge bone ou mauueise solom
lo[u]r descrecion pur queile chose bien & loialement garder & surier Rog' sauage
Will' le toneler mestr' Richard le heaum' Joh' tauy sount Jurres

[At the Hustings of the Common Pleas in the Guildhall before the Mayor, Aldermen,
and Sheriffs] with the agreement of Hugh Bungay, William Segrave, Roger Santige,
Thomas Copham, William Lanshull, Richard Kent, Gilot the hauberger, Hugh the
heaumer, Master Richard the heaumer, Simon the heaumer, Robert Skelton, John
Tavy, Henry Horpol, Elys Wodebergh, William the heaumer, Oliver the heaumer,
William Stamford, William Lyndeseie, John Kestevene, Robert Proude, Robert
Seymer, Renaud the hauberger, Roger Salter, and Richard Alakenhale, armourers. It
is ordained for the common good and agreement that henceforth armour made in
the City to be sold ought to be good and suitable according to the following form:
any aketon and gambeson covered with sendal (lightweight silk or very fine linen)
or silk cloth ought to be stuffed with new linen, cotton, cotton wool, and old sendal
and in no other manner. White aketons ought to be stuffed with old linen, cotton,
and new linen inside and out. Because there are lords or men who buy old, worn
out, and damaged basinets newly covered by men who know nothing of the craft
that are placed in secret places and carried into the country and into the City where
no man might know whether they are good or bad – these things being of great peril
and cause the ruin of the King and his people and is to the villainous slander of the
armourers and to all the City – it is ordained and agreed that no smith, nor any man
who makes the iron parts of basinets, may cover any basinet themselves to sell save
that it be sold out of his hand completely bare and un-equipped as was wont to be
done heretofore. They (the basinets) must remain un-equipped until they be viewed
by the four (masters of the craft) who shall be sworn in (or by two of them) who shall

decide whether they are suitable to be equipped or not. If any armour of any kind be found in an armourer's house or elsewhere for sale that is of poor quality or has not been inspected it shall immediately be taken and brought before the Mayor and Aldermen and judged by them to be good or bad at their discretion. Roger Savage, William le Toneler, Richard the heamuer, and John Tavy are sworn in

29

Kew, National Archives, C 145/87/12–25
Royal Inquisitions after the Battle of Boroughbridge on 16 March 1322, various Locations in Yorkshire

[…] vnu' Aketon' vnu' ensem & vnu' Buckeler' Armature Joh[an]nis de Eure videl' j haubergun j par de Jaumbers j par sotular' de plates vnu' par de plates Armatur' que fu[er]it Roger' de Thornton' videl[ice]t vnu' haubergun vnu' par' Cirotecar[um] de plates vnu' par de shynbaudes vnu' haubergun vnu' par de skynbaudes vnu' Bacynet' vnu' par cirothecar[um] de plates que fu[er]it Wil[e]l[m]i de Deer et vnu' par de plates vnu' colret vnu' Bacynet' j Aduentaill' vnu' pysane diu[er]sis armatura videl' quatuor Aketon' Tres Bacynettes duo p[ar]ia Cirotecar[um] de plate vnu' par de Jaumbers j par de polaynes iiij enses iiij Lancee & duo pyckhaches Duo haberguns j Aketon' j Bacynet' […] cirothecar[um] de plate j par' de quyssot' j par de poleyns vnu' Aketon' j hauberk j Bacynet' vnu' par cirothcar[um] de plate j par de quissot' vnu' p[ar]ia de Polayns j par de Jaumbers vnu' hauberk vnu' Bacynet' j Aduentaill' Nich[ol]us de Sutton' [and others] ceperunt q[u]inq[ue] p[ri]sones cum q[u]inq[ue] equis & vnu' haub[er]chun v s. D' quib[us] vnus equs mortuus est inf[r]a q[ui]ndecim dies p[ro] xi[m]o sequ[en]tes Et remane[n]t q[u]atuor equi vnde vnus lyard est in manu Nich[ol] i de Sutton' de empt[i]one est monoc[u]l[u]s xxx s. vnus equs est in manu Thom' hod d[imid]i marc' cu' vno haub[er]chun v s. vnus equs in manibus Rob[ert]i de Bellassis d[imid]i marc' vnus equis in manib[us] Nich[ol]i de Portigton' iiij s. Henr' & Alanus hod ceperu[n]t vnu' p[ri]sone' cum duob[us] equis & vnu' Aketon' vni' equi d[imid] i marc' & alt[er]ius duor[um] solid' & sex denar' Joh[an]nes de Barnebi & hugo de Pontefracto ceperu[n]t tres p[ri]sones cu' duob[us] equis & vnu' bacinet' Walt[eru] s Scutte ianitor Reg' inquir' de cat' eor[un]d' vnde inuent' fu[er]unt viij eq[u]os ij actones ij enses debil' Walt[eru]s Mere de Ingerthorp' & Joh[anne]s fil' Walt[er]i de Thorneton' ceperu[n]t corp' Wil[e]l[m]i Puncy & enim de duxeru[n]t ad p[ri]sona' ap[u]d Ripon' & h[ab]eueru[n]t de Wil[e]l[m]o Puncy j haketon' x s. s[er]iant Johan Cemeberall' & Johan Wodward […] vj cheuez j ackto' vj Bacynet' Gaunz de plat' espez Bokelers & aut[r]es menuz armurez pri' de Will[i]am Puncy vne Acketon' Rog' de Bretton' cep' de diu[er]sis rebell' armur' xl s Joh[ann]es de Kirketon' & Wil[e]l[mu]s le forester inuener' in Bosco in Holwelwod j cist' cu' arm' diu[er]sis de p[re]c' ignora[n]t & deuen' in manu Joh' de Richer Laur' de Ledewodhouses inuen' ij cofri & j herneys integ[r]a p[ro] vno milite cu' barhid q[ue] bon' fuer' in le herneys & in Cofr' ingora[n] t Joh[ann]es de Poncestre & Socii' sui' ceper' j milit' & arm[atur]am cu' ij equos palefr' & cu' al' bon' suis q[ue] bona ignora[n]t Joh[ann]es de fenton' j Rouncy xx s

66

hab[er]gon Acketon' x s Joh[ann]es schaldden h[ab]uit j Auberc j pisan Joh[ann]is de
Swyu[er]to[u]n ap[u]d bulto[u]n [...] vnu' scutum cum sella & duob[us] frenis Cent'
solid' vnu' haberione' cu' aduentail' pysan' & collaret sex' marc' t[ri]a haberiona viginta
solid' tres bacinett' t[ri]ginta solid' vnu' par' de gambers & q[ui]sseus & polleyns q[ui]
ndecim solid' duas balistas duaru[m] marc' duos gladios de guerra d[imid]i marc'

[...] one aketon, one sword, and one buckler, armour of John Eure viz.: one
haubergeon, one pair of jambers, one pair of plate shoes, one pair of plates, armour
which belonged to Roger Thornton viz.: one haubergeon, one pair of plate gauntlets,
one pair of schynbalds. One haubergeon, one pair of schynbalds, one basinet, one
pair of plate gauntlets which belonged to William Deer, and one pair of plates, one
basinet, one aventail, one pisan [...] divers armour viz.: four aketons, three basinets,
two pairs of plate gauntlets, one pair of jambers, one pair of poleyns, four swords,
four lances and two pickaxes, two haubergeons, one aketon, one basinet, one pair
of plate gauntlets, one pair of cuisses, one pair of poleyns, one aketon, one hauberk,
one basinet, one pair of plate gauntlets, one pair of cuisses, one pair of poleyns,
one pair of jambers, one hauberk, one basinet, one aventail, Nicholas Sutton [and
four others] captured five prisoners with five horses and one haubergeon 5s. – one
horse died within 15 days following and the remaining four horses (one of which is
a one-eyed dapple grey) are in the hands of Nicholas Sutton 30s., one horse is in the
hands of Thomas Hod half a mark with one haubergeon 5s., one horse in the hands
of Robert Bellassis half a mark, one horse in the hands of Nicholas Portington 4s.
Henry and Alan Hod captured one prisoner with two horses and one aketon, one
horse half a mark and the other 2s. 6d., John Barneby and Hugh Pontefract captured
three prisoners with two horses and one basinet, Walter Scutte, King's servant came
to inquire of their chattels and found that there were eight horses, two aketons,
two broken swords, Walter Mere of Ingelthorpe and John Fitz Walter of Thornton
captured William Puncy and thence led him prisoner to Ripon and they had from
William Puncy one aketon 10s., Sergeant John Camberwell and John Woodward
took six horses, one aketon, six basinets, plate gauntlets, swords, bucklers, and other
lesser arms [...] they took from William Puncy one aketon, Roger Breton captured
armour from divers rebels 40s., John Kirketon and William Forester found in the
wood at Howelwod one chest with divers arms the value of which they are ignorant
and came into the hands of John Richer, Laurence Ledewodhouses found two coffers
and one complete harness for a knight with a cart cover – he is ignorant of the goods
which comprised the harness and were in the coffers, John Poncestre and his servants
captured one knight and armour with two palfreys – they are ignorant of his other
goods, John Fenton took one rouncey 20s., one haubergon, and one aketon 10s. John
Schaldden had one hauberk and one pisan, John Swiverton had at Bolton [...] one
shield with saddle and two horse bits £100, one haubergeon with aventail, pisan, and
collar six marks, three haubergeons £20, three basinets £30, one pair of jambers and
cuisses and poleyns £15, two crossbows two marks, two war swords half a mark

30

Kew, National Archives, E 101/16/5
Account of Hugh Bungay, Armourer to King Edward II, Newcastle-up-on-Tyne, Northumberland, and London, 21 September 1322

vne heaume & vne creste apendaunt [...] armes le Roy deux bacinetz roundes garnies ou lour apurtenaunces deux pauilouns por pisanes deux peyre des gauntz de plates garniz vne peyre de trappes ouesques les apurtenaunces ouesques xx aunes de boltel por la lineure j peyre de Coffres roundes j peyre de boulges iiij peux de Cheuerel por faire diuerses correies vng peux de Cheuerel blaunk por couerir bacinetz quaunt mestier soit vn peyre de Jambers vne peyre poleyns vne peire des janbers vn chapel rounde od vne creste des armes le Roi vne ewme od vne creste de sendal des armes le Roi deus bacinez rondes garnitz deus pauylounetz p[u]r pussaignes deus peire des gaunt' de plates p[u]r lin[er]ez vne peire de trappes vne peire des coffres rondes p[u]r armurs a vne peire de boulges et demy dozeine pels rouges de cheuerolles p[u]r garneison

one helm and one pertaining crest of the King's arms, two round basinets equipped with their appurtenances, two covers for pisans, two pairs of equipped plate gauntlets, one pair of horse trappers with their appurtenances, one pair of (horse) trappers with 20 ells of bolting-cloth for the lining, one pair of round coffers, one pair of bags, four buckskins for divers leathering, one hide of white buckskin for covering basinets when it shall be necessary, one pair of jambers, one pair of poleyns, one pair of jambers, one round chapel de fer with a crest of the King's arms, one sendal (lightweight silk or very fine linen) crest of the King's arms, two equipped round basinets, two covers for pisans, two pairs of plate gauntlets, for lining a pair of horse trappers, one pair of round coffers for armour, a pair of bags, and a half-dozen red buckskins for equipping

31

Now-Lost Document printed in C. Dehaisnes, *Documents et extraits divers concernant l'histoire de l'art dans la Flandre, l'Artois & le Hainaut avant le XVe siècle*, 2 vols (Lille, 1886), I, pp. 238–48
Inventory of Arms and Armour of Robert, Count of Flanders, Courtrai/Kortrijk, 27 September 1322

un haubiert de boin clavre de Chambli un chamal de mesme unes manches et uns pans de Cambli a plates une gorgiere double pour capiel de Montauban une paire de chauches un camail coupe un camail entir de France un camail de Lombardie et une gorgiere de Lombardie delies une paire de caucons coupes une gorgiere de Cambli 2 gorgieres franchoises de demi clawre une paire de manches de Lombardie a plates et uns pans uns pans de France pour atakier a auketon une paire de wans de haubergerie de France un haubergon de Melan 2 piechetes de fier pour atakier a uns pans un noef auqueton de plates [*sic*] de rouge cendal a lendroit de vert a lenviers un auketon de plates rouges vies foure de vert chendal unes petites plates clauees dargent couvertes de samit de flours et unes manches et uns wans de ce mesme une paire de quissieus de plates et 2 paires wambisies 2 paires de quissieus de fier burnis et 3 paires de greves de ce mesme un bachinet a visiere et le colerete daciere et 2 demi visieres qui y apertiement un heaume a visiere et a un capiel de Montauban une paire de poulains 2 bachines couvriers de blanc cuir une paire de quissiens de ballaine des armes mgr une paire de quissieus de plates des armes mgr une estivalles de plates couviers de blanc cuir unes vieses greves une plates couvertes de un drap de soie estinchelet de rouges moletes a manches un bachinet couviert de blanc cuir 2 bourses a bachines et une heaumiere 2 vieses chemises de Chartres deus seles de tournoi

one hauberk of good nailing (i.e. all-riveted links) of Chambly (make), one aventail of the same (make), one (pair of mail) sleeves and one paunce of Chambly for (pairs of) plates, one double gorget (i.e. of two layers of mail) for a chapeau de Montauban, one pair of (mail) chausse, one cut-down aventail, one complete aventail of French (make), one aventail of Lombardy (make), and one worn-out gorget of Lombardy, one pair of cut-down chausse, one gorget of Chambly, two French gorgets of half nailing (i.e. not every link riveted), of pair of (mail) sleeves of Lombardy for (pairs of) plates and one paunce, one paunce of France to attach to an aketon, one pair of gloves of French mail-work, one haubergeon of Milan, two small pieces of iron to attach to a paunce, one new aketon of plates [*recte* as a foundation *for* a pair of plates] of red sendal (lightweight silk or very fine linen) on the outside and green inside, one old red aketon for (pairs of) plates fringed with green sendal, one little (pair of) plates nailed with silver covered with samite (shimmering silk fabric) (decorated) with flowers, and one (pair of) sleeves and one (pair of) gloves of the same (plate construction – i.e. gauntlets), one pair of plate cuisses and two gamboised pairs (i.e. made in the manner of a padded gambeson), two pairs of polished iron cuisses and three pairs of greaves of this same (type), one basinet with visor and steel collar and two appurtenant half visors, a helm with visor and one chapeau de Montauban, one pair of poleyns, two basinets covered with white leather, one pair of baleen cuisses (decorated with) the Lord's (heraldic) arms, one pair of plate cuisses of the Lord's arms, one (pair of) plate shoes covered with white leather, one (pair of) old greaves, one (pair of) plates with sleeves covered with silk cloth strewn (decorated) with red (heraldic) mullets (spur-rowels), one basinet covered with white leather, two bags for basinets and one for a helm, two old chemises of Chartres,[5] two tourney saddles

---

5   Moffat, '*The Manner of Arming Knights for the Tourney*', p. 10: 'a garment in the shape of, and that had come into contact with, the *sancta camisia* of Chartres cathedral'.

32

Kew, National Archives, DL 25/29
Inventory of the Goods of Humphrey, Earl of Hereford and Essex,
probably Pleshey Castle, Essex, 1322

j petite prente oue foilles dargent oue j frountele de saye pur j bacynet j hauberioun
qe est apele Bolioun & j peire des plates couertes de vert veluet' iiij espeies lun des
armes le dit Counte lautre de Seint George & le tierce Sarziney le quarte de Guerre
ij bacynet les lun couert de quir lautre bourni j peire de huses de Cordewan botonez
j corset' de fer j cou[er]ture pur j chiual des armes de h[er]eford'

one little prente with silver leaves with one fountele of silk (decorations) for one
basinet, one haubergeon called 'Bouillon' (i.e. belonged to Godfrey of Bouillon), and
one pair of plates covered with green velvet, four swords one (decorated) with the Earl's
(heraldic) arms, one of Saint George, the third of the (type used by the) Saracens, the
fourth for war, two basinets one covered with leather the other burnished (polished
steel), one pair of buttoned cordwain (high-quality Spanish leather) huces (shield
covers), one iron corset, one cover for one horse of the (heraldic) arms of Hereford

33

Kew, National Archives, E 101/16/5
Account of Hugh Bungay, Armourer to King Edward II, 1 May 1322–
13 September 1323

Hugon' de Bungeye de armaturis & aliis op[er]ib[us] f[ac]tis vno pari cirotec' de platis
empt' vj s. viij d. bokelett' & mordand' argent' cu' tissuta ceric' empt' et appo[n]
it' d[ic]tis cirotec' xvj d. s[um]ma viij s. vno pari de Jamb[er]is cu' polein' p[ro]
crurib[us] burnit' p[ro] d[omi]no Rege xxvj s. viij d. vno Casside burn' f[ac]to p[ro]
guerra p[ro] Rege xl s. vno clauon' deaurat' p[ro] cresta d[ic]to cass' cu' parcamen'
et penn' pauonu' empt' ad crestam vna cu' depinctura eiusdem aurea v s. bacinett'
cu' agulett' & garn' p[ro] Rege duob[us] bacinettis empt' xiij s. iiij d. agulett' argent'
laqueis cu' seric' & appo[n]it' bacinettis iij s. ij d. garnic[i]one eor[un]dem xiij s.

Hugh Bungay of the armour and all work done: one pair of plate gauntlets bought for
6s. 8d., silver buckles and mordants (buckle-tongues) with silk cloth bought and put
on these gauntlets 16d., one pair of burnished (polished steel) jambers with poleyns
for the legs of the lord King 26s. 8d., one burnished *casside* [an unknown helm type]
made for war for the King 40s., one gilt nail for the crest of this helm with parchment
and peacock feathers for the crest with its painting with gold 5s. Basinets with laces
and equipping: two basinets bought for the Lord King 13s. 4d., silver laces for the
straps with silk and put on the basinets 3s. 2d., for equipping them 13s.

34

London, British Library, Stowe Charter 622
Will of Sir Fulk Pembridge, Tong, Shropshire, 11 November 1325

Roger son lyt Jak' e barhuide e Cofres fouk' son fitz vne nue Acq[ue]tton blanke vn hauberioun de Acere vn peire de ces meilours plates vn bacinet pur le torney vn Auental e gauns de plat' quiseux e gr[e]ues de balencyn e vn Aut' peyre de quiseux e gr[e]ues blancs e vn autre peire de quisseux e poleyns e esquinebaus de Were e vn peire de gossetes e vn peyre de espaudlers vn quirre vn peire de Waynepayns vn peyre de Coters e vn healme pur torney e vn healme pur Were vn peyre de Couertours vn picer vn teister vn peire de chanfrouns vn espe pur torney e vn aut' pur Were vn peire de esperons Robert son fitz vn Aq[ue]tton blanc oue vn lyon rouge fourche la Cowe vn hauberioun vn corset de fer vn bacinet de Were vn auentail e vn colret vn healme orre vn peire de espaudlers quisseux e greues vn peire de gauns de plate vn peire de Waynepayns vn peire de chausons e vn espe William son fitz vn ganbesoun deus hauberiouns vn healme vn bacinet vn auentail e colret vn palet vn peire de espaudlers vn peire de gauns de plate quisseux e greues Payn son fitz deus hauberiouns e vn Jaceraunde

Roger his light jack, cart cover, and coffers, his son Fulk his new white aketon, one steel haubergeon, one of his best pairs of plates, a basinet for the tourney, an aventail, and plate gauntlets, cuisses and greaves of baleen, and another pair of white (polished steel) cuisses and greaves, another pair of cuisses and poleyns and schynbalds for war, a pair of (mail) gussets, a pair of spaudlers, a cuirie, a pair of gaignepains, a pair of couters, one helm for the tourney and one helm for war, a pair of (horse) covers, a peytral, a tester, a pair of shaffrons, a sword for the tourney and another for war, a pair of spurs, his son Robert a white aketon (emblazoned) with a red lion with forked tail, a haubergeon, a corset of iron, a basinet for war, an aventail and a collar, a gilt helm, a pair of spaudlers, cuisses and greaves, a pair of plate gauntlets, a pair of gaignepains, a pair of chausses, and a sword, his son William a gambeson, two haubergeons, a helm, a basinet, an aventail and collar, a pallet, a pair of spaudlers, a pair of plate gauntlets, cuisses and greaves, his son Payn two hauberks and a jazerant

35

Kew, National Archives, E 352/120, membr. 1–membr. 4
Arms and Armour at Caerphilly Castle, Principality of Wales, Hilary Term [January–March] 1326

j aketone de camoca viridi coop[er]to desup' de rubeo coreo cap[ri]oli ij loricis de Calibe vn' vno iac[er]ando cu' j pisano iac[er]ando ij pauilonib[us] p[ro] pisan no' p[er]fectis iiij loric' de ferro de alto inclauato j p[ar]i de pauns & bras de ferro lumbard' j alio p[ar]i de bras ij par' de musekinis de ferro lumbard' ij peciis de copura

vnius lorice j bracc' de mallea cu' tela p[er]tinente j pari chausonu' ferr' j p[ar]i de
plates coop[er]t' de velueto rubeo cu' brachiis de secta & vno loketto de argento
deaurato j p[ar]i de plates coop[er]t' de alb' lineo j bacinetto coop[er]t' de albo cor'
cu' auentali de calibe iac[er]and' j bacinetto cu' vmbraro furbato cu' auentali de ferro
iiij crestis de armis R' j p[ar]i de quissotz de plata coop[er]to de velueto paleato de
rubeo & p[u]rpur' j p[ar]i de quissotz de armis R' cu' puleis [sic] attachiat' j alio p[ar]
i polear[um] ij par' de jaumbers iiij p[ar]ib[us] de skynebaud' p[ro] R' j p[ar]i sotular'
de plata coop[er]t' de velueto rubeo j p[ar]i sabatonu' L augulett' de electro j scuto
de armis R' nobili j p[ar]i de frettes cu' lagulett' de electro j par' coop[er]torior[um]
p[ro] dext[ra]riis de ferro iac[er]ando j p[ar]i de trappis de armis R' j testar' de Cor'
p[ro] equis j zona de cerico rubeo p[ro] t[r]app' garnit' de electro j gladio garnit' ad
modu' Scoc' cu' pomello & hulto argentato cum chapa argent' & zona de cor' albo
j gladio garnito argento deaur' & aymelato de secta ramor[um] quercuu' cu' zona &
vagina de eadem secta talliatis j gladio cu' argento garnito deaur' & eymelato de armis
de Ispannia cu' zona & vagina de eadem secta j gladio cu' vagina de velueto viridi cum
zona de cerico viridi cu' argento garnito & ij Scuch' de armis lancastr' & Holand' cu'
pomello & hulto de calibe argent' j glad' nobili cu' zona & vagina de auro Broudat'
poudrat' de elegett' argent' argento garnitis eymelat' de armis Angl' & F[r]anc' vn'
pomellu' & hultu' sunt de argento ij glad' p[ro] iorneta vn' zona & vag' sunt de cor'
nigro dupplicato de cor' rubeo & de laqueis de cerico rubeo ij peciis de cor' albo
c[er]uino p[ro] j zona gladij xxix bideux & ij long' bideux de vascon' j fauchone ij
aunnell' p[ro] cultell' guerre iij par' magnor[um] cultell' p[ro] venac[i]one quolib[e]t
de iij cultell' j cultello longo de Wallia j cultello cu' manubrio nigro & puncto fracto
cu' argento gar' xl cultellettis xv ferris p[ro] lanceis iiij par' calcar' de vascon' deaur'
cu' tissutis de cerico ij masuell' j baculo p[ro] maceo j cornu de Welk' cu' balteo
& cerico viridi cu' argento garnito j p[ar]uo cornu de Bugle nigro cu' tissutis de
cerico iiij penuncell' p[ro] tub' de armis R' j chatena p[ro] leporar' xxj aketon' debil'
coop[er]t' cu' linea tela xl bacinett' vn' viij ad vmbraru' & viij sine vmbraro burnit' &
ali' cop[er]te de cor' albo v xx par' cerot' de plata xxiij loricis vn' vna nulli' valor' vij
auentalib[us] v palet' xxj capell' de ferro rotund' xix targeis de diu[er]sis armis iiij targ'
de lumbardia x hache' danor[um] xvj gisarmis vj ferr' p[ro] gisarmis xxix bundell'
de hastis p[ro] lanceis q[u]ol' bundello cont' xiiij hastas x xx xiiij ferr' lancear[um] j
viceo ad tendend' balistas ad viceu' cu' ij balistis ad viceu' m[i]l' C xxx quarell' cu' ere
pennat' xij bokett' de quarell' pennat' cu' anca maiore p[ar]te m[er]emij put[ri]da in
corbell' & in bokett' x garb' sagittar[um] in vno longo coffro xviij aketon' de armis
d[omi]ni Hug' le Despens' xlviij bacinett' xij bacinett' no' garnit' vj loricis ix auentalib[us] j pisano j colretto j p[ar]i de bras de plata vij galeis vij capell' ferr' ij capell' de
n[er]uo j p[ar]i de pauns ij muskynis j p[ar]i de Jaumbers xxiiij par' de plates j p[ar]i
de bras de plata vij galeis vij capell' ferr' ij capell' de n[er]uo ij bacinett' cu' vmbraro
xxiiij pauillonib[us] p[ro] auentalib[us] [sic] iiij testar' p[ro] equis j balista de belena
de tour xiij aliis balistis de balena ad duos pedes xiij balist' de balista ad vnu' pedem j
balista lignea de tour xv balist' ad vnu' pede' vj arcub[us] vj telar' p[ro] balist' fractis
ix balteis j doleo pleno de garrotis p[ro] sp[ri]ngald' & CCC p[ro] balist' de tour iiij
m[i]l' capitib[us] p[ro] quarell' p[ar]uis xvj lanceis & xvj ferr' p[ro] lanc' lxxij lanc'

sine ferr' v viceis ad balist' tendend' iiij hach' ad man' ij barell' de ter' iij barell' sulfur'
no' plenis d[imid]j b' de sulphur' vn' de calibe ferr' plumbo & canabo bona q[u]a[n]
ti[ta]te p[ro] munic[i]o[n]e Cast' xl aketon' xxxv lorice xxvj pauillon' p[ro] pisano &
auentall' ij par' de pauns v par de bras iiij par' musekyn' xxvj par' platar[um] v xx & v
bacinette ij pisani xix auentall' j colrett' ij par' quissor[um] vij galee ij par' poleor[um]
iij par' de Jaumber' iiij par' skynebald' j bracca de mallea cu' tela p[er]tinente j par
chausonu' j par de Couter' iiij crest' j par sotular' de plata j par sabatonu' de plata j
scut' j par coop[er]tor' p[ro] dex[tr]ariis v testar' p[ro] equis v xx par' cerot' de plata
v pallette xxiij targ' xxx capelle de ferr' & de neruo vij gladij iij par' cultell' p[ro]
venac[i]one ij cultell' & xl cultellett' j cultell' j fauch' ij masuell' j baculu' p[ro] mace
xiiij hach' daneor[um] & ad manu' xxxj bideux xvj gisarmi iiij xx viij lancee xij xxv
ferr' p[ro] lanceis DC iiij xx xvj hast' p[ro] lanceis vj ferr' p[ro] gisarm' xxxv baliste
m[i]l' C xxx quarell' pennat' cu' ere xij bokett' quarell' pennat' cu' anca ix baltee vj
vicee ad balist' tendend' vj telar' p[ro] balistis vj arcus vij sp[ri]ngald' iiij coffr' de
quib[us] iij sunt rotund' & trussabil' p[ro] armatur' ferr' & quartu' de ligno trussabil'
xv ferr' p[ro] lanceis j par de couters de cor' bullat' xij bukett' de quarell' pennat' cu'
anca maiore p[ar]te merem' put[ri]da in corbell' & in bokett' x garb' sagittar[um] in
j longo coffro xviij aketon' de armis d[omi]ni Hug' le Despens' vij sp[ri]ngald' garnit'
& j sp[ri]ngald' non garnit' j glad' coop[er]t' de velueto viridi & garnit' de armis
Comitis Lanc' & Rob[er]ti de Hol' j bacinett' & j auentall' que fuer' Rob[er]ti de
Hol' j loric' que fu[er]it Rob[er]ti de Hol' ij p[ar]ib[us] musekinor[um] de ferro de
Lumbard' lib' Wil[e]l[m]o le Haub[er]geour

one aketon of green camaca (silk fabric) covered over with red goatskin, two steel
hauberks one of which is jazerant with one jazerant pisan, two unfinished coverings
for pisans, three iron hauberks of high nailing (i.e. of all-riveted links), one pair of
iron paunce and (mail) sleeves of Lombardy (make), another pair of (mail) sleeves,
two pairs of iron musekins of Lombardy, two pieces of copper, one hauberk, one
mail sleeve with appurtenant coif, one pair of iron (mail) chausses, one pair of plates
covered with red velvet with sleeves en suite and a silver-gilt locket, one pair of plates
covered with white linen, one basinet covered with white leather with steel aventail
jazerant, one furbished (polished steel) basinet with umbrer with iron aventail, four
crests of the King's arms, one pair of plate cuisses covered with palled red and purple
velvet, one pair of cuisses with the King's arms with poleyns attached, one other pair
of poleyns, two pairs of jambers, three pairs of schynbalds for the King, one pair of
plate boots covered with red velvet, one pair of sabatons, one shield with the noble
King's arms, one pair of (decorative) frettes with amber laces, one pair of iron (mail)
covers for destriers jazerant, one tester of leather for a horse, one girdle of red silk for
(horse) trappers garnished with amber, one sword in the Scottish manner garnished
with silvered pommel and hilt with a silver chape and belt of white leather, one
sword garnished with silver-gilt and enamelled en suite with oak boughs with belt
and scabbard in the same suite, one sword garnished with silver-gilt and enamelled
with the (heraldic) arms of Spain with belt and scabbard of the same suite, one
sword with green velvet scabbard with belt of green velvet garnished with silver and

two escutcheons of the arms of Lancaster and Holland with the pommel and hilt of silvered steel, one noble sword with belt and scabbard embroidered with gold powdered (decorated) with silver eaglets garnished with silver enamelled with the arms of England and France the pommel and hilt of which are of silver, two swords for journeys (riding swords) the belt and scabbard of which are of black leather lined with red leather with straps of red silk, two pieces of white buckskin for one sword belt, 29 biddows and two long Gascon biddows, one falchion, two rings for war knives, three pairs of great hunting knives which consist of three knives, one long Welsh knife, one knife with black and dotted broken hilt garnished with silver, 40 knives, 15 lanceheads, three pairs of gilt Gascon spurs with fringes of silk, two maces, one haft for a mace, one horn of whelk (shell) with belt and green silk garnished with silver, one small black bugle with silk straps, four trumpet pennoncels of the King's arms, one chain for a greyhound, 21 worn out aketons covered with linen, 40 burnished (polished steel) basinets eight of which have umbrers and eight without umbrers and the rest covered with white leather, five score pairs of plate gauntlets, 23 hauberks one of which is of no value, seven aventails, five pallets, 21 round chapel de fers, 19 targes of divers arms, four targes of Lombardy, ten Danish axes, 16 gisarmes, six blades for gisarmes, 29 bundles of lance-staves each bundle containing 14 staves, ten score and 14 lanceheads, one vice for drawing vice-spanned crossbows, 1,130 quarrels fletched with copper, 12 buckets of quarrels fletched with goose the greater part of the timber rotten in the baskets and buckets, ten sheaves of arrows in a long coffer, 18 aketons of the (heraldic) arms of Lord Hugh Despenser, 48 basinets, 12 un-equipped basinets, six hauberks, nine aventails, one pisan, one collar, one pair of plate sleeves, seven helms, seven chapel de fers, one chapel of sinew, one pair of paunce, two musekins, one pair of jambers, 24 pairs of plates, one pair of plate sleeves, seven helms, seven chapel de fers, two chapels of sinew, two basinets with umbrers, 24 coverings for aventails, four testers for horses, one torsion crossbow of baleen, 13 other two-foot crossbows of baleen (i.e. for two-foot-long bow-staves), 13 one-foot crossbows (i.e. for one-foot-long bow-staves), one torsion wooden crossbow, 15 one-foot crossbows, six bows, one broken crossbow tiller (stock), one pipe full of garrots for springalds and three hundred for torsion crossbows, 4,000 small quarrel-heads, 16 lances and 16 lanceheads, 72 lances without lanceheads, five vices for drawing crossbows, four hand axes, two barrels of soil, three unfilled barrels of sulphur, half a barrel of sulphur, a good quantity of steel, iron, lead, and canvas for the castle's munitions, 40 aketons, 25 hauberks, 26 coverings for pisans and aventails, two pairs of paunces, five pairs of (mail) sleeves, three pairs of musekins, 26 pairs of plates, five score and five basinets, two pisans, 19 aventails, one silver-gilt locket, one collar, two pairs of cuisses, seven helms, two pairs of poleyns, three pairs of jambers, three pairs of schynbalds, one mail sleeve with appurtenant coif, one pair of chausses, one pair of couters, four crests, one pair of plate boots, one pair of plate sabatons, one shield, one pair of covers for destriers, five testers for horses, five score pairs of plate gauntlets, five pallets, 23 targes, 30 chapel de fers and one of sinew, seven swords, three pairs of hunting knives, two knives and 40 small knives, one ring for knives, one falchion, two maces, one haft for a mace, 14 Danish axes, 31 biddows, 16 gisarmes, four score and eight lances, 12 score and five lanceheads, 600 and four score lance-staves, six blades for gisarmes, 35 crossbows, 1,130 quarrels fletched with copper, 12 buckets of quarrels fletched with goose, nine belts, six vices for drawing crossbows, six crossbow tillers, six bows, seven springalds, four coffers three of which are round and trussable for iron (mail) armour and the fourth (also trussable) is of wood, 15 heads for lances, one pair of couters of cuir bouilli, 12 buckets of quarrels fletched with goose, most of the wood in the baskets and buckets is rotten, ten sheaves of arrows in one long coffer, 28 aketons of the (heraldic) arms of Lord Hugh Despenser, seven equipped springalds and one un-equipped, one sword covered in green velvet and garnished with the arms of the Earl of Lancaster and Robert Holland, one basinet and one aventail which belonged to Robert Holland, one hauberk which belonged to Robert Holland, two pairs of iron musekins of Lombardy (make) delivered to William the hauberger

36

Kew, National Archives E 101/17/37
Inventory of the Tower of London, 1327

This document is very fragmentary

xij Ak[…] Bacynetz veaux & p[ar][…] descou[er]tz xij peyre des gaunz de Baleyne febles ij pey[…] oue les pulleyns […]s febles xxxij chapeaux de fer roilez & desbour-nicez don[…] febles viij coffyns de quir p[ro] des ditz chapeaux vn escu darmes esquartilez des armes le Roi & des armes sire Pieres de Gau[…] xlix huses de Caneuas p[u]r les targes de diu[er]se conisaunces febles xvj launces de Guerre febles v laun[…] p[u]r les ioustes […] cotel galleys […] En la haute chaumbre en la Tour En la chape[…] & p[ar]tie sanz cordes dount les treis Telers roump[re] […] Chaumbre iiij haubercs iiij cou[er]t[u]res de fer p[u]r ch[…] peyre des chaussouns de fer vne peyre d[…] fust a viz […] vn quiuere de Oure sarceneys ou xxiiij q[…] quareaux & gros quareaux penne[…]

12 aketons […] basinets old and partly uncovered, 12 pairs of worn out baleen gauntlets, two pairs […] with worn out poleyns, 32 chapel de fers rusted and un-bur-nished of which […] are worn out, eight leather coffers for the said chapels, one shield with the (heraldic) arms quartered with the arms of the King and the arms of Sir Piers Gaveston, 49 worn out canvas huses (covers) for the targes of divers cogni-zances, 16 worn out war lances, five lances for jousts […] one Welsh knife […] in the high chamber in the Tower, in the Chapel […] and partly without cords of which the three tillers (crossbow stocks) are broken […] (in the) chamber three hauberks, four iron (mail) horse covers […] pair of iron (mail) chausses, one pair […] of wood with (crossbow spanning) vices […] one quiver of Saracen work with 24 quarrels […] quarrels and great quarrels fletched with […]

37

Unlocated Original Document from the State Archives of Turin, printed in C. Buttin, *Le Guet de Genève au XVe siècle et l'armement des ses gardes* (Geneva, 1910), p. 35
Household Account of the Counts of Savoy, Turin, Piedmont, 21 January 1327

Andree, pro reparacione unius paris plactarum copertarum zamelloto celesti prefati domini, in quo pari plactarum refecte fuerunt pecie septem de aczaro [no cost recorded]

to Andrew for repairing one pair of plates covered in sky-blue camlet (silk fabric) previously made for the Lord, in which pair of plates there were seven pieces of steel [no cost recorded]

38

Cambridge, Corpus Christi College Library, MS 174, fol. 156v: Extract from the Middle English Prose Brut Chronicle
Chronicle Account of Queen Isabella of England in Armour, January 1329

þe sente þe quene Isabelle and þe mortymer aft' hize retenue and aft' þe kingez retenue so þat þey had ordeynede amonges [t]ham an huge oste and þei councelede þe king so þat oppon anyzt þey reden xxiiij mile towarde Bedforde þer' þat þe erl of lancastr' w[a]s wiþ his companye and þouzte haue him distroiede & þat nyzt she rode bisides þe king hire sone as a knyzt armede for drede of deþ
　　And hit was done þe king Edwarde to vnderstende þat þe erl Henry of lancastr' & his companye woulde haue destoyede þe king and h' councele for eu[er]more

they sent Queen Isabella and [Roger] Mortimer [Earl of March] after his retinue and after the King's retinue so that they had ordained amongst themselves a huge host and they counselled the King (advising) that they ride by night the 24 miles towards Bedford as the Earl of Lancaster was with his company and thought to have him destroyed. And that night she rode beside the King her son as a knight armed for dread of death.
　　And King Edward was made to understand that Earl Henry of Lancaster and his company would have destroyed the king and his council for evermore

39

Kew, National Archives, C 145/114/2
Arms and Armour at Scarborough Castle, Yorkshire, 2 September 1330

j par' de T[r]appes coop[er]t' de veluet' & possu[n]t r[e]p[ar]ar' de vna marca xiij
Aketone de diu[er]sis color' que su[n]t nulli' valor' p[re]t' L Estoff xxxvij Aketon'
albe q[ue] possunt eme[n]dari de C s j par de quysotz de cendall' rub' q[ue] possunt
r[e]p[ar]ari de iij s j par de q[ui]ssotz coop[er]t' de veluet' q[ue] possunt r[e]p[ar]
ari de ij s j par de q[ui]ssotz de plat' cu' poleyn' q[ue] p[oss]u[n]t emen' de xviij d j
par de skynebauds q[u]e possunt eme[n]d[ar]e de ij s j par de Jambers j haub[er]gh
xl haub[er]ions x corsetz ij coleretz j par de chausouns j par cyrotec' de mayl' j par
cyrotec' de plat' xl coyfs de fer q[ua]t[u]or capell' cu' viser' viij bacynett' ij par' de
platz iiij pec' de ferr' format' p[ro] schynebauds & om[n]i isti su[n]t nulli' valor' p[re]
t' ferrj lx arblastur' & possunt emend' de lx s x m[i]l' C q[u]arell' q[ue] p' emend' de
xx s lxxij garoks penat' de ferr' q[ui]b[us] defect' capit' & possu[n]t emend' de xij ij
magna ingen' quor[um] j conf[r]actu' est & aliud e' debile & potest emend' de C s ij
sp[rin]galds nulli' valor'

one pair of (horse) trappers covered with velvet which can be repaired for one mark, 13
aketons of divers colours which are of no value save for the stuffings, 37 white aketons
which can be mended for 100s., one pair of cuisses of red sendal (lightweight silk or very
fine linen) which can be repaired for 3s., one pair of cuisses covered with velvet which
can be repaired for 2s., one pair of plate cuisses with poleyns which can be mended
for 18d., one pair of schynbalds which can be mended for 2s., one pair of jambers, one
hauberk, 40 haubergeons, ten corsets, two collars, one pair of chausses, one pair of mail
gauntlets, one pair of plate gauntlets, 40 iron (mail) coifs, four chapel de fers with visors,
eight basinets, two pairs of plates, four pieces of iron formed for schynbalds all this is of
no value save for the iron, 60 crossbows which can be mended for 60s., 10,100 quarrels
which can be mended for 20s., 72 garrots fletched with iron which lack heads and can be
mended for 12s., two large (siege) engines one of which is broken and the other is worn
out and can be mended for 100s., two springalds of no value

40

Cambridge, Gonville and Caius College Library, MS 424/448, pp. 88–90
Ordinance regulating Tournaments in England decreed at the Siege of
Stirling (April–24 July 1304), copied at Dartford, Kent, in 1331

*This is an extract. The whole document describes the locations, noblemen in charge,
heralds, and dates of the tourneying seasons.*

le Roi Edward fitz au roi henry ordena a g[r]ant siege de streuelyn q[u]ant il auoit la
t[er]re descoce conquis & mys en sa subiectio[u]n pur le p[ro]fyt de so[u]n Roialme

Cest assauoir p[u]r les countes & pur les barons & p[u]r touz aultres chiualers armes portanz quatr' t[u]rneme[n]tz en lan […] Et q[u]ant les ch[ai]rs serrount venuz en villes q[ue] eux ne p[or]tent tanqe ils eyent torneye Auxi fist ordener p[u]r s[er]uir les ch[ai]rs deux rois vn de North' lautr' de South & quatr' herraus suffisanz pur les quatr' marches Et auxi est ordene des armur[er]s louer pur corps de chiualer herneys de tiel entier deux trente leus xvj s Et pur esquier x s Et endroit de haubergers ceo q[ue] reison soit alower deins l leus de la cite de loundr[e]s vij s iiij d Et sils passe les l leus x s iiij d Auxi en mesme la manere des autr[e]s armerers si les passent les xxx leus soit entra p[ur] a gard des dysours Auxi les healmer[er]s p[u]r la pece vj s viiij d & les selers soient a la gard des disours

King Edward, son to King Henry, made a decree for the good of his realm at the great Siege of Stirling when he had conquered the Land of Scotland and placed it under his subjection – that is to say: there be four tournaments a year […] When the sides have come to the towns they may bear nought (no weapons and armour) but that with which they shall tourney. It has been decreed that two Kings of Arms serve the sides (one from the North the other from the South) and four heralds suitable for the four marches. It has been decreed that the armourers hire out complete harness of linen for the knight's body within 30 leagues (of the City of London) at 16s. and at 10s. for a squire. Haubergers are to hire out (mail armour) at 7s. 8d. within 50 leagues of the City of London or at 10s. 4d. beyond, but (in the same manner as the other armourers) if their clients pass beyond 30 leagues they should be compensated by those who have called the tourney. Heaumers (plate armourers) must hire out (plate armour) at 6s. 9d. a piece. Saddlers shall be compensated by the callers (of the tourney)

41

London, British Library, MS Cotton Otho D.v., fol. 1r–fol. 15v, printed in J. Paviot, *Projets de croisade (v. 1290–v. 1330)* (Paris, 2008), pp. 315–64 Sir Roger Stanegrave, *Li Charboclois d'Armes du Conquest Precious de la Terre Sainte*, 1331

This MS is severely fire damaged

Sir Roger was a knight of the Military Holy Order of the Hospitallers. He was imprisoned for 30 years in Egypt and here provides advice on re-taking the Holy Land and insight into the martial skills of his enemies.

Par valerous coers destable proesce a la prove de la destresce de chaumpele bataille espee encountre espee et heaume encountre heaume par covenable et complie

ordinance saunz nule feyntise de proesce darmes solonc les perillous fes de guerre pur
quoy lon est dist chivaler nobles et vaillant [...] sy [...] valour et de graunt renomee

jeo osereye enprendre a conquer la terre de XXX mil hommes darmes esprovetz de
vaillour et qe la moyte de lour fuissent arblasters a chival et lautre moyte lancier pur
espaules as arblasters Et ensi les uns garderount les autres et se defenderont desqes
archiers ont perdu lour vertue Reson coment Por ceo qe les arblasters [...] assetz
plus qe les arcs dont il avient a lherdoie qe les arblasters la moite tregetents et lautre
moite aident Et par ceo avent qe ly arblasters ne sessent ne faillent de terre par quoy
ly archier sentent par esprove si grant charge et si mortel damage qe suffrir nen puent
le herdoys des arblasters

[the Army of Saladin were] mountez sour ceux chivals arabiens et non montez sur
ces grantz chivals d'Espaine
la gent darmes de la rivere [Nile] de la mer aprocher et tant come le arblasters porra
son couverture de paves qest dist targes par dela qant les arblastes iront [...] entreant
les Sarazins [...] tres grevouse damage de eaux moyms ot

[...] de garoys acierre en les grauntz damage et graunt esbaissement du trait des garoys

Car encountre li Tartar qe sont meillour archiers qe li Sarazins lessent les arcz et
prenent les launces et encountre les Cristiens qe sont meilleur launciers qe li Sarazins
lessent les launces et prenent les arcz

With valorous hearts and steadfast prowess proved on the brutal field of battle –
sword against sword and helm against helm – in proper and strict discipline with
unflinching valour of arms according to the perilous feats of war, it is for this one is
called a noble and valiant knight [...] (known for) valour and great renown.

I would be courageous enough to conquer the (Holy) Land with 30,000
men-at-arms of proven valour. Half of them should be mounted crossbowmen and
the other half lancers to support these crossbowmen: thus one may guard and defend
the other. Archers, however, lose heart. The reason? Because crossbowmen are more
courageous than archers – half of them may shoot whilst the other half assist. In this
way the crossbowmen remain steadfast without losing ground. For it has been proven
that archers cannot withstand a massed charge and suffer such deadly harm that they
cannot possibly match the crossbowman's courage.

(The Army of Saladin) were mounted on their Arabian horses *not* on great horses
of Spain.

The men-at-arms advanced from the sea to the river (Nile). Now because the crossbowmen had pavises – called targes – to cover themselves, the crossbowmen could
sally forth engaging the Saracens; grievously harming them.

Steel-tipped garrots (springald quarrels) do great damage – their shot causes (the
enemy) to badly lose ground.

As the Tartars are better archers than the Saracens, they shoot their bows then resort
to the lance. But, as the Christians are better lancers than the Saracens, they (the
Tartars) cast their lances *then* resort to the bow.

42

Library of the Society of Antiquaries of London MS, SAL/MS/541
Account of William the Hauberger, Armourer to King Edward III, 1331

Wil[e]l[m]o le haub[er]ger Armatori Regis p[ro] xiij p[ar]ib[us] de pauntz & brach'
vij li. xj s. iiij d. j par de pauntz & brach' j par de mustiler' cu' quissot' & j par' de
Geynepayns xij s. vj d. vj auentaill' xx s. vj pisan' xv s. vj p[ar]ib[us] cirotecar[um]
de plat' xlvj s. j par de Gussett' ferr' v s. ij colerett' ferr' iij s. iiij glad' p[ro] To[u]
rniament' vj s. j bacinett' x s. largi[a]c[i]o[n]e vnu' par' de paunz & brach' de Calibe
p[ro] Rege xvj s. j pec' argent' p[ro] emend' & rep[ar]acione vnu' par' de chauson'
argent' p[ro] Rege xiiij s. ij lagen' olei' & iiij bussell fufur' p[ro] armatur' Regis
rolland' & ab erugine saluand' ij s. vj d.

William the hauberger, King's Armourer for 13 pairs of paunces and (mail) sleeves £7
11s. 4d., one pair of paunce and (mail) sleeves, one pair of mustilers with cuisses, and
one pair of gaignepains 12s. 6d., six aventails 20s., six pisans 15s., six pairs of plate
gauntlets 46s., one pair of iron (mail) gussets 5s., one iron collar 3s., four swords for
tourneying 6s., one basinet 10s., enlarging one steel pair of paunces and (mail) sleeves
for the King 16s., one piece of silver for mending and repairing one pair of the King's
silver (mail) chausses 14s., two flagons of oil and four bushels of bran for rolling the
King's armour and safeguarding it from rust 2s. 6d.

43

Kew, National Archives, E 101/333/4
Arms and Armour delivered to the Family of Roger Mortimer, Earl of
March, Wigmore Castle, Herefordshire, 1332

vne peire des plates cou[er]tz dun drap dor iiij vieles espores vn cote p[u]r les ioustes
de rouge veluet oue vne frette dargent oue papillons des armes de mortem[er] vne
cou[er]ture p[u]r lesen de mesme la sieute vn baner de cendal de mesme la sieute vn
herneys p[u]r les ioustes de veluet vert vn viel ban[er] des armes de mortem' batu
& vn autre de cendal deux peir despaulers oue bracers & vauntbracers vn bacynet
p[u]r le tornoyment vne peire deskynebaudz dorez poudrez des moletz p[er]cez trois
heaumes susorez p[u]r le tornoyment vn autre heaume p[u]r le tornoy trois bacynetz
p[u]r le tornoy treis peire des braz & paunz deux peire despaulers trois peire des
quisseux de quir boile deux peire des chauson vne peire deskynebauz susorrez vne
peire des plates cou[er]tz de rouge samyt vj corsetz de feer trois heaumes p[u]r la
guerre vn chapel de feer vne peire de cou[er]tures de feer

one pair of plates covered with cloth of gold, four old spurs, one coat for the jousts
of red velvet with a silver (decorative) fret with butterflies of the (heraldic) arms
of Mortimer, one horse cover for the same in the same suite, one banner of sendal

(lightweight silk or very fine linen) in the same suite, one harness for the jousts of green velvet, one old banner decorated with the arms of Mortimer and another of sendal, two pairs of spaudlers with bracers and vambrace, one basinet for tourneying, one pair of gilt schynbalds powdered with pierced mullets (decorated with heraldic spur-rowels), three gilt helms for tourneying, another helm for the tourney, three basinets for the tourney, three pairs of (mail) sleeves and paunces, two pairs of spaudlers, three pairs of cuisses of cuir bouilli, two pairs of (mail) chausse, a pair of gilt schynbalds, a pair of plates covered with red samite (shimmering silk fabric), six iron corsets, three helms for war, a chapel de fer, a pair of iron (mail) horse covers

44

Unlocated Original Document printed in J. Hunter, 'On Measures [...] for the Apprehension of Sir Thomas de Gournay, one of the Murderers of King Edward II', *Archaeologia* 27 (1838), pp. 274–97 (p. 292)
Purchase of Armour for Sir Thomas Gournay and his Companions at Pisa, Tuscany, 7–20 July 1333

p[ro] iij p[u]rpoyntz xj s vj d iij p[ar]ib[us] de plates xlvj s viij d iij p[ar]ib[us] de Paunces, braces, & Musekyns [&] avental' vj li xvj s viij d iij p[ar]ib[us] cyrotecar[um] de plate & iij bacinettes xvj s xj d p[ro] quodam sacco & quadam cista p[ro] p[re] d[ic]tis armaturis viij s viij d

for three pourpoints 11s. 6d., three pairs of plates 46s. 8d., three pairs of paunces, (mail) sleeves, and musekins, (and) aventails £6 16s. 8d., three pairs of plate gauntlets and three basinets 16s. 11d., for a certain sack and chest for the said armour 8s. 8d.

45

Kew, National Archives, E 361/3, membr. 28
Account of William Northwell, Keeper of the King's Wardrobe, 1 April 1335

lx hauberiou' xlix par' plat' j corsett' de calibe j corsett' de d[i]m[i]d' clauatur' lxxij par' de pauntz & braz j par' braz lx par' braz de coreo bulutt' xxxviij par' de vantbraz & rerbraz iiijo duoden' & xxix par' cirotec' de plat' CCiiij xx xvj pisan' sine pauillon' xliiij pisan' cum pauillon' CCxxxvij auentall' vj palett' de ferro lxvj bacinett' sine vmbrar' Cxxviij bacinett' cum vmbrar' Clxiij bacinett' Furbiz Cxxxv bacinett' nigr' verbat' xj galeis nigr' verbat' xxvij par' quissot' coop[er]t' de coreo xxxviij par' de quissott' de plat' cu' iamb[er]' de coreo bullito & xl quissott' de lumbardie empt' de diu[er]s' m[er] cator' ad diu[er]sa p[re]cia

60 haubergeons, 49 pairs of plates, one steel corset, one half-nailed corset (i.e. not all the mail links are riveted), 72 pairs of paunce and (mail) sleeves, one pair of (mail) sleeves, 60 pairs of sleeves of cuir bouilli, 38 pairs of vambrace and rerebrace, four score and 29 pairs of plate gauntlets, 200 four score and 16 pisans without covers, 44 pisans with covers, 237 aventails, six iron pallets, 66 basinets without umbrers (peaks), 128 basinets with umbrers, 163 furbished basinets, 135 black-beaten basinets (i.e. black from the hammer), 11 black-beaten helms, 27 pairs of cuisses covered with leather, 38 pairs of plate cuisses with jambers of cuir bouilli and 40 cuisses of Lombardy (make) bought from divers merchants at divers prices

46

Paris, Bibliothèque nationale de France, MS fr. 5287, extracts printed in *Documents relatifs au clos des galées de Rouen et aux armées de mer du roi de France de 1293 à 1418*, ed. A. Merlin-Chazelas, 2 vols (Paris, 1977–78), II, pp. 11–14
Arms and Armour provided by Thomas Fouques, Keeper of the Fortress of the Galleys of Rouen, Normandy, 1336 and 1339

1336
quatre paire de platez fourbiez, couvertes de drap de soie doré, huit platez couvertes de bourde, douze bachinez garnis, 1 garrot et une casse de carreaux a garrot

four equipped pairs of plates covered with silk cloth of gold, eight (pairs of) plates covered with bourde (cheap cloth), 12 equipped basinets, one garrot (Fr. for springald) and one case of garrot quarrels

1339
cinquante targez et pavois, cent chinquante lancez ferreez, deus cens dars ferrez, douze cassez de carreaux a 1 pié, un garrot garni de 2 vraies cordes et une fausse, une casse de carreaux a garrot, trente arbalestes, trente baudrez

50 targes and pavises, 150 headed lances, 200 headed darts, 12 cases of one foot (long) quarrels, one *garrot* equipped with two true cords and one false cord (a loose cord to assist with spanning), one case of *garrot* quarrels, 30 crossbows, 30 baldrics

47

London, British Library, MS Cotton Vespasian F. VII, fol. 11r
Report of French Forces mustering at Harfleur and Le Havre, Normandy, 1336

This manuscript is very fragmentary

CCC naues in q[uo]q[ue] c[on]tinet' hom' armator[um] xj xx et dict' xxx Galee fere'
& loric' […] fuer' compocte baliste & scutellata ad coop[er]iend' armatos & sic[u]t
Balistarij […] & Bombaci[ni]a al' cu' platis ferries que vix penet[ra]ri possunt p[er]
sagittas lanceas v[e]l al' armaturas […] hankeneys heaume' […]

300 ships each carrying II score men-at-arms (armed in) iron helms and hauberks
[…] they [the ships] are arraigned with crossbows and small shields to cover the
armed men who, like the crossbowmen, (are armed with) doublets others (armed
with reinforced) iron plates which can hardly be penetrated by arrows, lances, or
other weapons […] Hankeneys the heaumer (plate armourer) […]

48

Now-Lost Original Document printed in C. Faider, *Coutumes du pays et
comté de Hainaut*, 4 vols (Brussels, 1871–83), I, p. 29
Pleas to the Court of the Count of Hainaut, 1336

de l'armure qui à le liegiet appertient, li sires doit avoir le haubier, s'il y est, et les
cauches avoec, se elles y sont s'il n'y a haubier et il y ait haubregon, li sire doit le
haubregon avoir et le coiffe, se elle y est, les cauches de maille et les wans de maille,
s'il y sont. Et se coiffe n'y a, il doit avoir le barbière s'il n'y a ne haubier ne haubregon,
le sires doit avoir les pans et les manches, le barbière, les musekins, les cauchons et les
wans de maille, s'il y sont; car autre armure ke ly homs a d'armure de maille, ne puet
li sires avoir de demander

concerning the armour appropriate for lieges: lords ought to have a hauberk (if they
have one), and (be armed) with chausses (if they have them), if they have not a
hauberk but a haubergeon, the lord's haubergeon ought to have a coif (if there is one),
mail chausses, and mail gauntlets (if they have them), and if they have not a coif,
they ought to have a *barbière*, if he have no hauberk or haubergeon, the lords ought
to have paunces and (mail) sleeves, a *barbière*, and musekins, chausses, and gauntlets
of mail (if they have them). The lords cannot be ordered to have more armour than
that (required) of the mail-armoured men

49

Grenoble, Archives départementales de l'Isère, FR.AD38–9B2, fol. 59v–fol. 75r

Account of Jean de Poncy, Treasurer to Humbert, Dauphin of the Viennois, Grenoble, Dauphiné, 14 July–17 September 1336

bartholomeo lap mercatori pro vno paro de platis cum cosseriis et gampiis iij t[e]r' xij amonetto de chissiato p[ro] rep[ar]atura vni' Bacinetti d[omi]ni xx [ter'] lib[er]' amonetto de chissiato pro em[en]dis guantis p[ro] d[omi]no t[e]r' j [...] soluit p[ro] gamberijs cossalis braczerijs p[er] ant' & retro & guantis lattunatis ij t[e]r' xij p[ro] paro vno de caligis de lattono ij [ter'] p[ro] parib[us] duob' de arneuse de malia iij t[e]r' vj p[ro] arneuse vna de malia de aczario sine musachinjs & colla[r]io cu' paro vno de caligis v [ter'] p[ro] curettis trib[us] barbuta vna & cerbelleria vna iij t[e]r' xviij p[ro] vna panzeria dupla ij [ter']

Bartholomeo Lap, merchant for one pair of plates with cuisses and jambers 3 *lire* 12 *denari tertiole* (Milanese currency), Amonetto de Chissiato for repairing one of the Lord's basinets 20*l.*, paid to Amonetto de Chissiato for mending gauntlets for the Lord 1*l.*, [...] paid for jambers, cuisses, bracers for the front and back (of the limbs) and lattened gauntlets (i.e. decorated with latten) 2*l.* 12*d.*, for one pair of chausses of latten (links) 2*l.*, for two pairs of mail harness 3*l.* 6*d.*, for one steel mail harness without musekins and collar with one pair of chausses 5*l.*, for three *curettis* (torso defences), three *barbutas* (mail chin and throat defences), and one skullcap 3*l.* 18*d.*, for one (fabric) lined *panzeria* (mail shirt) 2*l.*

50

Kew, National Archives, E 101/387/25, membr. 7
Account of William Hoo, Keeper of the Wardrobe of Edward the Black Prince, 1337 (the Prince is just seven years old)

j heume ij bacenetz ij p[er]e de skynebauz de plate j pere de poleyns j pere de gauntz de plate j pere de paunz & braaz j pisane & j Aventaille ij p[er]re de plates vaunt braaz & ryrebraaz

one helm, two basinets, two pairs of plate schynbalds, one pair of poleyns, one pair of plate gauntlets, one pair of paunce and (mail) sleeves, one pisan and one aventail, two pairs of plates, vambrace and rerebrace

51

Now-Lost Document printed in C. Dehaisnes, *Documents et extraits divers concernant l'histoire de l'art dans la Flandre, l'Artois & le Hainaut avant le XVe siècle*, 2 vols (Lille, 1886), I, pp. 325–6
Inventory of Arms and Armour in the House of Jean Bernier, Banner-Bearer of Valenciennes, County of Hainault, 1337

uns pans un bras un barbiere un haubregon et uns caucons de fier unes plates burneys sans couvretures clauees sur cuir dengleterre unes plates couvertes de camokas un capiel couviert de vermel veluiel des armes Jehan Biernier les rutes et les boutons de pierles un hayaume de wiere et unes couvretures de vermel candal des armes Jehan Biernier un harnas de gambes

one paunce, one mail sleeve, one *barbière*, one haubergeon, and one (pair of) mail chausse, one (pair of) plates without covers nailed on English leather, one (pair of) plates covered with camaca (silk fabric), one chapel (de fer) covered with vermilion velvet (decorated with the heraldic) arms of Jean Bernier – the strap and buttons (decorated with) pearls, one war helm, and one (pair of horse) trappers of vermilion sendal (lightweight silk or very fine linen) of the (heraldic) arms of Jean Bernier, one (pair of) legharness

52

Kew, National Archives, E 101/338/11
Account of Gerard de Tourney, King's Heaumer (Plate Armourer), various Locations in England and the Low Countries, 1 April 1337–30 September 1342

deliu[er]ez en la garderobe en la To[u]r de Londr[e]s le p[re]m[er] iour de aueril lan xje [et] le moys de Janeuer Gerard de T[u]rney rend acompte de vne peire de plates couert de blanc quir l s vn chapel blank p[u]rbatuz xxvj s viij d vn Bacinet blank p[u] rbatutz xij s vj Chapels blancs p[u]rbatuz viij li le mois de Feuerer a Westm' vne peire de plates couert de blank quir l s j peire de plates cou[er]t de camoca quele le Roi dona a mons' Henri de Ferers l s vn Bacinet blancs p[u]rbatuz xij s viij Chapels blancs p[u]rbatuz x li xiij s iiij d la To[u]r de Loundres le moys de marz iij Chapels blancs p[u]rbatuz des queux le Roi dona a Henr' Dengaigne vn Chapel et a Joh' Brokaz vn autre iiij li p[u]r le recou[er]ir de vne peire de plat' couert de blanc quir oue scalopes dorez x s Westm' le mois dauerill vne peire de quissez couert de Camoca q[ue] le Roi dona a mons' Renaud de Cobeham xiij s iiij d vne peire de plates cou[er]t de blanc quir oue scalopes dorez l s vn Chapel blaunk p[u]rbatuz que le Roi dona a Piers de Beauchamp xxvj s viij d vn Chapel blanc p[u]rbatuz xxvj s viij d la Tour de Loundres vn Bacinet fo[u]rbiz quel le Roi donit a vn Chiual[er] de Cateloigne x s Burgh seint

Esmon el moys de Juyn vn Chapel garnisse xxvj s viij d Arewelle p[u]r le reclouer
Fourbir & garnisser de vne cou[er]t[u]re de plate p[u]r chiual vj li xiij s iiij d Anduers
au temps q[ue] les Justes illoq[ue]s estoient j peire de plates Couert de Camec' lx s
p[u]r le Fourb' & garnisser de vn Bassinet de Lumbardie le quel vn Chiualer dalem'
dona a le Roi vj s viij d p[u]r le Fourbir de ij maindefer ij s ij maindefer ij s vne peire
de Coutiers Fourbiz vj s viij d vne Poit[ri]ne p[u]r Justes xvj s p[u]r le recouerir de
vne peire de plates p[u]r sire Rob[er]t de Kingesto[u]n vj s viij d Brucelles j peire de
plates couert de drap dor a tut assai quele le Roi dona a mons' Joh' de Henau iiij li
Mountz en Henaud vne peire de plates p[u]r le corps le Roi cou[er]t de blank quir lx
s Mortelake vn maindefer vj s viij d la Chastel de Wyndes' el mois daprill as ioustes
illoeq[ue]z ordinez quen temps vindrent nouelles q[ue] le Counte de Salesbris estoit
p[ri]s de la mier iij peire de plates nouelles couertz de blancs quir vij li x s iij Poitrines
p[u]r les Joustes xlviij s iiij d Grates & iiij auant plates xx s xij Coronals xij s vne peire
de plates cou[er]t de veluet roie les queux plates le Roi dona a mons' Joh' le Melre l
s Arewelle a sa darreine passage as p[ar]ties de Flaundr' vne peire plates cou[er]t de
blanc quir p[u]r le corps le Roi lx s vn Bacinet p[u]r le Roi xvj s vne peire de plates
cou[er]t de veluet roie p[u]r mons' Joh' de Henau l s deliu[er]ez en la gard' a la
siege deuant T[ou]rney vn Bacinet xvj s a Gaunt p[ur] Guy de Brian as Justes q[ue]
illoeq[ue]z estoient a la reuenue le Roi de la siege de T[ou]rnei vn heaume vn Barber
vne peire de plates vne poitrine p[u]r Justes vne peire de rerebraz vn maindefer iiij
auantplates iiij Grates & vj Coronals vij li xij s ij Coronals ij s Norwiz contre les Justes
illoeq[ue]z vne Poitrine xvj s vne peire de rerebraz & auantbraz fourbiz p[u]r le corps
le Roi de la nouelle man[er]e xxx s iiij Grates & iiij auant plates xx s Langeleye contre
les Justes a la releuee la Roine le derrein iour de Septembr' lan xve vne poitrine p[u]
r le corps le Roi xvj s j peire plat' cou[er]t de blaunk quir lx s Westm' le derrein iour
de Septembr' l aketo[u]nes l li estaunford a son Aler v[er]s escoce j Chapel noir batuz
xviij s j h[er]nois de Jambers c[e]st [a]ssauoir Gr[eue]s xl s

Delivered to the Wardrobe in the Tower of London on 1 April in the 11th regnal year
[1337] and in January: Gerard de Tourney accounts for one pair of plates covered with
white leather 50s., one beaten white chapel de fer (i.e. of polished steel hammered
from scratch) 26s. 8d., one beaten white basinet 12s., six beaten white chapel de fers
£8. Westminster in February [1338]: one pair of plates covered with white leather 50s.,
one pair of plates covered with camaca (silk fabric) which the King gave to Sir Henry
Ferrers 50s., one beaten white basinet 12s., eight beaten white chapel de fers, £10 13s.
4d. Tower of London in March: three beaten white chapel de fers the King gave one
chapel de fer to Henry Dengaine and one other to John Brocas £4, for re-covering one
pair of plates covered with white leather with gilt scallops 10s. Westminster on 20 to
27 April: one pair of cuisses covered with camaca which the King gave to Sir Reginald
Cobham 13s. 4d., one pair of plates covered with white leather with gilt scallops 50s.,
one beaten white chapel de fer which the King gave to Piers Beauchamp 26s. 8d.
Tower of London [no date]: one furbished basinet which the King gave to a knight
of Catalonia 10s. Bury Saint Edmunds in June: one garnished chapel de fer 26s. 8d.
Orwell [no date]: for re-nailing, furbishing, and equipping one plate horse cover £6

13s. 4d. Antwerp at the time the jousts were held there: one pair of plates covered with camaca 60s., for furbishing and equipping a basinet of Lombardy (make) which a knight of Germany gave to the King 6s. 8d., for furbishing two manifers 2s., two manifers 2s., one pair of furbished couters 6s. 8d., one poitrine (i.e. breastplate) for jousts 16s., re-covering of one pair of plates for Sir Robert Kingston 6s. 8d. Brussels [no date]: one completely-assayed pair of plates (i.e. proofed by crossbow shot) covered with cloth of gold which the King gave to Sir John of Hainault £4. Mons in Hainault [no date]: one pair of plates for the King's body covered with white leather 60s. Mortlake [no date]: one manifer 6s. 8d. Windsor Castle in April for the jousts ordained to be held there at the time the news arrived that the Earl of Salisbury had been saved from the sea: three new pairs of plates covered with white leather £7 10s., three poitrines (breastplates) for the jousts 48s., four grappers and four vamplates 20s., 12 coronals 12s., one pair of plates covered with striped velvet the King gave these plates to Sir John Melre 50s. Orwell at the King's last passage to parts of Flanders [no date]: one pair of plates covered with white leather for the King's body 60s., one basinet for the King 16s., one pair of plates covered with striped velvet for Sir John of Hainault 50s. Delivered to the Wardrobe at the siege before Tournai [23 July–22 September 1340]: one basinet 16s. Ghent: for Guy Bryan for the jousts which were held there at the return of the King from the Siege of Tournai: one helm, one barber, one pair of plates, one poitrine for jousts, one pair of rerebrace, one manifer, four vamplates, four grappers, and six coronals £7 12s., two coronals 2s. Norwich [no date]: for the jousts there: one poitrine 16s., one pair of furbished rerebrace and vambrace for the King's body of the new manner 30s., four grappers and four vamplates 20s. Langley for the jousts for the recovery of the Queen on the last day of September in the 15th regnal year [1341]: one poitrine for the King's body 16s., one pair of plates covered with white leather 60s. Westminster on the last day of September: 50 aketons £50. Stanford [no date]: for the King's expedition to Scotland: one beaten black (unpolished) chapel de fer 18s. and one pair of legharness – that is to say: greaves 40s.

53

Now-Lost Flyleaf from London Metropolitan Archives, London Letter-Book F, printed in *Memorials of London and London Life,* ed. H. T. Riley (London, 1868), pp. 204–8
Inventory of Munitions of War provided by the City of London, 1339

in the house called *La Bretaske* near the Tower of London are 7 springalds and 380 *quarels* for the same feathered with *latone* and with heads and 500 *quarels* feathered with wood with heads and 29 cords called *strenges* also 8 bows of ash for the same springalds Alegate namely beyond the Gate thereof one springald with two strenges and one faussecord for the same also 20 quarels feathered with latone and headed with iron in *Camera Gildaulæ sunt sex Instrumenta de latone vocitata Gonnes et quinque*

roleres ad eadem, peletæ de plumbo pro eisdem Instrumentis quæ ponderant iiiic [*sic*] *libræ*
et dimidium xxxii libræ de pulvere pro dictis Instrumentis

in the building called *The Bretaske* (battlement) near the Tower of London are seven
springalds and 380 quarrels for the same fletched with latten and with heads and 500
quarrels fletched with wood with heads and 29 cords called strings also eight bows of
ash for the same springalds, Without Aldgate: one springald with two strings and one
false cord (a loose cord to assist with spanning) for the same also 20 quarrels fletched
with latten and headed with iron, in the Chamber of the Guildhall are six devices of
latten called guns and five rollers for them, lead pellets for these devices which weigh
400½ lb. [prob. 4½ lb.], 32 lb. of (gun) powder for the said devices

54

Now-Lost Document printed in A. Behault de Doron, 'Le Tournoi de
Mons de 1310', *Annales du Cercle Archéologique de Mons* 38 (1909), pp.
103–256 (pp. 115–16)
The Decision of the Count of Hainaut's Council on the Armour per-
mitted for Combat in the Lists between Jehan de Moustiers and Jehan
de Thians (known as Wafflart de Croix), Gentlemen, Mons, County of
Hainaut, 1 June 1339

chascun des campions doit pour son corps garder et deffendre estre armez comme
que bon lui semblera pour sen aise et pour sen prouffit doivent ils avoir chacun sa
glaive tout dune longhesse chacun son escut et chacun ij espees telles quil leur plaira
doivent ils avoir chacun j faulx estryer dune samblable fachon et de tel poix quil
plaira a chacun deaux pour luy doivent ils avoir chascun ung brocque de fer en sen
want destre et le chanfrein du cheval sans taillant et sans brocque et se remannant de
larmure du cheval telle quil plaira a chacun pour lui sans brocque et sans taillant ne
doivent ils avoir nul coutiel a pointe ne autre baston deffensaulle que dit est dessus
doivent ils avoir sielles a leurs chevaux qui naient plus darmures le ungs que ly autre
peuvent ils leurs dites armures lasquier et rastraindre deschi adont quils viennent au
camp a lentrer au camp doivent ils faire serment que autre armures ils naront sur
eux que cy devant est dit Et aussi quils naront sour eaux haulx noms propres noms
sorcheries ne chose nulle qui a dechevanche puist appartenir puelt chacun deaulx
rennier son chev' et amener ung tel au camp quil lui plaira

each of the combatants may be armed as they see fit for their ease and benefit to guard
and protect their bodies, their lances must be of the same length, each shall have a
shield, and each two swords as they please, each must have a false stirrup (poss. a
mace) of the same fashion and of such weight as is pleasing to each, each may have
an iron spike on their left gauntlet but the horse's shaffron shall be without sharpened
parts and without a spike, they may not have a pointed knife (i.e. for thrusting) nor

any other fighting weapon other than those stated above, on their horses' saddles: one may be no more armoured than the other, each may thus have their said arms strapped and fitted as soon and they come to the lists, on entering the lists they must swear that they bear no other arms save those stated above; and also that they do not have on them powerful spells, secret spells, nor sorcery, nor anything else that might be considered deceitful, each one of them may rein his horse and bring a cloth (i.e. horse cover) to the lists as they please

55

Kew, National Archives, SC 1/54/30
Unsigned Letter to King Edward III from the Scottish Pale, c. 1340

Johan Ker est mort par iouster de guerre de vne coupe qe vn de mes valetz lui ferst permy le corps et permy son haketon' et hauberioun

John Ker has been killed in a joust of war by one of my valets who struck him through the body and through his aketon and haubergeon

56

Paris, Bibliothèque nationale de France, MS fr. 5287, extracts printed in *Actes normands de la chambre des comptes sous Philippe de Valois (1328–50)*, ed. L. Déslisle (Rouen, 1871), pp. 258–64
Arms and Armour provided by Thomas Fouques, Keeper of the Fortress of the Galleys of Rouen, Normandy, 24 March and 24–28 May 1340

24 March
La barque de Jean Ligier: XL paire de pleatez, xx cote-pointez, LX bachinez, LX gorgerètez, XXX lanches, I coffre de carrais, I coffre de viretons de chiualz qui furent fais à Roen, III arbalestes, et LX que targes que paviers

24–28 May
Guillebert le Fèvre, mestre de la nef Saint Jehan de Hareflue: vint et huit plates, dont il en y a VI d'Allemaigne, douse bachinés, trente deuls targes et pavois, chinc arbalestes, sis baudrés, une arbaleste à II piez, trois casses de carreaux, une casse de viretons douze cousteaz et douze père de gantelez un garrot, et une casse de carreaux à garrot, et vint lanchez ferréez. Cogge de Guillaume de Bordeaux: trente plates, quinse bachinés, vint escus, vint pavois, vint et chinc lances, sis arbalestes prestes, une arbaleste à II piez, sept baudrés, quatre casses de carreaux à un pié, une casse de viretons, XII cousteux, une arbaleste à tour et le tour et une casse de carreaux pour icelle, un garrot et une casse de carreaux à garrot. Robin Danios, maitre de la nef le

Jehennet de Leure: vint plates de prove et de demie prove; Symon Coterel, maitre de la nef Sainte Marie de Leure: seze plates de demie prove. Guillaume de Tourneville, maitre de la nef Sainte Catherine de Leure: chinc arbalestes à I pié, une arbaleste de cor à deulz piez, sis baudrés, un haucepié à tendre arbaleste. Jehan Godeffroy, maistre du Christofe: cinquante plates, dont il en i a XXV d'Alemaigne et les autres de prove, vint bachinés, vint chinc escus, vint chinc pavois, cinquante lances ferrées, huit arbalestes à un pié, une arbaleste de cor à II piés, huit baudrés, un haucepié, une arbaleste à tour, le tour pour tendre la dite arbaleste, une casse de carreaux pour le trait d'icelle, trois casses de viretons où il a IIIm, deux casses de viretons où il a en chascune environ un millier, un garrot fourny, une casse de carreaux à garrot et vint couteaux. Martin Danois: trois cases de viretons où il a IIIm, une arbaleste à tour et le tour pour la tendre, une casse de carreaux pour ycelle, deuls cases de viretons qui sont environ IIm. Ph. Bouvet, maistre de la nef Saint George: vint plates d'Alemaine, deus cens pavois, quinze arbalestes de cor à deus piés, deus arbalestes de cor à tour, diz haucepiés, cent baudrés, vint paire de gantelés, huit cens sexante dars ferrés, six cens sexante quinze dars defferrés, six cens sexante treze fors dars, quarante deux lances, quatre cens quarante fers de lance en un coffre, sexante banères de Camelot des armes de France, deux baucens des dites armes, sept banères des armes d'Escosse, trois banères des armes monseigneur l'admiral, deux banères des armes sire Nicolas Behuchet, deux milliers de bochètes pour ferer dars et lances, chinquante huit milliers de clou melés

24 March

Jean Ligier's barque: 40 pairs of plates, 20 pointed (i.e. padded) coats, 60 basinets, 60 gorgets, 30 lances, one coffer of quarrels, one coffer of quarrels for horses (i.e. mounted crossbowmen) made at Rouen, three crossbows, and 60 (shields) both targes and pavises.

24–28 May

Guillebert le Fèvre Master of the Ship *Saint Jehan* of Harfleur: 28 (pairs of) plates six of which are German (i.e. of German steel), 12 basinets, 32 targes and pavises, five crossbows, six baldrics, one two-foot crossbow (i.e. for two-foot-long quarrels), three cases of quarrels, one case of quarrels, 12 knives, and 12 pairs of gauntlets, one *garrot* (Fr. for springald), one case of *garrot* quarrels, and 20 headed lances. Guillaume de Bordeaux's Cog: 30 (pairs of) plates, 15 basinets, 20 shields, 20 pavises, 25 lances, six crossbows ready for use, one two-foot crossbow, seven baldrics, four cases of quarrels for one-foot (crossbows), one case of quarrels, 12 knives, one torsion crossbow and the spanning device, one case of quarrels for it, one *garrot* (springald) and one case of *garrot* quarrels. Robin Danois, Master of the ship *Le Jehennet* of Eure: 20 proofed and half-proofed (pairs of) plates (i.e. shot at with a powerful device-spanned crossbow or with a hand-spanned bow or crossbow); Symon Coterel, Master of the ship *Sainte Marie* of Eure: 16 (pairs of) plates of half proof. Guillaume de Tourneville, Master of the ship *Sainte Catherine* of Eure: five one-foot crossbows, one horn two-foot crossbow, six baldrics, one crossbow spanning device. Jehan Godeffroy, Master of the *Cristofe*: 50 (pairs of) plates 25 of which are German and the others are proofed, 20 basinets, 25 shields, 25 pavises, 50 headed lances, eight one-foot crossbows, one horn two-foot crossbow, eight baldrics, one crossbow spanning device, one torsion crossbow, the device for spanning the said crossbow, one case of quarrels for it to shoot, three cases in which are 3,000 quarrels, two cases in which there are around 1,000 quarrels, one equipped *garrot* (springald), one case of *garrot* quarrels, and 20 knives. Martin Danois: three cases in which there are 3,000 quarrels, one torsion crossbow and the device for spanning it, one case of quarrels for it, two cases in which there are around 2,000 quarrels. Philippe Bouvet, Master of the ship *Saint George*: 20 (pairs of) German plates, 200 pavises, 15 horn two-foot crossbows, two horn torsion crossbows, ten crossbow spanning devices, 100 baldrics, 20 pairs of gauntlets, 860 headed darts, 675 darts without heads, 673 strong darts, 42 lances, 440 lanceheads in a coffer, 60 banners of camlet (fine fabric) of the (royal coat of) arms of France, two (smaller) banners of the said arms, seven banners of (the royal coat of) arms of Scotland, three banners of the arms of my Lord the Admiral, two banners of Sir Nicolas Behuchet's arms, 2,000 shafts for dart- and lance-heads, 58,000 nails of different sizes

57

London, British Library, Additional Charter 7198, printed in *A Catalogue of the Manuscripts Relating to Wales in the British Museum*, ed. E. Owen, 4 vols (London, 1900–22), III, pp. 675–9
Arms and Armour in the Castles of Conwy, Beaumaris, Caernarfon, Criccieth, Harlech, Lampeter, and Emlyn, Principality of Wales, 1341

Conewey
viij aketons feables couerts de blanc lynge teille j gambeison de petite value j pair des plates feables x bacinets feables xvj hauberjons iiij corsets bons e j feable x targes feables j coffre menue plein des quarels feables ij springalds oue tot le apparail estre les cordes a un de eux appuertenant j arblaste de viz apparaile ij costes e j coler de tax' pour arblastes de viz j coste pur un arblaste de ij pees xxx arblastes de un pee des queux x arblastes sunt suffisauntz xxj arcis manuel sanz cord iiijxx xiiij quarells de arein pennes suffisauntz xix baldres feables des queux iiij sunt sanz fers xx gaddis daster Et xvj pieces de fer

Beal mareis
viij aketonz suffisauntz couertz de blanch teile vij aketons veux e molt feables e vij aketons de nule value j pauelon de pesane blanc xvj bacinetz garnys de blanc couerture v bacinetz des queux j est burny e vernice xij hauberjons de fer des queux j est suffisaunt xj hauberjonz molt feables e vj hauberjons de nule value iiij corsetz de fer j coiffe de fer feable iij double gorgers de nule value vij pesanes des queux j est

sufficaunt e les altiers sunt molt feables vij auentailles des queux j est de nule value j paire quisots de fer de nule value j paire chauccis de fer de nule value un paire jambers de plate garniz de blanc quyr molt feable v coleretz de plate couvertz de carde ix chapeaux de fer molt febles des queux iij sunt oue visieres xxj targe de nule value vij quirs de boef veux e de nule value iiij p' le meind cont' de gros quarell pour les aspringalds pennes de arein iiij petites coffres pleins de menue quarels ne mye pennes ix dozeines de meryn pour flech ne mye ouertez xv launces feables dex queux x sunt sauntz testes j baril plein daster ccc gadd daster xxix summas de fer xxx arblasts suffi-cauntz e iij de corn des queux j est de viz x costers de arblasts xvj baudr' sufficauntz xxviij arcs manueles sufficauntz

Caiernaruan
iiij barrels plein daster iiij springald oue tot le apparail ij grauntz engynz xlviij grauntz pieces de plom viij jupel suffisantz xvj aketons suffisantz iij aketons de nule value vij bacinetz sauffisantz de queux un est burny ij paire des plates de queux un est feble iiij paire des gauntz de plate ij paire jambers xxx arblastz suffisantz ij paire polain Dc testes des quarels pour aspringaldes xlviij setes cc flacches saunz testes xxj arcs manueles febles ccclxxiiij testes des quarels pour arblastes de viz pennes darein xiij testes pour menues lances e ciiijxx testes pour gauelots

Cruckyth
x aketons de queux j est molt feble vj jupels suffisantz j paire des plates iij paire de gauntz de plate xij bacinetz suffisantz ix arblastes suffisantz viij baldrics de queux v sunt feables xviij pieces de plum xlvij pieces de fer

Hardelagh
vj haubergeons j hauberk ij corsets de fer dunt le une est de nule value e j coiffre de fer viij aketons suffisantz ij gambeisons xj bacinetz dunt vij sunt feble ne mye garniz iiij bacinetz suffisantz ij jupeles suffisantz iij paire des gauntz de baleyne xxvj arblestes dun pee perriz e de nule value estre le fer iij costes de arblastes de baleine non suffisantz iij costes de baleine pour arblastes de viz x baldrics suffisantz

Lampadar
xl pieces de fer iiij aketons nouelles vj aketons veux deux corsetz de fer ij haberjons de fer v paire des plates nouelles j paire plates veux v coleretz de plate nouelles j coleret de plate veil x bacinetz dunt les v sunt nouelles e v sunt veux iiij coleretz de fer pour bacinetz xv targes des armes le Roi xij launces un springald oue son apparail vjxx testes pour quarels des springalds iiijm quarells pour arblastes

Emelyn
vj aketons de petite value iiij bacinetz de nule value de nule maniere armure de fer ne des plates rienz remeint vj arblastes auqe bons j baudre de nule value vc quarells de petite value vj targes des armes Dangleterre vj launces
Fait a remembrer qe tote la garnesture de chaseteaux de Nortgales e Suthgales [...] en

touz ceux chastieux ny sunt pas armures a bien armer de lynge armures e de fer pour
lx homes Ne en touz ceux chasteaux ne sunt qe iiijxx ix arbalestes xxxviij baudress e
xxj arkes manuieles qe soient de value

Conwy: eight worn out aketons covered with white linen, one gambeson of little
value, one worn out pair of plates, ten worn out basinets, 16 haubergeons, four
good corsets and one worn out, one small coffer full of worn out quarrels, two fully-
equipped springalds with the appurtenant cord for one, one equipped vice-spanned
crossbow, two ribs and one attaching collar for vice-spanned crossbows, one rib for a
two-foot (long) crossbow, 30 one-foot crossbows ten of which are sufficient, 21 hand
bows (i.e. longbows) without cords, four score and 14 sufficient quarrels fletched with
copper, 19 worn out baldrics four of which are without iron (fittings), 20 gads of steel
and 16 pieces of iron

Beaumaris: eight sufficient aketons covered with white cloth, seven old and very
worn out aketons and seven aketons of no value, one white pisan cover, 16 basinets
equipped with white covers, five basinets one of which is burnished and varnished,
12 iron haubergeons one of which is sufficient, 11 very worn out haubergeons and
six haubergeons of no value, four iron corsets, one worn out iron coif, three double
gorgets of no value, seven pisans one of which is sufficient and the others are very
worn out, seven aventails one of which is of no value, one pair of iron cuisses of no
value, one pair of iron chausse of no value, one very worn out pair of plate jambers
garnished with white leather, five plate collars covered with carde (linen material),
nine very worn out chapel de fers three of which have visors, 21 targes of no value,
seven old cow hides of no value, four smaller (coffers) containing large quarrels for
springalds fletched with copper, four little coffers full of small, un-fletched quarrels,
nine dozen unworked wooden (shafts) for arrows, 15 worn out lances ten of which
lack heads, one barrel full of steel, 300 gads of steel, 29 loads of iron, 30 sufficient
crossbows and three of horn one of which is vice-spanned, ten crossbow ribs, 16 sufficient baldrics, 28 sufficient hand bows (i.e. longbows)

Caernarfon: four barrels full of steel, four fully-equipped springalds, two great
(siege) engines, 48 pieces of lead, eight sufficient jupels, 16 sufficient aketons, three
aketons of no value, seven sufficient basinets one of which is burnished, two pairs of
plates one of which is worn out, four pairs of plate gauntlets, two pairs of jambers,
30 sufficient crossbows, two pairs of poleyns, 600 quarrel-heads for springalds, 48
(heavy) arrows, 200 arrows lacking heads, 21 worn out hand bows (i.e. longbows), 374
quarrel-heads for vice-spanned crossbows fletched with copper, 13 heads for smaller
lances and 104 score heads for javelins

Criccieth: ten aketons one of which is very worn out, six sufficient jupels, one pair
of plates, three pairs of plate gauntlets, 12 sufficient basinets, nine sufficient crossbows,
eight baldrics five of which are worn out, 18 pieces of lead, 47 pieces of iron

Harlech: six haubergeons, one hauberk, two iron corsets one of which is of no value
and one iron coif, eight sufficient aketons, two gambesons, 11 basinets seven of
which are worn out and un-equipped, four sufficient basinets, two sufficient jupels,
three pairs of baleen gauntlets, 26 rotten one-foot (long) crossbows the iron of no

value, three insufficient baleen ribs for crossbows, three baleen ribs for vice-spanned crossbows, ten sufficient baldrics

Lampeter: 40 pieces of iron, four new aketons, six old aketons, two iron corsets, two iron haubergeons, five new pairs of plates, one old pair of plates, five new plate collars, one old plate collar, ten basinets five of which are new and five are old, four iron collars for basinets, 15 targes of the King's (heraldic coat of) arms, 12 lances, one fully-equipped springald, six score quarrel-heads for springalds, 4,000 crossbow quarrels

Emlyn: six aketons of little value, four basinets of no value, no manner of iron (mail) armour nor plate remains, six fairly good crossbows, one baldric of no value, 500 quarrels of little value, six targes of the (heraldic) arms of England, six lances

Let it be recorded that in all the victuals of the castles of North Wales and South Wales […] in all these castles there be good armour of linen or iron for but 60 men; in all these castles there are but four score and nine crossbows, 38 baldrics, 21 hand bows (i.e. longbows) that are of any value

58

Now-Lost Document printed in C. Dehaisnes, *Documents et extraits divers concernant l'histoire de l'art dans la Flandre, l'Artois & le Hainaut avant le XVe siècle*, 2 vols (Lille, 1886), I, pp. 341–2
Armour provided for Philippe, Count of Auvergne, by Jean de Beaumez and others, Hôtel d'Artois, Paris, 1342 and 1345

Jehan De Biaumes pour VI paire de harnas de jambes et unes greves IIII harnas de bras unes plates XLIII lb Andrieu Caret X harnas de jambes IIII harnas de bras III paire de gantelles III bachines II camaulx une gorgerette uns pans LXIIII lb Brebant le Hyaumier III paire de plates VII bachines I camail II paire de manches I haubregon et III gorgerettes uns pans uns cuisseux I harnas de bras uns gantelles IIIIxx XII lb Guillaume De Rains I bachinet III camaus III gorgerettes uns pans unes manches XVI lb Jehan De Dieval uns pans unes manches I bachinet I camial VIII lb maistre Gille larmurier IIII paire de plates uns gantelles XXXVIII lb Jehannot le haubregier unes manches I camail une gorgerette VIII lb Jaquemin Du Liege I pourpoint I harnas de bras IIII paires de gantelles uns saullers I bachinet unes plates XX lb Lambekin De Liege unes plates I harnois de bras et II paires de gantelles pour mons' Hughe de Viane XXIIII lb X s pour mons' Philippe De Chauvery pour I bachinet et I harnas de bras et de jambes et I haubregon XL lb a Jaquemart le Wantier pour I camail pour Martin escuier mons' Du Traynel IIII lb I harnas de maille pans et manches II camauls une colerette pour Hue de Berbenchon XXVI lb unes plates pour Hodie de Dampierre LX s Thomas le pourpointier pour I pourpoint XX s Lambekin De Liege pour mons' Jehan de Frolays II paire de harnas de gambes II paire de harnas de bras I bachinet une gorgerette III paire de gantelles XXIX lb XV s Lambekin Du Liege pour mons' Hughe de Viane une gorgerette un harnas de bras et uns cuisseux pour son escuier VIII lb XV s Andriu Caree uns harnas de gambes C s pour lescuier mons' Hughe a Brebant uns plates uns pans et unes manches I bachinet XXIIII lb pour mons' De Bouloigne Lambekin Du Liege I bachinet un harnas de gambes XXXI lb X s Guillaume De Rains I camail pour mons' Hughe de Viane XL s a Jehan De Biaumes larmurier pour le faichon des pourpoints et pour le gaurniere des II chanffrains apparer et pour colleretes X l V s Brebant le hiaumier pour une dousaine de lances ferrees pour banieres LXX s Robert Macefer le fourbisseur pour fourbir le harnas mons' heaumes harnas de gambes harnas de bras LVIII s Jaquemart larmurier pour aguillettes dargent et pour las de soie et pour VIII paius de vel IIII l VI s

ier août 1345 [...] a Brebant le heaumier pour recouvrir unes plates de cuir blanc XVIII s

Jean de Beamez for six pairs of legharness and one (pair of) greaves, four (pairs of) arm harness, one (pair of) plates 43l., Andrieu Caret ten (pairs of) legharness, four (pairs of) arm harness, three pairs of gauntlets, three basinets, two aventails, one gorget, one paunce 44l., Brebant the heaumer (plate armourer) three pairs of plates, seven basinets, one aventail, two pairs of (mail) sleeves, one haubergeon and three gorgets, one paunce, one (pair of) cuisses, one (pair of) arm harness, one (pair of) gauntlets, four score and 12l., Guillaume de Rains one basinet, three aventails, three gorgets, one paunce, one (pair of) mail sleeves 16l., Jean de Dieval one paunce, one (pair of mail) sleeves, one basinet, one aventail 8l., Master Gille the armourer four pairs of plates, one (pair of) gauntlets 38l., Jehannot the hauberger (mail-maker) one (pair of mail) sleeves, one aventail, one gorget 8l., Jaquemin de Liège one pourpoint, one (pair of) arm harness, four pairs of gauntlets, one (pair of) sabatons, one basinet, one (pair of) plates 20l., Lambekin de Liège one (pair of) plates, one (pair of) arm harness, and two pairs of gauntlets for Sir Hughes de Viane 24l. 10s., for Sir Philippe de Chauvery for one basinet and one (pair of) arm- and legharness and one haubergeon 40l., to Jacquemart le Wantier for one aventail for Martin, squire of my Lord Du Traynel 4l., one mail harness, paunce and (mail) sleeves, two aventails, one collar for Hughes de Berbenchon 26l., one (pair of) plates for Hodie de Dampierre 60s., Thomas the pourpoint-maker for one pourpoint 20s., Lambekin de Liège for Sir Jean de Frolays two pairs of legharness, two pairs of arm harness, one basinet, one gorget, three pairs of gauntlets 29l. 15s., Lambekin de Liège for Sir Huges de Viane one gorget, one (pair of) arm harness, and one (pair of) cuisses for his squire 8l. 15s., Andrieu Caree one (pair of) legharness 100s. for the squire of Sir Hughes, to Brebant (the heaumer) one (pair of) plates, one paunce, one (pair of mail) sleeves, one basinet 24l. for my Lord of Boulogne, Lambekin de Liège one basinet, one (pair of) legharness 31l. 10s., Guillaume de Rains one aventail for Sir Hughes de Viane 40s., Jean de Beaumez the armourer for making pourpoints and for preparing two shaffrons and for collars 10l. 5s., Brebant the heaumer for a dozen headed lances for banners 70s., Robert Macefer the furbisher for furbishing my Lord's harness: helms, legharness, arm harness 58s., to Jacquemart the armourer for silver lace-points and for silk laces, and for eight calf skins 4l. 6.

1 August 1345 [...] Brebant the heaumer for re-covering one (pair of) plates with white leather 18s.

59

Kew, National Archives, E 101/290/23
Arms and Armour brought from Brittany and the Isle of Wight to the Tower of London, 1–6 September 1343

Rep[ar]ac[i]o' diu[er]s' armatur' venientiu' de p[ar]tib[u]s Britanu' armatur' de mail j barello j par' pauns & braces xvij auentails iiij xx v pisans emedac[i]o[n]e cuiusdam vt[en]c[e]l[ii]s ferri fracti p[ro] barell' v[er]tendo vj d. iij lagen' olei p[ro] fraiac[i] o[n]e hi' armatur' ij s vj d j quart' furfur' p[ro] armatur' fraiand' xvj d corr' russet' p[ro] xiij auentails & j par de pans p[ro] armatur' quoru' corr' fuit putref[ac]t[u]m xij d filo magno p[ro] corr' sup[er] armatur' consuend' ij d Wil[e]l[m]o Haub[er]' & iij soc' suis conduct' p[ro] armatur' fraiand' v[i]z a p[rim]o die Sept' vsq[ue] vj die mens' vj s Ric[ard]o Hauberger & j soc' suo p[ro] diu[er]sis armatur' rep[ar]and' p[ro] idem temp' iiij s armatur' de plat' iij m[i]l' d' clau' minut' p[ro] iiij par' plat' de nouo coop[er]t' & p[ro] defect' alioru[um] xvj par' plat' venient' de p[ar]t' Britanu' rep[ar]ac' infra T[u]rr' London' p[re]c' mill' ij s xj d xl bokles p[ro] plat' vj d iiij par' de garnatz p[ro] plat' p[re]c' par' j d ob' vj d corr' russet' p[ro] tissuz deficient' sup[er] plat' faciend' iiij d vj vln' de carde de coloyn p[ro] iiij par' plat' coop[er]and' xxj d jacobo le Arm[u]rer & ij soc' suis p[ro] plat' clouand' & rep[ar]and' v[i]z a d[ic]to p[rim]o die Sept' vsq[ue] vj diem eiusde' mens' vj s Gilb[er]to le Fourbour & ij soc' suis conduct' p[ro] plat' mu[n]dand' & rep[ar]and' p[ro] idem te[m]pus vj s Ric[ard] o le Taillour & j soc' suo p[ro] coop[er]tor' plat' consuend' v[i]z se[cun]do die Sept' & t[er]cio die eiusdem mens' xij d filo p[ro] coop[er]tor' consuend' j d ob' Corset' de plat' v m[i]l' clau' minut' p[ro] xvj corsetz de plat' de nouo coop[er]t' clauand' & p[ro] defect' alior[um] lxvj corsetz de plat' p[ro] sagittar' d[omi]ni R' rep[ar]and' infra T[u]rr' London' iiij s ij d corr' albo p[ro] tissuz & al' defect' corset' rep[ar]and' viij d jacobo le arm[u]rer & iij soc' suis p[ro] corsett' clouand' & rep[ar]and' v[i]z a ix die Septembr' vsq[ue] xiij diem eiusdem mens' vj s viij d eidem jacobo & iij soc' suis a xv die Septembr' vsq[ue] xx diem eiusde' mens' viij s Certoece de plate m[i]l' clau' p[ar]uis p[ro] xviij par' cerotecar[um] de plat' venient' de Britanu' rep[ar]and' infra T[u]rr' London' vj d corr' albo p[ro] rep[ar]ac' ear[un]dem iiij d Joh[ann]i de Potenhale & j soc' suo p[ro] cerotec' clouand' & rep[ar]and' v[i]z a xxij die Septembr' vsq[ue] xxvij diem eiusdem mens' iiij s Rep[ar]ac[i]o' diu[er]s' armatur' venient' de Insula vecti armatur' de mail iiij lagen' olei p[ro] xxix par' de pans & braces & xxv auentails & xxv pisans venientiu' de Insula vecti fraiand' iij s iiij d j quart' furfur' p[ro] pans braces auentails & pisans fraiand' xvj d Wil[e]l[m]o Haub' & iij soc' suis p[ro] armatur' fraiand' v[i]z a ix die Sept' vsq[ue] xiij die' eiusde' mens' v s eide' Wil[e]l[m] o & iij soc' suis a xv die mens' Sept' vsq[ue] xix diem eiusde' mens' v s Ric[ard]o le Hauberger & j soc' suo p[ro] defect' armatur' rep[ar]and' a xv die Sept' vsq[ue] xx die' eiusde' mens' iiij s corr' russeto p[ro] xv auentails & vj par' de pans p[re]d[ic]tar[um]

armatur' quar[um] corr' fuit fractu' & putref[ac]tiu' xv d armatur' de plat' Wil[e]l[m]
o le Fourbour & ij soc' suis p[ro] xxx par' de plat' venient' de Insula vecti mundand'
infra T[u]rr' London' v[i]z a xxij die Septembr' vsq[ue] xxvij diem eiusde' mens' iiij
s vj d Joh[ann]i de Potenhale p[ro] plat' rep[ar]and' ab vlt' die Sept' vsq[ue] quart'
die' Octobr' xx d Rep[ar]ac' armatur' existentiu' in gard' Reg' infra T[u]rr' London'
armatur' de mail ij lagen' olei p[ro] iiij Loricis v par' de pans & braces & ij auentails
existent' in gard' d[omi]ni Reg' infra T[u]rr' London v[i]z in T[u]rri rotund' & v par'
de pans & braces ij auentails & iiij pisans ex[is]tentiu' in gard' sup[r]a aquam fraiand'
xx d iiij b' furfur' p[ro] armatur' fraiand' viij d Wil[e]l[m]o Haub' & iij soc' suis p[ro]
armatur' fraiand' a xxij die Septembr' vsq[ue] xxv diem eiusdem mens' iiij s j batello
p[ro] Cxxxv par' plat' nouis querend' de Westm' vsq[ue] T[u]rr' London' xx die [...]

Repair of divers armour come from parts of Brittany – Mail armour: one barrel, one
pair of paunces and (mail) sleeves, 17 aventails, four score and five pisans, mending
certain broken iron tools for the turning barrel (for scouring mail) 6d., three flagons
of oil for scouring this armour 2s. 6d., one quarter of bran for scouring the armour
16d., russet leather for 13 aventails and one pair of paunces for equipping the armour
as the leathers were rotten 12d., thick thread for sewing the leather over the armour
2d., William the hauberger and three of his servants for carrying the armour to be
scoured viz.: from 1 to 6 September 6s., Richard the hauberger and one of his servants
for divers repairs to the armour for the same time 4s. Plate armour: three and a half
thousand small nails for covering four new pairs of plates and for another 16 worn
out pairs of plates come from parts of Brittany for repair in the Tower of London for
each 1,000 2s. 11d., 40 buckles for the plates 6d., four pairs of fittings for the plates
6d., russet leather for making the straps that are lacking upon the plates 4d., six ells
of Cologne carde (cloth) for covering four pairs of plates 21d., James the armourer
and two of his servants for nailing and repairing the plates viz.: from 1 to 6 September
6s., Gilbert the furbisher and two of his servants to mend and repair the plates for
the same time 6s., Richard the tailor and one of his servants for sewing the covers
of the plates viz.: from 2 to 3 September 12d., thread for sewing these covers ½d.
Plate corsets: 5,000 small nails for covering 16 new plate corsets and for another 66
worn out plate corsets for the Lord King's archers repaired in the Tower of London
4s. 2d., white leather for straps and repairing those lacking on the corsets 8d., James
the armourer and three of his servants for nailing and repairing the corsets viz.:
from 9 to 13 September 6s. 8d., this James and three of his servants from 15 to 20
September 8s. Plate gauntlets: 1,000 small nails for 18 pairs of plate gauntlets come
from Brittany repaired in the Tower of London 6d., white leather for repairing them
4d., John Potenhale and one of his servants to nail and repair the gauntlets viz.:
from 22 to 27 September 4s. Repair of divers armour come for the Isle of Wight –
Mail armour: four flagons of oil for scouring 29 pairs of paunces and (mail) sleeves
and 25 aventails and 25 pisans come from the Isle of Wight 3s. 4d., one quarter of
bran bought for scouring these paunces, (mail) sleeves, aventails, and pisans 16d.,
William the hauberger and three of his servants to scour the armour viz.: from 9 to
13 September 5s., this William and his three servants for this purpose from 15 to 19

September 5s., Richard the hauberger and one of his servants for repairing the worn out armour from 15 to 20 September 4s., russet leather for the 15 aventails and six pairs of paunces from this armour the leather of which was worn out and rotten 15d. Plate armour: William the furbisher and two of his servants to mend 30 pairs of plates come for the Isle of White in the Tower of London viz.: from 22 to 27 September 4s. 6d., John Potenhale to repair these plates from 30 September to 4 October 20d. Repair of armour remaining in the Lord King's Wardrobe in the Tower of London – Mail armour: two flagons of oil for scouring three hauberks, five pairs of paunces and (mail) sleeves and two aventails remaining in the King's Wardrobe in the Tower of London viz.: in the Round Tower, and five pairs of paunces and (mail) sleeves, two aventails, and four pisans remaining in the wardrobe above the water 20d., four bushels of bran for scouring this armour 8d., William hauberger and three of his servants to scour this armour from 22 to 25 September 4s. One boat to carry 135 new pairs of plates found at Westminster to the Tower of London on the 20th day of [...]

60

Montauban, Archives départementales de Tarn-et-Garonne, registre G372, fol. 20v, fol. 41v, and fol. 121v
Register of the Bonis Brothers, Merchants of Montauban, County of Quercy, 1345 and 1348

1345
jª platas de mega proa xvj s' viij d' jª platas de mega proa lxv s

one fully-proofed (pair of) plates (i.e. shot at with a device-spanned crossbow) 16 *sous* 8 *deniers*, one fully-proofed (pair of) plates 65 *sous*

1348
jª platas de mega proa q[ue]lh trameze' p[ar] en B amis son cozi quant trames iiij omes darmas en peireguort a mo' lo sensecalt mo' arnaut despanha combrem las platas [no individual cost recorded]

one fully-proofed (pair of) plates which were brought by B. de Amis, his (the merchant's) cousin – which four men-at-arms received and brought the (pair of) plates to Périgueux to my Lord the Sénéchal my Lord Arnaut d'Espanha [no individual cost recorded]

61

Kew, National Archives, E 101/390/7
Armour in the Royal Wardrobe at the Tower of London, 25 January
1344–24 January 1345

This manuscript is very fragmentary

.j. haub[er]geo[n]e de grosse maille .j. bacinet round cou[er]t [...] j. auentaille feble
& roillez .j. haub[er]geon de mesm' p[u]r t[ur]noy .j. peire de q[ui]ssotz cou[er]
tz [...] ij aketon m[u]lt fieble cou[er]t de teille blaunk .j. peire des chaunceouns de
plate [*sic*] cou' de veluet v[er]mail.ij. haub[er]geons bons .ij. bacinetz .j. auentaille
.j. gorg[er]o double .j. pauillon' p[u]r pisane .ij. peire de poleins .ij. peire gantz de
plate .ij. peire de skinebaux .j. peire de sabatons [...] gantz de plate [...] les leop[ar]tz
brodez des [...] .j. peir quisseux de plate cou[er]tz [...] poleins .ij. peire de jamb[er]s
.j. healm doree od la creste .iiij. autres healmes de diu[er]se taille .j. chapel [...] autres
chapeux de diu[er]ses man[er]es .j. chapel round de nerfs depeint des arm[...] .j. peire
de treppes cou[er]tz [...] .ij. healmes p[ur] le t[or]noi vieux & de petite [...] .j. peal
de bazeyne rouge fieble .viij. [...] corroiee fieble .ij. peire despaudlers de petite value
iiij peals de vache corroiee fiebles de petite value .iiij. peire de jamb[er]s de quir de
petite [...] quissotz de quir de petite value quir de petite value .j. chapel de feer vieux
& roillez .iiij. coffres p[u]r trusser

one haubergeon of large mail (links), one round basinet covered [...] one old and
rusted aventail, one haubergeon in the same (rusted) condition for the tourney, one
pair of cuisses covered [...] two very worn out aketons covered with white linen, one
pair of plate chausses [*sic*], covered with vermilion velvet, two good haubergeons, two
basinets, one aventail, one double gorget (i.e. of two layers of mail), one cover for a
pisan, one pair of poleyns, two pairs of plate gauntlets, two pairs of schynbalds, one
pair of sabatons [...] plate gauntlets [...] the (heraldic) leopards embroidered with
[...] one pair of cuisses of plate covered [...] poleyns, two pairs of jambers, one gilt
helm with the crest, three other helms of divers size, one chapel de fer [...] other
chapel de fers of divers sorts, one round chapel of sinew painted with the King's arms,
one in the same suite, one pair of (horse) trappers covered [...] two old helms for the
tourney of little value, one worn out hide of red sheepskin, eight [...] of worn out
leather, two pairs of spaudlers of little value, four worn out cowhides of little value,
four pairs of leather jambers of little value [...] leather cuisses of little value, one
cuirie of little value, one old and rusted chapel de fer, four coffers for trussing armour

62

Unlocated Original Document printed in A. Way, 'Accounts of the Constables of the Castle of Dover', *Archaeological Journal* 11 (1854), pp. 381–8

Inventory of Dover Castle, Kent, 20 December 1344

in AULA j. barelle pro armaturis rollandis in FABRICA; ij. maides, ij. bicorn', iij. martellos magnos, iij. martellos parvos, ij. tenaces magnas, quinque tencaes parvas, ij. instrumenta ad ferrum cindendum, iiijor Instrumenta ferrea ad claves inficiendos, ij. paria flaborum, j. folour de ferro, j. mola de petra versatilis pro ferro acuendo, et ij. ligamina de ferro pro j. buketto in DOMO ARMORUM; iij. springald' magnas cum toto artill' preter cordas quinque minores springald' sine cordis, et iij. parve' springald' modici valoris, l. arcus de tempore Regis avi, clvj. Arcus de tempore Regis nunc, cxxvj. arbalistas de quibus xxxiiij. arbaliste de cornu ad duos pedes, et ix. de cornu ad unum pedem, et iij. magne arbaliste ad turrim xliij. Baudrys, vij. xx et ix. garbas sagittarum, lviij. Sagittas larg' barbatas, xxv. Haubergons debiles et putrefactos, xxij. basenett' deblies de veteri tour, xj. galee de ferro, de quibus vj. cum visers, xx. capellas de ferro, xxij. basenett' coopertos de coreo de veteri factura deblies et putrefactos, xxv. paria cirotecarum de platis nullius valoris, xij. capellas de nervis de pampilon' depictas, xxx. haketons et gambesons nullius valoris, iij. instrumenta pro arbalistis tendendis, cxviij. Lanceas quarum xviij. sine capitibus, j. cas cum sagittis Saracernorum, ciij. targett' quorum xxxiiij. nullius valoris, j. veterem cistam cum capitibus quarellorum et sagittarum debil', ij. barell', vj. bukett' cum quarellis debilibus non pennatis, j. cistam cum quantitate capitum quarellorum et quondam quantitatem de Calketrappis in j. doleo. m. vj.c et xxviij. garroks de majori forma. iiij. xx garroks de eadem forma sine capitibus. m. vj.c et xxiij. garroks de minori forma.

in the hall: one barrel for rolling armour, in the forge: two maides [NB this is unclear], two bicorns, three sledgehammers, three small hammers, two large (pairs of) tongs, five small (pairs of) tongs, two instruments for heating iron, four iron instruments for making nails, two pairs of bellows, one iron fuller, one grindstone for sharpening iron, and two iron bindings for one bucket, in the armoury: three great springalds with all their fittings save cords, five smaller springalds without cords, and three small spingalds of moderate value, 50 bows from the time of King's grandfather, 156 bows from the time of the present King, 126 crossbows of which 34 are two-foot crossbows of horn (i.e. for two-foot-long bow-staves), and nine one-footers of horn (i.e. for one-foot-long bow-staves), and three large torsion crossbows, 43 baldrics, seven score and nine sheaves of arrows, 58 large barbed arrows, 25 worn out and rotten haubergeons, 22 worn out basinets of the old height, 11 iron helms six of which have visors, 20 chapel de fers, 22 basinets worn out and rotten covered with leather, 25 pairs of plate gauntlets of no value, 12 painted chapels of sinew of Pamplona, 30 aketons and gambesons of no value, three instruments for spanning crossbows, 118 lances – 18 of which lack heads, one case with Saracen arrows, 103 targes – 34 of which are of no value, one old chest with worn out quarrel- and arrowheads, two barrels, six buckets with worn out un-fletched quarrels, one chest with a quantity of quarrel-heads and a certain quantity of caltraps in one dole, 1,628 garrots of larger form, four score garrots of the same form without heads, 1,623 garrots of smaller form

63

Nottingham University Library, Middleton MS, Mi I 40
Goods of Sir Baldwin Fryvill, Nottinghamshire, 13 June 1346

j sel p[u]r lez justes ij helmes j escu ij meyndeffers ou to' maner' autr' herneys apurtenantz x li'

one jousting saddle, two helms, one shield, two manifers with all manner of other appurtenant harness £10

64

York, Borthwick Institute, Abp Reg 10: William Zouche (1342–52), fol. 306r
Will of Sir Ralph Hastings, York, 21 November 1346

p[ro] mortuar' in Abath' vbi sepult' ero meliore' equ' cu' armis competent' om[ni] a arma mea fil' meo Rad[ulph]o Joh[ann]i Courcy unu' hauberk' Edm[un]d' de hastinges nepoti meo de Rouseby & Joh[ann]i de Kyrkeby istu' prisone' que' h' in bello ad diuidend' int[er] eos p[ar] equales porc[i]ones

for mortuary (gift) to the abbey in which I shall be interred my best horse and suitable arms, all my arms to my son Ralph, John Courcy one hauberk, my nephew Edmund Hastings of Roxby and John of Kirkby the (ransom) of a prisoner whom I took in battle divided between them in equal portions

65

York, Borthwick Institute, Abp Reg 10: William Zouche (1342–52), fol. 316v
Will of John, Earl Warenne, 24 June 1347

mon corps destre ent[er]re en Leglise saint Pancratz de Lewes en vne arche p[re]s del haut autier a la p[ar]tie senestre quele ieo ay fait faire quatre de mes g[r]auntz chiuaux destre armetz de mes armes les deux p[u]r guerre & les autr' deuz p[u]r pees deuant mon corps le io[u]r de mon ent[er]rement dount ceux de guerre soient cou[er]tz de fer et q[ue] mesmes les deus chiuaux demoergent & soient donez a Leglise de saint

Pancratz oue mes armes dount ceux q[ue] les chiuacherount s[er]ront armetz mons'
Rob[er]t de Holand les quissers oue le picer de quir q[ue] sount p[u]r mon destrer
mons' Otes de Holand le Cou[er]turs burnitz de plate q[ue] sount p[u]r mon destrer
mons' William de Warenne mon filz tout mon hernoys p[u]r le Jouster

my body be interred in the Church of Saint Pancras of Lewes in an arch near the high
altar on the left side which I have had made, four of my great horses be armed with
my arms – two for war and the other two for (jousts of) peace – processing before
my body on the day of my interment, those horses for war be covered with iron
(mail), these two of these horses be given to the Church of Saint Pancras with my
arms (and armour) with which those who shall ride are armed, Sir Robert Holland
the cuisses [sic] with the leather peytral which were for my destrier, Sir Otes Holland
the burnished (polished steel) covers of plate which were for my destrier, Sir William
Warenne, my son all my harness for jousting

66

London Metropolitan Archives, London Letter-Book F, fol. 142v
Articles of the Heaumers (Plate Armourers) of London, 23 October
1347

nul du mestier ne marchaunde ne teigne seude del mestier deinz la Franchise de
la Citee de Londres taunqe il eyt couuenablement achatee sa fraunchise les vsages
de la Citee s[u]r peyne de p[er]dre la marchaundie p[ur]ces q[ue] auaunt ces hures
ascunes gentz s[u]ruenauntz estraunges se sunt entremys & vn se entremettent a faire
heaumeries p[ar] la ou ils ne seuent pas lour mestier p[ar] q[ue] pluseurs grauntz &
autres du Roialme sunt este occys & periz en lour desante a graunt esclaundre du
mestier ordene est qe nul desormes ne se entremett' ne oeure heaumerie sil ne soit
p[ar] suffisaunt ouerour p[ar] les gardeyns du mestier s[u]r peyne de forfeture bon
couenable & suffisaunt heaumerie al oeps de la chambre troys ou quatre ou plusours
si mestier soit des meillours ou[er]ours du mestier soit eslutz & iuretz a reuler le
mestier com aperit bien & couenablent en seurte & sauuete des grauntz & autres du
Roialm e a p[u]r hon[o]r & p[ro]fit de la Citee & des ouerours del mestier nul app[re]
ntitz ne soit resceu de nul mestr' de meyndre t[er]me q[ue] de vij aunz & ceo sauntz
collusion ou fraude s[u]r peyne a payer a la Chaumbre .C. s. nul du mestier ne nul
autre de la fraunchise ne mette en oueraigne nul qe soit del mestier sil ne soit bon &
leal & p[u]r qi son mestre vodra respoundre de son bon port s[u]r peyne de payer a
la Chambre .xx. s. nul du mestier ne resoun ne mette en ouerayne autri app[re]ntitz
ne autri s[er]uaunt taunq[ue] le t[er]me de son mestre soit pleynement a compli s[u]
r peyne de payer a la Chaumbre xx s. nul app[re]ntitz ou s[er]uaunt du mestier q[ue]
soit endette en ascune su[m]me dargent a son mestre a la fine de son t[er]me ne s[er]
ue de cy enauaunt a nul autre fors a son mestr' ne de dep[ar]t de son s[er]ute soit
en ascune man[er]e resceu taunq[ue] il yet pleynement fait gree a son mestre de sa
dette Et celui q[ue] autre man[er]e resceuiera autri s[er]uaunt ou autri app[ren]titz

en autre man[er]e payera a la Chaumbre .xx. s. heaumerie & autr[e]s arm[ur]s q[ue]
sount forgez de martel q[ue] sount amenez de p[ar] [...] de ceste t[er]re ou dascune
autr' lieu a la Citee a uendre ne sorent de cy en auaunt nule man[er]e mys a la vente
p[ri]uement ne ap[ar]tement taunq[ue] ils soient couenablement p[ar] les gardeyns
& m[ar]chetz de lour signe s[u]r peyne de forfaire les heaum' et les arm[ure]s a la
Chaumbre q[ue] s[er]ount issunt mys a la vente chescun des ou[er]ours eyt son p[ro]
pre signe & m[ar]che issunt q[ue] ne contrefayt autri signe ne m[ar]che s[u]r peyne
de p[er]dre son fraunchise taunq[ue] il le rechatee & fait gree a celui qi signe il eyt
countrefayt & nequedent paye a la chaumbre xl .s. Custodes eiusdem mestreri el[ec]
ti a uis Rob[ertu]s de Shirwode Ric[ard]us Bridde Thom' Canoun

None of this craft or any merchant set up in this craft within the freedom of the City
of London lest he be suitable to purchase his franchise of the customs of this City
on pain of losing the right to sell. Heretofore certain men coming from abroad have
become involved (and continue to be involved) in making heaumeries (plate armour)
where they cannot have their workmanship viewed. Because of this several great men
and others of the realm have been slain and their safety imperilled to the great slander
of the craft. Thus it is ordained that none should henceforth involve themselves in
the work of heaumerie if he be not judged a suitable worker of good, proper, and
suitable heaumerie by the wardens of the craft on pain of forfeiture to the profit of
the Chamber (Guildhall). Three or four (or several) of the best workmen of the craft
should be elected and take turns to regulate the craft as seems good and proper for
the surety and safety of the great men and others of the realm and for the honour and
benefit of the City and the workers of the craft. No apprentice shall be received by
any master of the craft for less than the term of seven years and this without collusion
or fraud on pain of paying the Chamber 100s. None of the craft or anyone of the
freedom (of the City) shall set himself to work lest he be a good and legal member of
the craft, and to ensure this his master must answer for their good behaviour or pay
a fine of 20s. to the Chamber. None of the craft shall put to work any apprentice or
other servant until the term of his apprenticeship be fully complete on pain of paying
the Chamber 20s. No apprentice or servant of the craft who is in debt of any sum
of money can demand of his master the termination of his apprenticeship, nor may
he serve anyone else save his master before this, nor shall his oath be received in any
way until he has completely settled his debts with his master. Whosoever shall receive
– in any manner – any other servant or other apprentice shall pay the Chamber 20s.
Henceforth heaumerie and other armour that is forged with the hammer brought to
this land from elsewhere to be sold in the City shall not be in any way put up for sale
(be it privately or openly) until it has been found to be suitable by the wardens and
marked with their sign on pain of the forfeiture of the heaumerie and armour to the
Chamber so that they may be put up for sale. Each of the craftsmen must have their
own sign and mark and none counterfeit another's sign or mark on pain of losing
his freedom until he has bought it back and settled his debt to he whose sign he
has counterfeited and, nevertheless, to pay the Chamber 40s. Wardens of this Craft
elected viz.: Robert Sherwood, Richard Bridde, Thomas Canoun

67

Edinburgh University Library, MS 183, fol. 95v–fol. 96r and fol. 127v–fol. 127r
Mythical Royal Ladies send Letters of Challenge for their Champions to Joust, Composed at the Court of Edward III, 1350s

From Queen Pantesilia of Persia to Queen Florippé of France and Flanders, Princess of the Provinces of Little Troy, Written at the Castle of the Maidens

de Calangis pacis
pur la tresgrand fame & renoune q[ue] de iour en io[u]r se passe & vole des excellentes & famouses filz del bon Taro[ye]n Brutus nez & norriz en v[ost]re Court en queux honur & armes se delitent a demurrer Nous vous envoions vn n[os]tre Nurry venour de noz veisines forestes & desertz poy ou petit sachant si de chiens ou de chace noun Empriant tresentierement de trestout n[ost]re cuer de comaunder a lonurable Esquier demurrant en v[ost]re Court q[ui] porte lescu dargent oue sept losenges de goules p[er]se ouec vn molet de sable de lui deliu[er]er de sys copes de launce assis en bases selles en v[ost]re p[re]sence cest iour mesme tost ap[re]s manger Et celuy q[ui] plusours foiz voide la seele deinz les sys copees doigne a son compaigno[u]n vne anele dore en guerdo[u]n

Of the Challenges for (Jousts of) Peace
Not a single day passes without tell of the great fame and renown of the excellent and famous sons of the good Trojan Brutus born and raised in your court where there is great delight in honour and (feats of) arms. Thus we send you a hunter – as he was raised in nearby forests and deserts he knows of little else but hounds and hunting – praying that you command the honourable squire of your court who bears the (heraldic) shield argent seven lozenges persée gules with a mullet sable (Henry Braybrooke, Squire of the Black Prince) to deliver six lance thrusts seated on low saddles in your presence today; immediately after dining. Whoever receives the most knocks from their saddle within the (running of the) six thrusts must give his companion a gold ring as reward.

From Empress Judith of Egypt and Arabia to Queen Phelippé of King Arthur's Realm of the Lands of Great Britain, Written at the Marvellous Manner of Mount Sinai

de Calangis pacis
pur ce q[ue] de certain la sourse et fontaigne damour & darmes se tient toutdys en v[ost]re Courte come fount les oyseux en leir & les mariners deinz le mere sale de ce nous prent a purpose & tresgraund penser denvoier n[ost]re chier & bien ame

Esquier Bohors de Bassenne deu[er]s v[ost]re tr[es]honourable famose feste empriant
t[re]sentierme[n]t de cuer a v[ost]re roial noblay de comaunder a vaillant Esquier le
Vssher de v[ost]re Chambre le lundys matyn de lui deliu[er]er de tauntz des copees
de launce en bases scelles come ils purrount corere la longe nuyt de yuere la clere lune
luissant saunz escuier ou seruitour forsq[ue] soulement soy mesmes

Of the Challenges for (Jousts of) Peace
As birds fly in the air and sailors sail the salty sea so everyone considers your court
to be the source and fountain of love and (feats of) arms. To this end, it has thus
occurred to us to send our squire Bohors de Bassenne to your famous fête (of
jousting) praying you command the valiant squire the Usher of your Chamber on
Monday morning to deliver him (Bohors) as many lance thrusts in low saddles as they
can run throughout the long winter's moonlit night – just themselves alone without
squires or attendants.

From Niolas Queen of Nubia, of the Philistines, and the Pharaoh's People to
Elianore, Daughter of the King of the Romans, Princess of Great Britain, Written
at the Marvellous Manner of Mount Sinai

Purce que la Chiualrie dautres roiaux roiaumes enuers voz gentils genz darmes
nadautre comparison que les estoilles petites & meins enuers la lune lusaunte &
graunde de ce nous vient tresgraunde ioie & plesaunce denuoier deuers vostre tresfamouse court vne n[ost]re chier & bien ame Escuier nomez Sergramour lui desarmez
empriaunt que please a v[ost]re noble noblay dassigner vn de voz meillourz iolifs
ioustours li quel que plesir vous soit present par mains ou par toute v[ost]re festiuale
fest a le feste de Noel de lui deliuerer de sys coupes de launce le mardy prochein assys
en bases seeles saunz estre en nulle manere liez en v[ost]re presence pur lui enseigner
coment les chiualerouses chiualers de v[ost]re court soloient enseigner lour filz &
enfauntz de lour assaier as selles tenir

As the stars are outshone by the brighter light of the moon so the chivalrous (men)
of other realms cannot compare to your courteous men of arms. I take great joy and
pleasure to send, unarmed, to your court our squire named Sergramour praying that it
please your noblesse to assign one of your best jolly jousters at your fête (of jousting) at
the Feast of the Nativity to deliver him six lance thrusts seated on low saddles being in
no manner attached (thereto); in your presence. Thus he may learn how the chivalrous
knights of your court train their sons and youngsters to stay in the saddle.

From Empress Emely of Europe and Judea to Iscete, Eldest Daughter of the Line
of Aeneas, Queen of the Isles West of Greece, and of Great Britain, Written at the
Castle of Delight in the Realm of Joy

pur ce q[ue] nous auons du vraie entenduz que vous tiendrez v[ost]re tresfamouse
court plainere en v[ost]re paloys de plesaunte pres de v[ost]re Citee de Petite Troie
& auons vn n[ost]re treschier Cousin ioesne doncelle norriz en n[ost]re Chambre li

quel nous enuoions par deuers vous empriauntz de comaunder le meillour Chiualer deinz lage de cynquante ans & le meillour Chiualer deinz lage de quarante ans & le meillour Chiualer deinz lage de trente ans p[re]sent en v[ost]re tresfamouse feste que chescun des troys Chiualers lui plese deliuer de sys coupes de launce assys pur lui enseigner de soi tenir en son selle Nous reenuoiant si vous esperez nul bon en lui & sil soit vaillaunt de visiter les courtes roiaux destraunges roiaumes

Verily we have heard that you shall openly hold your famous court in your Palace of Pleasure near your City of Little Troy. Thus we send you one of our beloved cousins – young Doncelle – raised in our Chamber (i.e. close household) praying that you command the best knight under the age of 50, and the best knight under the age of 40, and the best knight under the age of 30 attending your famous fête (of jousting). All three of these knights are to deliver him six lance thrusts seated in such a manner that he may learn to keep himself in the saddle. Send him back to us if you find such good in him that he might be valiant enough to visit the royal courts of (other) foreign realms.

From Philippé, Daughter of Aeneas, Empress of Europe to the (unnamed) Queen of Albion, Princess of the Chivalrous People, written at the Unknown Castle

No[us] enuoions par deuers vous n[ost]re chier & foiau Chiualer mons' Frik de Frikaunce pur deliu[er]er les Chalenges que lui ount estee fait par lui noble vaillaunt sire de Chastillon ioesne ioli ioustour en v[ost]re roial court vous requerant honurement si dieu doint grace a n[ost]re dit Chiualer de parfournir le ditz chalenges saunz perdre sa vie ou sauntee qil ce face vous please comaunder le plus ioesne chiualer de lonurable compaignie du Jarter qest au present en v[ost]re noble court pur deliuerer n[ost]re dit Chiualer de troys coupes de launce sanz hurtier des chiuaux pur lui enseigner de soi le mieux adresser en fait darmes

We send you our dear and loyal knight Sir Frik de Frikaunce to deliver the challenges issued to him by the noble valiant Lord of Chastillon – a young, jolly jouster at your royal court – honourably requiring that, if God gives grace to our knight to perform (the feats of arms contained in) these challenges without facing the loss of life or limb, you command the youngest knight of the honourable companions of (the Order of) the Garter currently at your noble court to deliver our said knight three lance thrusts without the horses colliding so he may better learn to improve in (future) feats of arms.

68

Kew, National Archives, E 101/624/34
Armour purchased by Johan the Hauberger for King Edward III, 15 August, year not stated

pur les armours le Roy deus sakes & ij bahous iiij mars ij pair de coffers le vn pair pur xxiij s. lautre xiiij s. iij pair des bowges xx s. xij sakes pur freyere les armours xxiiij s. ij collerettes de pissaigne pur le corps le Roy xx s. ij collerettes ouertz pur son bazynet xxiiij s. ij peles de rouge quire vj s. quire achate & bockeles pur garnir iij pair couerturs de fere vj s. j corset & le brayel couere du sandale pur garnier vn paire de pawnse & braze d[em]j mark' j autre pair fait du quir iij s. pur j male de cordewane v s. iij liuers fyl de fere ij s. iij lj fyl de Letoun xviij d. j coffynet pur le chapew le Roy de quire boyly xij s. vn autre coffinet de quir boyly ix s. iij coffyns sengle vj s. vne charet alowe de Loundres a Nichole par vij iours pur les armours pur le corps le Roy xvij s. vj d. pur garnyr ij espays pur le Roy viij s. furbyr xxv espays xviij s. furbyr xxiiij chapewes & Hewmes xx s. blaunchyr C & lx hawbergouns & iiij pair des couerturs xxiiij s.

for the King's armour: two sacks and two cart covers 4 marks, two pairs of coffers one pair 23s. the other 14s., three pairs of bags 20s., 12 sacks for scouring the armour 24s., two pisan collars for the King's body 20s., two open collars for his basinet 24s., two hides of red leather for 6s., leather and buckles bought to equip three pairs of iron (horse) covers 6s., one corset and the brayer covered with sendal (lightweight silk or very fine linen) to equip a pair of paunces and (mail) sleeves half a mark, one other pair (of corsets and brayers) made of leather 3s., one pack of cordwain (high-quality Spanish leather) 5s., 3lb of iron wire 2s., 3lb of latten wire 18d., one coffer of cuir bouilli for the King's chapel de fer 12s., another coffer of cuir bouilli 9s., three plain coffers 6s., hire of one cart from London to Lincoln for seven days 17s. 6d., equipping two swords for the King 8s., furbishing 25 swords 18s., 24 chapel de fers and helms 20s., scouring 160 haubergeons and four pairs of (horse) covers 24s.

69

Chronicon Galfridi le Baker de Swynebroke, ed. E. M. Thompson (Oxford, 1889), pp. 113–14

A Chronicler describes a Duel between Frenchman Thomas de La Marche and Cypriot Giovanni Visconti, Palace of Westminster, 6 October 1350

Thomas in declarationem suae justitiae ejus adversarium superavit non tamen occidit quia nec potuit sufficienter armatum penetrare aliquo tormento invasiuo praeterquam in facie quam habuit nudam Post nempe hastiludia et pedestres congressus luctando simul in aream profusi Thomas quibusdam stimulis curtis et acutis quos manum dextram comprimendo digitorum nodi radicales id est chirotecis laminatis expresserunt et eos moderni vocant gadelinges nudam Iohannis faciem wlneravit E contra Johannes nullum tormentum habuit iacta curtum quo posset laedere faciem Thomae et hinc horribiliter ipso exclamante regio precepto duellum cessavit et Thome victoria adiudicatur qui victum Iohannem principi Walliae dederat captiuum atque suam armaturam sancto Georgio in ecclesia sancti Pauli optulit devote

Thomas defeated his adversary in his appeal for justice. He did not kill him, however, because he could not sufficiently penetrate his armour anywhere he might inflict pain: save his face which was left bare. After jousting well they fought on foot; brutally wrestling on the ground. Thomas injured Giovanni in his bare face with certain short, sharp spikes protruding from the round knobs of the right gauntlet's finger scales – these are called 'gadlings' in modern parlance. Giovanni, on the other hand, feeling no pain, had a short throwing (weapon) with which he would be able to strike Thomas's face. Dreading this, the King shouted the order to halt the duel and adjudged the victory to Thomas, who presented his defeated opponent Giovanni to the Prince of Wales, yet offered up his (Giovanni's) armour in devotion to Saint George in Saint Paul's Cathedral.

70

Kew, National Archives, E 36/278
Register of Edward the Black Prince, Calais, Gascony, London, Plymouth, Smithfield, and Windsor, 25 January 1351–24 January 1366

donez a Paulee tut vn herneys entier de maille liuerez a mons' Thomas de Dreuelee vn harneys entier de maille liuerez al Esquier Trussell j harneys entier de maille Watelot j harnoys entier de maille Henr' Breybrok j herneys entier de maille & j ketilhat Jakelet Piper' j ketilhat mons' Henr' Em deliu[er]a a vn Duchom[m]e j haub[er]geon j bacinet mons' Johan Dentree j peir plates cou[er]tz de noir veluet mons' Hugh de Wrotteslee j peir plates couertz de noir veluet vn heraud darmes j haub[er]geon j ketilhat al Frere mons' Johan Chaundos j haub[er]geon j ketilhat mons' James Daudelee j haub[er]geon mons' Baudewyn Buttord j harneys de maille dasser vn Duch chiualer j haubergeon dasser Olneye de la Chaumbre la Roine j haub[er]geon mons' Joh[a]n Chaundos iij bacynetz Thedryk van Dale j auentaill mons' Berth[olom]u Burgherssh j habergeon dasser James Daudelee j peir greues j peir vauntbratz mons' Johan de Lille j long sutill espeie p[u]r la guerr' Henr' Em j bacinet j auentaill liu[er]ez dep[ar] le Seign[eu]r p[ar] les mains sire Henr' de Blacbourn j harneys entier a Thederik van Dale j habergeon a Joh[a]n Chaundos j peir plates cou[er]tz de blu camaca a mons' Joh[a]n de Gystell j hab[er]geon a j autre Duchman j peir plates a Nich[ol]as Bonde j peir plates cou[er]tz oue blu veluet Bekesfeld ij habergeons j palet j auentaill j pair gauntz de plate vn Duchman j peir plates cou[er]tz de noir veluet pouudrez oue pennes Berth[olom]u de Burgherssh j bacinet oue j vicer Baudewyn Buttord j peir gauntz de plate mons' Hugh Griffyn j peir plates cou[er]tz de reuge veluet Berth[olom]u Burgherssh j hab[er]geon done a vn Chivaler Dalmaigne j baselard donez a Plomuthe a Baudewyn Buttord j peir gauntz de plate a mons' Johan Sully j peir gauntz de plate a Johan Chaundos j peir gauntz de plate & j peir quisseux au dit Johan j bacinet oue j Noumbrer a Sharnesfeld j habergeon a mons' Esmon Vauncy j peir gauntz de plate & j bacinet a mons' Peytenyn j pair gauntz de plate a mons' Rog' Cotesford j peir gaunz de plate a mons' William Soty j peir gaunz de plate a Johan Chaundos j habergeon a Geffrey Pauely j hab[er]geon a mons' Renaud de Cobham j bacinet Counte de

Oxeneford j peir gauntz de fer Baudewyn Buttord j peir gaunz de feer mons' Joh[a]
n de Cheureston' j peir gaunz de feer Counte de Suff j bacinet oue j auentaill dasser
James Daudelee j bacinet oue j viser j Nasell j auentaill j peir bratz courz de maille
dasser seign[eu]r de Mussedean j peir gaunz de plate orrez mons' Thomas de Felton'
j peir gauntz de plate mons' Edward Courtenay j peir plates Counte de Salesbirs j
bacineut oue j auentaill Berth[olom]u j espeie s[eigneu]r Eamond j bacinet oue j viser
j auentaill & j peir plates Counte de Salesbirs j peir plates oue pennes mons' Neel
Loryngg j bacinet oue j viser Barth[olom]u Burgherssh j peir gauntz de plate Joh[a]n
Chaundos j espeie mons' de Mounferaunt j peir gauntz de plate Baudewyn Buttord
j bacinet Thederyk Dale j entier harneys de maille James Daudele j auentaill dasser
Plates p[ar] la deliu[er]aunce meistr' Rich' Platemaker donez au Duc de Lancastr' j
peir plates p[u]r les justes & j brestplate doner [a] Gascoigne a mons' William t[r]
ussell j Cou[er]ture de chiual de maille al reto[u]rner mons[eigneu]r de Gascoign' a
les Justes q[ue] le Counte de la March' fist crier ap[re]s la feste de Wyndesore lan du
regne le Roi xxxij au Sign[eu]r de Grimegg' j paire plates couertz oue drap door &
j Brestplate & j paire vices liu[er]es au Seign[eu]r de Mountferaunte j seale p[u]r les
Justes ij stuffes p[u]r Justes a ij launces a Barth[olom]u de Burgherssh j seale p[u]r les
Justes & j Escu p[u]r les Justes mons' Rob[er]t de Nevill ij Rierrebraz Dasser countre
les Justes de Wyndesore a la feste de Wyndesore Counte de Salesbri' j heaume oue
vn cower garniz dargent & j seint[u]re al Barber del seute garniz dargent & orrez
le dymenge p[ro]sch' deuant la Pasq[ue] en lan le Roi xxxiij mons' Aleyn Cheyne j
haub[er]geon le xxj iour de may p[ro]sch' ens[uiv]ant s[eignue]r de Ware j heaume
p[u]r les Justes le dit iour p[ar] comand' James Daudelegh' mons' Rich' Benton' j
espeie Ducs de lancastre q[u]aunt il vient de Normandie p[ar] comand' le seign[eu]
r j paire plates countre les Justes de Smethefeld lan xxxiij Susdit feut a p[re]s[en]tez
a mons' Jahan Gistels p[ar] comand' le s[eigneu]r vn paire paunz & j Pisan Dasser
les queux il ne voet render arriere a les Justes de Smethefeld countre les Justes [pour
la] mariage le Counte de Richemond Barth[olom]u de Burghersse j escu q[ue] estoit
cornee de nouel s[eigneu]r de la Ware p[ar] la deliu[er]aunce James Daudelegh' j
auentaille Countre lassumption n[ost]re dame lan xxxiij James daudelegh meismes
prist en la Garderobe vn haub[er]geon lendemayn mons' a dona a le Roi vn Espeye
donez p[ar] comand' le s[eigneu]r a Gerard de Gascoingn' j paire Jambes j peyre
quisseux j peire poleyns & vn harneys entier de maille j peyre plates cou[er]ts de
veluet blu j Bacynet j peyre gauntz vn paire gauntz [sic] vn paire vauntbraz de quir
boillez j paire rierre braz dasser & j haube[r]geon liu[er]ez au filz Esmon Rose vn
legier haub[er]geoun p[ar] comand' James Daudelegh James daudelee j haberg' a
le Roi j espeie Berth[olom]u de Burgerssh j espee Bernard de Gascoigne j peaire
iaumbes j paire quisseux j peaires poleyns j herneis entier de maill' j peaire plates
cou[er]tes de veluet blu j bacynet oue j viser j peaire gauntz de plate j paire vanbraz de
querboill' j peaire rerebras dasser & j hab[er]g' deli[er]e au filz Esmon Rose j haub[er]
g' leg' mons' Arnaud de la Bret j bacynet oue vnes auentaill a Caleis p[ar] comand'
mons[eigneu]r mons' Rich' destafford j bacynet oue vn viser a Caleis Berth[olom]u
de Berghersh j bacynet j paire gauntz de plate Henr' Bernard j hauberg' en Fraunce
done a Berth[olom]u de Burgherssh j espee le harnies de quel espee de soi garnise

dargent feict donne au Counte de Richemond donn' en lound[re]s a mons' Johan
Celly j bacynet oue j nombrer & j espee James daudelee j paire gauntz de plates quant
les counseil feust a Caleis Nich' Peko j haub[er]g' p[u]r aler en Gascoinge Rog' des
Saham j hauberg' Stafford j peaire pauntz Berth[olom]u de Bergherssh j test' garnise
de laton & j pic' garnise des bolles large dasser

given to [Geoffrey] Paveley a complete harness of mail, delivered to Sir Thomas
Drevely a complete harness of mail, delivered to Squire Trussell one complete harness
of mail, Watelot one complete harness of mail, Henry Braybrooke one complete
harness of mail and a kettlehat, Jakelet Piper one kettlehat, Sir Henry Eam delivered
to a Dutchman one haubergeon, one basinet, Sir John Aintree a pair of plates
covered with black velvet, Sir Hugh Wrottesley a pair of plates covered with black
velvet, a herald-at-arms one haubergeon, one kettlehat, Sir John Chandos's brother
one haubergeon, one kettlehat, Sir James Audley one haubergeon, Sir Baudewyn
Buttord one harness of steel mail, a Dutch knight one haubergeon of steel, Olneye
of the Queen's Chamber one haubergeon, Sir John Chandos three basinets, Thedryk
van Dale one aventail, Sir Bartholomew Burghersh one steel haubergeon, James
Audley one pair of greaves, one pair of vambrace, Sir Johan de Lille one long thin
sword for war, Henry Eam one basinet, one aventail, delivered on behalf of the
Lord by the hands of Sir Henry Blackburn one complete harness, Thedryk van
Dale one haubergeon, John Chandos one pair of plates covered with blue camaca
(silk fabric), Sir Johan de Gystell one haubergeon, another Dutchman one pair of
plates, Nicholas Bonde one pair of plates covered with blue velvet, Bekesfeld two
haubergeons, one pallet, one aventail, one pair of plate gauntlets, a Dutchman
one pair of plates covered with black velvet powdered (decorated) with (heraldic)
feathers, Bartholomew Burghersh one basinet with one visor, Baudewyn Buttord one
pair of plate gauntlets, Sir Hugh Griffin one pair of plates covered with red velvet,
Bartholomew Burghersh one haubergeon, a knight of Germany one baselard, given
at Plymouth to Baudewyn Buttord one pair of plate gauntlets, Sir John Sully one
pair of plate gauntlets, John Chandos one pair of plate gauntlets and one pair of
cuisses, this John one basinet with one umbrer, Sharenesfeld one haubergeon, Sir
Edmund Vauncy one pair of plate gauntlets and one basinet, Lord Peytenyn one
pair of plate gauntlets, Sir Roger Cotesford one pair of plate gauntlets, Sir William
Soty one pair of plate gauntlets, John Chandos one haubergeon, Geoffrey Paveley
one haubergeon, Sir Reginald Cobham one basinet, the Earl of Oxford one pair of
iron gauntlets, Baudewyn Buttord one pair of iron gauntlets, Sir John Cheverston
one pair of iron gauntlets, the Earl of Suffolk one basinet with one steel aventail,
James Audley one basinet with one visor, one nasal, one aventail, one pair of short
sleeves of steel mail, Lord of Mussenden one gilt pair of plate gauntlets, Sir Thomas
Felton one pair of plate gauntlets, Sir Edward Courteney one pair of plates, the Earl
of Salisbury one basinet with one aventail, Bartholomew one sword, Sir Edmund
[Vauncy] one basinet with one visor, one aventail, and one pair of plates, the Earl
of Salisbury one pair of plates (decorated) with feathers, Sir Neil Loring one basinet
with one visor, Bartholomew Burghersh one pair of plate gauntlets, John Chandos

one sword, the Lord of Montferrat one pair of plate gauntlets, Baudewyn Buttord one basinet, Thedryk van Dale one complete harness of mail, James Audley one steel aventail. Pairs of plates delivered by Master Richard Platemaker: given to the Duke of Lancaster one pair of plates for the jousts and one breastplate, given at Gascony to Sir William Trussell one horse cover of mail, on the return of my Lord from Gascony to the jousts which the Earl of March had cried after the fête at Windsor in the 32nd regnal year [1358–59] to the Lord of Grimbergen one pair of plates covered with cloth of gold and one breastplate and one pair of vices (poss. to attach the breastplate to the pair of plates beneath), the Lord of Montferrat one saddle for the jousts, two staves for jousts for two lances, Bartholomew Burghersh one saddle for the joust and one shield for the jousts, Sir Robert Neville two steel rerebrace for the jousts at Windsor, given to the Earl of Salisbury at the fête at Windsor one helm with one cover garnished with silver and one strap for a barber (i.e. reinforcing plate) in the same suite garnished with silver and gilded, on the Sunday next before Easter in the 33rd regnal [1359] year given by order of the Lord Prince to Sir Alan Cheyne one haubergeon, on 21 May next following to the Lord De la Warr one helm for the jousts, on this day by order of James Audley given to Sir Richard Benton one sword, the Duke of Lancaster when he came from Normandy by order of the Lord Prince one pair of plates for the jousts at Smithfield in the 33rd year aforesaid, Sir Johan de Gystell was presented by order of the Lord Prince one pair of paunces and one steel pisan which he does not want to return, at the jousts at Smithfield for the jousts for the nuptials of the Earl of Richmond, Bartholomew Burghersh was given one shield which was newly-horned, the Lord De la Warr by James Audley one aventail, at the Assumption of Our Lady in the 33rd year [15 August 1359] James Audley himself took from the Wardrobe one haubergeon, the next day my Lord Prince gave the King one sword, given by the Lord's order to Gerard Gascoigne one pair of jambers, one pair of cuisses, one pair of poleyns, and one complete harness of mail, one pair of plates covered with blue velvet, one basinet, one pair of gauntlets, one pair of gauntlets [sic], one pair of vambrace of cuir bouilli, one pair of rerebrace of steel, and one haubergeon, delivered by order of James Audley to Edmund Rose's son a light haubergeon, James Audley one haubergeon, the King one sword, Bartholomew Burghersh one sword, Bernard Gascoigne one pair of jambers, one pair of cuisses, one pair of poleyns, one complete harness of mail, one pair of plates covered with blue velvet, one basinet with one visor, one pair of plate gauntlets, one pair of vambrace of cuir bouilli, one pair of rerebrace of steel, and one haubergeon, delivered to Edmund Rose's son one light haubergeon, Sir Arnaud de la Bret one basinet with one aventail at Calais on my Lord's order, Sir Richard Stafford one basinet with one visor at Calais, Bartholomew Burghersh one basinet, one pair of plate gauntlets, Henry Bernard one haubergeon (given) in France, given to Bartholomew Burghersh one sword the harness of this sword garnished with silver which he gave to the Earl of Richmond, in London to John Sully one basinet with one umbrer and one sword, James Audley one pair of plate gauntlets when the Council was held at Calais, Nicholas Peko one haubergeon to go to Gascony, Roger Saham one haubergeon, [Richard] Stafford one pair of paunces,

Bartholomew Burghersh one tester garnished with latten and one peytral garnished
with large silver balls

71

Norwich, Norfolk Record Office, NCR 5C–6, 7, 9
Muster Roll of the Men of the City of Norwich, Norfolk, 28 July 1355

Constabular' plen' armat' Will[el]m[u]s skie vn' constabular' armat' cu' dublet' plat'
& bacinett'
    cu' pisan' & Auentaill & bratz & Cerotec' Joh[an]nes de Canston' alt' constabular'
armat' eod[e]m modo j sagitt' Thom' Cole vn' vall' de Nowico armat' eod' mod' j sagitar'
    dimid' armat' Thom' de hornyngg' vint' armat' cu' dublett' plat' bacinett' cu'
Auental' & cerot' de plate'
    sagittar' Will[elmu]s de Frecan' Arcus sagitt' glad' & Cutell'
    Centenar' Joh[an]nes mounfort Centenar' armat' ut sup[r]a cu' hast' & Baner'
vinternar' Thom' de hornyngg' vyntener' armat' cu hasta & pyncell' Joh[an]nes de
heuyngham' wyex glad' & Cutell' Ric[ard]us taillo[u]r cu' glad' bacul' & Cutell'
Rob[er]tus Robleyerd cu' bacul' & Cutell' Will[elmu]s Terneys cu' wyex glad' & Cut'
Will[elmu]s labyngheth wyex glad' & Cutell'
    Rob' de Bungeye plene arm' cu' p[our]point brac[...] pisan' plat' bas' cu' auental'
vaunbras & rerbras cuters ferr' glad' cutell' Wa[...] plene armat' d[imid]i armat' sagittar'
Petrus de Woster plene armat' Will[elmu]s de Buston' d[imid]j armat' hug' de tostes
plene armat' Ric' de Colton' d[imid]j armat' Thomas de Conesforde plene armat'
    Centenar' Joh' de Welbe plene armat' Will[elmu]s de Worstede plene armat'
Ric[ard]us de multon' d[imid]j armat' henr' de Valle plene armat' [...] brac' plat' bac'
cu' auent[...] [...]th[u]s de Paletine d[imid]j armat' Joh' de hauenham j ho' armat'
cu' p[our]point plat' u[e]l haub' bacin' cu' auental' & Cirotec' glad' & Cutell' Joh'
Pere j h' armat' Joh' de Welbourn' j ho' armat' cu' p[our]point plat' bac' cu' auent'
glad' & Cut'
    Ho[m]ines ad arma armati sunt cu' p[our]poys & plate vel alketonium haub[er]
ionem Bacinettu' ad Aventail' Cirotec' de plat' glad' & cutell' Joh[ann]es de
heuyngham agistat' & arrayat' est ad vnu' ho[m]inem pedit' armatu' cu p[ou]rpoint
plat' u[e]l Alketonu' cu' hauberion' Bacinettu' cu' Auentall' Cirotecis de plate glad' &
cutell' Joh[ann]es Ric[ard]us de harpele d[imid]j armat' vidz haketon' plat' bac' cu'
auent' Cerotec' ferr' glad' & cult'

Fully-armed constables: William Skie one constable fully-armed with doublet, (pair
of) plates, and basinet with pisan and aventail, and (mail) sleeves, and gauntlets, John
Cranston another constable armed in the same manner (provides) one archer
    Half-armed: Thomas Horning, vintenar armed with doublet, (pair of) plates,
basinet with aventail, and plate gauntlets
    Archers: William Frecan bow, arrows, sword, and knife
    Centenars: John Mounfort, centenar armed as above (half-armed) with spear and banner

Vintenars: Thomas Horning, vintenar armed with lance and pennoncel, John Hevingham battle axe, sword, and knife, Richard Tailor with sword, staff (or club), and knife, Robert Robleyerd with staff and knife, William Terneys with battle axe and knife, William Labyngheth battle axe, sword, and knife

Robert Bungeye fully-armed with pourpoint, (mail) sleeves, pisan, (pair of) plates, basinet with aventail, iron vambrace and rerebrace, couters, sword, knife, Walter [...] fully-armed (provides) a half-armed (man) and archer, Peter Woster fully-armed, William of Buston half-armed, Hugh Tostes fully-armed, Richard Colton half-armed, Thomas Conesford fully-armed

Centenars: John Welbe fully-armed, William Worsted fully-armed, Richard Multon half-armed, Henry Valle fully-armed (with) (mail) sleeves, (pair of) plates, basinet with aventail [...] Paletin half-armed, John Havenham (provides) one man-at-arms with pourpoint, (pair of) plates or haubergeon, basinet with aventail, and gauntlets, sword and knife, John Pere (provides) one man-at-arms, John Welbourn (provides) one man-at-arms with pourpoint, (pair of) plates, basinet with aventail, sword and knife

Men-at-arms shall be armed with pourpoint and (pair of) plates or aketon (and) haubergeon, basinet and aventail, plate gauntlets, sword and knife, John Hevingham is arrayed as one armed footman with pourpoint, (pair of) plates or aketon with haubergeon, basinet with aventail, plate gauntlets, sword and knife, Richard Harpele half-armed viz.: aketon, (pair of) plates, basinet with aventail, iron gauntlets, sword and knife

72

London Metropolitan Archives, London Letter-Book G, fol. 45r
Goods of Stephen le Northerne, Upholder (dealer in household items), Parish of Saint Michael Cornhill, City of London, 6 January 1356

vnu' par cerotecar[um] de ferro & vnu' par de braces vj d' vnu' par de plates vnu' bacenet vnu' cultell' vna p[ar]ma v s' xv secur' p[ro] guerra vij s'

one pair of plate gauntlets and one pair of bracers 6d. one pair of plates, one basinet, one knife, one *parma* (Latin for a small, round, hand-held shield, prob. a buckler or targe) 5s. 15 axes for war 7s.

73

Liber Pluscardensis, ed. F. J. H. Skene, 2 vols (Edinburgh, 1877–80), I, pp. 300–1
A Chronicler recounts an Incident in the Aftermath of the Battle of Poitiers, 19 September 1356

Archibald Douglas was a natural son of Sir James Douglas. Sir James spent a lifetime fighting the English. On the death of his half-brother William, Archibald became Earl of Douglas. Known as Archibald 'the Grim', he and his dynasty were mortal foes to their enemies to the South.

Archebaldus vero de Douglas juvenis et bene armatus captus est a quibusdam eum magnum dominum propter armaturam putantibus de quo quia bastardus erat modicum compotum tenuerunt amici ejus Dum autem de sero venerunt captivi ad hospicium apud villam de Poictiers quidam nobilis miles dominus Willelmus de Ramsay de Colluthi ductus est in quodam loco ubi erat Archibaldus de Douglas nobilibus armis spoliatus cui dixerunt magistri capturis eorum Ecce hic habemus filium cujusdam potentis domini nobilissime armatum Quem intuens dictus miles dixit O proditor ribalde cui furatus es arma domini tui consanguinei mei Maledicta sic illa hora in qua nauts fuist Nam tota die quaeri te fecit et non inveniens in campo nudus egrediens transfixus est a sagitta volante quod oculis meis vidi Ipse enim Archibaldus niger erat nec aspectu formosus sed magis toto similabatur quam nobili cui iratus quasi furiose se fingens motum allocutus est dictus miles Veni huc dicens decalciare prius botas meas et vade poatea per campum in tali loco inter occisos et quaere corpus domini tui ut sacrise sacro sepultur crastino potermis commendare illud Alter vero percipiens prudenciam militis similiter finixit se tremebundum et transiens ministrabat ei eripiens unum ex botis suis quam concito miles in manu capiens eundem Archibaldum graviter circa buccas verberavit cui Anglici occurrentes dixerunt Cui ita nobilem sic vilipenditis eum sic injuriose verberando Quibus miles respondens dixit Non enim nobilis est ymmo lixa in coquina domini sui Quod credentes alii circumstantes eundem pro xl solidis redemptum dimiserunt Et sic prudenter dictus miles eum de minibus eorum extraxit quod si ipsi eum connouissent pro pondere suo auri non utique eum deliberassent

Archibald (truly a Douglas, although as he was a bastard his friends thought little of him) being a youth and well armed was captured by those who thought him to be a great lord on account of the armour he bore. In the evening, whilst the captives came to lodgings in the town of Poitiers, a certain noble knight Lord William Ramsay of Colluthy was led into a certain place where Archibald Douglas had been stripped of his noble arms. The masters with their captives said to him (Sir William): 'Here we have the son of some great lord, most nobly armed.' On hearing this, this knight exclaimed: 'Oh treacherous scoundrel! Cursed be the hour of your birth! Because you have armed yourself in *my* kinsman's – *your* lord's – armour, he searched for you all day and, as he was unable to find you in camp, marched unarmed and was struck by a flying arrow; this I saw with my own eyes!' Now Archibald was of a dark complexion and not particularly handsome but was very well built like a noble. This knight was so enraged and furious he was roused to bark: 'Come here and remove my boots! Now go and scour the field for your lord's corpse amongst the dead so that we might arrange his sacred burial this day!' Now this knight was truly canny. As soon as he had stopped trembling, he lunged – grabbing one of his boots – then proceeded to mercilessly beat Archibald about the mouth with it. Seeing this commotion, the

Englishmen exclaimed: 'Why do you beat this noble so badly and berate him so viciously?' To which the knight replied: 'Why, *he* is no noble! He is but a scullion in his lord's kitchen!' And so believing this, they released him for a ransom of 40 shillings. This knight was very canny to have had him released so cheaply: had they known who he was, they would not have ransomed him for his weight in gold.

74

Mons, Archives de l'État, Chartrier des archives de la ville, no. 146
Inventory of the Arms and Armour of Guillaume, Count of Hainaut, in the Armoury of Mons Castle, County of Hainaut, 15 August 1358

ij paires de plattes de wiere les vnes couuiertes dun drap dor les autres dun bleu velluiel j Escut des armez le Conte willaume ij paires de plattes a jouster de coy li vne est couuierte dun noir velluiel li autre dun bleu vne paire de plattes a jouster couuiertes dun drap dor vne paire de plattes a jouster ij paires de plattes de wiere des armes de haynau vij paires de plattes de le viese maniere vne paire de plattes de Rouge velluiel a ij kainnes dargent & j billet dargent vne paire de grandes plattes couuieretes dune Rouge torse viij haubrigons & j de deliet fier vj pans sen y a j de jaserant viij paires de manches les ij paires de jaserant ij autres paires de deliet fier ix barbieres les iij de jaserant ij collerettes de fort fier et vne de deliet fier iiij paires de kauchons de wiere vne paire doree vne paire de kauchons de tournoy & j despareil vne paire de longhes kauces de deliet fier de maille vne paire de plus gros fier de celi maniere et vne kauche despareille vne coiffe de le viese maniere a fleur de lis de laiton ij paires de musekins de jaserant iiij paires daut' de fier & vne piecette de deliet fier j auketon de noir kamouskat sa j haubrigon deuens vj poitrines a jouster vj hiaumes a jouster et vj baiuieres iij rondelles iiij hyaumes de wiere & j hyame xviij bachines viij paires de bras de fier a jouster & ij Rondelles a jouster de le viese maniere vne paire de bras de fier de wiere vne paire de les boucles dargent esmaillies des armes de haynau vne paire de bras de fier de wiere & vne paire de lons wans de wiere vj paires de lons wans de balaine les ij paires aescuces des armes de haynau les autres dun vert samit les autres paires dun Rouge veluiel vne autre paire couuiers de blanc cuir vij paires de wans de plattes les iij paires de laiton vne paire de cussuels a maniere de Rosettes & vne paire de laiton ij paires couuiers de veluiel li vne de vert li autre de Rouge iij paires de cussuels couuiers de noir cuir clawet de claus dores vne paire de noir cuir clawes de claus dores & de bendes dorees vj paires de cussuelz de Rouge cuir a boistes de fier sen ya vne paire clawes de bendes de latton vne paire de nouz cussuelz de noir cuir a escuces des armes de haynau ij paires de cussuelz de noir cuir ij paires de noires greues a bendes dorees et vne paire de noir cuir a escuces des armes de haunau vj pairez de noires greues encor iij paires de Rouge cuir iij paires de sorlers entrais xiiij paires de sorlers clawes vij paires dauans bras de cuir & x paires de aut' de bras deseur viij paires de couuretures a escuces de hacement des armes de haynau dun bleu samit viij houches descut xxij houches descut faissies de bleu samit & de Rouge vne espee estoffee dargent a j fouriaul de veluiel a pumiaul & haldure dargent vne petite espee a haldure dargent sa j pumiaul de Rouge piere encor vne espee a j fouriaul de Rouge cuir a j tissut de soye clawet dargent iiij espeis de wiere xij espees & ij brans ij espees de tournoy encor vne espee qui vint dauignon v lons fiers de glaue & ij cours j fier de bidaul & j plus estroit j espiet j timbre de haynau iiij Capiaus de fier li vns de j cercle dargent ij coiffes a jouster de le viese maniere vne targe de wiere a j lion qui porte le hiame de haynau vne petite targe a j escucet des armes de haynau vne petite targe couuierte dargent j pauet a j hiame mons' de biaumont j pauet de prusse ij paires de couuertures de cheuaus de fier de maillez & vne paire de couuretures de fier de plattes iiij escus a Jouster iiij coffres de bois fieres j lonc a ij cloustres iiij coffres de cuir ij paires despeurons de laiton vne paire de dores a boutons j arbalestre

two pairs of plates for war one of which is covered with cloth of gold the other with blue velvet, one shield of the arms of Count Guillaume, two pairs of plates for jousting one of which is covered with black velvet the other with blue, one pair of plates for jousting covered with cloth of gold, one pair of plates for jousting, two pairs of plates for war of the arms of Hainaut, seven pairs of plates of the old type, one pair of plates of red velvet with two silver chains and one silver billet, one large pair of plates covered in a red wreath, eight haubergeons one of weak iron, six paunces one of which is jazerant, eight pairs of (mail) sleeves two pairs are jazerant another two pairs of weak iron, nine bevors three of which are jazerant, two collars of strong iron one of weak iron, four pairs of chausses for war one pair of which are gilt (i.e. made of gilded mail links), one pair of chausses for the tourney and one similar pair, one pair of long mail chausses of weak iron (mail), one pair (of chausses) of much larger iron (mail links), one of this type and one similar chausse, one coif of the old type with latten fleur-de-lys, two pairs of jazerant musekins, four other pairs of iron (mail musekins) and one small piece of weak iron (mail), one aketon of black camaca (silk fabric) with one haubergeon inside, six poitrines (i.e. breastplates) for jousting, six helms for jousting, six bevors, three vamplates, four helms for war and one helm, 18 basinets, eight pairs of iron (mail) sleeves for jousting, two vamplates for jousting of the old type, one pair of iron (mail) sleeves for war and a pair of gauntlets the buckles of which are of silver enamelled with the arms of Hainaut, one pair of iron (mail) sleeves for war, one pair of long gauntlets for war, six pairs of long gauntlets of baleen two pairs escutcheoned with the arms of Hainaut the others (covered) with green samite (shimmering silk fabric) and others with red velvet, another pair covered with white leather, seven pairs of plate gauntlets three of which are of latten, one pair of cuisses (with nail-heads) in the manner of rosettes and one pair of latten, two pairs of (horse) covers of velvet one green and the other red, three pairs of cuisses covered with black leather nailed with gilt nails, one pair (of cuisses) of black leather nailed with gilt nails and with gilt bends (heraldic stripes), six pairs of cuisses of red leather with bosses of iron one pair of which are nailed with latten bends, one pair of new cuisses of black leather with escutcheons of the arms of Hainaut, two pairs of cuisses of black leather, two pairs of black (unpolished steel) greaves with gilt bends, and one pair of black leather with escutcheons of the arms of Hainaut, six pairs of black greaves, another three pairs of red leather, three pairs of formed sabatons (i.e.

of uncovered steel plates), 14 pairs of nailed sabatons (i.e. of plates riveted to a fabric base), seven pairs of leather vambrace and ten others with the (mail) sleeves above, eight pairs of (horse) covers with escutcheons of hatchments of the arms of Hainaut one is of blue samite, eight huses (covers) for shields, 22 huses for shields of blue and red samite, one sword garnished with silver with one scabbard of velvet with pommel and hilt of silver, a small sword with silver hilt its pommel of red stone, another sword with one scabbard of red leather with one strap of silk nailed with silver, three war swords, 12 swords and two blades, two swords for the tourney, another sword that came from Avignon, five long and two short glaive-heads, one biddow-blade and one narrower one, one spear, one crest of Hainaut, three chapel de fers one with a silver circlet, two coifs for jousting of the old type, one targe for war with one (heraldic) lion which bears the helm of Hainaut, a small targe with one escutcheon of the arms of Hainaut, a small targe covered with silver, one pavise with one (heraldic) helm of my Lord of Beaumont, one pavise of spruce, two pairs of mail horse covers of iron and one pair of plate (horse) covers of iron, four shields for jousting, four iron-bound wooden coffers, one long (coffer) with two enclosed sections, three coffers of leather, two pairs of latten spurs and one gilt pair (decorated) with rosebuds, one crossbow

75

Now-Lost Document recorded by J. Kirkpatrick (d. 1725), printed in W. Hudson, 'Norwich Militia in the 14th Century', *Norfolk Archaeology* 14 (1901), pp. 316–20
Muster of the Militia at Norwich, Norfolk, Easter 1359

Ric[ard]us de Byteryng 2 Dublets 1 Avental 2 Pisan 1 Bacinet' cu' Av' 2 paria Bras' cum 2 paribus de Musekyns [cost not recorded] Tho' de Bumpsted 1 haub[er]ion 1 par Plat 1 Avental 1 Pisan 1 Bacinet' c' av' 1 par Bras' de maille [cost not recorded] Joh' But 2 par' Plat 2 Avental 2 Pisan 2 Bacinet' 2 par Bras' de m' 1 par de vantbras & rerebras asceri £3 5s. Joh' de Elyngham + [sic] Dublet 1 par Plat 1 Avental 1 Pisan + [sic] Bacinet' 1 par Cerotec' de plat 1 Bras' de m' £1 15s. Will' de Blakene 1 par Plat 1 Pisan 1 Bacinet' cu' 2 av' & 2 pis' £2 16s. 4d. Edm[undu]s de Alderford 1 par Plat 2 Avental 2 Pisan 2 Bacinet' cu' 2 av' & 2 pis' £3 1s. 4d. Barth' Appelyerd 1 Dublet 1 par Plat 2 Avental 2 Pisan 1 Bacinet' c' av' 1 par Cerotec' de pl' 1 par Bras' asceri 1 par de m. £3 4s. 4d. Joh' de Gnateshale 2 par' Plat 1 Pisan 1 Bacinet' c' av' 1 par Cerotec' [cost not recorded] Joh' Pykyng + [sic] Dublet 2 par' Plat 1 Pisan 1 Bacinet' c' av' 1 par Cerotec' £3 11s. 4d. Rob' Heigh' 1 Dublet 1 Bacinet' cu' av' & pis' [cost not recorded] Will' de Gnateshale 1 Dublet 1 par Plat 1 Bacinet' cu' av' 2 paria Cerotec' £2 14s. Galf' Boteler 1 Dublet 1 par Plat 1 par Cerotec' de plat 1 par Bras' de m. [cost not recorded] Edm' Lent 1 Dublet 1 par Plat 1 Bacinet' cu' av' 1 par Cerotec' [cost not recorded] Simon Spencer 1 par Plat 1 Pisan 1 Bacinet' cu' av' 2 par Cerotec' de plat Avant Bras rerebras Coters de ferr' [cost not recorded] Hen' de Botelesham 1 Bacinet' cu' av' [cost not recorded] Rog' Midday 1 Dublet 1 par Plat 1 Pisan 1 Bacinet' 1 par Cerotec' de plat £1 1s. 8d. Tho'

Gronger 1 Pisan 1 Bacinet' cu' av' 1 par Bras' de m. £18 Joh' de Toftes 1 Plat 1 Pisan 1 Cerotec' de plat Rerebras vantbras coters asceri £1 12s. Rob' Spicer 1 Dublet 1 Pisan 1 Bacinet' cu' av' 1 par de Cerotec' de plat Vanbras rerebras asceri 1 par bras de maille £2 1s. Joh' Fairchild 1 Dublet 1 Pisan 1 Bacinet' cu' av' 1 par Cerotec' de plat 1 par Bras' de m. £2 1s. 4d. Roger de Halesworth 1 Dublet 1 Plat 1 Bacinet' cu' av' 1 hasta & glad' £1 1s. 4d. Joh[ann]es de Welburn 2 Dublet 2 par' Plat 2 Avental 2 Pisan 2 Bacinet' cu' av' 1 par Cerotec' de plat 2 par Bras' de m. 1 p[u]rpoint 1 par vantbras rerebr' asceri £6 4s. 8d. Will' de Wosted 1 par Plat 1 par Cerotec' de plat £1 1s. 4d. Joh' Palmere 1 Dublet 6s. 8d. Joh' de Berford 1 par Plat 1 Avental 1 Pisan 1 Bacinet' 1 par Bras' de m. £2 9s., [name not recorded] 1 Dublet 3s. Tho' Sherman 1 par Plat 1 Bacinet' cu' av' 1 par Cerotec' de plat vantbras rerebras asceri £2 12s. Joh' Latymer 1 Pisan 1 Bacinet' cu' av' 1 par Cerotec' de plat £1 1s. 4d. Andr' Berd 1 Bacinet' cu' umbrer 1 par de bras £1 Tho' de Bumpsted 1 par Plat 2 Avental 2 Pisan 2 Bacinet' 1 par Cerotec' de plat 2 par' Bras' de m. £4 1s. 4d. Joh' Deux 1 Avental 1 Bacinet' £2 4s. Rog' Hardegrey 2 Dublet 1 par Plat 1 Avental 1 Pisan 1 Bacinet' 1 Cerotec' 1 Bras' de m. £2 13s. 8d.

Richard Bittering: two doublets, one aventail, two pisans, one basinet with aventail, two pairs of mail sleeves, with two pairs of musekins [cost not recorded]; Thomas Bumpstead: one haubergeon, one pair of plates, one aventail, one pisan, one basinet with aventail, one pair of mail sleeves [cost not recorded]; John But: two pairs of plates, two aventails, two pisans, two basinets, two pairs of mail sleeves, one pair of steel vambrace and rerebrace £3 5s.; John Ellingham: one doublet, one pair of plates, one aventail, one pisan, one basinet, one pair of plate gauntlets, one pair of mail sleeves £1 15s.; William Blakeney: one pair of plates, one pisan, one basinet with two aventails, and two pisans £2 16s. 4d.; Edmund Alderford: one pair of plates, two aventails, two pisans, two basinets with two aventails, and two pisans £3 1s. 4d.; Bartholomew Appleyard: one doublet, one pair of plates, two aventails, two pisans, one basinet with aventail, one pair of plate gauntlets, one pair of steel bracers, one pair of mail sleeves £3 4s. 4d.; John Gnateshale: two pairs of plates, one pisan, one basinet with aventail, one pair of gauntlets [cost not recorded]; John Pickering: one doublet, one pair of plates, one pisan, one basinet with aventail, one pair of gauntlets £3 11s. 4d.; Robert Heigham: one doublet, one basinet with aventail, and pisan [cost not recorded]; William Gnateshale: one doublet, one pair of plates, one basinet with aventail, one pair of gauntlets £2 14s.; Geoffrey Butler: one doublet, one pair of plates, one pair of plate gauntlets, one pair of mail sleeves [cost not recorded]; Edmund Lent: one doublet, one pair of plates, one basinet with aventail, one pair of gauntlets [cost not recorded]; Simon Spencer: one pair of plates, one pisan, one basinet with aventail, two pairs of plate gauntlets, iron vambrace, rerebrace, and couters [cost not recorded]; Henry Bottlesham: one basinet with aventail [cost not recorded]; Roger Midday: one doublet, one pair of plates, one pisan, one basinet, one pair of plate gauntlets £1 1s. 8d.; Thomas Granger: one pisan, one basinet with aventail, one pair of mail sleeves £18; John Tofts: one pair of plates, one pisan, one pair of plate gauntlets, steel rerebrace, vambrace, and couters; Robert Spicer: one doublet, one pisan, one basinet with aventail, one pair of plate gauntlets, steel vambrace (and) rerebrace, one pair of mail sleeves £2 1s.; John Fairchild: one doublet, one pisan, one basinet with aventail, one pair of mail sleeves £2 1s. 4d.; Roger Halesworth: one doublet, one pair of plates, one basinet with aventail, one spear, and sword £1 1s. 4d.; John Welborne: two doublets, two pairs of plates, two aventails, two pisans, two basinets with aventails, one pair of plate gauntlets, two pairs of mail sleeves, one pourpoint, one pair of steel vambrace (and) rerebrace £6 4s. 8d.; William Worstead: one pair of plates, one pair of plate gauntlets £1 1s. 4d.; John Palmer: one doublet 6s. 8d.; John Barford: one pair of plates, one aventail, one pisan, one basinet, one pair of mail sleeves £2 9s.; [name not recorded]: one doublet 3s.; Thomas Sherman: one pair of plates, one basinet with aventail, one pair of plate gauntlets, steel vambrace (and) rerebrace £2 12s.; John Latimer: one pisan, one basinet with aventail, one pair of plate gauntlets £1 1s. 4d.; Andrew Berd: one basinet with umbrer, one pair of mail sleeves £1; Thomas Bumpstead: one pair of plates, two aventails, two pisans, two basinets, one pair of plate gauntlets, two pairs of mail sleeves £4 1s. 4d.; John Deux: one aventail, one basinet £2 4s.; Roger Hardgrey: two doublets, one pair of plates, one aventail, one pisan, one basinet, one pair of gauntlets, one pair of mail sleeves £2 13s. 8d.

76

Unlocated Original Document printed in A. Way, 'Accounts of the Constables of the Castle of Dover', *Archaeological Journal* 11 (1854), pp. 381–8

Inventory of Dover Castle, Kent, 26 January 1361

En la forge: ij andefeltes de fer, j. andefelte debruse, j. bikor[n]e, iij. slegges, iiij. hameres, vj. paires tanges dount deux grosses, iiij. pensons febles, iij. nailetoules pur claues en icels faire, iij. paire bulghes dount une novell, j. peer moler, ij. Fusels de feer aicele, j. paire de wynches as mesme le peer, j. trow de peer pur ewe, j. hurthestaf de feer, j. cottyngyre, j. markyngyre, une cable vels et pourz. En diversez tourez: noefs espringales ove tote lour necc[ec]ai[r]es et apparailz bonz et covenables dount ij. groses. En la meson des armours: vj. aketons covenables, xxvj. Ak[e]tons febles et de petit value, vj. paire de plates febles dount iiij. de nulle value, habrejons et autres hernous de maile de nulle value, xij. paire de gaunz de plate febles de nulle value, j. brustplate pur Justes, deux avantplates, xix. chapels de feer, xj. helmes febles, xiij. basynetez tinez ove umbres febles, et autre basynet et palet debruses et porus de nulle value, vj. capels de nerfs febles, xl. targes febles, l. launcez ove testes et xxvj. sanz testes, ij. cornals, j. grate pur joutes, xxvj. albalastes bones et covenables, xxiiij. Alblastes debrusez et poruz qe sont de nulle value, ij. cofres pleinz de quareles pur alblastes, ij. boketes et ij. bariles pleinz de quareles pur alblastes, xxxiij. Arcz bonez et covenables cx. Arcz feblez et veus dount plusours sont porus et debruses, iiij. xx garbes de seetes febles, j. viel cofre ove testes de quareles, iiij. cofres pleinz dez quareles pur espringales, j. paire polains, xxx. Baudreyes febles et porus, xxiiij. arc pur arblastes de corn saunz teilers, iiij. arcez et vis vels et febles, iij. vis pur les dit arcez tendre febles et porus, j. coffyn ov seetes pur j. arc' de Turkye, ij. toneaux dont en lautre une grant partie de kaltrappes, [et en] laut' cheinez et aultrez intrumentz de feer pur engynz

In the forge: two iron anvils, one worn out anvil, one bicorn, three sledgehammers, four hammers, six pairs of tongs two of which are large, four worn out pincers, three nail-tools in which nails are formed, three pairs of bellows one of which is new, one grindstone, two steel axles, one pair of winches for this grindstone, one stone water trough, one iron hearth staff, one cutting gear, one marking gear, one old rotten cable. In divers towers: new springalds with all their necessities well and suitably equipped two of which are large. In the armoury: six useable aketons, 26 worn out aketons of little value, six worn out pairs of plates four of which are of no value, haubergeons and other harness of mail of no value, 12 pairs of worn out plate gauntlets of no value, one breastplate for jousts, two vamplates, 19 chapel de fers, 11 worn out helms, 13 worn out tinned basinets with umbrers and other worn out and rotten basinets and pallets of no value, six worn out chapels of sinew, 40 worn out targes, 50 headed lances and 26 without heads, two coronals, one grapper for jousts, 26 good and useable crossbows, 24 worn out and rotten crossbows of no value, two buckets and two barrels full of crossbow quarrels, 33 good and useable bows and 110 old and worn out several of which are rotten, four score sheaves of worn out arrows, one old coffer with quarrel-heads, four coffers full of quarrels for springalds, one pair of pulleys, 30 worn out and rotten baldrics, 24 bows for horn crossbows without tillers (stocks), four old and worn out bows and a vice, three vices for spanning these bows worn out and rotten, one coffer with arrows for one bow of Turkey, two tuns in one of which is a great quantity of caltraps in the other chains and other iron tools for (siege) engines

77

London Metropolitan Archives, Plea and Memoranda Roll A10
Complaint of John Winchcombe, Armourer of London, 10 December 1364

Joh[ann]es de Wynchecombe Ciuis & Armurar' london' ven' coram Ad' de Bury & Ald[e]r[mann]i & monstrauit Eisdem q[uo]d Will[el]m[u]s atte halle filius margarete de Grubbelane app[re]ntic' suis no' vul[u]t irrotular se[cun]d[u]m cons' Ciuitatis p[ar] indentur' int[er] ces factas qua indent[ur]a lecta & audicta & ip[s] e cogn' bene p[ro] facto suo Et dicit Ideo comiss' p[er]sone de Neugate Et sup[er] hoc ven' margareta de Grubbelane mater d[ic]ti app[re]nticij & sic[u]ct q[uo]d talis commento' franguinta et p[re]d[ic]tus app[re]nt[ici]i hab[u]it acqu[ic]t' cons' est p[ar] Ad de Bury m' & pon' de nigram […]

John Winchcombe citizen and armourer of London came into the presence of Adam Bury and the Aldermen and pleaded to the same that William atte Halle son to Margaret of Grub Lane his apprentice did not wish to be enrolled according to the customs of the City by an indenture made between them which indenture having been read and heard and the same well understood to have been made by him. And the same (John) said that he had sent persons to Newgate and having come thither Margaret of Grub Lane mother of the said apprentice was asked where he was and the said apprentice had quit his lodgings. This was sworn before Adam Bury and recorded in the Black (Book)

78

London Metropolitan Archives, Plea and Memoranda Roll A20
Goods of Robert Payn, Fuster (Saddletree-Maker), in his House in
Wood Street, Parish of Saint Albans, City of London, December 1364

vnu' loricam vnu' par' vantbrace & Rerbrace & vnu' par' de serotecar[um] de plata vnu' blak jak vnu' chekere jak & vnu' jak de defens' vnu' bacinettu' cu' auentallo vnu' par' cerotecar[um] de plata vnu' par legherneys

One hauberk, one pair of vambrace and rerebrace, one pair of plate gauntlets, one black jack, one chequered jack, and one jack of defence, one basinet with aventail, one pair of plate gauntlets, one pair of legharness

79

Paris, Archives de la Préfecture de Police, cote AD 4, Collection Lamoignon, vol. II, fol. 309r
Statutes of the Armourers, *Coustepointiers* (Fabric Defence-Makers), and Heaumers (Plate Armourers) of Paris, 1 December 1364

This manuscript is a copy made before 1772 from the now-lost Livre vert vieil premier of the Châtelet de Paris.

Jehan Bernier, garde de la prevosté de Paris, a fait register et ordonnance pour iceluy mestier, en la fourme et manière qui s'ensuit: nul doresenavant ne puisse ouvrer ne faire ouvrer du mestier de armeurier ne de coustepointier, ne de choses qui y appartiengnent, se il n'est maistre ou ait esté apprentis ou souffisant personne de faire un chief d'euvre. Nul ne puisse lever ouvrouer du mestier tant qu'il n'ait fait une pièce d'oeuvre de sa main, bonne et souffisant, sur un des maistres du mestier; et se ainsy est que aucun leve ledit mestier, que il soit souffisant par le dit des maistres; il payera douze sols d'entrée, c'est assavoir huit sols au Roy et quatre sols aux maistres, se il n'est fils de maistre. Nulz compaignons du mestier ne puissant aller ouvrer, se ce n'est sur les maistres et ouvriers d'iceluy mestier, sans le congié des maistres et gardes du mestier; et que nul ne le puisse prendre a moins de terme de six ans. Nul ne puisse garnir bacinet neuf, se ce n'est de cendail neuf ou de toile neufve ou de bouguerant, et que les cervelières soient doubles jusques dessoubz le pertuis ou les cermeillières doivent estre clouées ou cousues, et que les languettes des cervelières, se le bacinet est garni de cendail, soient couvertes de cendail et arrière pointées. Nul ne face fonceau ou bassinet, se il ne lui est commandé, et que le feutre soit couchié de coton neuf sur vielz linge et enterin flotté et couvert et arrière pointé, sur cendail neuf comme dit est, et que nul ne fasse hourson a bassinet se l'envers n'est de toille neufve, et que il soit couchié de bon cotton souffisant ou de bourre de soye a point enfermé, et que il soit flotté de cendail, et contrendroit, de la couleur du cendail. Nul ne puisse [faire] pavillon à gorgière, se ce n'est de neufve estoffe, et que le colret soit arrière pointé et trait et que il y ait contrendroit, et que il soit houssé dedans de toille neufve ou de cendail, et soit dedens couchié de coton neuf. Nul ne face corsets ne brayers, se ils ne sont de cendail ou de toille neufve ou de souffisant estoffe neufve. Se il venoit aucun vieil bassinet à garnir, ou autres pièces, quelles que elles soient, regarnis de cendail neuf ou de neufve toille, ou de bouguerant neuf ou de si souffisant estoffe, comme il seroit regardé par les maistres, et qu'il seroit trouvé du contraire, que il soit en l'amande dessus, et que la besongne soit arsé au lieu accoustumé et ordené. Se l'en fair cottes gamboisiées, que elles soient couches durement sur neufves estoffes et pointées enfermes, faites à deux fois, bien et nettement emplies de bonnes estoffes, soie, coton ou autres estoffes, par les maistres. Quiconque fera euvre de gambesinem soit paletot, jupon, jacqués ou houppelandes gamboisiées, que les maistres puissent avoir visitation, en quelques lieux que elles soient faites, pour scavoir se l'euvre sera bonne et loyale et de loyaulx estoffes. Toute besongne qui sera quasiguesnée soit faite à deux fois et poins enfermés et le fer soit vernicé et estoffé souffisament, selon ce qu'il appartient, et de neufve estoffe. Nul ne puisse faire couverture de cheval gamboisiée, soit d'estamine ou d'autre chose, que ne soit faite de cendail, que il y ait contrendroit et que toutes les autres choses dessus soient gamboisiées. Nul ne puisse faire manches balenées, que il n'y ait contrendroit de forte toille, et l'endroit de chenevas ou de forte toille neufve. Nul ne puisse garnir heaume pour la jouste, qu'il ne soit garni de cotton entre deux toilles de cendail. Nul ne puisse faire espaulières pour le tournois, soit de cendail ou de toille ou de bougueran, qu'elles ne soient arrière pointées, et que il ait contrendroit et l'envers de toille neufve, qu'elle elle soit, et boutté de tuyaux emplis d'estouspes et de balene, et planché de baleine là ou il appartiendra; et les envers soient bons et loyaulx par le regard des maistres. Nul ne puisse garnir bassinet pour le tournois, qu'il ne soit vernicé dedans et dehors et garni de deux paires de cermailles toutes neufves, et couverts de bon cuir blanc courroyé, ou d'autre chose qui le vaille. Nul ne puisse couvrir cuiriée pour le tournois que elle ne soit premierement forgée, se elle n'est de cuir boulu, et gamboisiée dedans de cotton ou d'estouppe qui ainsi le vouldra. Nuls marcha[n]s venans à Paris et apportans denrées appartenans à l'armoyerie, iceulx marchans ne mettens en vente les denrées sans ce que ils appellent ou facent appeler l'un des jurez ou gardes du mestier de l'armoyerie commis à ce, pour savoir se les denrées seront souffisament garnies et estoffées, si comme il appartient; et que les maistres puissent aller paisiblement veoir les denrées, se aucuns marchans quels qu'ils soient, de Paris ou de dehors, les veulent mettre en vente; et que les maistres les puissent visiter bien et loyalment pour eschever aux perils dessus dits. Nul ne puisse doresnavant acheter harnois ne vendre, quel que il soit, en disant qu'il ait esté fait en la Ville de Paris, se fait ny a esté, sur paine de le perdre et de faire forfait, et seront ceulx qui feront le contraire de cet article a xxx sols parisis d'amende, c'est assavoir xx sols au Roy et x sols aux maistres. Nul ne puisse comporter pièces de harnois aval la Ville de Paris, appartenant a ladite armoyerie, si ils ne sont bonnes, loyaulx et souffisament faites et garnies. Quiconques fera aucunes besongnes contre l'ordonnance que icelles [armures] soient arses au carrefour de la heaumerie de Paris ou il appartiendra.

Jehan Bernier, Warden of the Office of the *Prévôt* of Paris, has recorded and it has been agreed by this craft in the following form and manner: That henceforth none may work, or cause to work, for the craft of the armourer or *coustepoint*-maker nor others related lest he be a master or has served apprenticeship or been made a chief craftsman by a suitable person. None may rise to the position of craftsman of the craft until he has made his good and suitable masterpiece by his own hand under the supervision of one of the masters of the craft. Any who rise to the craft, if he be found suitable by the masters, shall pay 12 Parisian *sous* ingress (if he be not a master's son) – that is to say: eight *sous* to the King and four *sous* to these masters. No members of the craft may work, if it be not under one of the masters and craftsmen of this craft, without the permission of the masters or wardens of the craft, and that none may serve an apprenticeship of less than the term of six years. None may equip a new basinet lest it be of new sendal, linen, or buckram, and that the linings be lined to cover the perforations where the linings ought to be nailed or sewn, and that the linings' straps – if the basinet be equipped with sendal – be covered with sendal and pointed on the back (i.e. padded like a pourpoint). None may make a pouch (i.e. for storage and transport) for the basinet lest he be ordered and that the felt be stuffed with new cotton on old linen and the whole flocked and covered and pointed at the back over new sendal. None may make hourson (aventail-cover) for the basinet lest the outside be of new linen, and it be stuffed with good suitable cotton or silk burrs with closed points and that it be flocked with sendal and faced with the colour of the sendal. None may make cover for gorget lest it be newly stuffed, and the collar be pointed at the back and drawn (with a drawstring) and that it be faced with new cotton. None may make corsets or brayers lest they be of new sendal or linen and suitably newly stuffed. Should it happen that any old basinet be equipped, or any other pieces (of plate armour) whatsoever be re-equipped, with new sendal, linen, buckram, or such suitable stuffing, then it shall be viewed by the masters and if it be found contrary (to these statutes) then he (the culprit) shall be fined as devised above and the workmanship shall be burnt in the customary and assigned place [the cross-roads of the Rue de la Heaumerie]. If making gamboised coats, they be strongly stuffed with new stuffing and pointed covers made of two layers – well and neatly filled with good stuffing, silk, cotton, or other stuffing by the masters' agreement. Whosoever works on a gambeson – be it gamboised paletot, jupon, jack, or overgown – the masters have the right of visitation (inspection) in any place where they are made to establish whether the work be good and legal and made of legal stuff. All workmanship of jazerant is to be made of two layers with pointed covers and the mail varnished and sufficiently stuffed accordingly with new stuffing. None may make gamboised horse covers – be they of wool or other things – lest they be made of sendal, and it be faced, and all the other parts above be gamboised. None may make baleen sleeves lest they be faced with strong linen and the inside of canvas or strong new linen. None may equip jousting helms lest they be equipped with cotton between two layers of sendal. None may make spaudlers for the tourney lest they be of sendal, linen, or buckram, pointed at the back and have facing and the back of new linen where it should be, and tubes full of tow, baleen, and planks of baleen where suitable. None may equip basinet for the tourney lest it be varnished inside and out and equipped with two pairs of completely new linings and covered with well-tanned white leather or other things as desired. None may cover cuirie for the tourney lest it be firstly forged (if it be not of cuir bouilli) and gamboised inside with cotton or tubes as desired. No merchants coming to Paris and importing armour goods may put these goods up for sale without summoning (or causing to summon) one of the appointed judges or wardens of the craft to find out if the goods be suitably equipped and stuffed as appropriate, and that the masters may peaceably go to appraise the goods of any merchant whatsoever of Paris or from outside wishing to put them up for sale, and that the masters may properly and legally inspect (them) to avoid the aforesaid perils (to the men of the realm). Henceforth none may buy or sell harness of any kind claiming that it has been made in the City of Paris if it has not on pain of its loss and forfeiture. Those who contravene this article shall be fined 30 *sous* – that is to say: 20 *sous* to the King and ten *sous* to the masters. None may import into the City of Paris pieces of harness for armour lest they be good, legal, and suitably made and equipped. Whosoever contravenes this ordinance in any way shall (have their substandard goods) appropriately burnt at the crossroads of the Rue de la Heaumerie of Paris.

80

Chaumont, Archives départementales de la Haute-Marne, 2 G 115
Arms and Armour of Jean de Suffres (or Saffres), *Chanoine* (Priest) of Langres, Duchy of Burgundy, 3 November 1365

vnu' bombiciniu' al' porpointu' de bisso sex grossos aliud bombiciniu' de bisso qui[n] decim grossos aliud bomiciniu' coop[er]tum de Samisio quindec' grossos vnu' gallice Jaque coop[er]tum de Camocas in quo sunt tres Cathene in pectore' vnu' florenu' florencie alium Jaque coop[er]tum de bisso duos florenos alium Jaque coop[er] tum de tela alba quatuor grossos vnam balistam neruata' de sup[er] tres francos auri aliam balistam magnam de ycio duos francos auri aliam balistam de duobus fustis neruatam desup[er] vnum florenu' tres balistas ad trahendum t[erti]um francoru' aur' tres vet[er]es balistas cum vno talerio vnu' florenu' vnu' baltheum nouu' qui[n] q[ue] grossos alium balthenum nouu' qui[n]q[ue] grossos alium balthenum de filo cum polia de Cupro quatuor grossos alium balthenum corij cum polia ferrea quatuor grossos alium balthenum veterem duos grossos vnu' gallice pauaix magnu' de duobus fustis vnu' francum auri alium pauaix octo grossos alium pauaix octo grossos aliu'

pauaix sex grossos alium pauaix sex grossos alium pauaix sex grossos aliu' pauaix
octo grossos alium pauaix sex grossos vnam targiam depictam cum quod' equite
armato quinq[ue] grossor[um] aliam targia' quinq[ue] grossos aliam targiam armis de
Saffris depictam qui[n]q[ue] grossos vnu' scutum in quo est depictus quidem eques
quinq[ue] grossos aliam targiam armis de Saffris ut dicitur depictam cu' quodam
ceruo depicto desup[er] quinq[ue] grossos aliam targiam ijsdem armis depictam duos
grossos aliam targiam depictam vnu' grossum vnam targiam rotundarij vnu' grossum
vna' p[ar]uam targiam vnu' grossum vnu' cutellum de vasconia qui[n]q[ue] grossos
alium cutellum vocatum de platez op[er]is lumbardie qui[n]q[ue] grossos alium
cutellum de platez duos grossos vnum gallice estoc vnu' francu' auri vnum spatam
op[er]is Coloniensis qui[n]q[ue] grossos aliam spatam operis boemie sex grossos vnu'
ensem op[er]is lombardie ad signu' scorpionis duos florenos alium ensem op[er]is
boemie qui[n]decim grossos vnu' piquetum vnu' grossum cu' dimidio vnu' Jesum
al' Jusarma' vnu' florenu' vnu' grossum baculum quadratum in quo sunt tres virole
argenti cum quatuor clauis octo grossos alium p[ar]uu' baculum radiatum in quo
est quedam daigua desup[er] duos grossos vnu' gallico godandud vnius grossi vnam
hacham aciam tres grossos aliam hacha' aciam dimidium grossum vnu' gallice espie
quatuor gross' aliud espie duos grossos vnam tunicam ferream decem florenas aliam
tunicam ferream dece[m]octo grossos aliam tunica' ferream quatuor florenos aliam
tunicam ferream dece[m]octo grossos vnu' bacinetum cum camali de Jaserand tres
florenos vna' gorgeriam op[er]is de Jaserant duodecim grossos vnu' bacinetu' cum
camali op[er]is rotundi quindecim grossos alium bacinetum cum camali duos gross'
vnu' clipeum ferreum vnu' grossum alium clipeum ferreum vnu' gross' vnu' bacinetu'
cum camali quinq[ue] grossos alium bassinetum cum camali duodecim grossos alium
bassinetum cum camali decem grossos alium bassinetum cum camali sex grossos
alium bassinetum cu' camali octo grossos alium bassinetu' cu' Camali octo grossos
aliu' bassinetum cu' camali octo grossos alium bassinetum cu' Camali tres grossos
vnu' Camale op[er]is rotundi vnu' florenu' aliud Camale vnu' grossum aliud Camale
dimidium grossum aliud Camale dimidium grossum vnam galeam veterem sub p[re]
cio qui[n]q[ue] grossorum aliam galeam qui[n]q[ue] grossos vnam cufa' ferream cum
vna pecia galee vnu' grossum arnesium tybiarum in quatuor peciis tres grossos aliud
arnesium ferreu' in quatuor peciis p[ro] tybiis armandis tres grossos aliud arnesiu'
ferreu' pro tybiis armandis in quatuor peciis tres grossos aliud arnesium de corio p[ro]
tibiis arma[n]dis vnu' grossum aliud arnesium p[ro] tybiis armandis coop[er]tum de
corio albo dimidiu' grossu' aliud arnesium p[ro] tybiis arma[n]dis coop[er]tum de
corio nigro dimid' grossum quasdam cyrothecas ferreas duos grossos alios cyrothecas
ferreas cum manucis vnum grossum alias cyrothecas ferreas eiusdem op[er]is duos
grossos alias cyrothecas vet[er]es ferreas cum q[u]od' arnesio brachior[um] f[a]c[t]
o de corio et quibusdam coutiers de ferro duos grossos vnu' clipeum depictum vnu'
grossum tres Jaculos de fraxino ferratos tres grossos sexdecim lanceas quaru' quatuor-
decim su[n]t ferrato et alio non ferrate duodecim grossos quatuor gallice Canons
ferri ad p[ro]iecte[n]d' garretos cum quadraginta qui[n]q[ue] garretos duos florenos
quasda' cyrothecas ferreas cum quod' arnesio de Corio ad armandu' brachia vnu'
grossum cum dimidio quoddam arnesium ferri ad armandu' brachia quatuor grossos

aliud arnesiu' de Corio pro brachiis arma[n]dis cum quibusd' vet[er]ib[u]s Cyrothecis duos grossos quasdam platas ad armandum duodecim grossorum alias platas cum t[ri]bus Cathenis in pectore coop[er]tas de fustana vnum florenu' alias platas vet[er] es coop[er]tas de panno viridi in quibus est scutu' rubeu' in pectori quinq[ue] grossos alias platas ad armandu' vet[er]es coop[er]tas de pa[n]no viridi sex grossos alias platas coop[er]tas de veluello croceo duodecim grossos alias platas ad arma[n]du' coop[er] tas de Corio albo vnu' francu' auri alias vet[er]es platas ad idem coop[er]tas de pa[n] no radiaco qui[n]q[ue] grossos alias platas non coop[er]tas duos florenos alias platas cum t[ri]bus Cathenis in pectore coop[er]tas de corio albo duodecim grossos alias platas vet[er]es coop[er]tas de corio albo qui[n]q[ue] grossos quasdam pecias ferreas ad arma[n]du' sex gross' quoddam arnesiu' de Corio p[ro] brachiis armandis cum quibusd' vet[er]ib[us] cyrotechis ferreis vnu' grossum aliud arnesiu' ad idem cum quibusd' vet[er]ib[us] cyrothecis ferreis vnu' grossum aliud arnesiu' cum vet[er]ib[us] cyrothecis vnu' grossum duos vet[er]es cyrothecas f[er]reas cum duab[us] peciis arnesii bracior[um] vnum grossum cum dimidio quasdam pecias platarum ferri dimidium grossum quosdam gallice pans de maille vnius floreni alios gallice pans cum corrigiis sex grossos alios pans quatuor grossos alios pans in duabus peciis vnu' g[r]oss' quasdam manucas ferreas ad armandum duodecim grossos alias manucas ad idem tres grossos duas pecias maillie duos grossos quasdam alias manucas maillie ad armandu' vnu' florenu' alias manucas ferreas ad idem sex grossos alias manucas ferreas ad idem duos grossos alias manucas ferreas ad idem vnu' grossu' alias manucas ferreas ad idem duos grossos quasd' cyrothecas de maillia cum quibusd' cyrothecis de tela vnu' grossum quatuor pecias vet[er]ib[us] maillie ad p[ar]andum arma tres grossos

a bombicinium otherwise known as a pourpoint of linen six groats, another bombicinium of linen 15*gr.*, another bombicinium covered with samite (shimmering silk fabric) 15*gr.*, one (defence) called in French a jack covered with camaca (silk fabric) in which are three chains in the chest one Florentine florin, another jack covered with linen 2*fl.*, another jack covered with white cloth 4*gr.*, a crossbow covered with sinew three gold francs, another large crossbow of yew 2 gold *fr.*, another crossbow with two wooden parts covered with sinew 1*fl.*, three torsion crossbows 3 gold *fr.*, three old crossbows with one tiller (stock) 1*fl.*, a new belt 5*gr.*, another new belt 5*gr.*, another cord belt with copper pulley 4*gr.*, another leather belt with iron pulley 4*gr.*, another old belt 2*gr.*, one (shield) called in French a pavise of two wooden parts 1 gold *fr.*, another pavise 8*gr.*, another pavise 8*gr.*, another pavise 6*gr.*, another pavise 6*gr.*, another pavise 6*gr.*, another pavise 8*gr.*, another pavise 6*gr.*, a targe painted with an armed horseman 5*gr.*, another targe 5*gr.*, another targe painted with the (heraldic) arms of Saffres (Suffres) 5*gr.*, a shield on which a certain horseman is painted 5*gr.*, another targe painted with the arms of Saffres (Suffres) with a certain hart painted on it 5*gr.*, another targe painted with these arms 2*gr.*, another painted targe 1*gr.*, a round targe 1*gr.*, a small targe 1*gr.*, a Gascon knife 5*gr.*, another knife called 'of plates' of Lombardy work 5*gr.*, another knife of plates 2*gr.*, a sword called in French an estoc 1 gold *fr.*, a *spatam* (prob. longsword) of Cologne work 5*gr.*, another *spatam* of Bohemian work 6*gr.*, a sword of Lombardy work with the sign of the scorpion 2*fl.*, another sword of Bohemian work 5gr., a pike 1½gr., a weapon known as a gisarme 1fl., a large quarterstaff on which there are three silver ferrules with four nails 8gr., another small radiating staff on which is a certain spike 2gr., one weapon called in French a godendag 1gr., a steel axe 3gr., another steel axe ½gr., one weapon called in French an espie (sword) 4gr., another espie 2gr., an iron tunic (mail shirt) 10fl., another iron tunic 18gr., another iron tunic 4fl., another iron tunic 18gr., a basinet with jazerant aventail 3fl., a gorget of jazerant work 12gr., a basinet with aventail of round work (i.e. round-sectioned wire links) 15gr., another basinet with aventail 2gr., an iron shield 1gr., another iron shield 1gr., a basinet with aventail 5gr., another basinet with aventail 12gr., another basinet with aventail 10gr., another basinet with aventail 6gr., another basinet with aventail 8gr., another basinet with aventail 8gr., another basinet with aventail 8gr., another basinet with aventail 3gr., an aventail of round work 1fl., another aventail 1gr., another aventail ½gr., another aventail ½gr., an old helm 5gr., another helm 5gr., an iron coif with one pièce (reinforcing plate) of a helm 1gr., harness for the shins in four pieces 3gr., another iron harness in four pieces for arming the shins 3gr., another iron harness for arming the shins in four pieces 3gr., leather harness for arming the shins 1gr., another iron harness for arming the shins in four pieces 3gr., another harness for arming the shins covered with white leather ½gr., another harness for arming the shins covered with black leather ½gr., certain iron gauntlets 2gr., other iron gauntlets with sleeves 1gr., other iron gauntlets of the same work 2gr., other old iron gauntlets with certain arm harness made of leather the couters of which are of iron 2gr., a painted shield 1gr., three darts of ash with heads 3gr., 16 lances 14 of which have heads and the others are without heads 12gr., four weapons called in French iron cannons for shooting garrots with 45 garrots 2fl., certain iron gauntlets with certain harness of leather for arming the arms 1½gr., certain iron harness for arming the arms 4gr., another harness of leather for arming the arms with certain old gauntlets 2gr., certain pairs of plates for arming 12gr., other pairs of plates with three chains on the breast covered with fustian (strong fabric made from any two of cotton, flax, or wool) 1fl., another old pair of plates covered with green cloth with a red escutcheon on the breast 5gr., another old pair of plates for arming covered with green cloth 6gr., other pairs of plates covered with yellow velvet 12gr., other pairs of plates for arming covered with white leather one gold fr., another old pair of plates for the same covered with striped cloth 5gr., other uncovered pairs of plates 2fl., other pairs of plates with three chains on the breast covered with white leather 12gr., another old pair of plates covered with white leather 5gr., certain pieces of iron for arming 6gr., certain harness of leather for arming the arms with certain old iron gauntlets 1gr., another harness of the same with certain old iron gauntlets 1gr., another similar harness with old gauntlets 1gr., two old iron gauntlets with two pieces of arm harness 1½gr., certain pieces of iron plates ½gr., certain defences called in French paunce of mail 1fl., other paunces with leathers 6gr., other paunces 4gr., other paunces in two pieces 1gr., certain iron (mail) sleeves for arming 12gr., other (mail) sleeves for the same 6gr., two pieces of mail 2gr., certain other mail sleeves for arming 1fl., other iron (mail) sleeves for the same 6gr., other iron (mail) sleeves for the same 2gr., other iron (mail) sleeves for the same 1gr., other iron (mail) sleeves for the same 2*gr.*, certain gauntlets of mail with certain gauntlets of cloth 1*gr.*, four pieces of old mail to equip the arms (voiders) 3*gr.*

81

State Archives of Prato, Fondo Datini (Extracts), 1366–99
Extracts transcribed by L. Frangioni, printed in 'Bacinetti e altre difese della testa nella documentazione di una azienda mercantile, 1366–1410', *Archaeologia medievale* 11 (1984), pp. 507–22

Francesco di Marco Datini (b. c. 1335, d. 1410) was a merchant arms dealer from the Tuscan city of Prato. He set up his business in Avignon, Provence in 1350.

1366

bacinetto di Avignone della guisa di Gentile, di 1/2 prova, visiera grande a ponte, camaglio d'acciaio laschetto, padiglione di zendado azzurro, farsata di tela vermiglia: f. 9; bacinetto di Avignone della guisa di Petrolo, di 1/2 prova, un poco magagnato, visiera piccola di Liegi a ponte, con anelline e senza farsata: f. 4; bacinetto di Avignone traversato della guisa di Petrolo, cioè il coppo con anelline: f. 3.14; bacinetto di Avignone traversato della guisa di Petrolo, visiera grande a ponte di Guastaferro, calotta di tela vermiglia: f. 6; bacinetto di Avignone della guisa di Petrolo, grandissimo, visiera grande, camaglio di ferro di Milano ottonato, padiglione e calotta di tela vermiglia: f. 7; bacinetto di Avignone della guisa di Petrolo, bello e netto, visiera piccola, camaglio di ferro lasco, padiglione di tela, calotta di zendado: f. 6; bacinetto di Avignone della guisa di Martino da Milano, cioè il coppo doppioni 'sanza niuno altro fornimento': f. 4; bacinetto di Avignone traversato della guisa di Tommasolo, senza doppioni e altro fornimento: f. 2.12; bacinetto di Parigi della guisa passata, visiera grande, camaglio di ferro grosso, padiglione e calotta di tela: f. 4; bacinetto di Liegi alla guisa, di 1/2 prova, visiera grande a ponte, camaglio di ferro, padiglione e farsata di zendado: f. 7.12; bacinetto di Liegi alla guisa, di 1/2 prova, con anelline senza farsata: f. 3; [NB when there is more than one item their quantity is not given] [several] bacinetti di Milano e di Pinerolo alla guisa, di 1/2 prova, con anelline e farsate di tela: f. 2 uno; bacinetto di Milano di 1/2 prova, all'antica, con 'ghotollo, visiera e girlanda', camaglio di ferro, farsata di tela: f. 2; bacinetto di Milano all'antica, visiera piccola di Milano all'antica, calotta di tela tinta: f. 1; bacinetto traversato, visiera, calotta al modo della 'Magna': f. 1.6; visiera di Avignone, di Guastaferro, grande a ponte: f. – [no price recorded]; visiera di Liegi, grande a ponte, traversata, con cerniere e chiodi: f. 1.6; visiera grande a ponte, arrotata, senza cerniere e senza chiodi: s. 12; visiera di Perottino, piccola, traversata, con cerniere: s. 18; elmo da giostra con baviera e senza colatta, 'di cattiva fazone', stazzonato: f. 1; vetta da arciere [*sic*], traversata, calotta di tela vermiglia: f. 2.12; vetta da arciere [*sic*], 'migliore, che la fe' Gentile', calotta di zendado: f. 4; cervelliere 'fiorentine, fate a Chascia e a San Donatto', da pedoni, nuove, colme, farsate di tela bianca: f. 1 una; cervelliera di Firenze, privata, scoperta: s. 8; cervelliera di Firenze da briganti, nuova, magagnata sull'orlo: s. 18; cervelliera di Milano da pedoni, nuova, colma, farsata bianca: f. 1; cervelliera privata, coperta, stazzonata: s. 6; cervelliera da briganti, vecchia, colma, ritraversata, magagnata, senza calotta: s. 9.7; cervelliera alta da briganti, vecchia, ritraversata: s. 15; cervelliera da garzoni, vecchia, rugginosa, cattiva, senza farsata: s. 4; cappello di ferro grandissimo, alla spagnola, con tre filari di chiodi intorno al coppo, stazzonato: s. 18; cappelo di ferro di Milano, a chiodi d'ottone, riforbito, buono e saldo: f. 1; capelli di ferro di Milano e della 'Magna', rugginosi, magagnati, vecchi: s. 9.6. uno; cappellina da arciere [sic], traversata alla guisa, farsata di tela: f. 2.12

one of Gentile's (i.e. made by an armourer called Gentile, or from his workshop – see 1392 below where the 'chasa' of Giacomuollo da Villa is referred to) basinets of Avignon type, of half proof (i.e. shot at with a hand-spanned bow or crossbow as opposed to fully proofed with a device-spanned crossbow), with large pointed visor, worn steel aventail, azure sendal (lightweight silk or very fine linen) aventail-cover, lined with vermilion cloth 9 florins; one of Petrolo's half-proofed Avignon basinets, a little corroded, with small Liège-type pointed visor, with perforations (in the skull for sewing on the padded lining), unlined 4 *fl.*; one of Petrolo's furbished Avignon basinets (i.e. of Avignon type), the skull has perforations 3*fl.* 14 *lire*; one of Petrolo's furbished Avignon basinets, large pointed visor (made by) Guastaferro, vermilion cloth collar 6*fl.*; one of the largest of Petrolo's Avignon basinets, large visor, Milan-made aventail of iron links coated in latten, vermilion cloth aventail-cover and collar 7*fl.*; one of Petrolo's Avignon basinets, fine and clean, small visor, loosely-attached iron aventail, cloth aventail-cover and sendal collar 6*fl.*; one of Martino da Milano's Avignon basinets, its skull coated [prob. with latten, see below], with no other fittings 4*fl.*; one of Tommasolo's furbished basinets without coating or other fittings 2*fl.* 12*l.*; one old-style Paris basinet, large visor, aventail of large iron links, cloth aventail-cover and collar 4*fl.*; one half-proofed Liège basinet, large pointed visor, iron aventail, sendal aventail-cover and lining 7*fl.* 12*l.*; one half-proofed Liège basinet with (lining) perforations, unlined 3*fl.*; [NB when there is more than one item their quantity is not given] [several] of Pinerolo's half-proofed Milan basinets with lining perforations and cloth linings 2*fl.* each; one old-fashioned half-proofed Milan basinet with 'cap, visor, and garland', iron aventail, cloth lining 2*fl.*; one old-fashioned Milan basinet, small, old-fashioned Milan visor, dyed cloth collar 1*fl.*; one furbished basinet, visor, collar in the 'great' style 1*fl.* 6*l.*; one of Guastaferro's Avignon visors, large at the tip *fl.* [no price recorded]; one furbished Liège visor, large at the tip, with hinges and rivets 1*fl.* 6*l.*; one visor, large at the tip, rotating [NB this prob. means that it is of a type that is interchangeable with other helmets], without hinges or rivets 12*s.*; one of Perottino's furbished visors, small, with hinges 18*s.*; one jousting helm with (reinforcing) bevor and without collar, of hollowed fashion, keeled (i.e. shaped with a frontal keel) 1*fl.*; one steel *vetta* (a type of small, close-fitting helmet usually fitted with 'little ears' – circular metal discs at the temples: see 1392 below where there is mention of helmets 'con orechiangnioli al modo di vette': 'with little ears in the manner of *vette*'), refurbished, vermilion cloth collar 2*fl*. 12*s*.; one steel *vetta*, the best of Gentile's making, sendal collar 4*fl*.; [several] Florentine (type) skullcaps made in Cascia and San Donato, of footsoldier's (type), new, ridged, lined with white cloth 1*fl*. each; one Florentine skullcap, hidden (i.e. of the type hidden beneath fabric), uncovered 8*s*.; one Florentine skullcap of (the type worn by) brigands (i.e. mercenaries), new, the edge corroded 18*s*.; one footsoldier's Milan skullcap, new, ridged, lined with white (cloth) 1*fl*.; one hidden skullcap, covered, keeled (i.e. shaped with a medial keel) 6*s*.; one brigands' skullcap, old, ridged, refurbished, corroded, without collar 9*s*. 7*d*.; one high brigands' skullcap, old, refurbished 15*s*.; one boy's skullcap, old, rusted, hollowed, unlined 4*s*.; one of the largest chapel de fers, in the Spanish style, with three lines of rivets around the skull, keeled (with a medial keel) 18*s*.; one iron Milan chapel de fer, with latten rivets, refurbished, good and soldered 1*fl*.; [several] 'great' iron Milan chapel de fers, rusted, corroded, old 9*s*. 6*d*. each; one steel capelline (a close-fitting helmet) of the furbished type, lined with cloth 2*fl*. 12*l*.

1368

bacinetto di Avignone traversato della guisa di Perottino, visiera grande, camaglio di ferro ottonato grosso, padiglione di tela, calotta di zendado: f. 10; bacinetto di Milano traversato, lungo, visiera grande, padiglione e calotta di tela, barbuta di ferro grossa con padiglione di zendado azzurro di sopra: f. 5.19; bacinetto di Milano lungo e basso, visiera grande, padiglione e calotta di tela, barbuta di ferro: f. 4.4; [several] bacinetti di Milano all'antica, vecchi e rugginosi, a guance e senza guance alla guisa vecchia, con farsate, grandi e piccoli di testa: s. 12 uno per l'altro; bacinetto forte con cannellina d'argento per portare la piuma, visiera grande, padiglione e calotta di tela, barbuta di maglia di ferro grossa a mezz'opera: f. 6.12; bacinetto basso, piccolo, vecchio e rugginoso, sanz'altro fornimento: s. 6.10; bacinetto rifatto, battuto e pertugiato, rozzo, senz'altro fornimento: f. 1.12; bacinetto 'ch'àe una peza in sul chochuzolo', rugginoso: f. 1; [several] bacinetti 'i quali si chiamano elmi crestuti all chatalana', alti all'antica, visiere grandi, vecchi e rugginosi: f. 1 uno per l'altro; visiera di Tommasino, grande, traversata, con cerniere e chiodi, salda e buona: f. 1.12; visiera grande, con cerniere e senza chiodi, cattiva e rugginosa: s. 6; visiera di Milano, piccola, traversata: s. 3; elmi crestuti: bacinetti 'i quali si chiamano elmi crestuti alla chatalana', alti all'antica, visiere grandi, vecchi e rugginosi: f. 1 uno; elmo da giostra con le viste: f. 1; elmo da giostra vecchio, rugginoso, cattivo: s. 2

one of Perottino's furbished Avignon basinets, large visor, large iron aventail – the links latten-covered, cloth aventail-cover, sendal collar 10*fl*.; one furbished Milan basinet, long, large visor, cloth aventail-cover and collar, mail *barbuta* (chin and throat defence) of large iron links, azure sendal aventail-cover over the top 5*fl*. 19*l*.; one Milan basinet, long and low, large visor, cloth aventail-cover and collar, iron *barbuta* 4*fl*. 4*l*.; [several] old-fashioned Milan basinets, old and rusted, with old-fashioned cheek-pieces and without cheek-pieces, large visor, and cloth collar, with large and small linings 12s. each; one strong basinet with silver plume-holder, large visor, cloth aventail-cover and collar, *barbuta* of large, half-riveted mail links (i.e. not every link is riveted) 6fl. 12l.; one low, small, old and rusted basinet without any fittings 6s. 10d.; one repaired basinet, dented and cracked without any fittings 1fl. 12l.; one rusted basinet which has a small hole patched with a plate 1fl.; [several] old-fashioned basinets called crested Catalan helms (i.e. of the Catalan type and shaped with a medial keel), large visors, old and rusted, 1fl. each; one of Tommasino's furbished visors, large, with hinges and rivets, and soldered and good 1fl. 12l.; one large visor, with hinges and without rivets, hollowed and rusted 6s.; one small, furbished Milan visor 3s.; [several] crested (i.e. keeled) helms, basinets, which are called Catalan crested helms, old-fashioned height, large visors, old and rusted 1fl. each; one jousting helm with the sight 1fl.; one old jousting helm, rusted, hollowed 2s.

1369
bacinetto traversato, visiera grande della guisa passata, 'stati all mostra', camaglio di ferro, padiglione e calotta di tela: f. 3; bacinetto all'antica, senza visiera, con nasale: s. 12; crestuta rugginosa, visiera grande: s. 12; nasali da bacinetto all'antica: d. 1 ½ uno; visiera di Averardo, traversata, con cerniere e chiodi: s. 18; visiera di Averardo, traversata, senza cerniere e senza chiodi: s. 12; elmo da giostra con baviera, forte, forbito: f. 1; elmo 'd'armare', vecchio, rugginoso: s. 2; cervelliera di Milano, alta, nuova, con farsata: f. 14; cervelliere di Milano e di Firenze, alte, forbite e verniciate: s. 18 una; cervelliere basse da villani, vecchie: s. 20; cappello di ferro di Milano, 'a chiovi intorno': f. 1

one furbished basinet, old-style large visor, to be shown (as a template), iron aventail, cloth aventail-cover and collar 3fl.; one old-fashioned basinet, without visor, with a nasal (defence) 12s.; one rusted crested (helm), large visor 12s.; [several] old-fashioned basinet nasals 1½d. each; one of Averardo's furbished visors, with hinges and rivets 18s.; one of Averardo's furbished visors, without hinges or rivets 12s.; one jousting helm with bevor, strong, furbished 1fl.; one arming helm, old, rusted 2s.; one Milan skullcap, high, new, lined 14fl.; [several] Milan and Florentine skullcaps, high, furbished and varnished 18s. each; [several] low villein's skullcaps, old 20s. (each); one Milan chapel de fer, with rivets around (the skull) 1fl.

1372
bacinetto 'al modo di crestuta': f. – [no price recorded]; visiera grande, vecchia: s. 3; visiera piccola, con cerniere: s. 2.4; visiera di Giannino, grande a ponte, traversata con cerniere e chiodi: f. 1.12; visiera piccola a ponte, vecchia, riforbita: s. 16; cervelliera di Firenze, alta, nuova, bella, con farsata: f. 1.3.6; cervelliera traversata, usata: s. 18; cervelliera privata, vecchia, coperta di tela bioda: s. 7

one basinet in the crested manner (i.e. medially keeled) fl. [no price recorded]; one large visor, old 3s.; one small visor, with hinges 2s. 4d.; one of Giannino's furbished visors, large at the tip, with hinges and rivets 1fl. 12l.; one visor small at the tip, old, refurbished 16s.; one Florentine skullcap, high, new, fine, lined 1fl. 3l. 6s.; one worn, refurbished skullcap 18s.; one hidden skullcap, old, covered with red cloth 7s.

1374
bacinetto di Milano lungo, della guisa passata, senza visiera, camaglio d'acciaio sotti-letto: f. 4.2; bacinetto della guisa 'dov'ebe 1 coroletto d'otone', visiera grande bordata d'ottone con doppioni e senza doppioni: f. – [no price recorded]; [several] bacinetti della guisa passata 'che si chiamavano cornutti', senza doppioni, di cattiva fazione, sono 'per recali a la guisa': f. – [no price recorded]

one Milan basinet, long, old-style, without visor, fine steel aventail (i.e. constructed of very small links) 4fl. 2l.; one basinet of the type that is fitted with one small latten-covered collar, large latten-bordered visor, with (prob. latten) coating and without coating fl. [no price recorded]; [several] old-style basinets which are called 'horned', without (latten) coating, of hollowed making, only of use as a model for the type [NB this is unclear] [no price recorded]

1375
visiera della guisa, traversata, a 2 viste, con cerniere e chiodi: f. 2.6

one furbished visor of the (standard) type, with two sights, with hinges and rivets 2fl. 6l.

1376
bacinetto di prova, della guisa, senza visiera, 'bordato il fronte d'ottone con dopioni dorati', senza farsata: f. 10

one proofed basinet of (standard) type, without visor, the front bordered with gilded-latten coating, unlined 10fl.

1378
visiera di Avignone della guisa di Daniello Coco, bordata d'ottone a bordo rilevato, con cerniere e chiodi ricorperti d'ottone: f. –

one of Daniello Coco's Avignon latten-bordered visors, with a border in relief, with hinges and rivets re-covered with latten fl. [no price recorded]

1379
cappelletto di Avignone della guisa di Martino da Milano, bordato d'ottone, 'da portare la piuma': f. 6; cappelletto di Avignone della guisa di Martino da Milano, con 2 piume 'e co' lo spechio di soto alle piume': f. 6; cappelletto della guisa, piccolo, bordato d'ottone, con tuello a 3 piume, senz'altro guarnimento: f. 4

one of Martino da Milano's Avignon small chapel de fers, bordered with latten, (made to) bear a plume 6fl.; one of Martino da Milano's Avignon small chapel de fers with two plumes made to mirror each other *6fl.*; one (standard) small chapel der fer, small, bordered with latten, with finial (i.e. decorative top piece) with three plumes, without any other garnishings *4fl.*

1382

bacinetto di Avignone della guisa di Daniello Coco, visiera bordata e posata con doppioni d'ottone, senza calotta, 'fatto a misura': f. 8; con calotta di tela: f. 8.3.6; bacinetto di Avignone della guisa di Daniello Coco, camaglio d'acciaio a bozza, padiglione e calotta di boccaccino bianco: f. 15.12; bacinetto di Avignone della guisa di Daniello Coco, 'chon uno picholo rolletto a la visiera', camaglio di ferro, padiglione e calotta di tela: f. 11.12; bacinetto di Avignone della guisa di Daniello Coco, tutto bianco, visiera, sanz'altro guarnimento: f. 12; bacinetto di Avignone della guisa di Martino da Milano, 'fato in Piamonte', camaglio d'acciaio a bozza, padiglione e calotta di tela tinta: f. 14; bacinetto di Avignone alla guisa, visiera bordata d'ottone con doppioni d'ottone, calotta di tela, 'fato in Lombardia per Martino': f. 7; bacinetto di Lione alla guisa, bordato 'cho' rolletto di dretro', calotta di tela: f. 6; bacinetto di Milano di prova, bordato, visiera bordata d'ottone, camaglio d'acciaio a bozza, padiglione di tela: f. 14; bacinetto di Milano di 1/2 prova, bordato, camaglio di ferro leggero: f. 7.4; bacinetto di Milano di 1/2 prova, di ferro pesante, bordato d'ottone alla guisa, calotta di tela: f. 4; bacinetto di Milano di 1/2 prova, bordato in Avignone, calotta di tela: f. 3.12; bacinetto di Milano di 1/2 prova, di ferro tutto bianco, senza calotta: f. 2.20; bacinetto verniciato nero, visiera con doppioni d'ottone, senza calotta: f. 3; bacinetto vecchio ritraversato, visiera, camaglio di ferro sottile, 'istofa' di zendado rosa con frangia nera: f. 3.12; visiera di Avignone, nuova, senza cerniere: f. 1; visiera di Milano, piccola, da bacineeti da fanti: s. 12; visiera vecchia, rugginosa: s. 7.2

one of Daniello Coco's Avignon basinets, the visor bordered and overlaid with a latten coating, without collar, made to measure *8fl.*, with cloth collar *8fl. 3l. 6s.*; one of Daniello Coco's Avignon basinets, riveted steel aventail, white buckskin aventail-cover and collar *15fl. 12l.*; one of Daniello Coco's Avignon basinets, which has a little wheel on the visor, iron aventail, cloth aventail-cover and collar *11fl. 12l.*; one of Daniello Coco's Avignon basinets, all white (i.e. polished metal), visor, without any other garnishing *12fl.*; one of Martino da Milano's basinets, made in Piedmont, riveted steel aventail (i.e. every link is riveted), dyed cloth aventail-cover and collar *14fl.*; one Avignon basinet, latten-bordered visor with latten coating, cloth collar, made in Lombardy by Martino *7fl.*; one Lyon basinet, bordered with a border that rolls from behind (i.e. from the inside of the helmet), cloth collar *6fl.*; one proofed Milan basinet, bordered, latten-bordered visor, riveted steel aventail, cloth aventail-cover *14fl.*; one half-proofed Milan basinet, bordered, light iron aventail *7fl. 4l.*; one half-proofed Milan basinet, of light iron, bordered with latten in (standard) style, cloth collar *4fl.*; one half-proofed Milan basinet, bordered in Avignon (i.e. the border affixed there), cloth collar *3fl. 12l.*; one half-proofed Milan basinet, of all-white iron, without collar *2fl. 20l.*; one black-varnished basinet, visor with latten coating, without collar *3fl.*; one refurbished, old basinet, visor, fine iron aventail, stuffed with rose sendal with black fringe 3*fl.* 12*l.*; one new Avignon visor without hinges 1*fl.*; one small Milan visor of a footsoldier's basinet 12*s.*; one old, rusted visor 7*s.* 2*d.*

1385

bacinetto di Avignone della guisa di Daniello Coco, bordato d'ottone, camaglio di ferro lavorato al bordo d'acciaio: f. 10.12; bacinetto di Avignone vecchio, verniciato nero, visiera piccola bordata d'ottone, 'fecie Daniello di nuova guisa': f. 2.8; bacinetto di Lione bordato d'ottone alla guisa, un poco usato e ritraversato, visiera con la baviera, senza calotta: f. 7.12; bacinetto di Lione alla guisa, bordato d'ottone a doppioni e ghirlanda d'ottone, visiera: f. 9.12; senza ghirlanda: f. 9; bacinetto di *Chiaramonte* (poss. Clermont) alla guisa, bordato d'ottone a doppioni, visiera: f. 6; coppo di bacinetto di *Chiaramonte* (poss. Clermont), senza visiera 'con una ventaglia al fronte': f. 3.12; bacinetto di Milano di prova, bordato d'ottone alla guisa, visiera a due viste: f. 6; bacinetto di Milano di prova, bordato d'ottone alla guisa, visiera a una vista: f. 5.18; bacinetto di Milano di 1/2 prova, bordato d'ottone, camaglio di ferro: f. 5.12; bacinetto di Milano di 1/2 prova, visiera non bordata a doppioni d'ottone, 'di buona fazone': f. 3.12; bacinetto di Milano di 1/2 prova, bordato d'ottone alla guisa a doppioni di ferro [*sic*]: f. 3.6; visiera di Milano della guisa, bordata d'ottone: f. 1.6; visiera di Milano della guisa, bianca, buona: f. 1.2; visiera da vette, piccole, cattive: s. 1 una; vetta di Milano 'all'inglese, con gli orechi', bordata d'ottone: f. 3.18; non bordata: f. 2.18; vetta di Milano da briganti, visiera piccola puntuta, con calotta: f. 1.20; vetta di Milano da briganti, visiera piccola rotonda, calotta di tela: f. 1.8; cerveliera di Milano segreta, fatta a scaglie, verniciata nera: s. 20; cerveliere di Milano da nave per balestrieri, forti ad aletta, bianche e venicate nere: f. 1.20 una; senza alette, 'no sono da balestriere, verniciate nere': f. 1.4. una; cerveliere di Milano da briganti, nuova, colma, con farsata: s. 22; cerveliera di Firenze, privata, verniciata nera, con calotta: s. 12; cerveliera privata, vecchia, coperta di tela con farsata: s. 8; cappelletto di Avignone della guisa di Daniello Coco, bordato d'ottone, con tuello d'ottone: f. 4; cappellina della guisa nuova, coperta di brunetta di Lierre, camaglio di ferro sottile: f. 6; cappellina della guisa nuova, coperta di velluto nero, camaglio d'acciaio a 1/2 bozza, padiglione e calotta di zendado vermiglio: f. 8.12; cappellina della guisa nuova, verniciata nera, da coprire: f. 1.20

one of Daniello Coco's Avignon basinets, bordered with latten, aventail of worked iron with steel border 10*fl.* 12*l.*; one old Avignon basinet, black varnished, small latten-bordered visor, made by Daniello in the new fashion 2*fl.* 8*l.*; one Lyon basinet, bordered with latten in the (standard) way, a little worn and refurbished, visor with bevor, without collar 7*fl.* 12*l.*; one Lyon basinet, standard latten border with coating and garland of latten, visor 9*fl.* 12*l.*, without garland 9*fl.*; one basinet of the Chiaramonte type, bordered with latten with coating, visor 6*fl.*; one Chiaramonte-type basinet skull, without visor, with a ventilation (aperture) at the front 3*fl.* 12*l.*; one proofed Milan basinet, standard latten border, visor with two sights 6*fl.*; one proofed Milan basinet, standard latten border, visor with one sight 5*fl.* 18*l.*; one half-proofed Milan basinet, latten border, iron aventail 5*fl.* 12*l.*; one half-proofed

Milan basinet, visor without latten border with coating of latten, of good making 3*fl.* 12*l.*; one half-proofed Milan basinet, standard latten border with coating of iron [*sic*] 3*fl.* 6*l.*; one latten-bordered Milan visor 1*fl.* 6*l.*; one Milan visor, white, good 1*fl.* 2*l.*; one small, hollowed, visor of a *vette* 1*s.*; one English-style Milan *vetta* with little ears (i.e. disc-shaped ear defences), bordered with latten, 3*fl.* 18*l.*, unbordered 2*fl.* 18*l.*; one brigands' Milan *vetta*, small pointed visor, with collar 1*fl.* 20*l.*; one brigands' Milan *vetta*, small round visor, cloth collar 1*fl.* 8*l.*; one secret Milan skullcap, made of scales, black varnished 20*s.*; [several] Milan skullcaps for shipboard crossbowmen, reinforced with little wings (i.e. defensive plates at the temples), white and black varnished 1*fl.* 20*l.* each – without little wings not being for crossbowmen, black varnished 1*fl.* 4*l.* each; one brigands' Milan skullcap, new, ridged, lined 22*s.*; one Florentine skullcap, hidden, black varnished, with collar 12*s.*; one hidden skullcap, old, covered with cloth, lined 8*s.*; one of Daniello Coco's Avignon small chapel de fers, bordered with latten, with latten finial 4*fl.*; one new-style capelline, covered with brown (fabric) from Lier (town near Antwerp), light iron aventail 6*fl.*; one new-style capelline, covered with black velvet, half-riveted steel aventail, vermilion sendal aventail-cover and collar 8*fl.* 12*l.*; one new-style capelline, black varnished, covered 1*fl.* 20*l.*

1386
bacinetto di Avignone della guisa di Daniello Coco, di prova, bordato d'ottone, camaglio d'acciaio a bozza, padiglione e calotta di boccaccino azzurro: f. 15; bacinetto di Avignone della guisa di Daniello Coco, di prova, bordato d'ottone, camaglio d'acciaio a 1/2 bozza, padiglione di boccaccino, calotta di tela: f. 12; bacinetto di Avignone della guisa di Daniello Coco, di prova, bordato d'ottone a doppioni d'ottone, buono: f. 7.8; bacinetto di Avignone della guisa di Daniello Coco, di prova, non bordato e senza doppioni, buono: f. 6.16; bacinetto di Milano di 1/2 prova, forte, bordato d'ottone, camaglio di ferro: f. 7.6; bacinetto di Milano di 1/2 prova, leggero, bordato d'ottone, camaglio di ferro: f. 6; cappellina di Avignone, della guisa, verniciata nera, da coprire: f. 1.19

one of Daniello Coco's proofed Avignon basinets, latten-bordered, riveted steel aventail, azure buckskin aventail-cover and collar 15*fl.*; one of Daniello Coco's proofed Avignon basinets, latten-bordered, half-riveted steel aventail, buckskin aventail-cover, cloth collar 12*fl.*; one of Daniello Coco's proofed Avignon basinets, latten-bordered with latten coating, good 7*fl.* 8*l.*; one of Daniello Coco's proofed Avignon basinets, unbordered and without (latten) coating, good 6*fl.* 16*l.*; one half-proofed Milan basinet, strong, latten-bordered, iron aventail 7*fl.* 6*l.*; one half-proofed Milan basinet, light, latten-bordered, iron aventail 6*fl.*; one Avignon capelline, black varnished, covered 1*fl.* 19*l.*

1387
bacinetto di Avignone della guisa di Daniello Coco, di prova, bordato d'ottone, camaglio d'acciaio *caciato* a bozza, padiglione e calotta di boccaccino bianco: f. 14; bacinetto di Parigi bordato d'ottone, rugginoso, camaglio di ferro della 'Magna': f. 5;

bacinetto vecchio ritraversato, bordato d'ottone, della guisa passata, camaglio vecchio rifatto: f. 4; bacinetto vecchio ritraversato all'antica, 'di mala fazone', camaglio leggero rifatto: f. 2.12; visiera di Avignone della guisa, bordata d'ottone: f. 1; visiere rozze, non cavate: s. 6 una; visiere rozze, cattive: s. 1 una; coppi rozzi, cavati: f. 1.16 il coppo; cappelletto di Avignone della guisa, bordato d'ottone: f. 4; cappelletto di Avignone della guisa, tutto bianco: f. 3; cappelletto di Milano della guisa, temperato, bordato d'ottone, bello e di bella fazione: f. 5; cappelletto di Milano della guisa, bordato d'ottone, camaglio fatto di lame a scaglie: f. 5.12; cappellina della guisa, verniciata nera, coperta di brunetta, camaglio d'acciaio a 1/2 bozza 'rifato di cota': f. 8; una rotella di ferro per fare una cappellina: s. 18

one of Daniello Coco's proofed Avignon basinets, latten-bordered, riveted steel aventail marked (i.e. the links are marked by its maker), white buckskin aventail-cover and collar 14*fl.*; one Paris basinet, latten-bordered, rusted, 'great' (sized) iron aventail 5*fl.*; one old, refurbished basinet, latten-bordered, old-fashioned, repaired old aventail 4*fl.*; one old, refurbished, old-fashioned basinet of poor making, repaired light aventail 2*fl.* 12*l.*; one latten-bordered Avignon visor 1*fl.*; [several] rough, un-hollowed visors (i.e. rough from the hammer, of flat sheet form ready for finishing) 6*s.* each; one rusted visor, hollowed 1*s.*; [several] rough (basinet) skulls, hollowed 1*fl.* 16*l.* each skull; one Avignon small chapel de fer, bordered with latten 4*fl.*; one Avignon small chapel de fer, all white 3*fl.*; one Milan small chapel de fer, tempered, bordered with latten, fine and of fine making 5*fl.*; one Milan small chapel de fer, bordered with latten, aventail made of lames (i.e. articulated metal plates) with scales 5*fl.* 12*l.*; one (standard) type capelline, black varnished, covered with brown (fabric), half-riveted steel aventail remade from a (mail) coat 8*fl.*; one iron disc to make a capelline 18*s.*

1388
cappellina della guisa, verniciata nera, coperta di velluto nero, camaglio d'acciaio di 1/2 bozza rifato, padiglione e calotta di boccaccino bianco: f. 7.12; cappellina della guisa, verniciata nera, coperta di brunetta nera di Lierre, camaglio di ferro rifatto, padiglione e calotta di boccaccino e di tela: f. 6; cappellina di ferro, verniciata nera, al modo inglese: f. 1

one (standard) type capelline, black varnished, covered with black velvet, repaired half-riveted steel aventail, white buckskin aventail-cover and collar 7*fl.* 12*l.*; one standard capelline, black varnished, covered with dark-brown (fabric) from Lier (town near Antwerp), repaired iron aventail, buckskin and cloth aventail-cover and collar 6*fl.*; one English-style iron capelline, black varnished 1*fl.*

1389
visiera di Avignone di Daniello Coco, bianca: f. 1.6; visiera di Milano, bianca: s. 20; cervelliere di Milano da nave per balestriere, con ventaglie per balestrieri, forti, verniciate nere, con calotte: f. 1.18 una; cappelletto di ferro della 'Magna', usato, vecchio e rugginoso: s. 12; cappellina della guisa, verniciata nera, coperta di panno nero,

camaglio d'acciaio a 1/2 bozza: f. 7; cappellina della guisa, verniciata nera, coperta di panno verde: f. 4; cappellina di ferro, verniciata nera, con ventaglia, senza fornimenti: f. 2; cappellina vecchia, coperta di panno nero, camaglio di ferro, tuello di ferro: f. 2; cappellina 'al modo guaschone', vecchia e usata, camaglio di ferro, capperone bigio: f. 1

one of Daniello Coco's Avignon visors, white 1*fl.* 6*l.*; one Milan visor, white 20*s.*; [several] Milan skullcaps for shipboard crossbowmen, with ventilations for crossbowmen, strong, black varnished, with collars 1*fl.* 18*l.* each; one small chapel de fer, of iron, of the 'great' (type), worn, old, and rusted 12*s.*; one capelline of (standard) type, black varnished, covered with black cloth, half-riveted steel aventail 7*fl.*; one standard capelline, black varnished, covered with green cloth 4*fl.*; one iron capelline, black varnished, with ventilations, without fittings 2*fl.*; one old capelline, covered with green cloth, iron aventail, iron finial 2*fl.*; one Gascon-style capelline, old and worn, iron aventail, grey hood 1*fl.*

1390
bacinetto di Avignone di maestro Stefano da Lione, bordato d'ottone, visiera, senza calotta: f. 7.12; bacinetto vecchio di Daniello Coco, verniciato nero, bordato d'ottone, visiera piccola: f. 2; coppi cavati, magagnati: f. 1 uno; 1 visiera rozza, s. 5; cappellina di ferro, verniciata nera, senza ventaglia: f. 1; cappellina di ferro, verniciata nera, con ventaglia: f. 1.12

one of Master Stefano de Lione's [Stephen of Lyon's] basinets, latten-bordered, visor, without collar 7*fl.* 12*l.*; one of Daniello Coco's old basinets, black varnished, latten-bordered, small visor 2*fl.*; [several] hollowed skulls, corroded, 1*fl.* each; one rough visor 5*s.*; one iron capelline, black varnished, without ventilations 1*fl.*; one iron capelline, black varnished, with ventilations 1*fl.* 12*l.*

1391
visiera di Tolosa, bianca, nuova, traversata: f. 1; coppi rozzi, cavati, buoni: f. 2 uno; cappelline, cioè vette di Milano da briganti, con ghirlanda di ferro [*sic*], calotta di tela: f. 1.12 una; cappelletto d'acciaio di Avignone della guisa di Daniello Coco, bordato d'ottone, bello: f. 4; cappellina verniciata nera, coperta di brunetta, camaglio di ferro leggero, con ghirlanda 'coverta da rieto', f. 2; cappellina di ferro di Avignone, della guisa, verniciata nera, senza fornimenti: f. 1.6; cappellina di scaglie di ferro, verniciata nera, camaglio di ferro fatto a scaglie con un bordo di maglia: f. 2.6

one furbished Toulouse visor, white, new 1*fl.*; [several] rough (basinet) skulls, hollowed, good 2*fl.* each; [several] capellines – namely brigands' Milan *vette*, with iron garland [*sic*], cloth collars 1*fl.* 12*l.* each; one of Daniello Coco's Avignon small chapel de fers, bordered with latten, fine 4*fl.*; one black-varnished capelline, covered with brown (fabric), light iron aventail, with a garland covering the rear 2*fl.*; one iron Avignon capelline, black varnished, without fittings 1*fl.* 6*l.*; one capelline of iron scales, black varnished, iron aventail made of scales with a mail border 2*fl.* 6*l.*

1392

bacinetto di Avignone di Daniello Coco, d'acciaio temperato, bordato d'ottone, baviera a 2 pezze: f. 7.18; bacinetto di Avignone di Daniello Coco, di nuova guisa 'che si chiama cane', bordato d'ottone: f. 7; bacinetto di Avignone di maestro Simone di Fiandra, di prova, bordato d'ottone a doppioni d'ottone, visiera: f. 6.6; bacinetto della 'Magna', visiera bordata d'ottone a doppioni d'ottone, camaglio d'acciaio: f. 8.12; bacinetto di Tolosa della guisa passata, bordato d'ottone, usato, camaglio d'acciaio a bozza: f. 9; visiera della 'Magna' di ferro, arrotata, con cerniere e chiodi: s. 12; coppi di ferro e d'acciaio rozzi, cavati, buoni, per fare bacinetti della guisa, 'àe a chasa Giacomuollo da Villa': f. 1.8 uno; coppo d'acciaio rozzo, cavato, buono per fare un bacinetto della guisa, 'àe Daniello': f. 1.18; vetta all'inglese, verniciata nera, con 'orechiangnoli', di cattiva fazione: f. 1; cappelline di ferro, verniciate nere, con 'orechiangnioli' al modo di vette, calotte vecchie: s. 18 una; cappello d'acciaio di Milano, della guisa, bordato d'ottone, con tuello d'ottone: f. 3; cappellina d'acciaio temperato di Milano, a barbozza di nuova guisa, visiera bordata d'ottone, camaglio piccolo d'acciaio *caciato*: f. 9; cappellina d'acciaio temperato di Milano, a barbozza, visiera bordata d'ottone, 'no sì bella', camaglio d'acciaio a bozza: f. 7.12; cappellina della guisa, verniciata nera, coperta di velluto nero in seta fine, bordata d'ottone, guarnita di zendado nero usato e ricamato 'da pie'', camaglio d'acciaio a bozza bordato: f. 11.12; cappellina della guisa, coperta di velluto nero in accia, bordata d'ottone, padiglione e calotta di boccaccino azzurro, camaglio d'acciaio suoro: f. 9; cappellina della guisa, verniciata nera, coperta di brunetta nera di Lierre, padiglione e calotta di boccaccino rosso, camaglio d'acciaio a 1/2 bozza: f. 6; cappellina della guisa, verniciata nera, coperta di brunetta nera di Lierre, padiglione e calotta di tela azzurra, camaglio di ferro rifatto: f. 4; cappelline di fero di Avignone, di Daniello Coco e di Simone di Fiandra, verniciate nere: f. 1.12 una; cappellina d'acciaio temperato di Milano, verniciata nera, usata: f. 1.12; cappelline di Milano, fatte a scaglie da portare segrete, verniciate nere, camagli fatti a scaglie 'con un pocho di malglia [*sic*]': s. 21 una; cappelline di ferro, verniciate nere, 'con orechiangnoli al modo di vette', con calotte vecchie: s. 18 una; cappellina di ferro, bordata d'ottone, coperta di panno rosso e azzurro, camaglio di ferro leggero: f. 1; cappellina a ventaglia, coperta di panno nero con 'caschavelli' bianchi, camaglio di ferro usato: f. 1.12; bacinetto verniciato nero, vecchio, rifatto, al modo di cappellina, camaglio di ferro: f. 2

one of Daniello Coco's Avignon basinets, of tempered steel, latten-bordered, two-piece bevor 7*fl.* 18*l.*; one of Daniello Coco's Avignon basinets, in the new style which is called 'dog', latten-bordered 7*fl.*; one of Master Simone di Fiandra's [Simon of Flanders'] proofed Avignon basinets, latten-bordered with latten coating, visor 6*fl.* 6*l.*; one 'great' basinet, latten-bordered visor with latten coating, steel aventail 8*fl.* 12*l.*; one old-style Toulouse basinet, latten-bordered, worn, riveted steel aventail 9*fl.*; one iron 'great' visor, rotating, with hinges and rivets 12*s.*; [several] rough iron and steel skulls, hollowed, good, to make basinets of the sort (made at) Giacomuollo da Villa's workshop 1*fl.* 8*l.* each; one rough steel skull, hollowed, good, for making a basinet in the style of Daniello 1*fl.* 18*l.*; one English-style *vetta*, black varnished, with little ears, of hollowed fashion 1*fl.*; [several] iron capellines, black varnished, with little ears in the manner of (those on) *vette*, old collars 18*s.* each; one steel Milan chapel de fer, bordered with latten, with latten finial 3*fl.*; one Milan tempered-steel capelline, with new-style bevor, latten-bordered visor, small steel aventail (the links) marked (by its maker) 9*fl.*; one Milan tempered-steel capelline, with bevor, latten-bordered visor, not so fine, riveted steel aventail marked (with a maker's mark) 7*fl.* 12*l.*; one capelline of (standard) type, black varnished, covered with finely-set black velvet, bordered with latten, garnished with worn black sendal and embroidered with 'pie" [NB this is unclear], riveted steel aventail with (decorative) border 11*fl.* 12*l.*; one standard capelline, covered with black velvet (woven into) linen, bordered with latten, azure buckskin aventail-cover and collar, gilt-steel aventail 9*fl.*; one standard capelline, black varnished, covered with dark-brown (fabric) from Lier (town near Antwerp), rose buckskin aventail-cover and collar, half-riveted steel aventail 6*fl.*; one standard capelline, black varnished, covered with dark-brown (fabric) from Lier, azure cloth aventail-cover and collar, repaired iron aventail 4*fl.*; [several] of Daniello Coco and Simon of Flanders' iron Avignon capellines, black varnished 1*fl.* 12*l.* each; one tempered-steel Milan capelline, black varnished, worn 1*fl.* 12*l.*; [several] Milan capellines, made from scales to be worn secretly, black varnished, aventails made of scales with a little mail 21*s.* each; [several] iron Milan capellines, black varnished, with little ears in the manner of a *vette*, with old collars 18*s.* each; one iron capelline, bordered with latten, covered with rose and azure cloth, light iron aventail 1*fl.*; one capelline with ventilations, covered with black cloth with white (metal) little round bells, worn iron aventail 1*fl.* 12*l.*; one black-varnished basinet, old, repaired, in the manner of a capelline, iron aventail 2*fl.*

1393

bacinetto a baviera della guisa, 'bordato in Avignone e fato per uno maestro di Parigi': f. 7; bacinetto di Lione a baviera della guisa, bordato, 'che non è sì bello': f. 6; bacinetto di Milano di prova, della guisa a visiera, bordato d'ottone, camaglio d'acciaio *caciato* di Simone Corrente, padiglione e calotta di boccaccino bianco: f. 14; bacinetto di Tolosa di prova alla guisa, doppioni di ferro [*sic*]: f. 5; bacinetto della 'Magna' alla guisa, bordato d'ottone, camaglio d'acciaio suoro: f. 7; camaglio d'acciaio a 1/2 bozza: f. 7; vetta di ferro di Milano da briganti, visiera piccola, con calotta: f. 1.12; cappelli di Milano tondi [*sic*], bordati d'ottone, 'fati alla guisa', con tuelli piccoli d'ottone: f. 2.6 uno; cappellina d'acciaio a barbozza di nuova guisa, usata, camaglio d'acciaio a bozza: f. 4.12; cappellina d'acciaio a barbozza, visiera piccola bordata d'ottone, senza camaglio: f. 4.8; cappellina della guisa, verniciata nera, coperta di velluto di grana, padiglione di velluto di grana, calotta di zendado rosso, bordata d'argento bianco che pesò once 4.8, senza camaglio: f. 11; cappellina d'acciaio, della guisa, verniciata nera, coperta di velluto nero in accia non molto buono, padiglione e calotta di tela vermiglia, camaglio d'acciaio a 1/2 bozza: f. 8; cappellina verniciata nera, coperta di brunetta di Lierre, padiglione e calotta di boccaccino azzurro, camaglio d'acciaio a 1/2 bozza: f. 6.12; cappellina verniciata nera, coperta di camoscio bianco, vecchia, camaglio d'acciaio rifatto: f. 3; cappelline fatte a scaglie, verniciate nere, 'per portare segrete soto il chapucio': s. 21 una

one standard basinet with matching bevor, bordered (with latten) in Avignon and made by a Paris master *7fl.*; one Lyon basinet with matching bevor, bordered, which is not so fine *6fl.*; one proofed Milan basinet with visor, latten-bordered, steel aventail marked (on a link) by Simone Corrente (its maker), white buckskin aventail-cover and collar *14fl.*; one proofed Toulouse basinet, coated with iron [*sic*] *5fl.*; one 'great' basinet, latten-bordered, gilded-steel aventail *7fl.*; half-riveted steel aventail *7fl.*; one iron brigands' Milan *vetta*, small visor, with collar *1fl. 12l.*; [several] round Milan chapel de fers, bordered with latten, (all) made to match, with small latten finials *2fl. 6l.* each; one new-style steel capelline with bevor, worn, riveted steel aventail *4fl. 12l.*; one steel capelline with bevor, small latten-bordered visor, without aventail *4fl. 8l.*; one capelline of (standard) type, black varnished, covered with (coarse) grained velvet, (coarse) grained velvet aventail-cover, red sendal collar, bordered with white silver weighing 4.8oz, without aventail *11fl.*; one standard steel capelline, black varnished, covered with black velvet (woven into) linen – not very well, vermilion cloth aventail-cover and collar, half-riveted steel aventail *8fl.*; one black-varnished capelline, covered with brown Lier (fabric), azure buckskin aventail-cover and collar, half-riveted steel aventail *6fl. 12l.*; one black-varnished capelline, covered with white camaca (silk fabric), old, repaired steel aventail *3fl.*; [several] capellines made of scales, black varnished, to be worn secretly beneath a hood *21s.* each

1394
bacinetto di Avignone di Simone di Fiandra, di prova, a baviera al modo di cane, bordato d'ottone, camaglio d'acciaio *caciato*, padiglione e calotta di velluto nero: f. 12.12; bacinetto di Avignone di Daniello Coco, di prova, a baviera al modo di cane, tutto bianco, camaglio d'acciaio a bozza, padiglione e calotta di boccaccino bianco: f. 13; bacinetto di Avignone di Daniello Coco, di prova, a baveria al modo di cane, tutto bianco: f. 8.12; bacinetto di Avignone di Giacomolo da Villa, di prova, 'al modo di cane a baviera, tuto bia[n]cho colla covertta [*sic*] dinanzi al modo di mezo elmo': f. 5; bacinetto di Avignone di maestro Stefano da Lione, di prova, a visiera della guisa, tutto bianco senza doppioni: f. 5.18; bacinetto di Chambéry di prova, bordato d'ottone, camaglio d'acciaio a 1/2 bozza, padiglione e calotta di tela tinta: f. 6; visiere di ferro rozze in piastra, 'per fare visiere da bacineto della guisa', non cavate, 'fate a Vigliana piue tenpo [*sic*] fa': s. 4 una; agugliette di ferro da visiere della guisa per bacinetti: d. 2 una; coppo rozzo al modo di cane, 'fe' Giacomolo da Villa': f. 2; cervelliere private, 'ritonde da portare segrette', vecchie: s. 10 una; cappellina d'acciaio a barbozza di nuova guisa, bianca, camaglio d'acciaio a 1/2 bozza: f. 5.12; cappello di Milano tondo [*sic*], bordato d'ottone, 'rafazonato in Vingonone e ritraversato': f. 2.6; cappellina della guisa, verniciata nera, coperta di velluto nero vecchio, bordata d'ottone, padiglione e calotta di tela rosa, camaglio d'acciaio fino suoro:

f. 5.12; cappellina della guisa, verniciata nera, coperta di brunetta nera di Lierre, padiglione e calotta di boccaccino azzurro, camaglio d'acciaio a 1/2 bozza nuovo: f. 6; cappellina della guisa, verniciata nera, coperta di brunetta nera di Lierre, padiglione e calotta di boccaccino bianco, camaglio d'acciaio a 1/2 bozza nuovo: f. 6; cappelline di ferro, verniciate nere, coperte di brunetta nera usata, padiglione e calotte di tela tinta azzurra e vermiglia: f. 2.6 una; cappellina di ferro, verniciata nera, coperta di camoscio bianco, calotta di tela rosa: f. 2; cappellina nera, con la ventaglia davanti, con calotta: f. 1

one of Simon of Flanders' proofed Avignon basinets, with bevor in the manner of a dog, latten-bordered, steel aventail (maker's) marked, black velvet aventail-cover and collar 12*fl.* 12*l.*; one of Daniello Coco's proofed Avignon basinets, with bevor in the manner of a dog, all white, riveted steel aventail, white buckskin aventail-cover and collar 13*fl.*; one of Daniello Coco's proofed Avignon basinets, with bevor in the manner of a dog, all white 8*fl.* 12*l.*; one of Giacomolo da Villa's proofed Avignon basinets, in the manner of a dog with bevor, all white, with neck (defence) covered with ventilations in the manner of a demi-helm 5*fl.*; one of Master Stephen of Lyon's proofed Avignon basinets, with matching visor, all white, without coating 5*fl.* 18*l.*; one proofed Chambéry basinet, latten-bordered, half-riveted steel aventail, dyed cloth aventail-cover and collar 6*fl.*; [several] iron visors in rough sheet (form), for making basinet visors of the standard type, un-hollowed, made in Avignon at various times 4*s.* each; [several] iron-tipped laces for standard basinet visors 2*d.* each; one rough skull in the manner of a dog made by Giacomolo da Villa 2*fl.*; [several] hidden skullcaps, rounded to be worn secretly, old 10*s.* each; one steel capelline with new-style bevor, white, half-riveted steel aventail 5*fl.* 12*l.*; one round Milan chapel de fer, bordered with latten, remade in Avignon and re-exported 2*fl.* 6*l.*; one capelline of (standard) type, black varnished, covered with old black velvet, bordered with latten, rose cloth aventail-cover and collar, fine gilt-steel aventail 5*fl.* 12*l.*; one standard capelline, black varnished, covered with dark-brown (fabric) from Lier (town near Antwerp), azure buckskin aventail-cover and collar, new half-riveted steel aventail 6*fl.*; one standard capelline, black varnished, covered with Lier dark-brown (fabric), white buckskin aventail-cover and collar, new half-riveted steel aventail 6*fl.*; [several] iron capellines, black varnished, covered with worn dark-brown (fabric), aventail-covers and collars of azure- and vermilion-dyed cloth 2*fl.* 6*l.* each; one iron capelline, black varnished, covered with white camaca (silk fabric), rose cloth collar 2*fl.*; one black capelline, with the ventilation at the front, with collar 1*fl.*

1395

visiera bordata d'ottone, arrotata, nuova: s. 12; cervelliere di ferro da briganti, vecchia, ritraversata: s. 12; cappellina verniciata nera, con la ventaglia, bordata d'ottone, coperta di velluto nero vecchio, padiglione e calotta di boccaccino nero, camaglio d'acciaio a bozza leggero: f. 8; cappellina verniciata nera, bordata d'ottone, coperta di velluto nero, calotta di boccaccino nero, senz'altro guarnimento: f. 3.12; cappellina di Manuello, verniciata nera, coperta di brunetta nera vecchia, padiglione e calotta di tela vecchia, camaglio di ferro leggero: f. 2.12; cappellina verniciata nera, a 2 ventaglie, coperta di brunetta nera usata, padiglione e calotta di tela: f. 2; cappellina verniciata nera, coperta di velluto nero, 'fata per meser Franciescho di Mettone', il coppo bordato d'ottone, camaglio d'acciaio suoro e a chiodi d'ottone: f. 7

one latten-bordered visor, rotating, new, 12s.; [several] iron brigands' skullcaps, old, refurbished 12s. (each); one black-varnished capelline, with a ventilation (aperture), bordered with latten, covered with old black velvet, black buckskin aventail-cover and collar, light, riveted steel aventail 8fl.; one black-varnished capelline, bordered with latten, covered with black velvet, black buckskin collar, without any other fittings 3fl. 12l.; one of Manuello's capellines, black varnished, covered with old dark-brown (fabric), old cloth aventail-cover and collar, light iron aventail 2fl. 12l.; one black-varnished capelline, with two ventilations, covered with worn dark-brown (fabric), cloth aventail-cover and collar 2fl.; one black-varnished capelline, covered with black velvet, made by Mr Franciescho di Mettone, the skull bordered with latten, gilt-steel aventail, and with latten (helmet) rivets 7fl.

1396

bacinetto di Avignone di Daniello Coco, di prova, baviera e visiera alla guisa, tutto bianco, senz'altro fornimento: f. 7; bacinetto di Avignone di Daniello Coco, di prova, baviera e visiera alla guisa, bordata la visiera, senz'altro guarnimento 'perch'ànno il mantello di dietro': f. 8.12; bacinetto di Avignone di Daniello Coco, di prova, a baviera dinanzi e di dietro, bordato d'ottone alla guisa, camaglio d'acciaio *caciato* piccolo, padiglione e calotta di boccaccino bianco: f. 13; bacinetto di Avignone di Bernardone di Condomo, di prova, a baveria dinanzi con visiera al modo di cane, bordato d'ottone, 'sanza niuno guarnimento': f. 9; bacinetto di Avignone di Simone di Fiandra, di prova, a baveria dinanzi e visiera alla guisa, tutto bianco, camaglio a bozza rifatto, padiglione e calotta di boccaccino bianco: f. 12; bacinetto di Avignone di Simone di Fiandra, di prova, a baviera dinanzi e visiera della guisa al modo di cane, bordato d'ottone, 'sanza niuno guarnimento': f. 8; bacinetto di Avignone di Giacomolo da Villa, di prova, a baviera e visiera della guisa al modo di cane, tutto bianco, 'colla coverta dinanzi fato al modo di mezo elmo': f. 5; bacinetto di Avignone 'al modo di chane ritondo con baviera e visiera', verniciato nero, coperto di velluto nero in seta, bordato d'ottone, camaglio d'acciaio *caciato*, padiglione e calotta di boccaccino nero: f. 14; bacinetto di Parigi di prova, baviera e visiera della guisa, bordato d'ottone, un poco usato, ritraversato, senz'altro fornimento: f. 7; bacinetto di Milano d'acciaio temperato, di prova, a baveria al modo di cane, tutto bianco, 'sanza niuno guarnimento': f. 8; visiera della 'Magna', arrotata, nuova: s. 12; vetta di Milano, della guisa, ad alette 'd'amendue le parti per balestriere': f. 2; vetta di ferro di Milano da briganti, visiera piccola, calotta di tela: f. 1.12; cervelliera di ferro da briganti, vecchia, verniciata nera: s. 16; cappelletto d'acciaio temperato di Milan, bianco, 'a ragi di solle' di nuova guisa: f. 3.12; cappellina di 1/2 prova, verniciata nera, coperta di fustagno nero, con calotta: f. 1.12

one of Daniello Coco's proofed Avignon basinets, matching bevor and visor, all white, without any other fittings 7*fl.*; one of Daniello Coco's proofed Avignon basinets, matching bevor and visor, the visor bordered (with latten), without any other fittings so as to have a hood at the rear 8*fl.* 12*l.*; one of Daniello Coco's proofed Avignon basinets, with ventilations (outside) and inside the bevor, latten-bordered to match, small (linked), (maker's) marked steel aventail, white buckskin aventail-cover and collar 13*fl.*; one of Bernardone di Condomo's proofed Avignon basinets, with ventilated bevor with visor in the manner of a dog, latten-bordered, without any garnishing 9*fl.*; one of Simon of Flanders' proofed Avignon basinets, with matching ventilated bevor and visor, all white, repaired riveted aventail, white buckskin aventail-cover and collar 12*fl.*; one of Simon of Flanders' proofed Avignon basinets, with matching ventilated bevor and visor in the manner of a dog, latten-bordered, without any other garnishing 8*fl.*; one of Giacomolo da Villa's proofed Avignon basinets, with matching bevor and visor in the manner of a dog, all white, the neck (defence) covered with ventilations made in the manner of a demi-helm 5*fl.*; one Avignon basinet in the manner of a dog, round, with bevor and visor, black varnished, covered with set black velvet (i.e. woven into a linen base), latten-bordered, steel aventail (maker's) marked, black buckskin aventail-cover and collar 14*fl.*; one proofed Paris basinet, matching bevor and visor, latten-bordered, a little worn, refurbished, without any other fittings 7*fl.*; one tempered-steel, proofed Milan basinet, with bevor in the manner of a dog, all white, without any other garnishing 8*fl.*; one 'great' visor, rotating, new, 12*s.*; one Milan *vetta* with little wings (i.e. defensive plates at the temples), converted for (use by) crossbowmen 2*fl.*; one iron brigands' Milan *vetta*, small visor, cloth collar 1*fl.* 12*l.*; one iron brigands' skullcap, old, black varnished 16*s.*; one tempered-steel Milan small chapel de fer, white, with sunbeams in the new style 3*fl.* 12*l.*; one half-proofed capelline, black varnished, covered with black fustian (strong fabric made from any two of cotton, flax, or wool), with collar 1*fl.* 12*l.*

1397
bacinetto di Avignone di Bernardone di Condomo, di prova, a baviera dinanzi 'de la guisa che si chiama chane', tutto bianco: f. 8; bacinetto di Avignone di Bernardone di Condomo, di prova, a baviera, rotondo di sopra a guisa d'elmetto di novella guisa, rifatto da un coppo vecchio, visiera e baviera tutte nuove, tutto bianco: f. 4.12; bacinetto di Avignone di Giacomolo da Villa, di prova, a baviera e visiera della guisa al modo di cane, tutto bianco, 'chol manteleto al modo di mez'elmo per chonbatere': f. 6; [several] bacinetti di Avignone di Daniello Coco e di Simone di Fiandra, di prova, senza baviera, bordati d'ottone, tutti nuovi, camagli d'acciaio a 1/2 bozza, padiglioni e calotte di tela bioda: f. 9.12; bacinetto di Parigi di *Sargan di Bataglia*, di prova, senza baviera, rotondo di sopra a guisa di cane, visiera grande tutta pertugiata, camaglio piccolo di maglia d'acciaio grossa suora fatto nella 'Magna': f. 7; [several] bacinetti di Milano di ferro, con visiere, bordati a *varvela* d'ottone della vecchia guisa, 'tuti isghuarniti, fati per più maestri': f. 3 uno; bacinetto di Milano della vecchia guisa, di prova, piccolo, bordato a *varvela* d'ottone: f. 3.12; bacinetto di 1/2 prova, piccolo, rotondo all'antica, camaglio di ferro a 1/2 opera, vecchio e ritraversato: f. 1.6;

visiera grande di ferro da elmo, 'da posare in su uno bacineto', con cerniere di ferro: f. 2; cervelliere di ferro vecchio, 'apuntate, da marina': s. 16 una; cappelletto d'acciaio temperato di Milano, bordato d'ottone, 'apuntato di sopra de la ghuisa pasata': f. 3; cappello d'acciaio temperato di Milano, tutto bianco, 'ritondo di sopra a la ghuisa di Ghabaseti': f. 2.12; cappelletto di ferro di Avignone, 'tondo di sopra': f. 2

one of Bernardone di Condomo's proofed Avignon basinets, ventilated bevor of the type called 'dog', all white 8*fl.*; one of Bernardone di Condomo's proofed Avignon basinets, with bevor, round on the top in the manner of a little helm of the new type (prob. an armet[6]), remade from an old skull, completely new visor and bevor, all white 4*fl.* 12*l.*; one of Giacomolo da Villa's proofed Avignon basinets, with matching bevor and visor in the manner of a dog, all white, with mantlet in the manner of a demi-helm for (single) combat 6*fl.*; one of Daniello Coco and Simon of Flanders' proofed Avignon basinets, without bevor, latten-bordered, completely new, half-riveted steel aventail, red cloth aventail-cover and collar 9*fl.* 12*l.*; one of Sargan di Bataglia's proofed Paris basinets, without bevor, round on top in the manner of a dog, large visor completely cracked, small aventail of large links made in the 'great' style 7*fl.*; [several] iron Milan basinets, with visors, bordered with old-fashioned latten staples (i.e. vervelles to attach the aventail), completely ungarnished, made by various masters 3*fl.* each; one old-style proofed Milan basinet, small, with latten staples (vervelles) 3*fl.* 12*l.*; one half-proofed basinet, small, round in the old fashion, half-riveted iron aventail, old and refurbished 1*fl.* 6*l.*; one large iron visor of a helm, for placing in a basinet [NB this is unclear], with iron hinges 2*fl.*; [several] old iron skullcaps, pointed, for marine (fighting) 16*s.* each; one tempered-steel Milan small chapel de fer, bordered with latten, pointed on top in the old style 3*fl.*; one tempered-steel Milan chapel de fer, all white, round on top in the style of a small basket (*cabasette*) 2*fl.* 12*l.*; one little chapel de fer of Avignon round on the top 2*fl.*

1398

bacinetto di Avignone di Bernardone di Condomo, di ferro, a baviera della guisa di cane, bordato, camaglio d'acciaio a bozza, padiglione e calotta di boccaccino bianco: f. 14; bacinetto di Avignone di Daniello Coco, di ferro, a baviera dinanzo e di dietro, camaglio d'acciaio *caciato*, padiglione e calotta di boccaccino bianco: f. 13; bacinetto di Avignone di Bernadone di Condomo, di ferro, a baviera della guisa di cane, bianco, camaglio d'acciaio a bozza, padiglione e calotta di boccaccino: f. 13; bacinetto di ferro di prova, a baviera, corto e rotondo di sopra all'antica, tutto bianco, calotta di boccaccino azzurro: f. 2.6; bacinetto di ferro, tondo [*sic*] di sopra all'antica, bianco, camaglio di ferro vecchio antico: f. 2.6; bacinetto di ferro di 1/2 prova, tondo [*sic*] di sopra all'antica, bianco, vecchio e ritraversato, 'isfornito, con visiera e tristo': f. 1; visiera di ferro, nera, rozza, buona, nuova, con camaglio [*sic*]: f. 2; agugliette di ferro per bacinetti e visiere: s. 15 centinaio; visiera di ferro, nera, rozza, buona, nuova, con

---

[6] A close-fitting helmet encompassing the entire head. It originated in Northern Italy at the very end of the century. More detail will be provided in the next volume.

cerniere: s. 20; visiera di ferro grande, bianca 'fata al modo d'elmo da posare in su uno bacineto, con charniera e anelo di sopra e soto': − [no price recorded]; elmo di ferro da giostra, corto, vecchio, dipinto di vermiglio: f. 1; vetta di ferro di Milano, bianca, della guisa, con alette 'd'amendue le ghote [*recte* ghale]': f. 2; vetta di ferro di Milano, bianca, della guisa, 'per fanti a pié', con calotta: f. 1.12; cervelliere di ferro di Milano, nere, 'apuntate, da ghalee': s. 16 una; cappellina di ferro nera, di 1/2 prova, all'antica, rotonda di sopra, camaglio di ferro di 'trista maglia': f. 1.18; cappello di ferro di Montalbano, all'antica, vecchio e 'roviglioso': s. 10; cappellina di ferro, verniciata nera, 'con ventaglia di sopra inn [*sic*] ischanbio di visiera', coperta di velluto nero, bordata d'ottone della nuova guisa, padiglione e calotta, camaglio d'acciaio a bozza buono: f. 6; cappellina di ferro, verniciata nera, con ventaglia di sopra, scoperta, con calotta dentro, senza camaglio: f. 1

one of Bernardone di Condomo's iron Avignon basinets, with bevor in the manner of a dog, bordered (prob. with latten), riveted steel aventail, white buckskin aventail-cover and collar 14*fl.*; one of Daniello Coco's iron Avignon basinets, with bevor ventilated (inside) and out, (maker's) marked steel aventail, white buckskin aventail-cover and collar 13*fl.*; one of Bernardone di Condomo's iron Avignon basinets, with bevor in the manner of a dog, white, riveted steel aventail, buckskin aventail-cover and collar 13*fl.*; one proofed iron basinet, with bevor, short and round on the top in the old fashion, all white, collar of azure buckskin 2*fl.* 6*l.*; one iron basinet, round on the top in the old fashion, very old mail aventail 2*fl.* 6*l.*; one half-proofed iron basinet, round on the top in the old fashion, white, old, and refurbished, fitted, with a visor and weak 1*fl.*; one iron visor, black, rough, good, new, with aventail [*sic*] 2*fl.*; [several] iron-tipped laces for basinets and visors 15*s.* per hundred; one iron visor, black, rough, good, new, with hinges 20*s.*; one large iron visor, white, made in the manner of a helm to place in a basinet, with hinges and (lining) perforations above and below [no price recorded]; one iron jousting helm, short, old, painted with vermilion 1*fl.*; one iron Milan *vetta*, white, converted with little wings (i.e. defensive plates at the temples) for (fighting on) the galleys 2*fl.*; one iron Milan *vetta*, white, for footsoldiers, with collar 1*fl.* 12*l.*; [several] iron Milan skullcaps, black, pointed, for (fighting on) galleys 16*s.*; one black, half-proofed small chapel de fer, old-fashioned, round on top, iron aventail of weak mail 1*fl.* 18*l.*; one iron chapeau de Montauban, old-fashioned, old and very dented 10*s.*; one iron capelline, black varnished, with ventilations throughout as found in a visor, covered with black velvet, bordered with latten in the new style, aventail-cover and collar, well-riveted steel aventail 6*fl.*; one iron capelline, black varnished, with ventilations throughout, uncovered, with collar inside, without aventail 1*fl.*

1399
bacinetto di Avignone a baviera, 'con manteleto di sopra de la ghuisa', camaglio d'acciaio a 1/2 bozza, padiglione e calotta: f. 10; bacinetto di Avignone d'acciaio di prova, senza baviera, bordato, camaglio d'acciaio *caciato* 'di 6 maglie', padiglione e colatta: f. 10; bacinetto di Milano d'acciaio di prova, 'a l'antica con ghran visiera senza baviera, ritondo di sopra per far fati d'arme, tuto isghuarnito': f. 5; bacinetto di ferro

nero, a baviera a guisa di cane, rifatto da un bacinetto vecchio, camaglio di ferro, padiglione e colatta: f. 2.12; vetta di ferro di Milano, visiera dell'antica fazione, 'per giente di muragle': f. 1.12; cappellina d'acciaio temperato, a barbozza, bianca, camiglio di ferro lavorato al modo d'acciaio, padiglione e calotta: f. 6.12; cappelli d'acciaio temperato di Milano, di prova, rotondi, bianchi: f. 2.12 uno; cappellina di ferro, verniciata nera, con ventaglia di sopra della guisa, coperta di velluto nero, con calotta, senza camaglio: f. 4; cappellina di ferro nera, aguzzata dinanzi alla guisa, coperta di panno nero, padiglione e calotta, camaglio di ferro a 1/2 bozza: f. 2.6; cappellina di ferro di Milano, nera, a scaglie, nuova: s. 18

one Avignon basinet with bevor, with matching mantlet over the top, half-riveted steel aventail, aventail-cover and collar 10*fl.*; one proofed steel Avignon basinet, without bevor, bordered (prob. with latten), (maker's) marked steel aventail of six links (i.e. six rings link through one – rather than the usual four through one), aventail-cover and collar 10*fl.*; one proofed steel Milan basinet, old fashioned with large visor without bevor, round on the top for (performing) feats of arms, completely ungarnished 5*fl.*; one black, iron basinet, with bevor in the manner of a dog, remade from an old basinet, iron aventail, aventail-cover and collar 2*fl.* 12*l.*; one iron Milan *vetta*, old-fashioned visor, for wall-scaling men (i.e. sieges) 1*fl.* 12*l.*; one tempered-steel small chapel de fer, with bevor, white, iron aventail worked in the manner of steel (i.e. to look like steel), (cloth) lining and collar 6*fl.* 12*l.*; [several] tempered-steel, proofed chapel de fers, round, white 2*fl.* 12*l.* each; one iron capelline, black varnished, of the type with ventilations throughout, covered with black velvet, with collar, without aventail 4*fl.*; one black, iron capelline, of the type with sharp-edged ventilations, covered in black cloth, aventail-cover and collar, half-riveted aventail 2*fl.* 6*l.*; one new, black, iron, Milan capelline, with scales 18*s.*

82

Now-Lost Document printed in C. Dehaisnes, *Documents et extraits divers concernant l'histoire de l'art dans la Flandre, l'Artois & le Hainaut avant le XVe siècle*, 2 vols (Lille, 1886), I, pp. 471–4
Inventory of the Goods of Aillaume d'Auberchicourt, Wax Merchant and Burgess of Douai, County of Flanders, 23 September 1367

Parties d'armures servans pour corps d'homme et ad ce appartenans une cote de fer com dit haubregon de haulte clavure VII escus uns avant bras de fer et les quenterons XX gros

Pieces of armour that serve (to protect) a man's body and appurtenances: one coat of iron called a 'haubergeon' of high nailing (i.e. all-riveted links), seven shields, one (pair of) iron vambrace and the elbow defences (couters) 20 groats

83

Carlisle Archives, DRC/1/2, pp. 170–1: Register of Thomas Appleby,
Bishop of Carlisle, 2nd Register
Will of Roger Beauchamp, Carlisle, Cumberland, 20 December 1367

loricam meam d[omi]no de Dacre ij paltokes d[omi]no Wil[he]l[m]o fr[atr]i meo
cu' capite & cirotecis ferreis & zonam meam argent' Thome fr[atr]i meo acton' p[atr]
is sui

my hauberk to Lord Dacre, two paltocks (fabric torso defences) to my brother
William with (steel) cap and iron gauntlets and my silver belt, my brother Thomas
his father's aketon

84

Original Document printed in *Rotuli Scotiae in Turri Londinensi* [...] ed.
D. Macpherson and others, 2 vols (London, 1814–19), II, pp. 916–17
Royal Decree granting permission for the Servants of Sir James Douglas
of Dalkeith and Sir Thomas Erskine to take Armour from London for 'a
duel between him and Thomas Erskine according to the Law of Scotland' ('duellu' int[er] ip[s]im et Thomam de Erskyn juxta legem Scot"),
Westminster, 8 December 1367 and Windsor, 5 January 1368

1367
For Sir James
unu' par de platis unu' haub[er]geone' unu' par cirotecar[um] afferis unu' helm' unu'
par de bracers & alias armatur' p[ro] corpore suo crurib[us] tibiis & pedib[us] suis
longas armatur' & coop[er]tur' p[ro] duob[us] equis duos cultellos caput uni' lancee
& quasdam alias armatur' p[ro] eodem duello necessar'

one pair of plates, one haubergeon, one pair of iron gauntlets, one helm, one pair of
bracers, and other armour for his body – his thighs, shins, and feet – long armour and
covers for two horses, two knives, one lancehead, and certain other armour necessary
for this duel

1368
For Sir Thomas
unu' par de plates unu' bacenettu' unu' par de braciers unu' par de quisseulx unu'
par de grieves unu' chanffreyn p[ro] uno equo unu' cultellu' unu' ensem longu' unu'
ensem curtum & unu' par cirotecar[um] de ferro p[ro] duello in partib[us] Scot'

one pair of plates, one basinet, one pair of bracers, one pair of cuisses, one pair of greaves, one shaffron for a horse, one knife, one longsword, one short sword, and one pair of iron gauntlets for the duel in Scottish parts

85

Caen, Archives du Calvados, G/279/1
Inventory of the Goods of Hugue du Chataignier, *Chanoine prébende* (Priest) of Rouen, Normandy, 21 August 1368

q[ui]nq[ue] bacinj ad armandu' cu' camail […] ad visiere gallice due alij bacinj seu bacineti & sex gorgete & q[u]atuor paria brachior[um] de melle due tunice de ferro q[ui]nq[ue] plate ad armandum sex ganteleti & q[ui]nq[ue] gladij gallice gleiues vnus gladius vnus pic et tres targe duo bacinj ad armandum iiijor plate ferree antique duo paria de ganteles antiquis duo harnes de cuisses & due Jamber' de fer gallice vn harnes de cuir pour bras & j godendart gallice vne coute pointe a escus blancs gallice vna securis norreise & vne guisarme gallice

five (bequests of what are known) in French as arming 'basins' (i.e. basinets) with aventails [some?] with visors, two other basins or 'basinets' and six gorgets and four pairs of mail sleeves, two shirts of mail, five arming (pairs of) plates, six (pairs of) gauntlets, and five bladed weapons – in French – glaives, one sword one pike and three targes, two arming basinets, four old iron (pairs of) plates, two pairs of old gauntlets, two thigh harnesses (i.e. cuisses) and two iron jambers – in French, one leather arm harness and one godendag – in French, one *coutepointe* with white (heraldic) escutcheons – in French, one Norse axe and one guisarme – in French

86

Kew, National Archives, E 101/29/38, membr. 1– membr. 2
Account of Ralph Spigurnel, Constable of Dover Castle, Kent, for 1369–71

Mortu' stauru'
iij p[ar]ib[us] furgear[um] ij alneis p[ro] pasta j furnace de plumbo iiij dresser' ij plumbis fixis j furnace grosso j morthr' fixo in terra j bokett' ferr' lig' cu' vna cathena ferr' j cabul' debil' j bokett' ferr' lig' p[ro] petr' tract' ij Incud' de ferr' j Incud' frac' j bicor[n]e iij slegges iiij hamers vj par' tenac' vnde ij gross' iiijor pynsons debil' iiijor nailtoles p[ro]c clau' fac' ij par' suffocal' j peir' molar' ij fusill' ferr' cu' j pari de Wynches ad eandu' petr' j alneo de petra p[ro] aqua j hert[s]taf' de ferro j kuttyngyr' j markyngir' j cabul' debil' & putrid' ix spryngaldis cu' sict[an]dis & app[er]at' vnde ij gross' vj aketon' bon' & xxvj aketon' debil' vj par' de platis debil' vnde iiijor par'

nullis valoris xij par' cirotec' de plat' debil' & null' valor' j brestplate p[ro] hastilud' ij
vantplatis xix capellis de ferro xj galeis debil' xiij bacenett' tinnat' ov' vmbr' debil' & al'
bacenett' & palettis frac' & putr' null' val' vj capell' de n[er]uo debil' xl target' debil'
l lanceis cu' capit' & xxxvj lanceis sine capit' ij coronal' j gr[a]te p[ro] hastilud' xxvj
balistis bon' iiijxx balistis frac' null' val' ij coffris plen' quarell' p[ro] balist' ij bokett' ij
barell' plen' quarell' xxxvj arc' bon' & Cx arc' debil' & vet' iiijxx garb' sagitt' debil' j
coffr' vet' cu' capit' quarell' iiij coffr' plen' quarell' p[ro] spryngadis j pari de poleynes
xxx bauder' debil' & putr' xxiij arc' p[ro] balist' de corum sine tellur' iij arc' de vyz
vet' & debil' iij vyz eisdem arc' tend' debil' & putr' j cophino cu' sagitt' p[ro] vno arc'
de Turkie ij dol' vnde j cu' calketrappes cathenis & al' instr[ament]is ferr' p[ro] ingen'

Dead stock
three pairs of moulds, two (pieces of) alder wood for paste, one lead crucible, four
dressers, two lead fasteners, one large crucible, one mortar set in the ground, one
iron-bound bucket with one iron chain, one worn out cable, one iron-bound bucket
for drawing stones, two iron anvils, one broken anvil, one bicorn (anvil), three sledgehammers, four hammers, six pairs of tongs two of which are large, four worn out
pincers, four nail-tools for making nails, two pairs of bellows, one pair of grinding
wheels, two iron axles with one pair of winches for these grindstones, one stone
(quenching) trough for water, one iron hearth staff, one cutting gear, one marking
gear, one worn out and rotten cable, nine springalds with fixings and apparatus two
of which are large, six good aketons and 26 worn out aketons, six worn out pairs of
plates four pairs of which are of no value, 12 pairs of worn out plate gauntlets of no
value, one breastplate for jousts, two vamplates, 19 chapel de fers, 11 worn out helms,
13 worn out tinned basinets with umbrers and other broken and rotten basinets and
pallets of no value, six worn out chapels of sinew, 40 worn out targes, 50 lances
with heads and 36 lances lacking heads, two coronals, one graper for jousts, 26 good
crossbows, four score broken crossbows of no value, two coffers full of crossbow
quarrels, two buckets, two barrels full of quarrels, 36 good bows and 110 old and worn
out bows, four score sheaves of worn out arrows, one old coffer with quarrel-heads,
three coffers full of springald quarrels, one pair of pulleys, 30 worn out and rotten
baldrics, 23 horn bows for crossbows without tillers (stocks), three old and worn out
vice-spanned bows, three worn out and rotten vices for drawing these bows, one
quiver with arrows for a bow of Turkey, two tuns one of which has caltraps, chains,
and other iron instruments for (siege) engines

87

Lambeth Palace Library, Register of Archbishop Whittlesey, VA6, fol.
98r–fol. 98v
Will of Bartholomew, Lord Burghersh, London, 4 April 1369

la charette en quel mon corps s[e]ra amesne soit couert de rouge cendal od vn lyo[u]n
de mes armes ma helme esteyant a mon teste & vn tiele drap de cendal de mes armes

mys sur mon corps en chescun eglise ou mon corps se resposera la mist le io[u]r qe s[e]rai encenely q[ue] soit mys sur mon corps vn drap de rouge cendal au vn lyo[u] n de mes armes & mon helme a mon teste & vn sierge a mon test & vn autre a mes pies & deux torches a lun couste & deux a lautre sire Wautre Pauely les armes entier p[u]r les joustez q[ue] fuist pur mon corps & le haub[er]geon q[ue] fuist p[u]r mon corps & vn espeye ro[u]nde q[ue] soleye porter arme

the hearse in which my corpse shall be led be covered with red sendal (lightweight silk or very fine linen) with a lion of my (heraldic) arms – my helm on my head. A cloth of sendal of my (heraldic) arms be placed on my corpse in each church where my corpse shall repose. On the day of my interment there be a cloth of red sendal with a lion of my arms placed on my corpse, my helm on my head, one serge (cloth hanging) at my head, another at my feet, and two torches on each side, Sir Walter Paveley, all the arms for the jousts which were for my body, the haubergeon which was for my body, and a curved sword with which I was armed

88

Carlisle Archives, DRC/1/2, p. 175: Register of Thomas Appleby, Bishop of Carlisle, 2nd Register
Will of William Arturet, Mayor of Carlisle, Cumberland, 19 August 1369

Ric[ard]o […] vnu' equu' vnu' bacinettu' armatu' cu' vno pal[…] [paltock]

to Richard […] one horse one arming basinet with one paltock (fabric torso defence)

89

Lambeth Palace Library, Register of Archbishop Wittlesey, fol. 110r–fol. 110v
Will of Thomas, Earl of Warwick, 6 September 1369

ieo deuise a mon eisne fiz Thomas lespe de Gy de Warrewyk & le hauberk It' ieo deuise & ordeigne q' tout ce q' app[ar]tient a ma Gardrobe de mes arm[u]res si bien de pees come de guerre soit ouelement dep[ar]tiz p[ar] entre mes fiz Thomas & William

I give to my eldest son Thomas the sword of Guy of Warwick and the hauberk. I will and ordain that all that appertains to my wardrobe of my armours (i.e. armoury), both for peace as well as for war, shall be equally shared between my sons Thomas and William

90

Carlisle Archives, DRC/1/2, p. 176: Register of Thomas Appleby, Bishop of Carlisle, 2nd Register
Will of Clement Crofton, Carlisle, Cumberland, 11 October 1369

d[omin]o Abbati de holmcolt[ra]ne loricam meam que in Inuentar' meo app[er]
eat[u]r ad lx s' Joh[ann]i fr[atr]i meo vnu' par de paunce & de braces & j Jac'
Clementi de Skelton' vnu' meu' bacynet' cu' vno drew auentayl d[omi]no [...]u' aliu'
Aventayll' melius & grossiar'

the Lord Abbot of Holm Cultram my hauberk valued at 60s. in my inventory, my
brother John one pair of paunces and (mail) sleeves and one jack, Clement Skelton
one of my basinets with a draw aventail (i.e. can be drawn tight by a thong), Lord
[...] my better and larger (basinet) with aventail

91

Lambeth Palace Library, Register of Archbishop Wittlesey, fol. 118v–fol.
119r
Will of Thomas, Earl of Oxford, 1 August 1371

d[omi]no albrito de vee[r] fr[atr]i meo j haubergeon de asc[er]e quod d[omin]us
Wil[e]l[mu]s de Wyngefeld' michi dedit & j Basynet nou' j par' cirotecar[um] nou'
de plat j Cursar' bad' & j al[ia]m cursar' in p[ar]co de lauenham cu' iiij ped' alb'

my brother Lord Albert de Vere one haubergeon of steel which Lord William
Wingfield gave me, and one new basinet, one new pair of plate gauntlets, one bay
courser and one other courser in the park of Lavenham with four white hooves

92

Kew, National Archives, E 101/397/10, membr. 1–membr. 3
Arms and Armour in the Tower of London, 1372

ij op[er]ar' p[er] dues dies vni' p[er] [sic - all] vnu' diem & dimid' vni' p[er] vj dies
& vni' p[er] xlj dies [all wokers above ad vj d. p[er] diem] op[er]ant' sup[er] mundac'
loric' bac' c[ir]otec' de plat' & al' diu[ersi]s hernes' misso cu' R[eg]e in venat' sua
vsq[ue] Wynton' a[nn]o xlvjo xxvj s. iij d. v lag' & dimid' olei p[re]c' lag' xvj d. vno
barell' p[ro] oleo imponend' viij d. vij b' fur' p[re]c' b' ij d. p[ro] h[er]nes' saluo
custodiend' ix s. ij d. vna pell' de Roo p[ro] garnistur' bac' xx d. vna cumba locat' de
Turri vsq[ue] Shene p[ro] hernas' vsq[ue] ib[ide]m cariand' vj s. viij d. portag' &
trussag' h[er]nes' de Garder' infra Turr' vsq[ue] cimbam iij s. quadd' batell' locat' de
Shene vsq[ue] Wyndesore p[ro] hernas' cariand' vj s. viij d. portag' hernas' de aq[u]a

vsq[ue] Castell' xx d. portag' h[er]nas' apud Wynton' & discartag' carect' p[er]
m[agistr]o Thome Maddyngle cl[er]ici Garder' hospic' Regis iij s. iiij d. vni' ho' ad iij
d. p[er] diem emit' cl[eric]i hernas' p[ro] emedac' & salua custodiend' morant' tam
apud Wynton' et apud Wyndesore a feste s[an]c[t]i Georg' vsq[ue] f[esti]m Nat'
d[omi]ni p[er] lix dies lxij s. iij d. p[ro] op[er]ar' p[er] vnu' diem portag' garb' sag' de
quadam Capell' in Cam[er]a s[an]c[t]i Thome iuxta Cam[er]am R[eg]is apud Turre
london' temp[or]e que Princeps venit' ib[ide]m vsq[ue] quadam domu' iuxta aq[u]am
v s. reportag' ear[un]dem temp[or]e recessus Principis de Turri iiij s. iiij d. duob[us]
doleis long' m[er]emio & clauis p[ro] salua custod' sagitt' xj s. iiij d. duor[um] op[er]
ar' p[er] xxxiij dies op[er]and' sup[er] mundac' diu[er]s[i]s hernas' de plat' & de
mayll' ordinat' p[ro] viag' R[eg]is sup[r]a mare xxxiij s viij lag' olei ij q[u]a[to]r furfur'
p[ro] mundac' xiiij s. vni' op[er]ar' p[er] xxxij dies vni' p[er] xxj dies & vni' p[er]
xxxiij dies [all ad vj d. per diem] op[er]ant' sup[er] mundac' & rep[er]ac' hernes'
temp[or]e aduent' Regis de mari xliij s. ij Fletchers p[er] xxxiij dies duor[um]
Fletchers p[er] xvij dies [all ad vj d. per diem] op[er]ant' s[upe]r triat' & emendac' ix
m garb' sagitt' miss' cu' R[eg]e in viag' suo sup[r]a mare l s. iiij q[u]a[to]r carbonu'
p[re]c' q[u]art' xj d. empt' & exp[e]n' c[ir]ca triat' eor[un]dem iij s. viij d. triu' op[er]
ar' p[er] iij dies vj p[er] vnu' diem & vj [pro] iiij dies [all at vj d. per diem] op[er]ant'
sup[er] capitac' & brurewyng [sic] lanc' p[ro] guerr' p[ro] viag' xix s. vj d. vj pell'
equor[um] p[re]c' pec' ij s. C clauis p[ar]uis iij d. & m[i]l' taknayll' p[ro] burreux &
capit' lanc' furnand' xiij s. vj d. heluyng viijto gunnor[um] & x hatchett' ad modem
Pycoys cu' quodam Joigno[u]r' xiij s. depict' Cvj targett' de arm' s[an]c[t]i Georg'
recept' de quad' Naui vocat' le g[r]acedieu in primo aduentu suo in angl' & lib'
Joh[ann]i de haytfeld' p[ro] viag' liij s. iiij d. vna pell' de hungry vij s. ij li. alis p[ro]
penn' quarell' xiij s. iiij d. iij pell' ou[u]m rub' xviij d. vj lb. visci ij s. vj lb. Cer' virid'
& rub' & ij lb. Code iij s. iiij d. p[ro] balist' & quarell' sup[r]a mare rep[ar]and' xxviij
s. viij d. vno barell' pro Caltraps p[ro] viag' imponend' x d. emendac' & rep[ar]ac' xx
p[ar]u[i]m coffr' long' p[ro] arc' & sag' imponend' coop[er]t' de coreo p[er] m[agistr]
o Petri Shepe p[ro] viag' xx s. vj port' p[er] viij dies portant' lanc' arcus & sagitt' de
diu[er]s[i]s domib[us] infra Turr' london' vsq[ue] Cam[er]am R[egi]s p[ro] intrussand'
xxiiij s. ij Fletchers ad vj d. p[er] diem p[er] xl dies emit' in diu[er]s[i]s nauib[us] de
p[re]cept' Regis p[ro] salua custodienda & emendac' arc' & sag' in viag' xl s. iiijor
op[er]ar' ad xj d. p[er] diem p[er] iiij dies portant' loric' bac' C[ir]othec' de plat'
hachett' & al' de Garderob' vlt[r]a aq[u]am vsq[ue] magnam aul' infra Turr' p[ro]
intrussand' viij s. portag' Coffr' de domo Wil[e]l[m]i Alblast' vsq[ue] Cam[er]am
Regis p[ro] sag' instrussand' iij s. vj d. C pauys vsq[ue] Sandewyc' in quodam
victualar' hug' Caluylle cariand' p[er] m[agistr]o Joh[ann]is Bernes valletti Nauis xx
s. v op[er]ar' ad vj d. p[er] diem p[er] iij dies op[er]ant' sup[er] heluyng de Ciiij xx
xiiij pycoys p[ro] viag' vij s. vj d. fraxino p[ro] heluis p[ro] eisd[e]m vna cu' vj d. solut'
p[ro] cariag' de domo cuiusdam Currior vsq[ue] Turr' vj s. vj d. duob[us] lighters &
ij batell' locat' p[ro] cariag' hernes vsq[ue] le victailler stant' in Thamis & nauem
R[eg]is vocat' le Poule stant' apud Redeclyf xxxiiij s. xj d. cons' portag' & bat' h[er]
nes' apud Sandewyc' de d[i]c[t]is victailler & naui Regis vsq[ue] al' diu[er]s[i]s naues
Regis ib[ide]m xxiij s. iiij d. oleo & furfur' p[ro] diu[er]s[i]s hernes' Regis de mayll'

& plat' apud haddele saluo & munde' custodiend' p[er] m[agistr]o Thome horslak
vall[ett]i arm' ib[ide]m vj s. x d. iij C d[imid]j Talwode viij s. xvj q[u]art' & d[imid]
j Carbonu' p[re]c' q[u]art' ix d. exp[e]n' infra Turro c[ir]ca rep[ar]ac' sagitt' & salua'
custod' arm' xl s. iiij d. ob. cariag' Talwode & Carbon' de Baynardescastell' vsq[ue]
Turr' iiij s. duor[um] Fletchers ad vj d. p[er] diem p[er] Cl dies op[er]ant' s[upe]r
emendac' & rep[er]ac' cap' & sag' dimiss' in Garder' necnon sag' miss' v[er]sus Cales
vij li. x s. iij op[er]ar' ad vj d. p[er] diem p[er] iij dies triu' ad vj d. p[er] diem p[er] v
dies portant' & trussant' arcus sagitt' & cord' ad arcus apud Turr' v[er]sus Burdegal'
xij s. cariag' pip' de diu[er]s[i]s domib[us] vbi emebant[u]r vsq[ue] Turrim london' iij
s. triu' op[er]ar' ad vj d. p[er] diem p[er] duos dies op[er]ant' immundac' & sictant'
pip' iij s. lxiij Circ[u]lis p[ro] doleis ligand' v s. iiij d. clauis p[ro] Circulis firmand'
viij d. lyght' locat' de Turr' vsq[ue] Billyngesgate p[ro] pip' vsq[ue] q[u]anda' nauem
stant' ib[ide]m locat' p[ro] eisdem vsq[ue] Plomouth' cariand' p[er] duas vic' iij s. iiij
d. Polyfs & al' diu[er]s[i]s instrument' locat' p[ro] pip' in Nauem de lyght' hauriend'
iiij s. iiij d. duor[um] op[er]ar' ad vj d. p[er] diem p[er] xxxv dies op[er]ant' sup[er]
emendac' & rep[ar]ac' plat' antiquor[um] recept' de antiquo Galey venient' de Bayon'
& miss' sup[r]a mar' in nouo Galey xxxv s. coop[er]tur' & rep[ar]ac' vj xx v palett'
recept' de antiquo Galey & miss' sup[r]a mare v s. viij d. factur' duor[um] Springald'
& vni' balist' sauage p[er] m[agistr]o Wil[e]l[m]i herland Carpentar' p[ro] viag' R[eg]
is iiij li. xv s. viij d. mundac' & rep[ar]ac' gladior[um] & al' armatur' p[ro] corp[or]e
R[eg]is in Custod' Ric[ard]i de [sic] Arm' infra Turr' london' existent' iiij li. xvj s. viij
d. iiij Coffyns p[ro] iij bacinett' j galea & j scut' R[eg]is x s. viij d. iiij C Clau' deaur'
Cno iij s. iiij d. C fol' argent' xij d. v lb. plat' de laton' p[re]c' lb. viij d. xij vln' rubant
aur' stric' p[re]c' vln' xvj d. expendit' sup[er] emendac' armor[um] p[ro] corp[or]e
R[eg]is & Thome de Wodestoke apud Sandewyc' xxxiij s. viij d. xj op[er]ar' p[er] duos
dies vni' p[er] ix dies vj p[er] iiij d. vni' p[er] xlj dies triu' p[er] iij dies vni' p[er] xviij
dies vni' p[er] v dies vni' p[er] viij dies duor[um] p[er] lxiij dies vni' p[er] lxvj dies viij
p[er] vj dies vni' p[er] xj dies vni' p[er] xij dies vni' p[er] xxxiij dies vni' p[er] liiij dies
vni' p[er] lxx dies vni' p[er] vnu' diem [all ad vj d. per diem] op[er]ant' s[upe]r
mundac' loric' bac' C[ir]othec' de plat' palett' plat' hachett' gladior[um] & al' diu[er]
s[i]s h[er]nas' de mayll' existent' in Garder' R[eg]is infra Turr' london' in custod'
Wil[e]l[m]i de Garder' p[er] manus Wil[e]l[m]i xiij li. xviij s. iij d. xvj lag' olei p[re]
c' lag' xvj d. v lag' olei p[re]c' lag' ij s. p[ro] mundac' h[er]nas' lv s. iiij d. vno barell'
p[ro] oleo imponend' viij d. et p[ro] clau' p[ro] rep[ar]ac' plat' & Cowers & al' h[er]
nas' in Garder' xx d. vna pell' de Roo p[ro] auentaill' sup[er] bac' firmand' xx d. j q[u]
art' d[imid]j furfur' p[re]c' q[u]art' ij s. viij d. iij q[u]art' d[imid]j furfur' p[re]c' q[u]
art' xviij d. vno q[u]art' furfur' ij s. vj d. ij q[u]art' d[imid]j furfur' p[re]c' q[u]art' ij
s. p[ro] salua custod' & mundac' h[er]nas' xvj s. ix d. furfur' & oleo empt' apud
Sandewyc' p[ro] salua custodia armatur' Regis exstent' in naui sua sup[r]a mare p[er]
m[agistr]o Thom' Maddyngle xiij s. iiij d. vna pell' de coreo p[ro] garnistur' bacinett'
in naui vij s. iiij d. emendac' vni' coffr' antiqui in Custod' Rad[ulph]i Tyle p[ro] viag'
xvj d. portag' cariag' & batillag' balistr' loric' & al' rer[um] diu[er]s[i]s vsq[ue]
Westm' Rethertheth' & alibi de p[re]cepto Regis xviij s. ix d. talliatur' & elarg' Ciiij
xx xvj loric' rec' de Joh[ann]e Salman' p[re]c' pec' xij d. p[er] m[agistr]o Gerkyn

153

hauberger' ix li. xvij s. xxxviij arc' depict' empt' & lib[er]at' in Cam[er]am Regis p[ro]
venac' p[re]p[ar]' p[er] m[agistr]o Rad[ulph]i Tyle vall[ett]i Cam[er]e Cx s. factur' &
depictur' xxxj arc' p[ro]uenient' de tot' lign' hib[er]n' miss' Regi vsq[ue] Westm' p[er]
manus Rad[ulph]i iiij li. xiij s. x houces de tel' antiquor[um] p[ro] cons' [arc'] venac'
Regis p[er] m[agistr]o Rad[ulph]i xxix s. v[er]nysshyng vni' scutu' magni p[er]
m[agistr]o Rad[ulph]i xij s. vno par' sufflator' p[ro] offic' Wil[e]l[m]i heum' p[ro]
viag' R[eg]is xxvj s. viij d. vj par' rotar[um] magn' p[ro] mantilett' iij par' rotar[um]
pro Rybaudes empt' & p[ro]uis' p[ro] m[agistr]o Joh[ann]is Smert p[ro] viag' xj li.
duor[um] op[er]ar' p[er] vnu' diem & dimid' duor[um] p[er] x dies vni' p[er] iij dies
duor[um] p[er] xiiij dies & vni' p[er] xij dies [all at vj d. per diem] op[er]ant' s[upe]
r factur' pulu[er]is & palettes de plumbo p[ro] gunnes apud Turr' london' xxxiij s.
vno q[u]art' Carbonu' x d. d[imid]j C Talwod' iiij s. iiij d. p[ro] plumbo fundend' &
pulu[er]ib[us] sictand' v s. ij d. Ciij q[u]artron' fagot salicis p[ro] pulu[er]e fac' Cm
iiij s. viij s. iiij trays de lign' p[re]c' pec' iij d. & ollis & patell' ereis p[re]c' in toto xiij
d. empt' p[ro] pulu[er]e sup[r]a ignem & ad soleni sictand' ij s. j d. bagg' de coreo
p[ro] pulu[er]ib[us] imponend' x s. viij d. duob[us] morter' eneis iij pestell' ferr' xij
coclear' ferr' p[ro] pil' plumb' fundend' x form' de laton' pil' fac' j par' balanc' p[ro]
pulu[er]e ponder' xxx barell' p[ar]uis cu' garnett' haspis & stapul' p[ro] pil' plumb'
imponend' & custodiend' viij aliis barell' maior' p[ro] pulu[er]e xxx Serrur' p[ar]u'
pend' p[ro] xxx barell' CC xx lb. sal' petr' ij sarces xviij belowes xxiiij bagg' de coreo
p[ro] pulu[er]e delib[er]and' ollis & patell' terr' p[ro] pulu[er]e ad ignem & soleni
sictand' iiij C fagot Salic' p[ro] Carbon' inde fac' p[ro] pulu[er]e & C Talwode &
d[imid]j C fagot empt' ad diu[er]s[i]s p[re]c' p[ro] Joh[ann]em Derby Cl[er]icum
necnon batellag' portag' & cariag' plumbi gunnor[um] barell' & alior[um] nec[ess]
itior[um] p[er] diu[er]s[i]s loc' vna cu' duor[um] op[er]ar' & iij op[er]ar' op[er]antiu'
& laboranciu' sup[er] factur' pulu[er]e pil' & Carbon' p[er] xxij dies [...] Joh[ann]i
Groue Armator' london' p[ro] trib[us] p[ar]ib[us] plat' de Arm' R[eg]is & d[omi]ni
Thome de Wodestok p[re]c' par' empt' ab eo london' p[ro] R[eg]le & d[omi]no pro
viag' R[eg]is sup[r]a mare xiiij li. Wil[e]l[m]o Swynley p[ro] septem bac' p[er] ip[su]
m fact' de p[re]cept' R[eg]is in primo aduentu suo apud T[u]rrim & remanent' in
staur' ib[ide]m xiiij li. iij s. vj d. vno par' legh[ar]neys & vno bac' p[ro] d[omi]no
Thom' de Wodestok & vno bac' p[ro] Joh[ann]e holand' empt' ab eo apud Turr' de
p[re]cept' R[eg]is in gross' vj li. duob[us] par' C[ir]othec' de plat' p[re]c' par' xx s. &
vno par' vauntb[r]as & rereb[r]as p[re]c' par' xlvj s. viij d. empt' p[ro] d[omi]nis de
p[re]cept' R[eg]is p[er] m[agistr]o Ric[ard]i de Arm' p[ro] viag' iiij li. vj s. viij d.
Ric[ard]o Glou' p[ro] duob[us] par' legh[ar]neys plumtez cu' swages de laton' deaurat'
p[ro] R[eg]le & D[omi]no Britanu' p[re]c' par' x li. v s. empt' ab eo london' p[er]
m[agistr]o Ric[ard]i de Arm' xx li. x s. vno par' vauntb[r]as & rereb[r]as cum cout[er]
s op[er]at' cu' swages de laton' de eodem op[er]e p[ro] R[eg]le liij s. iiij d. vno par'
vauntb[r]as & rereb[r]as cum cout[er]s de ac[er]e p[ro] d[omi]no Thom' de Wodestok
xl s. vno par' C[ir]othec' de plat' cu' knokels deaurat' xxvj s. viij d. vno bac' xl s. empt'
p[ro] d[omi]no Thom' p[er] manus Ric[ard]i viij li. Ric[ard]o de Arm' p[ro] vno
pauys nouo de arm' R[eg]is depict' p[ro] viag' R[eg]is xxvj s viij d. vij m[i]l' m[i]l' arc'
alb' fac' D iiij xx iij duoden' & iiij arc' p[re]c' xijno xiij s. iiij d. ij C lx arc' depict' p[re]

c’ pec’ ij s. empt’ de Adam haket & al’ arcar’ diu[er]s[i]s apud london’ iiij C xiiij li’
xvij s. ix d. Bodekyn Joignor p[ro] iiij C xliiij lanc’ guerr’ long’ cu’ capit’ p[re]c’ pec’
ij s. & p[ro] lxiiij lanc’ guerr’ p[re]c’ pec’ x d. empt’ ab eo london’ p[ro] viag’ R[eg]is
sup[r]a mare xlvij li. xvj d. Godefr[id]o Sadeler’ p[ro] lvj targett’ de cornu p[re]c’ pec’
xiij s. iiij d. empt’ ab eo london’ p[er] Ric’ de Arm’ ad opus R[eg]is de p[re]cept’
eiusdem p[ro] vaig’ xxxvij li. vj s. viij d. Rob[er]to Joignor p[ro] Cxiiij pauys’ long’
depict’ de Arm’ S[an]c[t]i Georg’ p[re]c’ pec’ iij s. iiij d. empt’ ab eo london’ xix li.
Thome Essex p[ro] xij haucepes p[ro] balist’ tendend’ p[re]c’ pec’ iij s. iiij d. empt’ ab
eo london’ xl s. Joh[ann]i Stringer p[ro] C gross’ Cordar[um] ad arcus p[re]c’ gross’ v
s. empt’ ab eo london’ xxv li. Petro vansand’ p[ro] xxx lb. fili p[ro] balist’ p[re]c’ lb.
xviij d. empt’ ab eo p[ro] viag’ xlv s. Steph[an]o Warde p[ro] v Sp[r]ingald’ magn’
p[re]c’ pec’ C s. vno Spryngald’ minor[um] liij s. iiij d. empt’ ab eo london’ xxvij li.
xiij s. iiij d. Cxxxv coffr’ curt’ p[ro] sagitt’ imponend’ p[re]c’ pec’ xxij d. liij coffr’
long’ p[ro] arc’ imponend’ p[re]c’ pec’ iij s. vj d. xxxvij coffr’ long’ ferr’ ligat’ p[ro]
arc’ imponend’ p[re]c’ pec’ vj s. empt’ & p[ro]uis apud Turrim p[ro] viag’ xxxij li. xv
s. Petro Joignor p[ro] ij C xv Coffr’ p[ar]u’ pec’ v d. empt’ ab eo p[ro] quarell’ intruss’
vna cist’ Flandr’ p[re]c’ v s. vj d. vno gonne de laton’ cu’ iij pot’ xx s. empt’ Cxv s. j
d. Steph[an]o Smyth’ p[ro] CC pycoys p[re]c’ pec’ xij d. xiij patell’ ferr’ p[ro] gunnes
p[re]c’ pec’ v s. ij gunnes gross’ ferr’ p[re]c’ pec’ xl s. vj martell’ ferr’ p[ro] gunnes p[re]
c’ pec’ x d. xxviij driuelles ferr’ p[ro] gunnes p[re]c’ pec’ iij d. xxviij firyngirnes p[re]
c’ pec’ ij d. x par’ forcipu’ ferr’ x s. Cxx capit’ quarell’ p[ro] Spryngald p[re]c’ pec’ j
d. empt’ ab eo london’ p[ro] viag’ xix li. xx d. Joh[ann]i Wayte p[ro] vno barell’ gross’
p[re]c’ xvj d. empt’ p[ro] arc’ & sag’ vsq[ue] burdegal’ intrussand’ lvj s. vij d. x
bacynett’ iij par’ plat’ iij par’ legh[ar]neys iij par’ C[ir]othec’ de plat’ iij par’ vauntb[r]
as & rerb[r]as Cxv pauys’ vij m[i]l’ arcus alb’ ij C lx arcus depict’ lvj targett’ de cornu
iiij C xliiij lanc’ guerr’ lxiiij Capit’ lanc’ guerr’ xij haucepes C gross’ cord’ ad arc’ j cist’
Flandr’ x par’ forcipu’ ferr’ xxx lb. fili p[ro] cord’ balist’ vj Spryngald’ Cxxxv Coffr’
curt’ iiij xx x Coffr’ long’ CC xv Coffr’ p[ar]u’ ij C pycoys xiij patell’ ferr’ iij Gunnes
vnde j de laton’ & ij de ferr’ vj martell’ ferr’ xxviij Fyryngirnes xxviij dryuels Cxx
Capit’ q[u]arell’ p[ro] Spryngald’ xxij pip’ j barell’ viij galee xxxiij palet’ x Capell’ ferr’
m[i]l’ Cxlvij auent’ ij C vj pisanz iiij C lxv loric’ iiij xx vij par’ paunz j par’ paunz &
braz Clxxij braz j par’ bracc’ de mayll’ Cxliij standard’ p[ro] loric’ iij par’ gussett’ ix
pec’ de mayll’ p[ro] coop[er]tur’ equor[um] iiij xx xviij par’ plat’ DCvj par’ C[ir]
othec’ de plat’ v par’ quisseux & iij par’ poleyns vn’ j par de laton’ iij par’ Chasons xj
par’ splentes ij par’ tibial[iu]m vn’ j de coreo j par’ greues de coreo iiijor grates xv stufs
lanc’ sine auantplat’ vn’ xij p[ar]u’ xxxij Coronaux j mayndefer xij scut’ xxx Cathene
ferr’ p[ro] loric’ Ciiij gladij iij actons xlviij doublett’ Clxxiij Jaks xvij quirez p[ro] t[o]
rniament’ v pec’ p[ro] t[o]rniament’ op[er]at’ cu’ ymaginib[us] lvij cropor’ equor[um]
xxiiij testor’ equor[um] j mantellett’ & j testor’ de rub’ ray cordle iij Chanfreyns lxvj
pic[er]s j lapkyn p[ro] j galea iij C xxiiij balist’ vn’ vij de cornu j ad vic’ Cxxv baudryk
ij C lign’ p[ro] balist’ ij vic’ ad tendend’ balist’ xviij stirops p[ro] balist’ lxxvj mil’ D
iiij xx xv quarell’ m[i]l’ m[i]l’ quarelshaftes C arcus alb’ ij C xlv arc’ depict’ m[i]l’ m[i]
l’ liij bowestafs xxij gross’ v duoden’ & ij cord’ ad arc’ xxxij m[i]l’ D CCCCxxij garb’
sag’ cu’ capit’ viij m[i]l’ D arowshaftes xxiiij m[i]l’ iij C iiij xx viij capit’ sagitt’ Ciiij xx

viij hachett' xlv targett' de cornu viij pauys long' j spryngald' xxvij gunnes DC petr'
p[ro] Ingen' & tribegett' xx m[i]l' Caltraps xxix Coffr' p[ro] arc' & sag' inpon' iiij
anfeldes iij C shouels j standard' magn' ferr' lig' vj Cist' magne ferr' lig' j frayngbarell'
viij cornua iiij coffr' p[ro] Armatur' R[eg]is intruss' j par' bulgear[um] iiij barell'
Osemond' ij Tressett' de ferr' ij gratours iiij barell' sulphur' vi[uoru]m j pip' & ij
barell' sal' petr' ponder' l lb artillar' Joh[ann]i Byker balistar' R[eg]is infra Turr'
london' j magna ballista ad vice de cornu vet' logitudi[n]e vj pedu' vij baliste nou'
quar[um] v de ij pedib[us] ij haucepes iij balist' nou' de cornu ij balist' voc' pee de
cornu ij springald' de cornu vn' j virid' & j springald' voc' sauag'

two craftsmen for two days, one for 1½ days, one for six days, and one for 41 days all
at 6d. per day working on mending hauberks, basinets, plate gauntlets and other
divers harness sent with the King from his hunting lodge to Winchester in the 46th
regnal year [1372] 26s. 3d., 5½ flagons of oil 16d. per flagon, one barrel for the oil to
be put in 8d., seven bushels of bran for the safekeeping of the harness 9s. 2d., a roe
hide for equipping basinets 20d., a skiff brought from the Tower to Sheen for the
harness and for carriage 6s. 8d., portage and trussing the harness from the Wardrobe
in the Tower to the skiff 3s., a boat brought from Sheen to Windsor for carriage of
the harness 6s. 8d., for portage of harness by water to the castle [not specified] 20d.,
portage of the harness at Winchester and carriage and carts in the same place by
Master Thomas Maddyngle, Clerk of the King's Wardrobe 3s. 4d., one man at 3d. per
day sent by the Clerk for the harness and for mending and safekeeping and for so
remaining at Winchester and at Windsor from the Feast of Saint George [23 April]
until the Feast of the Lord's Nativity [25 December] for 59 days 62s. 3d., wages for
craftsmen and their workers at 6d. for one day for portage of sheaves of arrows from
a certain chapel in the Chamber of Saint Thomas beside the King's Chamber at the
Tower of London at the time the Prince came there to a certain house beside the water
5s., portage at the same time as the return of the Prince to the Tower 4s. 3d., two long
timber pipes and nails for safekeeping the arrows 11s. 4d., two craftsmen and their
servants at 6d. per day for 33 days working on mending divers harness of plate and
mail ordered for the King's voyage across the sea 33s., eight flagons of oil, two quarters
of bran bought for mending them 14s., one craftsman for 32 days, one for 21 days,
and one for 33 days all at 6d. per day working on mending and repairing the harness
for the time of the King's arrival at sea 43s., two fletchers for 33 days, two fletchers for
17 days all at 6d. per day working on shot and mending 9,000 sheaves of arrows sent
with the King on his voyage across the sea 50s., four quarters of charcoal expended
on the shot 3s. 8d., three craftsmen for three days, six for one day, and six for four
days all at 6d. per day working on attaching lanceheads and burrs (grips) to war lances
for the voyage 19s. 6d., six horsehides 2s. each, 100 small nails 3d., 1,000 tack-nails
for equipping the lances with burrs and lanceheads 13s. 6d., for helving (fitting with
stocks) eight guns and ten hatchets in the manner of picks by a certain joiner 13s.,
painting 106 six targes with the arms of Saint George taken in a certain ship called Le
Grace Dieu on its first arrival in England and paid to John Hatfield for the voyage 53s.
4d., a hide of Hungary leather 7s., 2lb of wings for fletching quarrels 13s. 4d., three

red sheepskins 18d., 6lb of lime 2s., 6lb of green and red wax, and 2lb of cod (grease) 3s. 4d. for repairing crossbows and quarrels on the sea 28s. 8d., one barrel for storing caltraps for the voyage 10d., mending and repairing 20 pairs of long coffers for storing bows and arrows covered with leather by Master Peter Shepe for the voyage 20s., six porters at 6d. each per day for eight days for the portage of lances, bows, and arrows from divers buildings in the Tower of London to the King's Chamber there and for trussing them 24s., two fletchers at 6d. each per day for 40 days sent in divers ships at the King's command for the safekeeping and mending of bows and arrows for the voyage 40s., four craftsmen at 11d. each per day for four days for the portage of hauberks, basinets, plate gauntlets, axes and suchlike from the Wardrobe above the water to the Great Hall in the Tower for trussing them there 8s., portage of coffers from the house of William the crossbow-maker to the King's Chamber for trussing arrows there 3s. 6d., 100 pavises (brought) to Sandwich that a certain victualler Hugh Calville had carried by Master John Bernes valet of this ship 20s., five craftsmen at 6d. each per day for three days working on helving 104 score and 14 pikes for this voyage 7s. 6d., ash for helving them along with 6d. spent on their carriage from the house of a certain currier to the Tower 6s. 6d., two lighters and two boats located for the carriage of the harness to the victualler berthed in the Thames and the King's ship called *Le Poule* berthed at Redcliff 34s. 11d., portage and shipping the harness at Sandwich from the victualler and the King's ship along with divers of the King's ships there 23s. 4d., and bran for safekeeping of divers of the King's harness of mail and plate at Hadley by Master Thomas Horslak, valet-at-arms there 6s. 10d., 300 halves of firewood price 8s., 16½ quarters of charcoal 9d. per quarter expended in the Tower on the repair of arrows and safekeeping of the armour during this time 40s. 4½d., carriage of the firewood and charcoal from Baynards Castle to the Tower 4s., two fletchers at 6d. each per day for 150 days working on mending and repairing heads and arrows in the Wardrobe as well as the arrows sent to Calais £7 10s., three craftsmen at 6d. each per day for three days, three at 6d. each per day for five days for the portage and trussing of bows, arrows, bowstrings at the Tower towards (a campaign in) Portugal 7s., carriage of the pipes from divers buildings so that they might be mended in the Tower of London 3s., three craftsmen at 6d. each per day for two days working on mending and forming the pipes 3s., 63 hoops for binding these pipes 5s. 4d., nails for affixing the hoops 8d., a lighter located from the Tower to Billingsgate for (loading) the pipes onto a ship berthed there for carriage of them to Plymouth 3s. 4d., pulleys and other divers instruments located (to load) the pipes onto the lighter 4s. 4d., two craftsmen at 6d. each per day for 35 days working on mending and repairing old pairs of plates received from the old galley that came from Bayonne and were sent across the sea in a new galley 35s., covering and repairing six score pallets received from the galley and sent across the sea 5s. 8d., making of two springalds and one 'savage' crossbow by Master William Herland, carpenter for the King's voyage £4 15s. 8d., mending and repairing swords and other armour for the King's body in the keeping of Richard the armourer in the Tower £4 16s. 8d., four coffers for three of the King's basinets one helm and one shield 10s. 8d., 400 gilt nails 3s. 4d., 100 silver leaves 12s., 5lb of latten plates 8d. per lb, 12 ells of gilded striped ribbon 16d. per ell expended on mending armour for the King's body and for Thomas of Woodstock at Sandwich 33s., 11 craftsmen for two days, one for nine days, six for 41 days, three for three days, one for 18 days, one for five days, one for eight days, two for eight days, two for 63 days, one for 66 days, eight for six days, one for 11 days, one for 12 days, one for 33 days, one for 54 days, one for 70 days, one for one day all at 6d. per day working on mending hauberks, basinets, plate gauntlets, pallets, pairs of plates, axes, swords and other divers harness of mail remaining in the King's Wardrobe in the Tower of London in the keeping of William of the Wardrobe through the hands of this William £13 18s. 3d., 16 flagons of oil 16d. per flagon, five flagons of oil 2s. per flagon for mending the harness 55s. 4d., a barrel for storing oil 8d., nails for repairing pairs of plates and (horse) covers and other harness in the Wardrobe 20d., a roe hide to affix an aventail upon a basinet 20d., 1½ quarters of bran 2s. 8d. per quarter, 3½ quarters of bran 18d. per quarter, one quarter of bran 2s. 6d., 2½ quarters of bran 2s. per quarter for safekeeping and mending the harness 16s. 9d., bran and oil bought at Sandwich for the safekeeping of the King's armour remaining in his ship upon the sea by Master Thomas Maddyngle 13s. 4d., a leather hide for equipping basinets in this ship 7s. 4d., mending an old coffer in the keeping of Ralph Tyle for this voyage 16d., portage, carriage, and shipping of crossbows, hauberks, and other divers things from Westminster to Rotherhithe and elsewhere by the King's command 18s. 9d., fitting and enlarging 104 score and 16 hauberks received from John Salman 12d. each by Master Gerkyn [sic] the hauberger £9 17s., 38 painted bows for hunting bought and delivered to the King's Chamber by Master Ralph Tyle, Valet of the Chamber 110s., making and painting 31 bows all of wood that were brought from Ireland to Westminster at the King's command by the hands of Ralph £4 13s., ten houces (housings) of old cloth to protect the King's own hunting (bows) by Master Ralph 29s., varnishing one large shield by Master Ralph 12s., a pair of bellows bought for the office of William the heaumer for the King's voyage 26s. 8d., six pairs of large wheels for mantlets (gun shields), three pairs of wheels for rybaudes (field guns) bought and provisioned by Master John Smert for this voyage £11, two craftsmen for 1½ days, two for ten days, one for three days, two for 14 days, and one for 12 days all at 6d. per day working on making powder and lead pellets for guns at the Tower of London 33s., a quarter of charcoal 10d., a half-hundred of firewood 4s. 4d. for casting lead and making powder 5s. 2d., 103 quarters of faggots of willow for making powder 4s. 8d., three trays of wood 3d. each, pots and pans of copper 13d. bought for (making) powder in the same place above the fire and to dry it 2s. 1d., a leather bag for storing the powder 10s. 8d., two copper mortars, three iron pestles, 12 iron winders for casting lead balls, ten latten formers for making these balls, one pair of scales for weighing powder, 30 small barrels with hinges, hasps, and staples to store and keep the lead balls, eight other large barrels for powder, 30 small hanging locks for the 30 barrels, 220lb of saltpetre, two sieves, 18 bellows, 24 leather bags for carrying powder, earthenware pots and pans for fire-powder and drying, 400 faggots of willow from which charcoal for the powder can be made, a hundred of firewood and a half-hundred of faggots bought for divers prices for John Derby, clerk as well as shipping, portage, and carriage of the lead, guns, barrels, and other necessities to divers places along with the two craftsmen and three craftsmen working and labouring on the production of powder, balls, and charcoal for 22 days [...] John Grove, armourer of London for three pairs of plates (decorated with the heraldic) arms of the King and Lord Thomas of Woodstock bought from him in London for the King and Lord for the King's voyage across the sea £14, William Swynley for seven basinets made by him at the King's command on his first coming to the Tower and remaining in store there £14 3s. 6d., a pair of legharness and a basinet for Lord Thomas of Woodstock and a basinet for John Holland bought for him at the Tower by the King's command in gross £6, two pairs of plate gauntlets 20s. per pair, a pair of vambrace and rerebrace 46s. 8d. per pair bought for this Lord by the King's command by Master Richard the armourer for the voyage £4 6s. 8d., Richard Glover for two pairs of legharness leaded (affixed with lead) with swages of gilt latten for the King and the Lord of Brittany £10 5s. per pair bought from him in London by Master Richard the armourer £20 10s., a pair of vambrace and rerebrace with couters worked with swages of latten of the same workmanship for the King 53s. 4d., a pair of vambrace and rerebrace with couters of steel for Lord Thomas of Woodstock 40s., a pair of plate gauntlets with gilt knuckles 26s. 8d., a basinet 40s. bought for Lord Thomas through Richard's hands £8, Richard the armourer for a new pavise painted with the King's arms for the King's voyage 26. 8d., 7,000 white bows, 500 and four score three dozen and four bows 13s. 4d., 260 painted bows 2s. each bought from Adam Haket and other divers bowyers in London £414 17s. 9d., Bodekyn the joiner for 444 long war lances with heads 2s. each, 64 war lances 10d. each bought from him in London for the King's voyage across the sea £47 16d., Geoffrey the saddler for 56 targes of horn bought from him in London by Richard the armourer for the use of the King by his command for the voyage £37 6s. 8d., Robert the joiner for 114 long pavises painted with the arms of Saint George bought from him in London £19, Thomas Essex for 12 spanning devices for drawing crossbows bought from him in London 40s., John Stringer for 100 gross of bowstrings bought from him in London £25, Peter Vansand for 30lb of cord for crossbows bought from him for this voyage 45s., Stephen Warde for five large springalds 100s. each and for a small springald 53s. 4d. bought from him in London £27 13s. 4d., 135 short coffers for storing arrows 22d. each, 53 long coffers for storing bows 3s. 6d. each, 37 long iron-bound coffers for storing bows 6s. each bought and provisioned at the Tower for this voyage £32 15s., Peter the joiner for 215 small coffers 5d. each bought from him for trussing quarrels, a Flanders chest 5s. 6d., a gun of latten with three chambers 20s. bought for 115s. 1d., Stephen Smyth for 200 pikes 12d. each, 13 iron patels for guns 5s. each, two large iron guns 40s. each, six iron hammers for guns 10d. each, 28 iron drills for guns 3d. each, 28 firing-irons 2d. each, ten pairs of iron tongs 10s., 120 quarrel-heads for springalds 1d. each bought from him in London for the voyage £19 20d., John Wayte for one large barrel 16d. bought for trussing the bows and arrows to (be taken to) Portugal 56s. 7d., ten basinets, three pairs of plates, three pairs of legharness, three pairs of plate gauntlets, three pairs of vambrace and rerebrace, 115 pavises, 7,000 white bows, 260 painted bows, 56 targes of horn, 444 war lances, 64 war lanceheads, 12 crossbow spanning devices, 100 gross of bowstrings, one Flanders chest, ten pairs of iron tongs, 30lb of cord for crossbows, six springalds, 135 short coffers, four score and ten long coffers, 215 small coffers, 200 pikes, 13 iron patels, three guns one of which is latten and two of iron, six iron hammers, 28 firing-irons, 28 drills, 120 quarrels for springalds, 22 pipes, one barrel, eight helms, 33 pallets, ten chapel de fers, 1,147 aventails, 206 pisans, 465 hauberks, four score and seven pairs of paunces, one pair of paunces and mail sleeves, 173 mail sleeves, one pair of mail sleeves, 143 standards for hauberks (i.e. separate mail neck defences), three pairs of (mail) gussets, nine pieces of mail for horse covers, four score and 18 pairs of plates, 606 pairs of plate gauntlets, five pairs of cuisses and three pairs of poleyns one pair of which are of latten, three pairs of chausses, 11 pairs of splints for the shins one of which is of leather, one pair of leather greaves, four grappers, 15 lance-staves without vamplates 12 of which are short, 32 coronals, one manifer, 12 shields, 30 iron chains for hauberks, 104 swords, three aketons, 48 doublets, 173 jacks, 17 cuiries for tournaments, five peytrals for tournaments worked with (decorative) images, 57 horse cruppers, 24 testers for horses, one mantlet, and one tester of red striped cloth, three shaffrons, 66 peytrals, one lapkyn (decoration) for one helm, 324 crossbows seven of which are of horn and one vice-spanned, 125 baldrics, 200 wooden parts for crossbows, two vices for drawing crossbows, 18 stirrups for crossbows, 76 dozen four score and 15 quarrels, 2,000 quarrel-shafts, 100 white bows, 245 painted bows, 2,053 bow staves, 22 gross five dozen and two bowstrings, 32,922 sheaves of arrows with heads, 8,500 arrow shafts, 24,300 four score and eight arrowheads, 100 four score and eight axes, 45 targes of horn, eight long pavises, one springald, 27 guns, 600 stones for (siege) engines and trebuchets, 20,000 caltraps, 19 coffers for storing bows and arrows, three anvils, 300 shovels, one large iron-bound case, six large iron-bound chests, one scouring barrel, four coffers for trussing the King's armour, one pair of bags, four barrels of Osmund (iron), two iron trestles, two graters, four barrels of quick sulphur, one pipe and two barrels of saltpetre weighing 50lb. Artillery (made) by John Byker, King's crossbow-maker in the Tower of London: One large vice-spanned crossbow of horn six feet in length, seven new crossbows five of which are two-footers (i.e. for two-foot-long quarrels), two crossbow spanning devices, three new crossbows of horn, two crossbows called 'pee' (feet: poss. affixed on a stand) of horn, two springalds of horn one of which is green, and one springald called 'savage'

93

Now-Lost Document printed in *Cartulaire des Comtes de Hainaut, de l'avènement de Guillaume II à la mort de Jacqueline de Bavière (1337–1436)*, ed. L. Devillers, 6 vols (Brussels, 1883–96), II, pp. 201–2 Ordinance of the Count of Hainaut's Court at Mons concerning the Armour which the Count of Fauquemberg and the Seigneur de Soriel have the right to use for Combat in the Lists, 14 June 1372

se presenterent li comte de Faukemberge comme appiellans et le sires de Soriel comme deffendans armet et montet sur leur chevaulx et fu par lordonnance de le court li armure diaux et de leur chevaulx rewardei Si fu ordonne que leur glaves devoient avoir XIJ piez de long de le pointe du fier jusques au debouth de le glave desoubz et pour ce que li glave du comte estoit trop longhe il fu ordonnet par le court de la racourchir par certaine ensaigne fu ordonnet que les croissans de fier qui estoient a larchon deriere de le selle du comte et li sautoir de fier estoient a larchon devant fuissent hostet et en ce lieu mis a larchon devant une kaisne de fier ainsi que a une selle de gherre et non plus que li taillant du canfrain de sen cheval fust hostez et ossi quil pendesist sen faulx estrier veulsist dedens ou dehors se sielle et li mesist ung cordiel pour lanchier en sen brach sil lui plaisoit et sans ce quil tenist a kaisne ne a corde fu ordonnet ainsi pour le s[ei]g[neu]r de Soriel que li sires de Sorile fesist hoster le taillant de canfrain de sen cheval que li miroir de se selle soient taint de le couleur de larchon et ossi que a larchon de se sielle devant nait que une kaisne de traviers et que li bors de larchon devant soit remplis et se kaisne qui estoit a larchon devant du lonck hostee et quil penge sen faulx estrier dedans ou dehors sen archon ainsi quil li plaist mais quil ne tiengne a kaisne ne a cordielle

the Count of Fauquemberg as appellant and the Seigneur de Soriel as defendant presented themselves armed and mounted on their horses and, by the Court's command, their armour and that of their horses was inspected. Thus it was ordained that their lances must be 12 feet long from the tip of the lancehead to the end of the lance beneath and, as the Count's lance was too long, the Court ordained that it be shortened using a certain sign (of measurement); it was ordained that the iron saddle-steels on the Count's saddle's rear saddlebow and the iron saltire (St Andrew's cross-shaped fitting) on the front saddlebow be removed and replaced with an iron chain affixed to the front saddlebow like unto a war saddle – nothing more; that the sharpened part of his horse's shaffron be removed and also that he hang his false stirrup (poss. a mace) – as he wishes – within or outwith his saddle and that he attach a thin cord to his arm for casting it (the false stirrup) – if he please – and, if not employing this (set-up), that he hold it with neither chain nor cord. Thus it was ordained for the Seigneur de Soriel: that the Seigneur de Soriel remove the sharpened part of his horse's shaffron; that his saddle's (dazzling-ly-polished) reflection be dyed the same colour as the saddlebow, and also that the front saddlebow have nought but one chain across (it), and that the rear saddlebow's wooden (frame) be filled (in), and that the chain the length of the rear saddlebow be removed, and that he hang his false stirrup within or outwith his saddlebow if it please him thus – but that he not hold it with chain nor thin cord

94

Kew, National Archives, E 101/397/10, membr. 3–membr. 5
Arms and Armour issued from the Tower of London, 18 June 1372–23 August 1374

Joh[ann]e Derby [...] x formul' de laton' Ciiij xx iiij lb' pulu[er]is p[ro] gu[n]nes p[ro]uenient' de Cxxxv lb' sal' Pet' & xlix lb' Sulphur' viui Ccxlij lb' sulphur' viui pur'

Wil[e]l[m]o de Redenesse victualar' Cales' p[ro] garnistur' ville C arcus m[i]l' m[i]l'
m[i]l' garb' sagitt' xx m[i]l' quarell' xl balist' de ligno viij balist' de cornu vnde j ad
vice xl baudriz viij haucepes j vice p[u]r tendre balast' xx gross' cord' p[u]r arks [sic]
x m[i]l' Caltraps j gonne gross' oue trois peecz v m[i]l' capit' sagitt' xxx lb' de fil' de
flandres iij C petr' ingenior[um] iiij xx xij coffr' p[ar]u' j Coffr' curt' p[ro] quarell'
intruss' Wil[e]l[m]o de Latym' const' Castr' Douorr' p[ro] ij C Petr' ingeninor[um]
Viginti quatuor Carpentar' [pro] fabr' p[ro] viag' Regis sup[r]a mare lxiij arcus lxiij
garb' sagitt' Cxxvj cord' ad arcus Ph[ilipp]o de Courteneye p[ro] eod' viag' xx arcus
xl garb' sagitt' iiij xx cord' ad arcus Canone Robesart' Capitanio de Arde p[ro]
garnistur' ville C arcus alb' m[i]l' m[i]l' garb' sagitt' Edwardo le Despenser p[ro] viag'
Regis sup[r]a mare vj xx arcus ij C garb' sagitt' ij C cord' ad arcus Wil[e]l[m]o de
Redenesse victualar' Cales' p[ro] garnistur' ville C arcus alb' m[i]l' m[i]l' garb' sagitt'
xx gross' cord' ad arcus hug' de Caluerleye xl pauys long' de arm' s[an]c[t]i Georg'
Rob[er]to de Wykford' Constab[u]l' de Burdeux m[i]l' C arcus alb' v m[i]l' garb'
sagitt' lx gross' cord' ad arcus xxij pipes j barell' p[ro] sag' & cord' intruss' miss' cu'
diu[er]s[i]s Nauib[us] R[eg]is in viag' suo sup[r]a mare lxxij arcus iiij xx iiij garb'
sagitt' m[i]l' vj C iiij xx xj quarell' iiij gross' cord' ad arcus m[i]ss' in mari vij hachett'
xvij lanc' long' xxxvj capit' lanc' ij baudriz iiij par' C[ir]othec' de plat' iiij par' plat'
coop[er]t' de coreo j hausepe iiij pauys xix pycoys Reg' Castell' iiij m[i]l' quarell'
antiq' lib[er]ac[i]o[n]es de dono R[eg]is Thome de Wodestok j bac' cu' j auent' j par'
C[ir]othec' de plat' j balist' cu' vno baudryk Joh[ann]i holand' j loric' ferr' j p[ar]
C[ir]othec' de plat' j p[ar] vauntb[r]as j p[ar] rereb[r]as j bac' cu' j auentaill' henr' st[r]
amy j par' plat' de s[er]ico coop[er]t' j bac' cu' j auentaill' j loric' ferr' j p[ar] C[ir]otec'
de plat' j doublett' Wil[e]l[m]o de holm' s[u]rigico R[eg]is j gladius Rob[er]to hull' j
bac' cu' j auentaill' Joh[ann]i Islani j par' paunz j par' braz In Cam[er]a Regis p[er]
manus Ric[ard]i de Arm' iiij auent' de ac[er]e armatur' & artillar' lib' diu[er]s[i]s
nauib[us] R[egi]s sup[r]a mare & exp[e]n' ib[ide]m tempore quo d[omin]us Rob[er]
tus de Asshton' erat admirall' iiij palett' ij Jakkes xij arcus Cij garb' sagitt' armatur' &
artillar' lib' vsq[ue] le nou' Galeye p[ro] s[e]c[un]do viag' sup[r]a mare iij par' plat'
coop[er]t' de cor' v palett' vj m[i]l lx quarell' iiijo Cressett' de ferr' p[ro] igno iactand'
xij pauys long' xliij Coffr' p[ar]u' p[ro] quarell' intruss' artillar' lib' magne barg' R[eg]
is p[ro] viag' m[i]l' m[i]l' ij C quarell' xvj Coffr' p[ar]u' p[ro] quarell' intruss' artillar'
lib' Wil[e]l[m]o Graylyng p[ro] garnistur' cuiusdam barg' capt' sup[r]a mare in
eodem viag' vj m[i]l quarell' xxxv Coffr' p[ro] quarell' intruss' artillar' lib' Barg' Regis
Galey & le Balyng' tempore quo helming leget existebat patronus eiusdem Gales &
amiss' & vastat' sup[r]a mare m[i]l' vj C quarell' nou' xj Coffr' p[ar]u' m[i]l' viij C
quarell' vn' iiij C nou' xj Coffr' p[ar]u' m[i]l' quarell' nou' xiiij pauys xij arcus alb' Cxx
cord' ad arcus ix palett' lxviij garb' sagitt' vij Coffr' p[ar]u' Joh[ann]i haytefeld' p[ro]
coop[er]tur' & emendac' diu[er]s[i]s Jakkes antiquor[um] p[ro] nauib[us] in Custod'
sua existent' lxv vln' tel' lin' henaud' xxiiij vln' hen' Clxxj tel' lin' xvj pec' diu[er]s[i]s
color' Worst' lxv vln' Canab' iiij gross' cord' ad arcus j barell' v[er]nyssh ponder' xx
viij lb' rep[ar]ac' & emendac' & coop[er]tur' plat' antiquor[um] recept' de quod'
antiquo Galey stant' apud le Redeclyf necnon p[ro] stufs fac' p[ro] Cxx palett'
antiquis recept' de eod' Galey p[er] m[agistr]o Berkyng' xlvj vln' Canab' iij lb' diu[er]

s[i]s color' fili Joh[ann]i Derby Cl[er]ico p[ro] offic' gunnor[um] Reg' p[ro] viag'
R[eg]is sup[r]a mare j Cist' flandr' xxix gonnes ferr' vj martell' ferr' xxviij driuelles
ferr' xxviij fyringyrnes xiij patell' ferr' x par' forc' ferr' vna Carrata & vj Wag' plumbi
vna pipa & ij barell' sal' petr' pond' liiij lb' talliatur' & elargat' Ciiij xx xvj loric' rec'
de Joh[ann]e Salman' xxiij loric' ferr' Cxliij stand' p[ro] loric' Joh[ann]i de Foxley
Constab[u]lar' Castr' de Quenesburgh' p[ro] staur' Cxxvj lb' de sulfur' vyf' xxx lb' de
poudr' p[u]r gunn' lib[er]ac' diu[er]s[i]s rer[um] arc' alb' m[i]l' m[i]l' viij C iiij xx xix
Sagitt' xij m[i]l' Clvij garb' sag' xliij m[i]l' CCClj quarell' Balist' xlix balist' vnde viij
de cornu & xlj de ligno Bauderiz xliij haucepez ix vicez j vice p[ro] balist' tendend'
Cord' ad arc' Cxj gross' vij duoden' & x cord' ad arc' Caltraps x m[i]l' Gunnes ferr'
xxix Gunnes de laton' j gunne g[r]oss' cu' iij peetz Capita sag' v m[i]l' cap' sag' fil' de
Flandr' xxx lb' Petr' Ingenior[um] C petr' Ingen' Coffr' p[ar]u' & curt' Ccxlij vnde j
curt' Pauys long' lxx Pip' vac' xxij Barell' vij hachett' vij lanc' long' xvij Capit' lanc'
xxxvj C[ir]otech' de plate v par' plat' viij par' vn' vij par' coop[er]t' de cor' Pycoys xl
Bacinett' iiijor Auentall' viij loric' vnde iiijor de ac[er]e loric' de ferr' xxv Standard'
p[ro] loric' Cxliiij vauntb[r]as j par' Rerebras j Doublett' j Gladij j Paunz j par' braz
j par' palett' viij Jackes ij Cressettes ferr' p[ro] igno iactand' iiij xx vln' tel' lin' hen'
xxiiij vln' tel' lin' Custanc' Clxxj vln' Worst' diu[er]s[i]s color' xvj pec' Canab' vxx xj
vln' barell' v[er]nyssh' j ponder' iiij xx viij lb' filu' diu[er]s[i]s color' iij lb' j q[u]art'
diu[er]s' color' Ciste flandr' j martell' ferr' vj Dryuell' ferr' xxviij Fyryngyrnes xxviij
patell' ferr' xiij forc' ferr' x par' Plumbu' j carrat' & vj Wag' Sal' petr' j pip' & ij barell'
pond' l lb' pulu' p[ro] gu[n]nes lx lb' moldes voc' formes p[ro] pelett' fac' v Sulphur'
vif' Cxxvj lb' Et remanent CCC iiij xx j bac' iiij xx xiij par' plat' iij par' legh[er]neys
vj C iiij par' c[ir]othec' de plat' iij par' vauntb[r]as & rereb[r]as Cxviij par' vauntb[r]
as ij par' rereb[r]as liij pauys' iiij m[i]l' ij C j arc' alb' v C v arc' depict' Cj targett' de
cornu iiij xx vij lanc' de guerr' xxviij capit' lanc' v haucepes x gross' ix duoden' iiijor
cord' ad arc' xj springald' Cxxxiiij coffr' curt' Cxix coffr' long' Ciiij xx j pycoys Cxx
capit' quarell' p[ro] springald' viij galee xxv palett' x Capell' ferr' m[i]l' Cxxxix
auentaill' ij C vj pisanz iiij C xl loric' iiij xx vj par' paunz j par' paunz & braz Clxij
braaz j par' braccal' de mayll' iij par' Gussett' ix pec' de mayll' p[ro] coop[er]tur'
equor[um] v par' quisseux iij par' poleyns vn' j de laton' iij par' chausons xj par'
splentes ij par' tibialiu' vn' j de cor' j par' Greues de coreo iiijor grates xv stufs lanc'
sine auantplat' vn' xij p[ar]u' xxxij Coronaux j mayndefer xij scuta xxx cathene ferr'
p[ro] loric' Ciij gladij iij Actons xlvij doublett' Clxxj Jakkes xvij quirrez p[ro] t[u]
rniament' v pec' p[ro] t[u]rniament' op[er]ac' cu' ymaginib[us] lvij croper' equor[um]
xxiiij testor' equor[um] j mantellett' j testor' de rub' ray cordele iij chanfreyns lxvj
pic[er]s j par' allett' j lapkyn p[ro] j galea ij C iiij xx ix balist' vn' j magn' ad vice de
cornu antiq' de longitud' vj ped' & j sauage [sic] iiij xx ij baudriz ij C lign' p[ro] balist'
j vice p[ro] balist' tend' xviij stirops p[ro] balist' xxxij m[i]l' ij C xliiij quarell' m[i]l'
m[i]l' liij bowestafs x m[i]l' iij C lxv sagitt' cu' cap' vij m[i]l' C arughshaftes xix m[i]
l' iij C iiij xx viij capit' sag' Ciiij xx j hachett' C petr' p[ro] Ingenijs & tribigect' x m[i]
l' Calt[r]aps iij anefeld' ij C j standard' magn' ferr' ligat' vj ciste magne ferr' ligat' j
frayngbarell' iiijor coffr' p[ro] armatur' R[eg]is intrussand' j par' bulgear[um] iiijor

barell' Osemond' ij g[r]atours iiijor barell' sulphur' vyf' Cxxiiij lb' puluer' p[ro] gunnis Cxvj lb' sulphur' viui v moldes de laton' voc' formule

John Derby: ten latten formers, 100 and four score and 4lb of gunpowder made from 135lb of saltpetre and 49lb of quick sulphur, 242lb of quick sulphur, William Redness, Victualler of Calais for equipping the town: 100 bows, 3,000 sheaves of arrows, 2,000 quarrels, 40 wooden crossbows, eight horn crossbows one of which is vice-spanned, 40 baldrics, eight crossbow spanning devices, one vice for drawing crossbows, 20 gross of bowstrings, 10,000 caltraps, one large gun with three (chamber) pieces, 5,000 arrowheads, 30lb of Flanders thread, 300 stones for (siege) engines, four score and 12 little coffers, one short coffer for trussing quarrels, William Latimer, Keeper of Dover Castle: 200 stones for (siege) engines, 34 carpenters, 24 latten-workers, and 15 smiths for the King's voyage across the sea: 63 bows, 63 sheaves of arrows, 126 bowstrings, Philip Courteney, for the same voyage: 20 bows, 40 sheaves of arrows, four score bowstrings, Canon Robesart, Captain of Ardres for equipping the town: 100 white bows, 2,000 sheaves of arrows, Edward Despenser for the King's voyage across the sea: six score bows, 200 sheaves of arrows, 200 bowstrings, William Redness, Victualler of Calais for equipping the town: 100 white bows, 2,000 sheaves of arrows, 20 gross of bowstrings, Hugh Calveley: 40 long pavises of the arms of Saint George, Robert Wykford, Keeper of Bordeaux: 1,100 white bows, 5,000 sheaves of arrows, 60 gross of bowstrings, 22 pipes, one barrel for trussing these arrows and strings, sent with divers of the King's ships in his voyage across the sea: 72 bows, four score and four sheaves of arrows, 1,600 four score and 11 quarrels, four gross of bowstrings, seven hatchets, 17 long lances, 36 lanceheads, two baldrics, four pairs of plate gauntlets, four pairs of plates covered with leather, one hausepe (crossbow spanning device), four pavises, 19 pikes, Reginald Castle: 4,000 old quarrels. Gifts of the King – Thomas of Woodstock: one basinet with one aventail, one pair of plate gauntlets, one crossbow with one baldric, John Holland: one iron hauberk, one pair of plate gauntlets, one pair of vambrace, one pair of rerebrace, one basinet with one aventail, Henry Stramy: one pair of plates covered with silk, one basinet with one aventail, one iron hauberk, one pair of plate gauntlets, one doublet, William Holm, King's Surgeon: one sword, Robert Hull: one basinet with one aventail, John Islani: one pair of paunces, one pair of (mail) sleeves, in the King's Chambers by the hands of Richard the armourer: four steel aventails. Armour and artillery delivered to divers of the King's ships on the sea and expenses at the time Robert Ashton was Admiral: four pallets, two jacks, 12 bows, 102 sheaves of arrows, armour and artillery delivered to the new galley for the second voyage across the sea: three pairs of plates covered with leather, five pallets, 6,060 quarrels, four iron cressets for shooting fire, 12 long pavises, 43 little coffers for trussing quarrels, artillery delivered to the King's great barge for the same voyage by the hands of Francis de La Mare: 2,200 quarrels, 16 little coffers for trussing quarrels, artillery delivered to William Grayling to equip a certain barge upon the sea for this voyage: 6,000 quarrels, 35 coffers for trussing quarrels, artillery delivered to the King's barge, galley, and ballinger at the time that Helming Leget was captain of these galleys: 1,600 new quarrels, 11 little coffers, 1,800 quarrels 400 of which are new, 11 little coffers, 1,000 new quarrels, 14 pavises, 12 white bows, 120 bowstrings, nine pallets, 68 sheaves of arrows, seven little coffers, John Hatfield for covering and mending divers old jacks for ships in his keeping: 65 ells of Hainaut linen, 24 ells of Hainaut, 171 ells of Constance linen, 16 pieces of divers colours of worsted (woollen cloth), 65 ells of canvas, four gross of bowstrings, one barrel of varnish weighing 80lb, repair and mending and covering of old plates received from a certain old galley birthed at Redcliff as well as for stuffed linings made for 120 old pallets received from this galley by Master Berkyng: 46 ells of canvas, 3lb of divers coloured thread, John Derby, Clerk of the Office of the King's Guns for the King's voyage across the sea: one Flanders chest, 29 iron guns, six iron hammers, 28 iron drills, 28 firing-irons, 13 iron pattels, ten pairs of iron tongs, one wagon and six lead swages, one pipe and two barrels of saltpetre weighing 54lb, refitting and enlarging 100 four score and 16 hauberks received from John Salman: 23 iron hauberks, 143 standards for hauberks, John Foxley, Keeper of Queensborough Castle for the stores: 126lb of quick sulphur, 30lb of gunpowder. Divers expenses: 2,800 four score and 19 white bows, 12,157 sheaves of arrows, 43,351 quarrels, 49 crossbows eight of which are of horn and 41 of wood, 43 baldrics, nine crossbow spanning devices, one vice for drawing crossbows, 111 gross seven dozen and ten bowstrings, 10,000 caltraps, 29 iron guns, one large latten gun with three (chamber) pieces, 5,000 arrowheads, 30lb of Flanders thread, 100 stones for (siege) engines, 242 little coffers one of which is short, 70 long pavises, 22 pipes, one barrel, seven hatchets, 17 long lances, 36 lanceheads, five pairs of plate gauntlets, eight (more) pairs seven pairs of which are covered with leather, 40 pikes, four basinets, eight aventails four of which are of steel, 25 iron hauberks, 144 standards for hauberks, one pair of vambrace, one pair of rerebrace, one doublet, one sword, one pair of paunces, one pair of mail sleeves, eight pallets, two jacks, four iron cressets for shooting fire, four score and nine ells of Hainaut linen, 171 ells of Constance linen, 16 pieces of worsted (woollen cloth) of divers colours, five score and 11 ells of canvas, one barrel of varnish weighing 80lb, 31¼lb of thread of divers colours, one Flanders chest, one iron hammer, 28 iron drills, 28 firing-irons, 13 iron pattles, ten pairs of iron tongs, one wagon and six swages of lead, one pipe and one barrel of saltpetre weighing 50lb, 126lb of quick sulphur. Remains (in the Tower): 300 four score and one basinets, four score and 13 pairs of plates, three pairs of legharness, 604 pairs of plate gauntlets, three pairs of vambrace and rerebrace, 118 pairs of vambrace, two pairs of rerebrace, 53 pavises, 4,201 white bows, 505 painted bows, 101 targes of horn, four score and seven war lances, 28 lanceheads, five crossbow spanning devices, ten gross nine dozen and four bowstrings, 11 springalds, 134 short coffers, 119 long coffers, 100 four score and one pikes, 120 quarrel-heads for springalds, eight helms, 25 pallets, ten chapel de fers, 1,139 aventails, 206 pisans, 440 hauberks, four score and six pairs of paunces, one pair of paunces and (mail) sleeves, 163 (mail) sleeves, one pair of mail sleeves, three pairs of gussets, nine pieces of mail for horse covers, five pairs of cuisses, three pairs of poleyns one of which is latten, three pairs of chausses, 11 pairs of splints, two pairs of shin defences one of which is leather, one pair of greaves of leather, four grappers, 15 lance-staves without vamplates 12 of which are short, 32 coronals, one manifer, 12 shields, 30 iron chains for hauberks, 103 swords, three aketons, 47 doublets, 171 jacks,

17 cuiries for tournaments, five peytrals for tournaments worked with images, 57 horse cruppers, 24 horse testers, one mantlet, one tester of striped corded red cloth, three shaffrons, 66 peytrals, one pair of ailettes one lapkyn (decoration) for one helm, 200 four score and nine crossbows one of which is large with a vice of old horn of six foot in length and one (crossbow called) 'savage', four score and two baldrics, 200 bindings for crossbows, one vice for drawing crossbows, 18 stirrups for crossbows, 32,244 quarrels, 2,053 bow staves, 10,365 arrowheads, 7,100 arrow shafts, 19,300 four score and eight arrowheads, 100 and four score hatchets, 100 stones for (siege) engines and trebuchets, 10,000 caltraps, three anvils, one large iron-bound trunk, six large iron-bound chests, one scouring barrel, four coffers for trussing the King's armour, one pair of bags, four barrels of Osmund (iron), two graters, four barrels of quick sulphur, 124lb of gunpowder, 116lb of quick sulphur, five moulds of latten called formers

95

London, British Library, Sloane Charter XXXI 2
Inventory of the Effects of Sir Edmund Appleby, Appleby Magna, Leicestershire, 1374

j basenet cu' aduentayle ij mar' Justy[n]gherneys test' & piser sella scuto […] iiij hauburjounes quor[um] vnu' p[ro] corp[orum] & duo al' xiij mar' ij p[ar]ia cirotecar[um] de plate vj s viij d ij ketelhattes & ij paletes vj s viij d

one basinet with aventail two marks, jousting harness: tester, and peytral, saddle, shield […] three haubergeons one of which was for his body and two others 13 marks, two pairs of plate gauntlets 6s. 8d., two kettlehats and two pallets 6s. 8d.

96

Kew, National Archives, E 41/472
Will of William Laxman, Manor of Wickensands in Sussex, or London, April 1374

Joh[ann]i Brokas j loricam que est apud Arundell' et j auentayle exist' london' in custod' Ph[illi]pi Broune Armorer' Thome Salman' j par' de plates exist' apud Wyke Joh[ann]i de la Botelry j palet cu' j auentayll coop[er]to cu' pannobip[ar]tito existent' in custod' d[ic]ti [Broune]

John Brokas one hauberk which is at Arundel and one aventail in London in the keeping of Philip Broune, armourer, Thomas Salman one pair of plates at Wickensands, John de la Botlery one pallet with aventail covered with parti-coloured cloth in the keeping of the said (Philip)

97

State Archives of Turin, Comptes des trésoriers généraux de Savoie, Vol. 39, fol. 33r and fol. 163r, printed in C. Buttin, *Notes sur les armures à l'épreuve* (Annecy, 1901), p. 15 and p. 22
Household Payments of the Counts of Savoy, Turin, Piedmont, 1375 and 1392

1375
duorum auberjonorum seu panceronorum pro domino, unius videlicet de maillia plata, et alterius rotonda

two haubergeons or paunces for the Lord, viz.: one of flat mail and the other round (i.e. the section of the wire links)

1392
I bacigniet et de I camail d'acier de toute botte, une piece d'acier, un arnes de brach tout entier, uns gantelles et un arnes de chambes tout entier Achettez de Symond Brulafer, arm[uri]eur XXXIIIJ frans, I auberion d'acier de botte cassé duquel toutes les mailles sunt seigniez du seigniet du maistre XL frans

one basinet and one steel aventail of complete riveting (i.e. all the links riveted), one *pièce* (reinforcing plate for the torso), a complete arm harness, one (pair of) gauntlets and one complete arm harness bought from Symond Brulafer, armourer 34 francs, one steel haubergeon with broken rivets that has each of the mail links marked with the master's (maker's) mark 40 francs

98

London Metropolitan Archives, Plea and Memoranda Roll A20
Complaint of Robert Wormwell, Apprentice to John Scot, Armourer of London, 22 March 1375

Rob[er]tus Wormwell app[re]ntiti' Joh[ann]is Scot armurer lib[er]ant hic quand^{a}m billam in hec v[er]ba – As t[re]shon[o]rables S[eign]o[r]s & g[r]acoiuses meire & Recor' de le Citee de lundr[e]s supplie humblement Rob[er]t Wormwell app[re]ntiz Joh[a]n Scot armurer q[ue] come le dit Rob[er]t ad s[er]ui bien & loialment son mestr[e] a cest Pask p[ro]schein venant p[ar] sys anz & deux anz de son t[er]me sont auenirs le quele Joh[a]n est voide hors de la Citee & ad lesse son dit app[re]ntiz aler vacat & v' sanz nuls coustages lui trouer ou lui mettre a ascun autre de son mestier ou il p[o]roit sa sustenaunce gayner Issint q[ue] le dit app[re]ntiz est Ou point destre p[er]due si bein pur defance de sa prise p[u]r le temps auenir come p[o]r sa sustenance ap[re]sent qar nul ho[m]me del mestier ne lui voet accepter de lui ap[re]

ndre ne sustiner p[a]r cause qil est app[re]ntiz Plese a v[ost]re tresg[r]aciouse S[igno]
rie pur dieu & en oeure de charite eut ordiner dus remedie issunt q[ue] le suppliant
son temps en defesance de lui en temps auenir Et sup[er] hoc concessum est p[ar]
maiorem & aldermannos q[uo]d Rob[er]tus s[er]uire posit aliam alt[er] de eod[e]m
mustero donec mag[ist]r' ven[ire]nt & en[i]m sustin[ir]e & doc[er]e posit & c'

Robert Wormwell apprentice to John Scot armourer here presented a certain bill
with these words: To the most honourable sirs and gracious Mayor and Recorder of
the City of London, Robert Wormwell apprentice to John Scot armourer humbly
supplicates that, as the said Robert has well and legally served his master until this
Easter next to come for six years and as two years of his term are yet to be served, the
said John has vacated to outside the City and has left his apprentice to go wanting
and unable to provide his expenses or place himself under another of his craft where
he might earn his keep – thus the apprentice is at the point of being ruined. Both for
the protection of his esteem for the future, as well as for his sustenance at present, no
man of the said craft wishes to accept him to teach nor sustain because he is still an
apprentice. May it please your most gracious lordships by God's grace and work of
charity that they might ordain and issue deliverance that the supplicant's future time
(to serve apprenticeship) be annulled. And upon this it was conceded by the Mayor
and Aldermen that Robert might serve any other of the same craft until his master
return and thus be able to be sustained and taught etc.

99

Kew, National Archives, E 101/509/26
Goods of Sir Richard Lyons, Merchant of London, 1376

La garderobe iiij jakk' de guerre cestassauoir iij de silk et camaca j autre de fustayn
vj l xiij s iiij d La petit garder' vj bacenettes saunz aventailles vsez xx s iij pair de
legharnoys vsez xxx s ij pair de legharnoys plus feblez vj s viij d j peir de vaimbras et j
peir de splentes feble j s vj arblastes vsez xxvj s viij d j basenet oue aventaille et healme
vsez xxij s j hache vsez iij s iiij d j espee le gayn et ceynture garnise dargent endor'
iiij mars j peir de plates couerez de rouge velvet xx s j pauad [sic] garnise darg' vsez
xiij s iiij d j coppegorge auncien iij s iiij d j bedewe garnise darg' iij s iiij d j dagger
garnise darg' ij s ij peir de gauntes de plate ij peir vaunbras ij peir de rerebras ij pair de
sabatons j bristplate vsez x s j peir de paunces ij peir brace et ij aventailles febles x s x
hastes de launces viij s iiij d Vendita iij arblastez xx s j coffyn oue viritons j bauderik
et j poley' iij s iiij d j Gleyue hernoys oue argent endor' x sperschaftes26s.

The Wardrobe: four jacks for war – that is to say: three of silk and camaca (silk fabric)
and one other of fustian (strong fabric made from any two of cotton, flax, or wool) £6
13s. 4d., the Small Wardrobe: six worn out basinets without aventails 20s., three pairs of
worn out legharness 30s., two pairs of even more worn out legharness 6s. 8d., six worn
out crossbows 26s. 8d., one worn out basinet with aventail and a helm 22s., one worn out

axe 3s. 4d., one sword the grip and belt garnished with silver-gilt four marks, one pair of plates covered with red velvet 20s., one old pavise garnished with silver 13s. 4d., one old coppegorge [lit. cutthroat] 3s. 4d., one biddow garnished with silver 3s. 4d., one dagger garnished with silver 2s., two pairs of worn out plate gauntlets, two pairs of vambrace, two pairs of rerebrace, two pairs of sabatons, one breastplate 10s., one worn out pair of paunces, two pairs of (mail) sleeves, and two aventails 10s., ten lance shafts 8s. 4d. To be sold: three crossbows 20s., one coffer with (crossbow) quarrels, one baldric and one pulley 3s. 4d., one glaive harnessed with silver-gilt, ten spear shafts

100

Lambeth Palace Library, Register of Archbishop Sudbury, fol. 90v
Will of Edward the Black Prince, Palace of Westminster, 7 June 1376

s[u]r quel [tombe] nouz voloms q' vn ymage d[…] signe leuez de latoun suzorrez soit mys en memorial de no[u]s tout armez de fier de guerre de nous armez quartillez & le visage nue oue n[ost]re heaume du leopard mys dessouz la teste del ymage […] q' n[ost]re corps soit menez p[ar]my la ville de Cant[er]bire tantis' a la Priorie deux destrez cou[er]tez de noz armez & deux ho[…] armez en noz armez & en noz heaumes voisent deuant dit n[ost]re corps Cest assauoir lun pur la guerre de noz armez entiers quartillez & lautre po[u]r la paix de noz badges des plumes dostruce oue quatre h[…] de mesme la sute & q' ch[as]cun de ceux q' porteront lez ban[er]s ait sur sa teste vn chapeau de noz armez

upon which [tomb] we will that an image of a design of raised gilt latten shall be placed in memorial of us completely armed in readiness for war with our quartered (heraldic) arms and face bared with our helm of the leopard (crest) placed beneath the head of the said image […] that our corpse be led through the town of Canterbury, thereafter to the Priory [with] two destriers trappered with our (heraldic) arms and two men in our arms and in our helms to be seen before our said corpse. That is to say: one for war with our entire quartered (heraldic) arms and the other for peace with our badge of ostrich feathers with four men in the same suit and that each of those who bear the banners have on his head a cap of my arms.

101

Paris, Bibliothèque nationale de France, MS fr. 26013, no. 1834, printed in *Documents relatifs au clos des galées de Rouen et aux armées de mer du roi de France de 1293 à 1418*, ed. A. Merlin-Chazelas, 2 vols (Paris, 1977–78), II, pp. 160–1
Inventory of the Château of Rouen, Normandy, 19 December 1376

en une chambre dite la chambre la royne, en 42 barilz viez, huit cens et quarante costes de fer, en un viel tonnel, neuf vins poulains et cuissos de l'ancienne façon, ou dit tonnel, trois coupes de bacinés enroulliés qui gaires ne vallent, neuf cens cinquante nuef bacinés chascun a camail, visiere et hourson, lesquieux il faut reglacier; et en y a de telz qui ont les hoursons et les cervelieres mengees de ras et d'autre vermine, huit cens vint et deux paire de gantelez, 1,057 paire de bracelés, quatre barilz viez a tout leurs piez a esclarcir armeures, un viel poinçon, une mine de sablon d'Estampes, ou environ, pour esclarcir armeures, en la chambre qui est dessoubz la dicte chambre, cinq viez bans a polir hernois. Ensuivent les reparacions qui neccessairement escon-viennent estre faites aus dictes armeures, pour les dictes 840 cotes de fer blanchir et appareiller ce qui est de neccessité, chascune cote 18 d., pour les dis 180 paire de poulains et cuissos de l'ancienne façon polir, appareillier et mettre a leur droit point et y trouver courroies et bougleites, chascune paire 18 d., pour les dis 959 bacinés, polir, appareillier et mettre en bonne ordenance, blanchir les camaux, appareillier la garnison dedens les bacinés, pour adjuster les visiers et charnieres, trouver les civres [prob. civelles] des camaux et yceux faire et mettre aus bacinés, chascun bacinet 6 s., pour 822 paire de gantelez appareillier bien et deurement, chascune paire 12 d., pour 1,057 bracelos polir, appareillier et y faire et trouver couroies et boucleites, chascun paire 18 d.

In a chamber called The Queen's Chamber: in 42 old barrels 840 coats of mail, in an old tun nine score old fashioned poleyns and cuisses, in this tun three rusted basinet skulls of no value, 959 basinets each with aventail, visor, and hourson (aventail-cover) which need to be polished, there are some which have had the hoursons and the linings eaten by rats and other vermin, 822 pairs of gauntlets, 1,057 pairs of bracers, four old barrels with their feet for scouring armour, an old punch, a *mine* (type of measure) or thereabouts of crushed sand for scouring armour. In the chamber above the said (Queen's) Chamber: five old strops for scouring armour. Here follow the necessary repairs for the armour: to equip and scour the 840 coats of mail as is necessary 18 *deniers* a coat, for polishing, equipping, and fixing the 180 pairs of old fashioned poleyns and cuisses and for sourcing straps and buckles 18d. a pair, for polishing, equipping, and fixing to good use the 959 basinets, scouring the aventails, equipping basinets' insides (linings), to adjust the visors and hinges, sourcing and making the *civelles* (leather tabs) for the aventails and attaching them to the basinets 6 *sous* a basinet, for strongly fitting the 822 pairs of gauntlets 12d. a pair, for polishing, equipping, and sourcing and making leathers (i.e. straps) and buckles for the 1,057 bracers 18d. a pair

102

London Metropolitan Archives, London Letter-Book H, fol. 39r
Royal Order to the Mayor of London for the release of Armour made for George, Scottish Earl of March, Westminster, 8 June 1377

mandam[us] vob' q[uod] om[n]ia hernesia que Joh[ann]es Wardelawe de Scocia fieri fecit ad opus Comitis marchis de Scocia vid[e]l[ice]t quinq[ue] bacynettes quatuor paria de plates quinq[ue] brestplates sex paria de braciers integr' sex garnesturas p[ro] lanceis octo paria cerotecar[um] de ferr' duo scuta & sex sellas bastardes que p[er] vos arestata existunt sine dil[ati]one dearestar' & p[re]fato Joh[ann]i delib[er]ar' P[er] billam testim' henr' de P[er]cy

We command that all the harness that John Wardlaw (merchant) of Scotland had made for the use of the Earl of March of Scotland viz.: five basinets, four pairs of plates, five breastplates, six pairs of complete bracers, six fittings for lances, eight pairs of iron gauntlets, two shields, and six bastard saddles that were confiscated by you be released without delay and delivered to the said John – by the bill witnessed by Henry Percy

Unlocated Original Document printed in Calendar of Documents Relating to Scotland, AD 1108–1516, ed. J. Bain and others, 5 vols (Edinburgh, 1886), IV, no. 592, undated. A French version of the document above

The Mayor of London is to deliver all the 'hernoises' arrested by him that John Wardelawe of Scotland had made for the Earl of March of Scotland viz.: five 'bacynettes', four pair of 'platez', with five 'brestplatez', six pair of 'braciers entiers', six 'garnicementz pour launces eit paire de gauntez de ferre deux escuez sys selles bastardes Par Henry Sire de Percy'

103

Unlocated Original Document from Archives Ville d'Angers, Comptes de la cloison d'Angers, no. 6, printed in V. Gay, *Glossaire archéologique du Moyen Âge et de la Renaissance*, 2 vols (Paris, 1887–1928), II, p. 768 Purchase of Crossbow Quarrels for Proofing Armour, Angers, Duchy of Anjou, 1378

Pour deux milliers de fer pour viretons, *partie d'espreuve* et autre partie de fer commun

For 2,000 heads for crossbow quarrels, half of them for proofing (i.e. for shooting to test armour) and the other half standard heads

104

London Metropolitan Archives, Plea and Memoranda Roll A10 Complaint against Stephen atte Fryth, Armourer of London, 19 March 1378

Steph[an]o atte Fryth de london' am[ur]er [and three others] Sum' fuer[u]nt ad respond' Thoma younge & Alicia vx[or]i eius [...] vici vocat' Watlyngstynstrate [...] fabrica leuata cui' fabrica tuellus est bassior q[u]am de iure esse deb[er]et fabricam

& mannopus cu' grossis malleis diu[er]sas magnas pecias ferri vocat' Osmond' op[er]
and' & faciend' inde diu[er]sas armat[ur]as vid[e]l[ice]t Brestplates quyssers Jambers
& alias armat[ur]as Ita q[uo]d p[ar] grossas ut' mallior[um] sup[er] uicendem fabrice
cadenan' tant' Sont' & tremer' euenit & rediuidat q[ou]d p[er]reces domor[um] de
petris & t[er]ra fact' contreu[er]e facit & sos om[n]io cadere & disrump[ar]e uecrion
Thom' & Alic' & S[er]uients suos die ac nocte niquietant & p[er]turbant & vinu[m]
& s[er]uisiam in celario & dominib[us] posita mispissant & aduichilant Et Ecia' fetor
fumi de carbonib[us] maris in Ead' fabrica acridentib[us] exiens uicrat in aulam &
cam[er]as nocumet' & pannor[um] s[u]or[um]

Stephen atte Fryth, armourer of London [and three others] were summoned to
answer to Thomas Young and Alice his wife [...] in the street called 'Watling Street'
[where they had] built a forge the chimney of which was made lower than legal and
with handiwork with sledgehammers made and worked divers great pieces of iron
called 'osmunds' into divers armours viz.: breastplates, cuisses, jambers, and other
armour. And by the blows of these sledgehammers working in the forge their house
(although made of stone and earth) is caused to shake and crumble so that Thomas
and Alice, and their servants are disturbed with noise both day and night and the
wine and beer in the cellar and house is spoilt and the fetid smoke of the sea coal
burnt in this forge blows into the hall and rooms spoiling their bread

105

Latin: Kew, National Archives, C 66/301/5; French: Kew, National
Archives, C 81/456/349
Royal Grant of Arms and Armour to Sir Robert Salle, 3 May 1378

unu' hernesiu' integru' p[ro] guerra vi[de]l[ice]t unu' p[ar] de braceys de ferr' unu' p[ar]
de sabatons de ferr' unu' integru' hernesiu' de jambes de ferr' cu' poleyns quisseux et
voiders una' tunica' de ferr' et unu' p[ar] de plates panno aur' coop[er]t' unu' bresteplate
rubea' unu' jak de aur' un' cu' bokles et pendentiis argent' deaurat' unu' bacinetu' cu'
un' aventall' de acer' si[mu]l cu' lestaples bacinet' unu' chaplet' argent' deauratu' una'
galea' cu' un' cresta unu' p[ar] cerotecar[um] de plat' unu' gladiu' et unu' dagger' de
guerr' unu' secur' de Burdeux unu' scutu' de corn' platatu' de acer' una' lancea' rubea' cu'
capit' de burdeux et unu' pavys alb' cu' un' capit' nigr' de aquil' racet' vn hernoys entier

pur la guerre cestassavoir vn peir de brays de fer vn peir de sabatons de fer vn entier
hernoys de iambes de fer ouesque poleyns quisseux et voiders vne cote de fer et vne
peire de plates couertes de drap dor vn brestplate rouge vn iak dor ouesque les bocles
et pendantz dargent susorrez vne bacynet ouesqes vn auentaill' dascer ouesque les
estaples du bacynet et vne chapelet dargent susorrez vne heaume ouesqes vn crest vne
peire de gantz de plate vn espeye et vn dagger de guerre vn hache de Burdeux vn escu
de corn platez dasser vne lance rouge oue la teste de Burdeux et vne pauys blanche
ouesqes vne teste noir degle racez

one complete harness for war viz.: one pair of iron bracers, one pair of iron sabatons, one complete legharness with poleyns cuisses and voiders, one mail shirt, one pair of plates covered with cloth of gold, one red breastplate, one jack of gold with silver-gilt buckles and pendants, one basinet with steel aventail along with the staples of the basinet, one silver-gilt chaplet (headdress), one helm with a crest, one pair of plate gauntlets, one war sword and one dagger, one axe of Bordeaux (make), one horn shield plated with steel, one red lance with Bordeaux head, and one white pavise with (the heraldic blazon of) an erased eagle's head sable

106

Winchester, Hampshire Record Office, Register of Bishop William
Wykeham, 21M65/A1/11
Will of Sir John Foxle, Apulderfield, Kent, 5 November 1378

Thome Paynel nepoti meo equu' meu' dun vnu' hab[er]geon de alto clowo[u]r ac vnu' basynet largiorem cu' le vyser & auentaille ad eund[e]m Joh[ann]i Feghelere nepoti meo equu' meu' vocat' morelhale vnu' hab[er]geon vnu' basynet' cu' le vyser & auentaill' ad eund[e]m

my nephew Thomas Paynel my dun horse, one haubergeon of high nailing (i.e. all the links riveted), with one large basinet with its visor and aventail, my nephew John Feghelere my all-black horse, one haubergeon, one basinet with its visor and aventail

107

Rotuli Parliamentorum [...] *tempore Ricardi R. II*, ed. J. Strachey and
others, 4 vols (London, 1767–77), III, 82
Act of Parliament regarding the Armour of Men living in Certain Parts
of the English Realm, 1379–80

come gentz demurrantz sur les Costes de Meer, sur les Marches d'Escoce, & autres Marches, la leur Persones & Vikers apres la mort des tielx demandent lours armures en noun des mortuaires c'est assavoir plates, haubergeons, bacinettes, aventailles, gauntz de plates, actons, palettes, jackes defensibles, & autres armures

After the death of men living on the sea coasts, on the marches of Scotland, and other marches their parsons and vicars may demand their armour in the name of mortuary (offerings), that is to say: (pairs of) plates, haubergeons, basinets, aventails, plate gauntlets, aketons, pallets, jacks of defence, and other armour

108

Carlisle Archives, DRC/1/2, pp. 303–4: Register of Thomas Appleby,
Bishop of Carlisle, 2nd Register
Will of Robert Goldsmyth, Goldsmith of Carlisle, Cumberland, 31
January 1379

Ric[ard]o Orfeure vnu' Paltok bloid de defens' Joh[ann]i fil' meo & hered' vnum
bacenet cu' j auentaill' vnu' par cirotecar[um] de plate vnu' paltok de defens' ij
pesaynes vnam securiu' Argentat' & vnam ensem trenchant Joh[ann]i de Dundrawe
baslardu' meu' argent' Joh[ann]i Austyn J par de plates

Richard Goldsmith one blue paltock of defence (fabric torso defence), my son and
heir John one basinet with one aventail one pair of plate gauntlets one paltock of
defence two pisans one silvered axe and one sword with cutting edge, John Dundrawe
my silver baselard, John Austyn one pair of plates

109

York, Borthwick Institute, Register of Archbishop Neville, fol. 374r
Will of Sir Robert Swylyngton, Junior, York, 23 May 1379

lego no[m]i[n]e mortuar' mei melius a[n]i[m]al' meu' cu' Cotearmo[u]r helme scuto
& vno gladio Wil[he]lmo de Swilyngton' fr[atr]i meo o[mn]ia arma mea & gladiu'
meu' & duos equos meos viz Bayerd le Bekwith' & Bartram

for my mortuary (gift to a religious foundation for his interment) my best animal
with coat armour, helm, shield, and one sword, William Swilyngton my brother all
my arms and my sword and two of my horses viz.: Beyard le Beckwith and Bartram

110

*Le Livre des fais du bon messire Jehan le Maingre, dit Bouciquaut, mare-
schal de France*, ed. D. Lalande (Geneva: Droz, 1985), pp. 24–6
Exercises of Maréchal Boucicaut to Harden Himself to a Life in Arms in
His Youth, 1380s

Ci devise les essais que Bouciquaut faisot de son corps pour soy duire aux armes. Dont
maintenant s'essayast a saillir sus le coursier tout armé; puis autre fois couroit ou aloit
longuement a pié, pour accoustumer a avoir longue aleine et souffrir longuement traveil;
autre fois feroit de une coignee ou d'un mail grant piece et longue, pour bien se duire
ou harnois et endurcir ses bras et ses mains a longuement ferir, et qu'il s'acoustumast a
legierement lever ses bras; pour lesquielz choses excerciter duisi telement son corps que,

en son temps, n'a esté veu nul autre gentilhomme de pareille appertise; car il faisot le soubresaut armé de toutes pieces fors le bacinet, et en dansant le faisoit armé d'une cotte d'acier. Item, sailloit sanz metre le pié en l'estrief sus un coursier, armé de toutes pieces. Item, a ung grant homme monté sur ung grant cheval sailloit de terre a chevauchons sur ses espaules, en prenant le dit homme par la manche a une main sans autre avantage. Item, en mettant une main sus l'arçon de la selle d'un grant coursier et l'autre emprés les oreilles, le prenoit par les crins en plaine terre et sailloit par entre ses bras de l'autre part du coursier. Item, se .II. parois de plastre fussent a une brasse l'une pres de l'autre, qui fussent de la haulteur d'une tour, a force de bras et de jambes, sanz autre ayde, montast tout au plus hault sanz cheoir au monter ne au devaler. Item, il montoit au revers d'une grant eschele dreciee contre un mur, tout au plus hault, sanz toucher des piez, mais seulement sautant des .II. mains ensemble d'eschelon en eschelon, armé d'une cotte d'acier, et ostee le cotte a une main sanz plus montoit plusieurs eschelons.

Here are described the bodily exercises that (the young) Boucicaut did to harden himself to arms. By now he could leap onto a horse completely armed, on other occasions he would run for a long time on foot to accustom himself to breathing and undertaking exertion, on another occasion he would do this with a large and long axe or hammer so as to harden himself to harness so his arms and his hands could thus endure longer and so he would become accustomed to easily raising his hands. Because of these exercises his body was in such good condition that there was no other gentleman in his day who could match him for he did somersaults armed at all points (except the basinet) and would dance armed in a coat of mail. Then he would leap onto a courser armed at all points without putting his foot in the stirrup. Then he would leap from the ground to ride on the shoulders of a large man mounted on a large horse grabbing this man by the sleeve with one hand – without any other assistance. Then, placing one hand on the saddlebow of the saddle of a great courser and the other (hand) between its ears, he would take it by the mane from standing on the ground and leap between his arms to the other side of the courser. Then two plaster walls, the height of a tower, would be placed at arms width apart. With only the strength of his arms and legs, without any (other) assistance, he would climb to the top without slipping as he ascended and descended. Then, armed in a coat of mail, he would climb on the underside of a large scaling ladder leant against a wall at the highest point without using his feet, leaping from rung to rung just using two hands together – and if without a coat of mail he could climb several rungs with only one hand.

111

Rotuli scaccarii regum Scotorum; The Exchequer Rolls of Scotland, Vol. III, A.D. 1379–1406, ed. G. Burnett (Edinburgh, 1880), p. 654
Royal Payments for Arms and Armour for Stirling Castle, 1380

duodecim lorice xxiiij li., duodecim bacineti cum ventalibus et aliis xviij li., duodecim paria cirothecarum, xlviij s., sex paria armaturarum tibialium, viij li., duodecim targete, vj li. [no. not given] capelli de calibe dicti ketilhattis, viij li.

12 hauberks £24, 12 basinets with aventails and all (their fittings) £18, 12 pairs of gauntlets 48s., six pairs of armour for the shins £8, 12 targes £6, [no. not given] steel hats called kettlehats £8

112

Chroniques de Froissart, ed. J. A. Buchon, 15 vols (Paris, 1826), II, p. 107

A chronicler describes an incident during a lull in the fighting during the Hundred Years War, Toury-en-Beauce, Duchy of Orléans, 1380

un ecuyer de Beausse gentilhomme et de bonne volonte qui savanca de son fait sans mouvement dautrui et vint a la barriere tout en escarmouchant et dit aux Anglois ya til la nul gentilhomme qui pour lamour de sa dame voulsist faire aucun fait darmes Si il en y a nul veez moi ci tout pret pour issir hors arme de toutes pieces monte a cheval pour jouter trois coups de glaive ferir trois coups de hache et trois coups de dague Si en ait qui peut et tout pour lamour de sa dame Or verra ton entre vous Anglois si il en y a nuls amoureux Et appeloit on lecuyer francois Gauvain Micaille Cette parole et requete fut tantot epandue entre les Anglois Adonc se trait avant un ecuyer anglois appert compagnon et bien joutant qui sappeloit Jovelin Kator et dit Oil oil je le vueil delivrer et tantot faites le traire hors du chastel Le marechal de lost vint aux barrieres et dit a [the English captain] Faites venir votre ecuyer hors il a trouve qui lui delivrera tres volontiers ce quil demande et lassurons en toutes choses Gauvain Micaille fut moult rejoui de ces paroles et sarma incontinent et laiderent les seigneurs a armer de toutes pieces moult bien et monta sur un cheval que on lui delivra Si issit hors du chastel lui troisieme et portoient ses varlets trois lances et trois dagues Et sachez que il fut moult regarde des Anglois quand il issit hors et lui tenoient celle emprise a grand outrage car ils ne cuidoient mie que nul Francois corps a corps sosat combattre contre un Anglois Encore en cette empeinte y avoit trois coups depees et toutes trois Gauvain les fit apporter avec lui pour laventure du briser

a squire from Beauce (being a gentleman of firm resolve) moved by his own volition – not by anyone else's – came to the barrier in the midst of the skirmishing and cried out to the English: 'Is there any gentleman who wishes to perform any feat of arms for the love of his lady? If there be anyone – see that I am completely prepared to sally forth armed at all points, mounted on horseback to joust three lance-strokes, deliver three axe blows, and three dagger thrusts. Is anyone prepared to undertake all this for the love of his lady? Is there none among you English who be so love-struck?' Now this French squire was called Gauvain Micaille. When word of his challenge spread amongst the English, there came forward an English squire called Jovelin Kator who was clearly his match as he was a good jouster. He called back: 'Aye, Aye, I will immediately deliver (you of your feat of arms) outside the castle!' The maréchal of the host came to the barriers and called to the English captain: 'Send out your squire. He will soon discover if he can deliver (these feats of arms of) his challenge, for we assure you all will be fair!' Gauvain Micaille was overjoyed at his words and immediately armed himself – for the (great) lords ensured he was very well armed at all points and mounted on a horse provided for him. Thus he sallied forth from the castle with three valets bearing three lances and three daggers. Know you that, for the English, this was some sight to see! So flabbergasted were they at his nerve; for they could hardly believe that a Frenchman would even dare to take on an Englishman corps-à-corps (i.e. in single combat)! Furthermore, Gauvain had (arranged for) three sword blows in this fight, thus he had three (swords) carried with him in case they should break!

113

York, Borthwick Institute, Register of Archbishop Neville, fol. 115v
Will of Henry Snayth, Cleric, London, 3 February 1380

mag[is]tro Walt[er]o de Skyrlowe zona' mea' stipal' cu' rotis arge[n]teis & deurat' cu' baslardo appendent' Ric[ard]o lely duas loricis ferr' duas bacinett' cu' ventall' & duas Jakkys coop[er]t' cu' fust'

Master Walter Skyrlowe my belt stippled with silver-gilt bosses with the hanging baselard, Richard Lely two iron (mail) hauberks, two basinets with aventails, and two jacks covered in fustian

114

Carlisle Archives, DRC/1/2, p. 325: Register of Thomas Appleby, Bishop of Carlisle, 2nd Register
Will of Sir William Stapilton, Carlisle, Cumberland, between June and July 1380

ieo ueuolle q[ue] nulle armo[u]rs soyent offerres ne deuus al eglise [...] le haubarioune q[ue] ieo auay de Richard de Grysby & le basynete darrayn fet & mon court espe o vn payr des Gayntes de plate & vn targete & mo[u]n gr[a]unt sainto[ur]e de argent a William mon fil' & Joh[a]n mo[u]n fil' le haubarioune q[ue] mo[u]n [NB word missing, prob. 'pere'] mei dona & le basinete en quel ioe su arme si il soit venant tanq[ue] al age de xviij anz Roulande vaus la basinete qil ad en sa gard vn iac mo[u] n brestplate vn par des Gayntes de plate a Joh[a]n de Calste'

I will that no armour be offered nor given to the church [...] to my son William the haubergeon which I had from Richard Grysby and the recently-made basinet and my short sword with one pair of plate gauntlets and one targe and my large silver belt, to my son John when he has reached the age of 18 years the haubergeon which my [prob.

father] gave me and the basinet in which I was armed, Roland Vaus the basinet which he had in his keeping, John Calste one jack my breastplate one pair of plate gauntlets

115

Carlisle Archives, DRC/1/2, p. 326: Register of Thomas Appleby, Bishop of Carlisle, 2nd Register
Will of John Dundrawe, Carlisle, Cumberland, 16 July 1380

Wil[he]l[m]o de Dundrawe co[n]sanguinio meo meu' optimu' Akton' cu' vno bacinetto Armato Walt[er]o consanguinio meo vnu' par de plates cu' vno bacinetto Armato·

my cousin William Dundrawe my best aketon with one arming basinet, my cousin Walter one pair of plates with one arming basinet

116

Carlisle Archives, DRC/1/2, pp. 329–30: Register of Thomas Appleby, Bishop of Carlisle, 2nd Register
Will of Thomas Sandforth, Carlisle, Cumberland, 29 August 1380

filio meo armat[u]ram meam Rob[er]to fil' meo longu' cultellu' meu'

my armour to my (eldest) son, my son Robert my long knife

117

Carlisle Archives, DRC/1/2, p. 331: Register of Thomas Appleby, Bishop of Carlisle, 2nd Register
Will of Thomas Karlton, Rector of Castle Carrock, Cumberland, 1 September 1380

Joh' fr[atr]i suo vnu' arcu' cu' sagitas & gladiu'

his brother John one bow with arrows and one sword

118

Thomas Walsingham, *Historia Anglicana*, ed. H. T. Riley, 2 vols (London, 1864), II, pp. 7–8

A Chronicler tells of the Deeds of Henry, Bishop of Norwich, during the Peasants' Revolt, Norfolk, June 1381

[…] de ordine militari et plures e patria generosi qui delitescebant timore communium vedentes Episcopum militem induisse et galeam assumpsisse metallicam et loricam duram quam non possent penetrare sagittæ necnon gladium materialem acipitem arripuisse ejus lateri se junxerunt Episcopus itaque cum pervenisset ad locum stipatus turba decenti reperit rusticos bellatorum fossata circumcinxisse locum en quem convenerant et super fossam tabulas fenestras et ostia cum palis in defensionem sui fixisse A tergo autem conspicit eorum cargiagum et carectas locatas tanquam de fuga minime cogitarent Nec mora Episcopus Martius aperto Marte pugnaturus commotus super audacia nebulonum jubet tubicinibus et clarigatoribus suis canere et ipse arrepta dextra manu lancea urget cornipedem acutis calcaribus et tanta animositate tanta audacia efferatur in eos ut cursu velocissimo fossam præoccuparet citatior sagittis suis nec erat opus arcitenentibus sagittariis cum res jam manu ad manum comminus ageretur Antistes ergo belliger velut aper frendens dentibus sibi nec hostibus suis parcens ubi majus conspicit esse periculum dirigit tentum suum et hunc perforando illum dejiciendo alium vulnerando non cessat lædere vehementer donec omnis turba quæ eum secuta fuerat nacta fossa ad confligendum parata foret

The local knights and many of the landed gentry were in hiding for fear of the common folk. Seeing the bishop as a knight, donning a metal helm and tough hauberk which arrows could not pierce – even wielding a sword (not one of spiritual power but an *actual* sword) – those who had been hiding flocked to him. And so the bishop, having arrived at the place, found it well surrounded by the mob – the peasants as warriors. The place they had gathered was encircled by a ditch and above the ditch were tables, window shutters, and doors affixed with stakes for defence. Worse, at the top he saw their wagons and carts arranged so that it was clear they had no thought of flight. Nevertheless, the martial bishop like a warrior of Mars was enraged by the gall of the scum. He ordered the trumpeters to sound their trumpets and he himself snatched up a lance in his right hand, urging on his steed with sharp spurs, and with such wrath, such bravery, charged at them riding with such speed that he gained the ditch before his archers' arrows! The archers didn't even have a chance to span their bows as he took on the peasants hand to hand. The bishop had become a warrior grinding his teeth like a wild boar – sparing none of his enemies. With a complete disregard for the great danger he knew himself to be in, by slashing so that he struck down one and injured another, he did not stop brutally wounding until all the force who followed him from the bottom of the ditch were able to engage (the enemy).

119

Thomas Walsingham, *Historia Anglicana*, ed. H. T. Riley, 2 vols (London, 1864), I, p. 457

A Chronicler's Account of the Revolting Peasants' Destruction of John of Gaunt's Savoy Palace, Near the City of London, June 1381

Deinde arreptum quoddam vestimentum pretiosissimum ipsius quale jakke vocamus et impositum lanceae pro signo ad sagittas suas statuerunt et cum parum dampni inferre sagittando valerent depositum securibus et gladiis confregerunt

Then they seized a certain item of clothing (the costliest) – which we call a 'jack' – and hoisted it up on a lance as a target at which to shoot their arrows. And when they only did a little damage shooting forcefully at it, they pulled it down and rent it with axes and swords.

120

Besançon, Bibliothèque municipale, MS 865, fol. 75r–fol. 75v. MS images reproduced in *HRI Online Froissart*, ed. P. Ainsworth and G. Croenen (Sheffield, 2013)

A Chronicler Describes an Incident During the Peasants' Revolt, Norwich, June 1381

The Captain of the City of Norwich, Sir Robert Salle, rides out to meet the peasants. Reminding him of his low birth – the son of a mason – they entreat him as one of their own to be their leader, enticing him with a quarter of the realm as his reward. On hearing of their treachery, he berates them as a 'shower of shite', promising them that they shall have nought but the certainty of swinging from the gallows ('mardaille que vous estes [...] vous feussiez penduz ainsi que vous serez').

A ces coups Il cuida Remonter sur son cheual mais il failly de lestrief et le cheual seffroya Adonc saherdirent a luy a luy et crierent a la mort Quant il ouy ces mots il laissa aler son cheual et trayst vne belle et longue espee de bourdeaulx que Il portoit et vous commance a escarmouschier et a faire place autour de luy que ce estoit grant beaute du veoir ne nul ne losoit approuchier aucuns lapprouchoyent mais de chascun coup quil gettoit sur eulx Il leur couppoit ou pie ou teste ou bras ou Jambe ne Il ny auoit si hardy quil ne le ressoingnast Et fist la cilz messire robert tant darmes que merueilles mais ces mescheans gens estoyent plus de xl m Sy gettoient la[n]coyent et traioyent sur luy et Il estoit tous desarmez et au voir dire sil eust este de fer ou dacier si conuenist Il quil feust demourez mais il en tua douze tous mors sans ceulx quil mes haigna et affoula finablement Il fut atterrez et lui decoupperent les Jambes et les bras et le detranchierent piece apres autre Ainsi fina mess' Robert salle dont ce

fut dommaige et en furent en angleterre depuis courrouciez tous les ch[eualie]rs et
escuiers q[uan]t Ilz en sceurent les nouuelles

With these insults he intended to remount his steed but he missed the stirrup and
his horse was spooked. Then they attacked him crying: 'Put him to death!' Hearing
these words, he let go of his steed and drew a long, fine Bordeaux sword which he
wore (at his hip) and as he prepared himself and began to skirmish it was a most fair
sight to see – none dared approach him. Whosoever came near received such a blow
that with each stroke dealt he cut off a foot, or head, or arm, or leg; being so brave
he feared none! The feats of arms that Sir Robert performed there were wondrous,
but these miscreants numbered more than forty thousand. They cast (missiles), thrust
spears, and shot arrows at him for he was completely unarmed (with body armour).
It is true to say that, had he been (protected) by iron or steel, he might have escaped
death: but 12 he killed outright not counting those he wounded and maimed. Finally,
he was floored and they cut off his legs and arms and rent him apart piece by piece.
Thus was the fate of Sir Robert Salle. Such a great loss. All the knights and squires of
England were enraged when they heard the news.

121

Now-Lost Document printed in *C. Dehaisnes, Documents et extraits
divers concernant l'histoire de l'art dans la Flandre, l'Artois & le Hainaut
avant le XVe siècle*, 2 vols (Lille, 1886), II, p. 578
Testament of Nicaise de Mons, Widow of Jacques Pilatte, Burgess of
Douai, County of Flanders, 12 December 1381

Jehan Wallet le jouene sen boin haubregion de le clavure de Cambely Thomas Pilatte
un haubregon de demy clavure qui fu le bastart Pilatte sen cousin

Jean Wallet, the younger his good haubergeon of Chambly nailing (i.e. all-riveted
links made at Chambly), Thomas Pilate a haubergeon of half nailing (i.e. not all links
are riveted) which belonged to the Bastard Pilatte his cousin

122

London Metropolitan Archives, Plea and Memoranda Roll A23
Complaint against John Hood, Armourer of London, 25 June 1383

joh[ann]es hood arm[u]rer m' est p[ar] Will[el]m' Thornhull & Thomam hogecote ad
assend' hic coram maiore & ald[e]r' quo sub po[en]a Et vlt[er]ius Jur' est d' d' nullu'
bassynet de Flandr' vend' p[ro] bassinet london' fact' nec apone' c[ui]li' bassinet' de
Flandr' n[e]c alt' armatur' pr[ou]d p[re]d[ic]to aliquod Signu' ho' london' sub' po[en]
a &c'

John Hood, armourer, was appealed by William Thornhull and Thomas Hogecote to appear here in the presence of the Mayor and Aldermen under pain etc. and furthermore it was sworn under oath that he should sell no basinet of Flanders as basinet of London make nor place upon any basinet of Flanders or other armour as aforesaid any sign (mark) of London (crafts) men under pain etc.

123

State Archives of Prato, Fondo Datini (Extracts), 1384 and 1394 Extracts transcribed by R. Brun, printed in 'Notes sur le commerce des armes à Avignon au XIVe siècle', *Bibliothèque de l'École des chartes* 109 (1951), pp. 209–31

Francesco di Marco Datini (b. c. 1335, d. 1410) was a merchant arms dealer from the Tuscan city of Prato. He set up his business in Avignon, Provence in 1350. Here his agents write from Valencia and Barcelona to report on the sale of his stock.

Letter from Giovanni de Stefano in Valencia to Matteo di Lorenzo in Avignon, 14 May 1384

Jo o fatto vendita per te d'armadure a uno armaduriere XII chamagli di mezza bozza VI cotte di mezza bozza; XII paia di ghuantaletti bordati; XII paia di ghauntaletti bianchi; XII cappelletti bordati simili a quelli ebbe da voi Bido di Causa e sieno fatti a Lione in sul Rodano o chosti, non vorebbono costa piu di f. 6 ½; XXIIII carette di bacinetti grandi e aghute e bene fatte, sieno di chasa o a Leone in sul Rodano; XII bacinetti fatti chosti ho al Leone in sul Rodano, e sieno della ghuisa e alla forma che vi mando la mostra disegnata in questa (f.n. 1 [drawing lost]); X balloni d'accaio del segno della crocetta e di l'elmo; X grosse di fibbie per arnesi di ghamba e bracciali; XIIᵐ di bulletta stagniate con buoni capi; IIIIᵐ baghette d'ottone di Melano per bacinetti; XII arnesi di ghamba e di coscia da cavalere e VI da schudere

Of the armour, I have sold to an armourer for you: 12 half-riveted aventails (i.e. not all the links are riveted), six half-riveted (mail) coats, 12 pairs of gauntlets bordered (with latten), 12 pairs of white (i.e. polished steel) gauntlets, 12 small chapel de fers bordered (with latten) – similar to those (prob. the agent) Bido di Causa got from you – made at Lyon-on-the-Rhône – I do not want to sell them for less than 6½*fl.*, 24 basinet punches (for making lining perforations etc.) – large, sharp, and well made, of the (Avignon) workshop or of Lyon-on-the-Rhône, 12 basinets like those made at Lyon-on-the-Rhône of the type and form shown in this drawing [NB sadly, now lost], ten balls of steel (marked with) the sign of the little cross and of the helm, ten gross (weight) of buckles for legharness and bracers, 12,000 tinned nails with good heads, 4,000 rods of Milan latten for basinets; 12 (pairs of) legharness and cuisses for cavalry and six (pairs of defences) for shins

Letter from an Unnamed Agent in Avignon to an Unnamed Agent in Barcelona, 10 March 1394

di II balle d'armi e merce da Milano mandamo a Barzalona a di deto a Francescho di Marcho e Lucha del Sera, le qua sono di Francescho di Marcho e chopagni da Vignone, lequali vendete per lo chorso di chosta. Nela prima balla: II chote di maglia d'acaio a boza minute, bele f. XXXV di corenti; IIII chamagli d'acaio, II chacoti e II a boza f. XVII; III ghrose di fibie di fero stangnate f. I s. VIII; IIII ghrose di fibie di fero stangnate da bracali e arnesi di ghanba f. I s. V. Nela sechonda balla: I chota di maglia d'acaio a boza minuta, bela f. XVII s. XII; II chote di maglia d'acaio a meza boza f. XXII; II falde di maglia d'acaio a boza f. VIII; II chamagli d'acaio a meza boza f. VI s. XII; XII paia di ghuanti di fero bordati d'otone, beli, di Milano, pero sono di pui beli se facino f. XVIII

of the two bales of arms and goods from Milan sent to Barcelona by Francesco di Marco and Lucha del Sera, those of Francesco di Marco and the Avignon Company shall be sold at the following prices. From the first bale: two fine steel mail coats with small rivets 35 florins, four steel aventails – two marked (with a maker's mark) and two (fully) riveted 17*fl.*, three gross (weight) of tinned-iron buckles 1*fl.* 8*s.*, four gross of tinned-iron buckles for bracers and legharness 1*fl.* 5*s.* From the second bale: one fine steel mail coat with small rivets 17*fl.* 12*s.*, two half-riveted steel mail coats 22*fl.*, two riveted steel mail skirts 8*fl.*, two half-riveted steel aventails 6*fl.* 12*s.*, 12 fine pairs of iron gauntlets bordered with latten, of Milan (make) – some of finer making than others 18*fl.*

124

Dijon, Archives départementales de la Côte-d'Or, B1463, fol. 76v and fol. 78r
Household Account of Philip, duke of Burgundy, 4 January 1384 and 5 April 1385

1384

henriet tallemont forbisseur pour vj haches fourbir & nettoier ij frans ij espees garnies de veluyau noir vne de parement & vne autre petite xxiiij s' p' vn bran dacier vne espee de castille deux espees de bourdeaux ij espees de langres et deux aut[re]s espees garnies de foureaulx neuf pour ij aut[re]s espees nettoier et garnir tout a neuf de cuir de vache pour la grant espee de mons' garnie de veluyau Rouge de parement vne autre petite espee a monter doree ij frans xiiij s' p' cloux charni[er]es et bossett' xvj s' iij lances pour mons' xxiiij s' p' hennequin le fourbissuer pour polir et nottoier ij bacines & iiij paires de h[ar]noiz de Jambes touz ent[ier]s pour mon seign[eu]r iij frans p[ier]re dufour pour deux bacinie[re]s de bacinet vne bouge a mettre h[ar] noiz vne vestices pour mettre la cotte dacier de mon sign[eu]r iij frans iiij s' p' Jehan gauill[aum]e espicier pour viij aulnes destamine pour enuoleper [*sic*] le dit h[ar]noiz de Jambes xx s' parisis

1384

Henriet Tallemont, furbisher, for furbishing and equipping six axes 2 Parisian francs, two swords garnished with black velvet – one patterned and another small 24 Parisian *sous*, one steel blade, one sword of Castile, two swords of Bordeaux, two swords of Langres and two other swords equipped with new scabbards, two other swords fitted and garnished as new with cow leather, my Lord's great sword (i.e. longsword) garnished with patterned red velvet, and one other small sword with gilt mounts 2 francs 20 *sous*, nails, hinges, and little bosses 16 *sous*, three lances for my Lord 24 *sous*. Hennequin the furbisher, for polishing and equipping two basinets and three pairs of complete legharness for my Lord 3 francs. Pierre Dufour for two basinet cases, one bag in which to place harness, and for one vestment-carrier in which to place my Lord's coat of mail 3 francs 4 *sous*. Jehan Guillaume, spice-merchant, for eight ells of wool to wrap the said legharness 20 *sous*.

1385

Clement briseson vallet de chambre de mess' ph[ilipp]e de bar pour acheter vn arnoiz de Jouste entier pour le dit messier ph[ilipp]e Lxxiij fr[a]nz v s' par' guill[aum]e de bruges armeurier pour vn bacinet senz camail piece h[ar]noiz de bras dess' & de soubz ij pieces de gantelet h[ar]nois de Jambes et soulers lesquell' chous' il a f[ai]tes par lecom[m]and de mon seigneur pour mess' ph[ilipp]e de bar

1385

Clement Briseson, *valet de chambre* of Sir Philippe de Bar (a younger son of Robert, count of Bar), to purchase a complete jousting harness for the said Sir Philippe 73 Parisian francs 5 *sous*. Guillaume of Bruges, armourer, for one basinet without aventail, *pièce* (reinforcing plate for a breastplate), arm harness above and below (prob. to protect the arm in these areas), two *pièces* (reinforces) of gauntlets, legharness and sabatons, which he has made by order of my Lord for Sir Philippe de Bar

125

Paris, Bibliothèque National de France, Clérembault, titres scellés, vol. 216, p. 9737, printed in H. Terrier de Loray, *Jean de Vienne, Amiral de France, 1341–96* (Paris, 1878), pp. lxxiv–lxxxvi
French Royal Payments for a Military Expedition to Scotland, Paris, 24 December 1384

Jehan Choque, maistre du cloz de noz galéez dez Rouen dix sept mile et deux cens frans d'or c'est assavoir: pour faire faire deux cens milliers de viretons renduz touz prests en nostre clos, ferrez, empannez et encoffrez, dont le bois sera pris en nostre forest de Rouvroy, pour nectoier et bien faire rappareillier noz armeures estans en nostre chastel de Rouen et à Harefleur; achater onze cens glayves de bonnes hantes et bien ferrez, cent bons falloz neufs et deux milliers de sarpes, et faire rappareiller et ordener mil pavez, certaine quantité de dars, lances, canons, et neuf vins et un millier de viretons, qui sont ès garnisons de nostre clos, et faire faire cinquante banières, deux quatre grans et larges estandars chascun de huit aulnes de long et quatre aulnes de lé, à noz armes; pour l'achat de onze cens jaques de fustaine que doivent faire et délivrer, par marchié fait, Jehan Le Grant et ses compaignons pourpointiers, demourans à Paris, à trois frans huit solz parisis chascun jaque; pour l'achat de cinq cens paires de harnois garniz de cote de fer, bacinet à visière et à camail de nouvelle façon, une pair de bracelez et une paire de gantelez, que doit délivrer Gillet Le Clerc, nostre haubergier à seize frans chascun harnois entire, et trois cens paires de harnois de jambs garnis de mailles, que doit délivrer ledit Gillet, à cinq frans huit solz parisis le harnois

Jehan Choque, Master of the Fortress of Our galleys at Rouen 17,200 gold francs that being: for having 200,000 crossbow quarrels made and delivered completely ready in Our fortress, with heads, wrapped and fitted in coffers – the wood taken from Our forest of Rouvroy, to prepare and repair Our armaments in Our château of Rouen and at Harfleur, to buy 1,100 glaives with good hafts and heads, 100 good new fire-arrows, and 2,000 billhooks, to repair and equip 1,000 pavises, a certain quantity of darts, lances, cannons, and nine score and 1,000 crossbow quarrels which victual Our fortress, and having 50 banners, four large and long standards – each eight ells long and four ells wide – of Our (royal coat of) arms made, 1,100 fustian (strong fabric made from any two of cotton, flax, or wool) jacks purchased from Jehan Le Grant and his companions – pourpoint-makers of Paris – at 3 Parisian francs and 8 *sous* each jack, to buy 500 pairs of harness equipped with a coat of mail, basinet with visor and with an aventail of the new fashion, one pair of bracers, and one pair of gauntlets to be delivered to Gilet Le Clerc, our hauberger, at 16 francs for each complete harness, and 300 pairs of legharness equipped with mail to be delivered to Gilet at 5 francs 8 *sous* a harness

126

Paris, Bibliothèque nationale de France, MS lat. 16928, fol. 199r, printed in *Documents relatifs au clos des galées de Rouen et aux armées de mer du roi de France de 1293 à 1418*, ed. A. Merlin-Chazelas, 2 vols (Paris, 1977–78), II, pp. 170–1

Royal Payments to Gilet Le Clerc, Hauberger of Paris, and Agnes, Widow of a Paris Hauberger, to provide Armour for the Fortress of the Galleys of Rouen, Normandy, 11 February, 1385

Gilet Leclerc, haubergier et varlet de chambre du roy et Agnes, jadiz femme de feu Jehan des Portes, dit Benedicte, a son vivant haubergier et varlet de chambre du dit seigneur, confesserent avoir receu de Jehan Choque, dit Desramé, maistre du clos des galees de Rouen la somme de neuf mil six cens et cinquante frans d'or, pour le marchié par eulz fait audit Chocques de cinq cens paires de harnois a armer homme, c'est assavoir: cote de fer bonne, large, longue et souffisante, pesant vint cinq livres et au dessus; bacinet bon et souffisant, de nouvelle façon, garny de bon hourson, visiere et de bon camail bien sarré, pesant ainsi garny et estoffé quatorze livres et au dessus; bons avans bras et bons gantelez pour chascun harnois, une paire bien estoffez et garniz; trois cens paire de harnois de jambes bons et bien souffisans et garniz de maille par derriere; pour et parmy, c'est assavoir chascun harnois a armer homme, seize frans d'or et chascune paire de harnois de jambes, cinq frans d'or

Gilet Le Clerc, hauberger and King's *Valet de Chambre* and Agnes, widow of Jehan des Portes (called Benedict) who in life was a hauberger and King's *Valet de Chambre* confirm to have received from Jehan Choque (called Desramé), Master of the Fortress of the Galleys of Rouen the sum of 9,650 gold francs for their sale to the said (Jehan) Choque of 500 pairs of harness for arming men, that is to say: good, suitable, large, and long coat of mail weighing 25 *livres* or more, good and suitable new-style basinet equipped with a hourson (aventail-cover), visor, and good secure aventail weighing 14 *livres* or more equipped and fitted thus, good vambrace and good gauntlets for each harness – each pair well-equipped and lined, 300 pairs of good and sufficient legharness equipped with mail at the back (of the leg) and throughout (i.e. behind the knee), that is to say: 16 gold francs for each harness for arming men, 5 gold francs for each pair of legharness

127

Durham Cathedral Archives, Accounts of the Sacrists and Hostillers of Durham Priory, 1385–88

Sacrist's Account, 1385–86
vno Jak x s' j lancia xiiij d' j brestplate v s' ij capitib[us] p[ro] launcijs ij s'

Hostiller's Account, 1385–86
In diu[ers]is armis empt' v[i]z in iiij gonnys ij palets j brestplat vambras ij lanc' j hast' v arcub[us] v shafe j batelax cu' al' intrument' p[ro] eisd' – Ciij s iiij d ob'

Hostiller's Account, 1387
vno basinet cu' ventale & cop[er]toris p[ro] ead' xl s'

Hostiller's Account, 1387–88
in rep[ar]ac[i]o[n]e quator[um] arcu' & empt[i]o[n]e cordar[um] xv d' p[ro] eisdem rep[ar]ac[i]o[n]e catapult' & eor[um] capit' iiij s' j d' & in empt[i]o[n]e capit' vni[um] lancie x d' in duob[us] Jaks p[ro] Stuffo domus liij s' iij d'

Sacrist's Account, 1385–86
one jack 10s., one lance 14d., one breastplate 5s., two lanceheads 2s.

Hostiller's Account, 1385–86
for divers arms bought viz.: three guns, two pallets, one breastplate [one pair of] vambrace, two lances, one lance-shaft, five bows, five sheaves (of arrows), one battle axe with other tools for them – 103s. 4½d.

Hostiller's Account, 1387
one basinet with aventail and one cover for the same 40s.

Hostiller's Account, 1387–88
for the repair of four bows and cords (i.e. strings) bought for them 15d., repair of the catapult and its head 4s. 1d., and the purchase of one lancehead 10d., for two jacks for equipping the house (i.e. the defence of the Priory) 53s. 3d.

128

Now-lost Document printed in G. A. Lobineau, *Histoire de Bretagne*, 2 vols (Paris, 1707), II, columns 672–7
Agreement of the Arms and Armour for a Judicial Duel between the Seigneur de Tournemine and the Seigneur de Beaumanoir, Duchy of Brittany, 1386

Premierement je eslis vestu de chemise & de brayes de toile de lin [...] sur ma chemise & mes brayes [aura] d'une cotte a armer d'un toile de lin, & de chanvre, & de cendal estoffe de cotton & de bourre de soye o boucles & hardilons & d'aguillettes de cuir, ou tresses de chanvre, garni de boucles & hardillons de fer, d'acier, & de letton, ou de l'un d'eux, [NB the choice of these metals is repeated in each instance] pour attacher les pieces & estoffes de mon harnois [...] chausses de toile de lin, & de chanvre, & de cendal [NB the choice of these materials is repeated in each instance], un solers de cuir [...] une braconniere de maille de fer, d'acier estoffe de toiles de lin [etc.] [...] soleres, greves, poulains, & cuissols garnies de samgnies [*sic*] de haubergerie & estoffez souffisament, clouees o cloux de fer ou de leton, un haubregon vestu & arme de maille de fer & d'acier & de leton, de telle longueur & leze comme me semblera estre profitable pour le corps & le bras attache d'aiguillettes de cuir ou tresses de chanvre, garnis [etc.] ceint par dessus o ceinture de corde de fil de chanvre ou tessus de soye, une collerette appelle faux camail de maille de fer & d'acier, garnir de couroyes de cuir ou tresses [etc.] garni d'estoffes de toile de lin [etc.] [aura] de plates estre arme sur mon haubregeon de fer [&] d'acier, garnier de cuir, de toile de chanvre, de avantbras & gardebras de fer & d'acier, garnis de maille, boucles & hardillons, courroyes de cuir, ganetelets de fer, d'acier, & de leton, garni dedans la main de haubrege de fer [etc.] garnis de cuir, de boucles, hardillons, de cloux & de rivez der fer [etc.] un basinet & visiere de fer [etc.] estoffe de cerueliers de toile de lin [etc.] & verteuells de fer [etc.] attachees audit bacinet, & cousu o cloux tenans le bacinet, qui seront de fer [etc.] & aura boucle d'argent, de fer [etc.] qui sera cousue & tendra a mon haubregeon ou a mes plates o attaches de cuir & clouz der fer [etc.] attache avec un hourson d'estoffes de bourre de soye, de coton, couvert de cendaux, de toiles de lin [etc.] un camail de fer [etc.] garni de barbiere de fer [etc.] dessur attache au bacinet & camail, garni de cuir & mailles de fer [etc.] attache au bacinet & aux verteuelles attache avec le hourson dessusdit o courroye de cuir [etc.] avec les plates ou haubregeon, sera couvert mon camail d'un cendal double de toile ou sangle, une cotte de cendal armoiee de mes armes, doublee de linge, unes chouces par mon harnois de cuisses de jambs & de pied de drap vermeil, ou de cendal, deux espees de fer & d'aicer o croez & plomme de fer & d'acier & d'autre metail o platesne devant la croez, de fer [etc.] garnies de fuerres de bois & de cuir cousu dessus, une desdites espees sera garnie de renges de cuir ou de soye, garnie de boucles de fer & d'acier, mise & ceinte a mon coste, ou attache a une courroye de cuir, & a un annelet de fer [etc.] attache a mes plates ou haubregeon, & lautre espee garnie de fuerre de boais couvert de cuir, attachee a l'arcon de la selle ou anneux de fer [etc.] une desdites espees sera de deux pieds & demy de longeur avant la main un poucle estache moins, ou environ; & la tenue & plomee d'un pied & poulce ou environ; & lautre espee est plus courte de deulx poulces estachez ou environ avant la main, une dague de fer [etc.] o manche de fer, d'acier, de cor, ou de boais, de longueur de demy pied & plein paume avant la main, ou environ; desquelles espees & dagues seront monstrees les mesures devers la Cour, pour plus a certain en savoir les mesures, eslis un cheval enselle de selle dont les arsons sont de boais, garnie de cor lie & garnie de fer [etc.], les arsons haults devant & derriere, ouvert ez deux costez, ma selle garnie de peitral & de croupiere de cuir, anneaux de fer [etc.] a attacher une de mesdites espees, un chanffrain de fer [etc.] pour armer la teste de mon cheval, garni de courroies de cuir attachez o cloux de fer [etc.] mon chanffrain garni dedans de toile estoffee de coton ou d'autres estoffes, sera garni de maille de fer [etc.] & d'estoffes de linge [etc.] mon chanffrain affis sur la teste & attache o les crains du cheval o tresses de chanvre, sera mon cheval couvert, estoffe, & arme devant & derriere & en tous endroits de linges de beluteaux, par dessus estoffe de bourre de soye ou de coton, couverte, point, & cousu ensemble, sera attache & mis hernois de maille de fer [etc.] une couverte de linge de toile de chanvre ou de lin, & de cendal points & cousus ensemble, telles & de si grande longueur comme il me plaira

Firstly I choose to be dressed in a chemise and brayer of linen cloth [...] over my chemise and brayer shall be an arming coat (i.e. arming doublet) of linen cloth, and canvas, and of sendal (lightweight silk or very fine linen) stuffed with cotton and silk burrs with buckles and chapes, and with leather laces with canvas straps equipped with buckles and chapes of iron, steel, and latten, or of one of them [NB the choice of these metals is repeated in each instance] to attach the plates and fittings of my harness [...] chauses of linen cloth and of canvas and of senal [NB the choice of these materials is repeated in each instance], leather shoes [...] a brayette of iron and steel mail equipped with linen cloth (etc.) [...] sabatons, greaves, poleyns, and cuisses equipped with sections of mail and suitably equipped, nailed (i.e. riveted) with latten or iron nails. I shall be armed bearing a haubergeon of iron, steel, and latten mail, of such length and weight as I see fit to be suitable for the body, and the mail sleeves shall be attached with leather laces or canvas straps equipped (etc.) belted above with canvas-twine cord or straps of silk, a collar called a 'faux camail' (lit. 'false aventail' in Fr. – not explained) of iron and steel equipped with leather linings with straps (etc.) equipped with linings of linen cloth (etc.). Over my haubergeon I shall be armed with (a pair of) plates of iron and steel equipped with linings of linen cloth (etc.), with vambrace and pauldrons of iron and steel equipped with mail, buckles and chapes, linings of leather, gauntlets of iron, steel, and latten equipped with mail of iron (etc.) on the inside of the hand equipped with leather, buckles, chapes, nails, and rivets of iron (etc.), a basinet and visor of iron (etc.) equipped with a helmet lining of linen (etc.) and affixed with nails holding the basinet which shall be of iron (etc.), and shall have a buckle of silver [sic], iron (etc.) which shall be affixed to – and held by – my haubergeon or my (pair of) plates with leather straps and nails of iron (etc.) attached with a hourson (aventail-cover) equipped with silk burrs, cotton, covered with sendal, linen cloth (etc.), an aventail of iron (etc.) equipped with a *barbière* of iron (etc.) attached to the basinet and to the vervelles attached with the aforesaid hourson with leather straps (etc.) to the (pair of) plates or haubergeon, my aventail shall be covered with sendal doubly or singly lined with linen, (I shall bear) a coat of sendal armed with my (heraldic) arms doubly lined with linen, a (pair of) vermilion (velvet) or sendal chausses for (i.e. to cover) my (leg) harness – thighs, shins, and feet, two swords of iron and steel with cross (guards) and pommels of iron and steel and other metal with sheet-metal before the cross of iron (etc.) equipped with grips of wood with leather affixed thereon, and one of these swords shall be equipped with (sword) straps of leather or silk equipped with buckles of iron and steel, placed and belted at my side or attached with a leather strap and a ring of iron (etc.) attached to my (pair of) plates or haubergeon, and the other sword equipped with a wooden scabbard covered with leather attached to the arson (pommel) of the saddle with rings of iron (etc.) one of these said swords shall be two and a half feet in length before the hand – an inch or less (or thereabouts) [NB this is unclear] and the grip and pommel of one foot and one inch (or thereabouts) and the other sword shorter than two inches [NB this is unclear] (or thereabouts) before the hand, a dagger of iron (etc.) with grip of iron, steel, leather, or wood of a half-foot in length and a good palm (or thereabouts) before the hand. These swords and daggers shall be openly measured before the court so that all might be certain of the measurements. I choose (to be mounted on) a horse saddled with a saddle the arsons of which shall be of wood equipped with tanned leather and equipped with iron (etc.), high arsons in front and behind and open on both sides. My saddle (shall be) equipped with leather peytral and crupper, rings of iron (etc.) to attach one of my said swords, a shaffron of iron (etc.) to arm my horse's head equipped with leather straps attached with nails of iron (etc.), the shaffron (shall be) equipped within with linen stuffed with cotton or other stuffing, and shall be equipped with mail of iron (etc.) and linings of linen (etc.). The shaffron (shall be) affixed upon the horse's head and attached to its crinnet with canvas straps, my horse shall be covered, equipped, and armed before and behind and all around with linen, bolting-cloth, above (this) equipped with silk burrs or cotton, covered, pointed (i.e. padded like a pourpoint), and sewn together, mail harness of iron (etc.) shall be attached and placed with a cover (i.e. horse trapper) of linen cloth, canvas or linen [sic] and sendal pointed and sewn together in such manner and of such length as I see fit

129

Westminster Abbey Muniment 5446
Goods of Nicholas Litlyngton, Abbot of Westminster, Delivered and Sold, January 1386

lib[er]at' W Colchestr' abb[at]i vj loric' j pisan j standard' vij basnett' cu' vij ventailes j ketelhat j par' platys j basnet cu' j ventaill' legharneys vambras Rerebras j par' cirotec' plat' ij par' Rerebras j par' rub' plat' & iiijor cap' lancear[um] W Asshewell' emit j arcu' cu' j garb' sagittar[um] de pauon' [with some clothing] xiij s' iiij d' J Snellyng vnu' arcu' xviij d' R Wyke j arcu' cu' j garb' sagittar[um] de pauon' v s' W Belden' j arcu' cu' j garb' sagitt' de anca iij s' iiij d' J holbeth' j arcu' cu' quibusd' sagitt' ij s' fr[at] ris Ric[ard]i M[er]lawe xvij arc' xx s' j garba' catapultar[um] x s' ix garbas sagittar[um] de pauon' xviij s' iiijor garb' sagittar[um] de anca v s' iiij d'

Delivered to Abbot William Colchester six hauberks, one pisan, one standard, seven basinets with seven aventails, one kettlehat, one pair of plates, one basinet with one aventail, legharness, vambrace, rerebrace, one pair of plate gauntlets, one pair of rerebrace, one red pair of plates, and four lanceheads, W. Asshewell bought one bow with one sheaf of arrows of peacock (i.e. fletched with peacock's flight feathers) [with some clothing] 13s. 4d., J. Snellyng one bow 18d., R. Wyke one bow with one sheaf of arrows of peacock 5s., W. Belden one bow with one sheaf of arrows of goose (fletchings) 3s. 4d., J. Holbeth one bow with certain arrows 2s., Brother Richard Merlawe 17 bows 20s., one sheaf [prob. of missiles] for catapults 10s., nine sheaves of arrows of peacock 18s., four sheaves of arrows of goose (fletchings) 5s. 4d.

130

Truro, Cornwall Record Office, Arundell Family of Lanherne and Trerice AR/15/2
Goods from a Shipwreck at Holeclyff, Hundred of Hartland, Devon, 17 January 1386

j lorica cu' j venteyl debil' xiij s' iiij d' j paire de plates debil' & j brustplate vj s' viij d' ij pailettes xij d' j garb' de antiquis sagitt' xij d' j doblet' xx d' one worn out hauberk with one aventail 13s. 4d., one worn out pair of plates and one breastplate 6s. 8d., two pallets 12d., one sheaf of old arrows 12d., one doublet 20d.

131

Oxford, Bodleian Library, MS Eng. hist. b. 229, fol. 4r–fol. 10r
Inventory of the Effects of Sir Simon Burley, London and Elsewhere, 1387

Armo[u]r pur les ioustes j paire plates de laton argente & s[u]rdorer ou[er]e de stakes j par' vambras & rerebras j pair' de legh[er]nois & sabatons & j paire gantelets tout de mesme suyte j autre plate graue de stakes sanz cou[er]ture j par' vambras & rerebras j pair' gauntz de fer j pair' de legh[er]nois & sabatons tout de mesme suyte j autre plate oue vambras & rerebras gantz de fer legh[er]nois & sabatons tout del suyte sus dit j autre plate tout blanc & j paire vambras & rerebras j plate cou[er]e de veluet blanc stake de vert j paire vambras & rerebras & legh[er]nois & sabatons de cuierboyll stake de veluet blanc & vert iiij plates cou[er]e de cuer blanc stake de vert vj vamplates v grates & xij cornals j autre plate de stakes j autre plate cou[er]e de rouge cuier vij helmes blancs peyntez de stakes vert ij vambras p[u]r la mayn destre & ij gantz de feer p[u]r la mesme mayn & ij mayndefer' & j pair' rerebras iiij autr[e]s vambras veilles iiij mayndefers ij gantz de fer p[u]r la mayn destre & iij pair' rerebras j doublet du drap dalisaundre p[u]r les ioustes j Cote p[u]r les plates de Tartaryn vert Batu de stake j Cote p[u]r les plates de Tartaryn vert stake de Tartaryn blanc j Cote p[u]r les plates de Tartaryn blanc stake de Tartaryn vert ix chap[er]ons petits p[u]r les helmes batuz de stake j paire manchez de veluet blanc ou[er]ez de clowes s[u]rdorez v celles p[u]r ioustes de pees vj testers p[u]r le destre & vj pisers dont deux sont de cuer blanc ij pair' chauc' batuz de corones j pair' chauc' batuz de stake iiij pair' chauc' stakez de Tartaryn j pair' Chauc' de drap vert j pair' Chauc' vert de Tartaryn poynez j pair' Chauc' de cuier blanc iiij pair' Esporons p[u]r les ioustes s[u]rdorez viij escutz p[u]r les ioustes de pees Armo[u]r pur la guerre iiij basynets oue iiij ventails vj ferr' de launces p[u]r la guerre j Target p[u]r iouster en guerre ij Polhaches p[u]r la guerre j paller [sic] de asser j palet de quierboyll cou[er]e de stakes blanc & vert ij dagers dont lun est h[er]nois' dargent s[u]rdore j pancher de mayl cou[er]e de drap noir j doublet blanc stuffe de vn h[au]bregon' j doublet de worstede noir p[u]r armo[u]r j Chap[er]on de drap lyne stuffe de mayl j ketilhate peynte de stakes j pauys de vert stake de blanc ij steropes surdorez Espeies iij espees de Turkye dont lun est h[er]nois' dargent & s[u]rdore de penk' j espe descoce hernois' de laton s[u]rdore & cou[er]e de veluet stake de vert ij espees de passou sanz h[er]nois' iiij Axes descose j petit hache de Turkye vj espees ij Axes descose Arblastes & Arcz & seytes iiij arcz p[u]r le boys iij Arblastes vj arblastes de Turkye xxix seites de null' vaillo[u]r xj seites de Turkye & j case p[u]r les mesmes iiij arcz p[u]r le boys j hantbowe de Turkye j Case de cuier & xviij seites p[u]r mesme de null' value ij arblastes j Bauderyk Autres petitez Choses a Baynard Castell j petit gonne de feer viij Cotelx de Prak' sanz vagynes j dagger de beryll hernois' dargent dorez iij cotelx dont ij garnisez dargent & le tierce dargent doree j jak de vert & blanc botonez de botons s[u]rdorez j espee a luy sanz h[er]nois en la garde de Tunbrigge j arblast a Joce pluso[u]rs seites [a] Clifford j chafo[u]r large j clothsake j borehyde j feer dune launcegay

Armour for the jousts: one pair of plates of silvered latten and over-gilt worked with (decorative) stakes, one pair of vambrace and rerebrace, one pair of legharness and sabatons, and one pair of gauntlets all of the same suite, one other pair of plates engraved [*sic*] with stakes without covers, one pair of vambrace and rerebrace, one pair of iron gauntlets, one pair of legharness and sabatons all of the same suite, one other pair of plates with vambrace and rerebrace, iron gauntlets, legharness and sabatons all of the same suite, one other pair of all-white (polished steel) plates and one pair of vambrace and rerebrace, one pair of plates covered with white and green velvet, one pair of vambrace and rerebrace and legharness and sabatons of cuir bouilli (covered) with white- and green-staked velvet, four pairs of plates covered with white- and green-staked leather, six vamplates, five grappers, and 12 coronals, one other pair of plates with stakes, one other pair of plates covered with red leather, seven white helms painted with green stakes, two vambrace for the right hand (i.e. arm) and two iron gauntlets for the same hand, and two manifers, and one pair of rerebrace, three other old pairs of vambrace, four manifers, two iron gauntlets for the right hand, and three pairs of rerebrace, one doublet of cloth of Alexandria for the jousts, one coat for pairs of plates of green tartaryn (silk fabric) decorated with stakes, one coat for pairs of plates of green- and white-staked tartaryn, one coat for pairs of plates of white- and green-staked tartaryn, nine little chaplets for the helms decorated with stakes, one pair of (plate) sleeves of white velvet worked with over-gilt nails, five saddles for jousts of peace, six testers for destriers and six peytrals two of which are of white leather, two pairs of chausses decorated with crowns, one pair of chausses decorated with stakes, four pairs of chausses staked with tartaryn, one pair of chausses of green cloth, one pair of pointed (padded) chausses of green tartaryn, one pair of chausses of white leather, four pairs of over-gilt spurs for the jousts, eight shields for jousts of peace. Armour for war: four basinets with four aventails, six lanceheads for war, one target for jousting in war, two pollaxes for war, one pallet of steel, one pallet of cuir bouilli covered with white and green stakes, two daggers one of which is harnessed with silver-gilt, one mail paunce covered with black cloth, one white doublet stuffed with a haubergeon, one doublet for armour (i.e. arming doublet) of black worsted (woollen cloth), one chaplet (hood) of linen cloth stuffed with mail, one kettlehat painted with stakes, one pavise of green staked with white, two over-gilt stirrups. Swords: three swords of Turkey one of which is harnessed with silver and over-gilt with feathers, one sword of Scotland harnessed with over-gilt latten and covered with green-staked velvet, two swords of Passau without harness, four axes of Scotland, one small axe of Turkey, six swords, two axes of Scotland. Crossbows, bows, and arrows: four bows for hunting, three crossbows, six crossbows of Turkey, 29 arrows of no value, 11 arrows of Turkey and one case for them, four bows for hunting, one hand (spanned) bow of Turkey, one case of leather and 18 arrows for it of no value, two crossbows, one baldric. Other small things at Baynard's Castle: one small iron gun, eight pricking knives without scabbards, one dagger of beryl (crystal) harnessed with silver gilt, three knives two of which are garnished with silver and the third with silver-gilt, one jack of green and white (velvet) buttoned with over-gilt buttons, one of his swords without harness. In the Wardrobe at Tunbridge: one crossbow, at Joce: several arrows, at Clifford: a large chafer, one cloth sack, one cart cover, one lance-gay-head (head for a casting spear)

132

Nouveau recueil de comptes de l'argenterie des rois de France, ed. L. Douët d'Arcq (Paris, 1874), p. 152
Household Account of Louis, Duke of Touraine (then 15 years old), 31 July 1387

pour la façcon de un petit doublet fait de 3 aulnes de toile de Rains pour mons. de Thouraine pour envoyer en Lombardie pour faire unes plates pour trois aulnes de fine toile de Reins pour faire un patron à un petit pourpoint pour mons. le Duc de Thouraine pour envoier en Allemaigne pour faire et forger unes plates d'acier pour son corps

for making a little doublet for my lord of Touraine made of three ells of Rheims cloth to send to Lombardy to make a (pair of) plates, for three ells of fine Rheims cloth to make a pattern for a little pourpoint for my lord the Duke of Touraine to send to Germany to make and forge a steel (pair of) plates for his body

133

Sir Philippe de Mézières, *Le Songe du Vieil Pelerin*, ed. G. W. Coopland, 2 vols (Cambridge: University Press, 1969), Extracts

Sir Philippe (c. 1327–1405) was a well-travelled soldier and avid writer. In his 1389 work he casts himself as an 'Old Pilgrim' (Vieil Pelerin). He offers advice to his sovereign the King of France through the words of the allegorical Queen of Virtue.

On the Battles of the Present
[…] s'il leur souvenoit bein des batailles du jourduy qui en une heure ou en deux, et aucunesfoiz ennamis, sont desconfites de commun cours, et veoit on peu que la partie desconfite repreigne cuer et se ressemble et par vaillance ait victoire finable de ses ennemis.

It is usually the case that battles of today last but an hour or two and sometimes enemies are defeated in the usual way, and seldom is it seen that the defeated side take heart again and rally and by valour have the final victory over their enemies.

On Suitable Recreations

[...] aucune honneste recreation, comme de jouer a l'arbaleste, et a l'arc aussi, de gecter une lance ou un javelot; et ce soit publiquement aux heures ordonnees et a ce legitime. Se tu joues a la paume un jeu ou deux; et que ce soit en lieu secret et non pas longuement, la chose se puet passer. Et si te doys garder de gecter une grande perre ou une barre de fer, ne faire les grans et perilleux saulx qui en ta haulte voulente viennent souvent au devant, car ce faisant a ta personne royalle le peril y est trop grant, et par espicial de jouster. Je ne dy pas, que s'il venoit aucun roy ou tresgrant prince estrange pour toy visiter, ou aucunes grans nopces et sollennelles, que tu ne peusses bien jouster quatre ou cinq lances pour la compaignie honourer, et non pas jouster ou l ou lx ou c lances comme tu as acostume. Et ce que dit est du jouster se puet dire du dancier avec les dames.

(You make partake of) any honest recreation such as shooting the crossbow and also the bow, casting a lance or javelin – this should be done in public during the legitimate and regulated hours. If you play at handball, let it be one or two games in a secret place and don't spend too long at it. And see that you take care when casting a large stone or an iron bar, don't make big and dangerous jumps which you have done too often up to now: for in doing this the danger to your royal person is too great. Especially avoid jousting. I'm not saying that if some great foreign king or prince comes to visit you, or at any great nuptials or celebrations, you cannot joust (running to break) four or five lances to honour the company. But do not joust fifty or sixty or one hundred lances as you are accustomed to do. And what I say about jousting also applies to dancing with ladies.

On the Defence of the Realm

[...] voire en laissant toutes autres occupacions et esbatemens et le fait d'armes auquel tu es enclin, sicomme en ta jeunesse tu l'as bien moustre. Et tout ce qui appartient honnourablement et profitablement a fait d'armes, c'est assavoir au propoz et non pas en dances, es jeux des dez, es joustes, es chasses, ne es tournois, mais a la defence de l'eglise gallicane, de ta couronne, et du people francoys.

See to it that by abandoning all other occupations, amusements, and feats of arms to which you are inclined – as was demonstrated in your youth – feats of arms be honourable and beneficial, that is to say: not wasted in dances, games of chess, jousts, hunting, nor tourneys, but in the defence of Mother Church, your crown, and the French people.

On Godfrey of Bouillon (d. 1100), Conqueror of Jerusalem

Godeffroy de Buillon, qui devant l'empereur de Romme se combaty en champ, et en combatant s'espee lui rompy empres la croyx, et fu sanz espee, et lors ses amis vouldrent traictier de la paix pour la paour qu'ilz avoient que le noble duc ne fust desconfit, auquel traictie le vaillant duc respondy qu'il n'estoit pas temps a son honneur de traicter de la paix, et confiant de Dieu, coury sus a son ennemy et du pommeau de l'espee brisee abaty son ennemy a terre, et quant il le tint dessoubz lui et qu'il eut la puissance de le mectre a mort, il lieva sa main dextre a toute s'espee brisee et a haulte viox dist a ses amis qu'il estoit temps de traictier de la paix.

When Godfrey of Bouillon was fighting in the lists before the Roman Emperor his sword broke near the cross (guard) and he was without a sword. So then his friends wanted him to treat for peace for they feared that the noble Duke would be defeated. On hearing their entreaty, the valiant Duke replied that, on his honour, this was no time to treat for peace, and – trusting in God – rushed at his enemy and bashing him with the pommel of his broken sword beat his enemy to the ground. And when he had him pinned down and having it in his power to put him to death he lifted his right hand and the broken sword and said to his friends in a loud voice that *now* was the time to treat for peace.

On Trial by Battle

Tu ne doyes pas souffrir devant ta royale mageste aucun champ de bataille. Sicomme en Henaul ou Liege et es parties d'entour se trouvera champion qui se combattra pour argent et non pas pour verite. Et en y a de telx qui ont desconfit trente ou quarante foiz en champ de bataille, mais en la fin communement telx champions sont occis ou champ et raisonnablement vont tout droit en enfer comme souverains bouchiers de leurs freres crestiens.

You must not allow any trial by battle before your royal majesty. For in Hainaut and Liège and the surrounding area one finds champions who fight not for truth but for money. And, although there are some who have defeated (their opponents) thirty or forty times in the field of battle (i.e. lists), in the end most of these champions are killed in the lists and justly go straight to hell being chief butchers of their Christian brothers.

On Jousts and Tournaments

[…] que toutes grans festes, joustes et vaines assemblees et noces trop sumptueuses du tout en tout soient condempnees et sus grans peines qui sera convertie a la preperacion du dit saint passage.

(I advise) that all great fêtes, jousts, and vain gatherings, and overly sumptuous nuptials be condemned outright and thoroughly fined and this (money) be spent on preparations for the Holy Passage (i.e. Crusade).

134

Westminster Abbey Muniment 25355
Will of Walter Leycestre, King's Sergeant-at-Arms, 3 September 1389

Joh[ann]i Drap' vnu' basenet cu' auentaile quod de me nu[n]c h[abe]t in sua custodia vnu' haubergon' vnu' par' cirotecar[um] de plate & vnu' par' de shinebaux Rob[er] to Sausemer vnu' basenet cu' auentaile meu' optiumu' vnu' haubergon' vnu' par' de legharneys & vnu' par' cirotecar[um] de plate Thome stanes vnu' equu' meu' optimu' cu' vna sella eid[e]m

John Draper one basinet with aventail of mine which he has in his keeping, one haubergeon, one pair of plate gauntlets, and one pair of schynbalds, Robert Sausemer my best basinet with aventail, one haubergeon, one pair of legharness, and one pair of plate gauntlets, Thomas Stanes my best horse with its saddle

135

Leeds, Royal Armouries Library, MS RAR.0035(I.35), fol. 13r–fol. 13v
Declaration of Jousts to be held at Smithfield, near the City of London, 9 October 1390

La criee des Joustes
Oez seigneurs Cheualiers et escuiers nous vous faisons assauoir vng tresgrand faict darmes et vnes tresnobles Joustes les quelles seront faictes par vng cheualier qui portera vng escu de gueulles et sus vng blanc serf ayant vne couronne entour le col auecq vne chayne pendant dor sur vne trasse verte Et Icellui cheualier acco[m]paignye de vingt cheualiers tous abillez dune couleur Et de puis le dimenche ixe Jour doctobre prouchain vena[n]t en la neufue abbaye pres de la tour de londres Et dicellui lieu ces mesmes ch[eua]l[ie]rs seront menez par vingt dames vestues dune liuree et de la dessusdicte couleur et seute des dessus ditz cheualiers tous oultre et parmy la noble cite dicte la neufu troy aultrement appellee londres Et tout oultre celle mesme porte lesditz cheualiers tendro[n]t champ appelle Smitfelde et par lostel de saint Jehan appelle Clerkwelle Et la ilz danceront et hoeuront et meneront Joyeuse vie Et le la[n] demain le lundj lesditz vingt cheualiers en vne liuree co[m]me est dit deua[n]t en ce mesme champ de Smitfelde armez et montez sur les Rencz dedens lheure de haulte prime pour deliurer toutes manie[re]s de ch[eua]l[ie]rs qui vouldront la venir pour Jouster ch[asc]un deulx six lances telles comme ilz trouuernt sur les Rencz lesquelles lances seront portees a lestandare le quel estandare sera en ce mesme champ par le quel estandare seront mesurees toutes les lances dune longue[u]r Et lesditz vingt ch[eua]l[ie]rs Jousteront en haultes selles Et que les lances aient Raisonnables Roques Et les escutz desditz cheualiers ne seront couuers en nulle maniere de fer ne dacier lesquelles Joustes les nobles dames et damoyselles donneront au cheualier qui Joustera mieulx dehors vng cor garny dor Et a cellui q[u]i mielx dedens Joustera vng blanc leurier auec vng colier dor en tour de son col Et le landemain le mercredj ensuiua[n]t les mesmes vingt cheualiers dessus no[m]mez seront eus ou deuandit champ pour deliurer tous cheualiers et escuiers quelzco[n]ques auecques au tant de lances comme[n]t il leur plaira a Jouster Et la sera donne par les dames a celluy Jour et a celuy qui mieulx Joustera dehors vng cercle dor Et a cellui qui mieulx Joustera dedens vne saincture doree Et a la dame ou damoiselle qui mieulx dancera ou qui menera plus Joyeuse vie les troys Jours deua[n]tditz qui est a entendre le Dimenche le lundj et le mardj sera

donne par lesditz cheualiers vng fermail dore Et a la dame et damoyselle qui mieulx dancer et Reueillera apres elle qui est a entendre le second pris desditz troys Jours sera donne vng anel dor auecq vng diamant Et quiconque Joustera lesditz troys Jours de lance qui ne soit de la mesure de lestandare ne emportera ne luy s[er]a donne nulle maniere de pris ne gre Et qui Joustera lesditz troys Jo[u]rs de non Raisonnables Roques perdra son cheual et son harnoys Et le mercredj ensuyuant lesditz troys Jours desdites Joustes seze escuiers portans escuz de gueules Et dessus les escuz vng griffon dargent montez armez et cheuauchans en haultes selles comment il est dit deuant tendront le champ et deliurero[n]t tous cheualiers et escuiers qui venir y vouldront au tant de lances que bon leur semblera Et sera donne en ce mesme champ a cellui qui mieulx Joustera dehors vng noble coursier selle et bride Et a celui que mieulx Joustera dedens vng beau chapellet bien ouure de soye Et sera seurete par la vertu de cest noble pardon darmes a tous estrangiers cheualiers et escuiers qui vouldront venir a la susdite feste Et pour demourer et passer vingt Jours deuant la feste et xv Jours apres par la vertu des treues donnees et acordees par les deux Roys sans aucun empescheme[n]t leur donner Et sur cela auoir saufconduit a tout homme qui auoir le vouldra du Roy n[ost]re souuerain seigneur

To Cry a Joust

Hear ye, lords, knights, and squires, know ye that a most grand feat of arms and most noble jousts shall be held by a knight who shall bear a shield (charged with the heraldic arms) gules and over this a white hart with a crown around its neck with a hanging chain or on a tress vert. And this knight shall be accompanied by 20 knights all arrayed in the same colour from Sunday 9 October next in the new abbey near the Tower of London. These same knights shall be led to this place by 20 ladies dressed in a livery of the same colour and suit as the knights' right out and through the noble City of New Troy, otherwise called London. And all out of this same gate the knights shall take the field called Smithfield by the residence of Saint John called Clerkenwell. And there they shall dance, revel, and make merry. And, on the following Monday, the 20 knights in one livery as aforesaid shall appear in this same field of Smithfield armed and mounted in the ring within the hour of high prime to deliver all manner of knights who should wish to come there to joust. Each of them shall have six lances such as they shall find in the ring. These lances shall be carried to the standard which shall be in this same field and all the lances shall be measured by this standard; and all shall be of a length. And these 20 knights shall joust in high saddles and the lances shall have reasonable coronals. And the knights' shields shall not be covered in any manner of iron or steel. In these jousts the noble ladies and damsels shall give to the knight from without who jousts best a horn garnished with gold. And a white greyhound with a golden collar round its neck to he who shall have jousted the best from within. And on the following Wednesday the same 20 knights forenamed shall be in the said field to deliver all knights and squires whosoever and to joust with whatsoever type of lance as they please. And on this day there shall be given there a golden circlet to whoever jousts best from without. And to whoever jousts best from within a gilt girdle. And to the lady or damsel who shall dance best or who shall make most merry during the three days aforesaid – which is to say on the Sunday, Monday, and Tuesday – shall be given a gilt brooch by the knights. And to the lady or damsel who shall best dance and revel after her – which is to say the second prize of these three days – shall be given a gold ring with a diamond. And whosoever shall have jousted for these three days with a lance that was not of the measure of the standard shall not carry away, nor shall he be given, any manner of prize or praise. And he who shall have jousted with unreasonable coronals for these three days shall lose his horse and his harness. And, on the following Wednesday of these three days of the jousts, 16 squires bearing shields (charged) gules a griffon argent, mounted, armed, and riding in high saddles as aforesaid shall hold the field and deliver all knights and squires who might wish to come with such lances as they see fit. And in this same field a noble courser with saddle and bridle shall be given to whoever jousts best from without. And a beautiful chaplet well worked with silk to he who shall have jousted best from within. And there shall be surety to all foreign knights and squires who wish to come to the above said festivity by the virtue of this noble *pardon d'armes*. And to remain and spend 20 days before the festivity and 15 days after by the virtue of the truce granted and accorded by the two kings without giving any impeachment to them. And under this to have safe conduct to all men who wish to have it of the King our sovereign lord.

136

Household Account of Louis, Duke of Touraine (and Duke of Orléans from 1392), Paris, 10 May 1391–19 January 1393
Glasgow Museums, R. L. Scott Library, MS E.1939.65.1174, fol. 9r [10 May 1391]

Robert thierry m[ar]chant demour' a par' pour vj piesses de satins de vj coulours po[u]r couu[er]tir un h[ar]noiz de Jouste de mon s' lx fr' ij auln' de veluau vermeil fin fil pour housser vne selle de Jouste vj fr' iij auln' de veluau de vj coulours po[u]r f' le demj corpz dunes plates ix fr' vne auln' de veluau de iiij coulours po[u]r escheuer la d[i]te besoigne iij fr'

Robert Thierry, merchant of Paris 60 francs for six pieces of satin of six colours for covering one of my Lord's jousting harnesses, two ells of vermilion velvet of fine thread for housing one jousting saddle six francs, three ells of velvet of six colours for making the demi-corps of a pair of plates (lit. 'half-body' – poss. a polished pair of plates partly covered with fabric) nine francs, one ell of velvet of four colours to carry out the work three francs

Glasgow Museums, R. L. Scott Library, MS E.1939.65.1174, fol. 11r [13 September 1391]

Robert thierry m[ar]chant demour' a par' pour v aulnes de veluau sur soie lune noire lune vert lune azuree lune blanche & lautre vermeille dont il en y a iiij aulnes qui val[en]t au pris ch[asc]une de vj fr' & laut' viij fr' val[en]t xxxij fr' lequel veluau a este baille a Boniface pour faire couurir les plates de mon s' pour Jouster

Robert Thierry, merchant of Paris for five ells of velvet on silk – one black, one green, one azure, one white, and the other vermilion four ells of which each cost six francs and the others eight francs, for a total of 32 francs, which velvet was given to Boniface (de Morez) for covering my Lord's pair of plates for jousting

London, British Library, Additional Charter 2571 [9 July 1392]

Colin pilleur n[ost]re armeurier vint frans dor pour vn camail dacier quil a baille & deliure pour n[ost]re bassinet et pour auoir fait garnir n[ost]re dit bassinet pardedens de Satin de hourson et aut[re]s estoffes pour garnir n[ost]re h[er]nois de Jambes p[ar] dedens de Satin & pour Recouurer deux paire de plates

Colin Pilleur, our armourer 20 gold francs for a steel aventail which he has given and delivered for our basinet and for having garnished our said basinet on the inside with satin, with the hourson (aventail-cover), and other stuffing, and garnished our legharness on the inside with satin, and for re-covering two pairs of plates

London, British Library, Additional Charter 2574 [19 January 1393]

gilet le clerc haubergier et valet de chambre de monseigneur le Roy Trente Cinq frans pour vne cote dacier mise en vn gazigant et deux paires de braces dacier dont nous auons donne les vnes a n[ost]re ame Le mareschal Bouciquaut et les autres nous auons fait mett' en n[ost]re armure

Gilet Le Clerc, King's hauberger and *valet de chambre* 35 francs for a coat of steel (mail shirt) placed in a jazerant, and for two pairs of steel (mail) sleeves one of which we have given to our friend the *Maréschal* Boucicaut and the others we have had placed in our armoury

137

Edinburgh, National Records of Scotland, GD 150/62
Will of Sir James Douglas of Dalkeith, Dalkeith Castle, near Edinburgh, 19 December 1392

Jacobo de Douglas filio meo vnum par' de playts pro hastiludio de guerra cum basineto et lorica cirotecis ocreis ferreis et aliis armaturis pro hastiludio de guerra compentibus et melius Jack quod habeo et cuschewis Jacobo de Douglas filio meo naturali vnum par' de platys pro duello et Residuum vnis armatura pro hastiludio de guerra Wilhelmo fratri meo aliam armaturam secundum Nicholao de Douglas fratri meo vnam armaturam residuum omnium armourm in castro de Dalketh pro ipsius

tutela et defensione perpetuo remansurum volo quod auentale cum cirotecis de plate
que fuernt Johannis Ker sibi vel heredibus suis restitantur

my son James Douglas a pair of plates for jousts of war, with basinet, hauberk, iron
gauntlets and greaves, and other armours suitable for jousts of war and the best jack
that I have, and cuisses, my natural son James Douglas a pair of plates for the duel
and the residue of an armour for jousts of war, my brother William another second
best armour, my brother Nicholas Douglas an armour, the residue of all the armour in
Dalkeith Castle is to remain in perpetuity for its protection and defence, the aventail
with plate gauntlets belonging to John Ker be returned to him or his heirs

138

Kew, National Archives, DL 28/1
Account of John Dounton, Keeper of Armour to Henry, Earl of Derby,
London, 1393–94

Egidio de T[u]rry p[ro] j helm empt' de eo p[ro] Thoma de Beauford p[ro] hastilud'
pac' apud hertforde xl s Joh[ann]i Groue p[ro] j par' de plates alb' furbisiat' p[ro]
corp[or]e d[omi]ni empt' erga ead[e]m hastilud' vj li j par' plates furbis' p[ro] Thoma
Beauford p[ro] hastil' iiij li St[ep]h[a]no atte Fryth' p[ro] j mayndefer empt' p[ro]
Thoma Beauforde xiij s iiij d j Cerothec' de plate empt' p[ro] hastilud' p[ro] Tho[m]
a Beauf' iij s iiij d j vambras cu' j Besagu p[ro] hastilud' vj s viij d j Rerebras p[ro]
dexter' humer' vj s viij d j Rerebras p[ro] humer' sinistr' iij s iiij d Ade Smastret p[ro]
ij pesans de ferr' empt' p[ro] hastilud' pac' x s j par' Gussettes de mayl de steell' p[ro]
d[omi]no xxxiij s Ric[ard]o Pecok' p[ro] clouura vni' par' Cerothec' de plat' iij s iiij d
Clouura vni' mayndefer & p[ro] mu[n]dac[i]o[n]e eiusd[e]m vj s viij d clouura duaru'
Cerothec' de plat' p[ro] hastilud' iiij s Garnisura de ij Rerebras & mu[n]dac' eiusd[e]
m xij d j nou' Certothec' de plate & j vantbras cu' j besag' p[ro] hastil' xiij s iiij d iij
Grates iiij coronalx & ij vantplates x s ij peces p[ro] j helm d[omi]ni vj s viij d j lb
de Emery p[ro] mu[n]dac[i]o[n]e h[ar]nis' d[omi]ni xij d j par' Cerothec' nou' & j
par' vambras p[ro] d[omi]no xvj s viij d Ric[ard]o Stuffer p[ro] lin[u]ra vni' coler' de
plate p[ro] d[omi]no xvj d stuffura vni' helm' xx d lin[u]ra vni' pysen d[omi]ni vj d
laurencio Joyno[u]r p[ro] xij lanc' empt' p[ro] hastilud' pac' apud h[er]tforde viij s vj
Burrewes lanc' ij s iiij Burrewes p[ro] brach' xiiij d Ric[ard]o Sadeler p[ro] j sell' cu'
tester & pyser nou' empt' p[ro] hastil' pac' apud hertforde Cvj s viij d emendac' de
ij scut' p[ro] hastilud' pac' viij s eme[n]dac[i]o[n]e vni' sell' p[ro] Thoma Beauford
p[ro] hastilud' ordin' vna cu' j nou' panell' & nou' styropes cu' corijs eor[un]d[e]m x
s emendac[i]o[n]e alt[er]ius sell' alt' de staur' p[ro] hastilud' pac' cu' j nou' panell' &
styrops & corijs eor[un]d' v s eme[n]dac[i]o[n]e vni' sell' Bastard' coop[er]t' in cor'
rub' cu' stuffura eiusd[e]m iij s stuffura vni' test' p[ro] dext[r]ar' d[omi]ni vj d j fren'
empt' p[ro] dext[r]ar' d[omi]ni c[ontr]a hastilud' ij s vj d iij Boreux p[ro] scut' &
p[ro] j felt' empt' p[ro] hastil' ij s j scuto empt' p[ro] hastilud' p[ar]at' xviij s j tester
& pyser & j scut' empt' p[ro] hastilud' xliij s Joh[ann]i Donacstr' p[ro] j cathena de

cupr' deaur' p[ro] j barb' j helm' d[omi]ni viij s iij d p[er] man' Joh[ann]is Dyndon' ij
stripes de mayl ad ponend' inf[r]a vni' capuc' d[omi]ni xij d p[ro] clau' empt' london'
p[ro] stuffur' lanc' d[omi]ni erg' hastuld' pac' xij d Joh[ann]i Widmer Joyno[u]r p[ro]
j armariolo empt' p[ro] officio armat[u]re d[omi]ni xl s car' eiusd[e]m de ecc[lesi]a
s[anc]ti Jacobi de Garlekhythe vsq[ue] hospic' d[omi]ni ad Baynardyscastell' iiij d
car' h[er]nis' armatur' d[omi]ni v[i]z de sell' testers pysers Ad pictore' & de ib[ide]
m ad hospic' d[omi]ni x d Ric[ard]o Stuffer p[ro] Stuffur' ij basenett' d[omi]ni apud
london' j virg' j q[ua]r' Satyn rub' & j virg' Satyn blod' p[ro] ij par' plat' d[omi]ni
v[i]z ad ponend' int' coop[er]tur' & les plates iij vln' tel' flandr' Joh[ann]i Dyndon'
p[ro] Stuffura vni' Jakke d[omi]ni bald' ceric' alb' & rub' cu' al' stuffura de Coton'
& Cadas xviij vln' & d' tel' de braban' [...] Joh[ann]i Groue p[ro] j par' de plates
nou' empt' de eo coop[er]t' in bald' nigr' iiij li vj s viij d cloueur' vni' par' de plat' de
staur' d[omi]ni coop[er]t' in veluet blod' xxvj s viij d vni' Brestplat' d[omi]ni nou'
xxvj s viij d j par' de plates empt' & dat' Petro de melbo[u]rne coop[er]t' in cor'
rub' iiij li vj s viij d Joh[ann]i Shirwode p[ro] j palett' d[omi]ni coop[er]t' cu' veluet'
nigr' postmod' dat' Wil[e]lmo hikelyng vj s viij d j par' Cerot' de plate e[m]pt' p[ro]
d[omi]no xviij s j par' Cerot' coop[er]t' in cor' alb' xij s p[ro] cloueura & rem' vni' par'
Cerot' d[omi]ni de Staur' vj s viij d Joh[ann]i Sendall' p[ro] j basenet nou' xxxvj s viij
d Ste[p]h[an]o atte fryth' p[ro] j par' de legh[ar]noys empt' p[ro] d[omi]no xl s Et j
auentall' de steel p[ro] j palett' d[omi]ni que d[omi]no ded[i]t W[i]l[e]lmo hikelyng
x s vj d Ric[ard]o Stuffer p[ro] Stuffur' vni' basenett' d[omi]ni que Sendall' fec[i]t iiij
s iiij d Stuffur' vni' basenett' d[omi]ni empt' in anno p[re]c' de mag[ist]ro Egidio in
turri iij s iiij d Stuffur' vni' palett' d[omi]ni coop[er]t' in veluet nigr' iij s iij d laurenc'
Joyn[e]ro p[ro] iij hasegayes p[ro] d[omi]no iij s xij lanc' empt' temp[or]e eq[ui]t'
cont[r]a Duc' hib[er]n' xviij s x lanc' empt' c[ontr]a t[r]ansit' d[omi]ni in Scot' xvj s
viij d Nich[ol]o Dour' p[ro] conduit' vni' h[arn]ois p[ro] arm' d[omi]ni mu[n]dand'
apud kenil' viij d cor' p[ro] ij auentall' d[omi]ni enarmand' ij d oleo p[ro] h[ar]nis'
d[omi]ni et p[ro] bran iiij d Mag[ist]ro Egidio de Turry p[ro] ij Basenettes de guerra
de ip[s]o empt' lxxiij s iiij d ij helm' p[ro] hastilud' pac' Cvj s viij d j Basenet p[ro]
guerra cu' ij visers lxxiij s iiij d emendac' vni' helm' d[omi]ni ac vni' viser' eid[e]
m xiij s iiij d p[er] Joh[ann]es Dounton' Ric[ard]o Pekoc' p[ro] clouura vni' par'
Cerothec' de plate & garnisura vni' par' Rerebras iij s iiij d j mayndefer nou' empt'
p[ro] d[omi]no p[ro] hastilud' xvj s viij d ij par' Cerothec' de plate xx s j par' vantbras
cu' j ala p[ro] hastilud' vj s viij d j par' Rerebras v s p[ro] j vantbras cu' vna ala p[ro]
hastilud' vj s j par' sabatons v s j Rerebras p[ro] hastilud' ij s clouura vni' Cerothec'
de plate p[ro] hastilud' xx s ij par' Cerothecar[um] de plate xx s ij par' vantbras x s
j par' Rerebras ij s ij lb Emry p[ro] Offic' armat[u]re [...] Joh[ann]i Groue p[ro] j
par' plates nou' furbis' fact' tam p[ro] pac' q[u]am p[ro] guerra vj li clouura vni' par'
Briganters coop[er]t' in bald' aur' de cipr' xl s clouura vni' par' manic' p[ro] plates vj
s viij d clouura vni' par' de plates palat' cu' veluet & cheu[er]ond' liij s iiij d Steph[a]
no Frith' p[ro] j par' legh[ar]neys empt' p[ro] d[omi]no xxxvj s viij d garnisura vni'
par' legh[ar]neys d[omi]ni de staur' vj s viij d j Grate & j Coronall' xviij d Ric[ard]o
Stuffer p[ro] stuffura de ij helm' pro d[omi]no v s stuffura de iij Basenettes d[omi]ni
x s Botenynge vni' lorice d[omi]ni ij s j labell' de mayl p[ro] loric' d[omi]ni ij s p[ro]

armynge de ij auentayles p[ro] basenett' d[omi]ni xvj s Ric[ard]o Sadeler p[ro] deaur' vni' hilte & pomell' & vni' riuett' p[ro] j glad' d[omi]ni de pass' vij s Laurent' Joyn[e] ro p[ro] xviij lanc' empt' erga hastilud' apud Brembeltee x s vj d xviij lanc' empt' erg' hastilud' pac' apud Waltham x s vj d Ric[ard]o Sadeler p[ro] viij helmthonges cu' pluscul' empt' p[ro] hastilud' xx d P[er] manus Joh[ann]is Dounton' p[ro] ij styles empt' p[ro] mu[n]dac' glad' d[om]ni x d ij scaberdes empt' p[ro] ij glad' d[omi]ni xvj d j pell' nigr' p[ro] scabe[r]des fac' viij d emendac[i]o[n]e & augmentac[i]o[n] e vni' lorice d[omi]ni dat' d[omi]no p[er] Ric[ardi]m Chelmeswik x s Lodewico fil' mag[ist]ri Egidij de Turry p[ro] ij ferr' lanc' p[ro] hastilud' guerre & p[ro] vj Coronalx p[ro] hastilud' pac' empt' p[ro] d[omi]no x s j auentayle j paire legh[ar]neys j pair' vantbras j pair' Rerebras & j par' Cerothec' de plate empt' de Joh[ann]e leghton' ad xxiiij s viij d

Giles of the Tower for one helm bought from him for Thomas Beaufort for the joust of peace at Hertford 40s., John Grove for one white (polished steel) pair of plates furbished for the Lord's body bought for this joust £6, one furbished pair of plates bought for Thomas Beaufort for the joust £4, Stephen atte Fryth for one manifer bought for Thomas Beaufort 13s. 4d., one plate gauntlet bought for the joust for Thomas Beaufort 3s. 4d., one vambrace with one besagew for the joust 6s. 8d., one rerebrace for the right arm 6s. 8d., one rerebrace for the left arm 3s. 4d., Adam Smastret for two iron pisans bought for the joust of peace 10s., one pair of gussets of steel mail for the Lord 23s., Richard Peacock for nailing one pair of the Lord's plate gauntlets 3s. 4d., nailing one manifer and for mending it 6s. 8d., nailing two plate gauntlets for the joust 4s., equipping two rerebrace and mending them 12d., one new pair of plate gauntlets and one vambrace with one besagew (circular armpit defence) for the joust 13s. 4d., three grappers, three coronals, and two vamplates 10s., two pièces (reinforcing plates) for one of the Lord's helms 6s. 8d., 1lb of emery for mending the Lord's harness 12d., one new pair of gauntlets and one pair of vambrace for the Lord 16s. 8d., Richard the stuffer for lining one plate collar for the Lord 16d., stuffing one helm 20d., lining one of the Lord's pisans 6d., Laurence the joiner for 12 lances bought for the joust of peace at Hertford 8s., 6 lance burrs (grips) 2s., 4 burrs for arms [NB this is unclear] 14d., Richard the saddler for one new saddle with tester and peytral bought for the joust of peace at Hertford 106s. 8d., mending two shields for the joust of peace 8s., mending one saddle ordered for Thomas Beaufort for the joust along with one new panel and new stirrups with leathers for it 10s., mending another high saddle from the store for the joust of peace with one new panel and stirrups and leathers for it 5s., mending one bastard saddle covered with red leather with stuffing the same 3s., stuffing one tester for the Lord's destrier 6d., one bridle for the Lord's destrier for the joust 2s. 6d., 3 burrs for shields and for one fewter for the joust (support pendant from the saddle in which to rest the wielder's end of the lance) 2s., one equipped shield bought for the joust 18s., one tester and peytral and one shield bought for the joust 43s., John Doncaster for one gilt-copper chain for one barber (i.e. reinforcing plate) for one of the Lord's helms 8s. 3d. Through the hands of John Dounton: two strips of mail to be placed inside one of the Lord's hoods 12d., nails bought in London for equipping the Lord's lances for the joust of peace 12d., John Widmer, joiner for one armoire bought for the office of the Lord's Armourer 40s., for its carriage from the Church of Saint James Garlichythe to the Lord's lodgings at Baynard's Castle 4d., carriage of the Lord's harness and armour viz.: saddles, testers, peytrals to the painter and from the same place to the Lord's lodgings 10d., [...] one ell and one quarter of red satin and one ell of blue satin bought at London by Richard the stuffer for stuffing two of the Lord's basinets and three ells of Flanders cloth for two of the Lord's pairs of plates viz.: to place between the covers and the plates, baldachin (exotic silk woven with gold thread), white and red silk, with other stuffing of cotton and cotton wool, 18½ ells of Brabant cloth was bought by John Dounton for stuffing one of the Lord's jacks [...] John Grove for one new pair of plates bought from him covered with black baldachin £4 6s. 8d., for nailing one pair of the Lord's plates from store covered with blue velvet 26s. 8d., one new breastplate for the Lord 26s. 8d., one pair of plates covered with red leather bought and given to Peter Melbourne £4 6s. 8d., John Sherwood for one pallet covered with black velvet afterwards given to William Hikelyng 6s. 8d., one pair of plate gauntlets for the Lord 18s., one pair of gauntlets covered with white leather 12s., nailing and repairing one pair of the Lord's gauntlets from store 6s. 8d., John Sendall for one new basinet 36s. 8d., Stephen atte Fryth for one pair of legharness bought for the Lord 40s., one steel aventail for one of the Lord's pallets which the Lord gave to William Hikelyng 10s. 6d., Richard the stuffer for stuffing one of the Lord's basinets which (John) Sendall made 3s. 4d., stuffing one of the Lord's basinets bought in the previous year from Master Giles in the Tower 3s. 4d., stuffing one of the Lord's pallets covered with black velvet 3s. 3d., Laurence the joiner for three hasegayes (casting spears) for the Lord 3s., 12 lances bought at the time he rode against the Duke of Ireland 18s., ten lances bought for the Lord's passing to Scotland 16s. 8d., Nicholas Dour' for carrying one of the Lord's arming harnesses to be mended at Kenilworth 8d., leather for arming two of the Lord's aventails 2d., oil for the Lord's harness and bran 4d., Master Giles of the Tower for two basinets for war bought from him 73s. 4d., two helms for jousts of peace 106s. 8d., one basinet for war with two visors 73s. 4d., mending one of the Lord's helms and one of its visors 13s. 8d., paid by John Dounton: Richard Peacock for nailing one pair of plate gauntlets and equipping one pair of rerebrace 3s. 4d., one new manifer for the Lord for jousts 16s. 8d., two pairs of plate gauntlets 20s., one pair of vambrace with one wing for jousts (i.e. the arm defence shaped to protect the crook of the elbow) 6s. 8d., one pair of rerebrace 5s., one vambrace with one wing for jousts 6s., one pair of sabatons 5s., one rerebrace for jousts 2s., nailing one plate gauntlet for the joust 20s., two pairs of plate gauntlets 20s., two pairs of vambrace 10s., one pair of rerebrace 2s., 1lb of emery for the Office of the Armourer [...] John Grove for one newly-furbished pair of plates made both for (jousts of) peace and for war £6, nailing one pair of brigandines covered with baldachin of Cypriot gold 40s., nailing one pair of sleeves for pairs of plates 6s. 8d., nailing one pair of plates (decoratively) palled with velvet and (heraldic) chevrons 53s. 4d., Stephen atte Fryth for one pair of legharness for the Lord 36s. 8d., equipping one pair of the Lord's legharness from store 6s. 8d., one grapper and one coronal 18d., Richard the stuffer for stuffing two helms for the Lord 5s., stuffing three of the Lord's basinets 10s., buttoning one of the Lord's hauberks 2s., one label of mail for the Lord's hauberk 2s., arming two aventails for the Lord's basinets 16s., Richard the saddler for gilding one hilt and pommel and one rivet for one of the Lord's swords of Passau 7s., Laurence the joiner for 18 lances bought for the joust at Brambletye 10s. 6d., 18 lances bought for the joust of peace at Waltham 10s. 6d., Richard the saddler for eight helm-thongs with buckles bought for the joust 20d. By John Dounton's hands: for two (sharpening) steels bought for mending the Lord's swords 10d., two scabbards bought for two of the Lord's swords 16d., one black hide for making scabbards 8d., mending and augmenting one of the Lord's hauberks given to the Lord by Richard Chelmeswick 10s., Ludovicus, son of Master Giles in the Tower for two lanceheads for jousts of war and for six coronals for jousts of peace for the Lord 10s., one aventail, one pair of legharness, one pair of vambrace, one pair of rerebrace, and one pair of plate gauntlets bought from John Leighton 24s. 8d.

139

Chippenham, Wiltshire and Swindon Archives, Register of John Waltham, Bishop of Salisbury, fol. 230r
Will of Sir Hugh Calveley (d. 1394), Salisbury Cathedral, Wiltshire

no[m]i[n]e p[ri]ncipal' eccl[es]ie meum optim' equu' falerat' cum ho[m]i[n]e to[t] alit' armat' p[ro] Guerra vnu' aliu' equu' totalit' armat' p[ro] pace cum vno ho[m] i[n]e armat'

in my principal name to the Church [prob. at Bunbury] my best mighty horse with a man totally armed for war, one other horse totally armed for peace with one armed man

140

London Metropolitan Archives, Court of Husting Roll 128 (17)
Will of Simon Winchcombe, Armourer of London, 7 April 1396

Ric[ard]o P[er]son' seruienti meo de om[n]ib[u]s armaturis meis vj integra hernezia p[ro] ho[m]i[n]e v[i]z vj p[ar]ia de Jambes vj habergeons de ferr' vj Bacnenett' de factur' de london' cu' vj auentailes vj p[ar]ia de vambras vj p[ar]ia de rerebras vj brest-plates & vj p[ar]ia de cerotec' de plate et vnde om[n]ib[u]s armaturis meis exec' mei eligant' primo tria integra hernezia de meliorib[u]s om[n]i armatur[am] mear[um] & Ric[ard]us Person' tunc eligat p[er] se alia tria harnezia Et tunc it[er]ato exec' mei elegant alia tris harnezia intergr' Et tunc it[er]to Ric[ard]us eligat alia tria harnezia integra de armaturis pred[ic]tis Ric[ard]o Persoun vnu' Barell' anfeltz Bicornes strakes ham[u]res tongs sheres & alia om[n]ia instra' & vtensilia mea p[er]tinent' shope mee de arte armurarij om[n]is residuu' armat[u]rar[um] mear[um] vbicumq[ue] existent' execut' meis ad vendend' my servant Richard Person six complete harnesses for men from all my armour viz.: six pairs of jambers, six iron haubergeons, six basinets of London make with six aventails, six pairs of vambrace, six pairs of rerebrace, six breastplates, and six pairs of plate gauntlets, my executors shall have the first choice from all my armour of three of the best complete harnesses of my armour, Richard Person shall then choose another three harnesses, then my executors shall – in turn – chose three complete harnesses, then Richard shall – in turn – choose another three complete harnesses from this armour, Richard Person a barrel, anvils, bicorns, stakes, hammers, tongs, shears, and all my other instruments and tools appurtenant to my shop of the armourer's craft, all the residue of my armour (wherever it shall be) to be sold by my executors

141

Ramón de Perellós, *Viatge al Purgatori*, ed. J. Tiñena (Barcelona, 1988), p. 42
A Catalan Knight, Sir Ramón de Perellós, describes the Bodyguard of Niall Mór Ó Néill, King of Tír Eoghain (Tyrone), Ireland, 1397

E aquest ha bé cent quaranta hòmens a cavall e s'armen de cota de malla e porten les sens cintes ab gorjarets de malla e capells de fer redons a manera dels moros o de sarracins e havia ne a manera de bernes ab espases e coltells e llances fort llongues e primes a la manera de les llances altres antigues són de does brasses les espases són aitals com les dels sarracins que nosaltres apellam genoeses lo pom e la crou són d'altra manera que és quasi com una mà estesa los coltells són llongs e estrets com lo dit menuell e són fort tallants

He has 140 horsemen, they are armed with coats of mail and wear them un-girded, and they have mail gorgets and rounded chapel de fers in the style of the Moors or Saracens with swords and knives and lances very long – but very thin in the manner of ancient lances – and they are two fathoms long; the swords are like those of the Saracens, which we call Genoese; the pommel and the hilt are of another kind: the pommel is like an extended hand. The knives are long and narrow like the little finger – and they cut very well.

142

Kew, National Archives, C 145/262/12
Inventory of the Effects of Sir William Castleacre, Great and Little Eversden, Cambridgeshire, 1397

iij haberiouns v marc' ij Euentayll' xx s j paunes vj s viij d j basenet xx s vombras & rerebras x s j par' cloues de plate vj s viiij d j brestp[...] xxvj s viij d j launcegay vj s viij d ij speres iij s iiij d v arblastes ij baudrykes xx s xi arc' x shef de arwes xxj s ij glad' xiij s iiij d j pollex iij s iiij d j ex & billes vj s viij d

three haubergeons 5 marks, two aventails 20s., one paunce 6s. 8d., one basinet 20s., vambrace and rerebrace 10s., one pair of plate gauntlets 6s. 9d., one breastplate 26s. 8d., one lancegay 6s. 8d., two spears 3s. 4d., five crossbows, two baldrics 20s., 11 bows, ten sheaves of arrows 21s., two swords 13s. 4d., one pollaxe 3s. 4d., one axe and (several) bills 6s. 8d.

143

Kew, National Archives, E 163/6/13
Inventory of the Arms and Armour of Richard, Earl of Arundel, Arundel Castle, Sussex, 1397

This manuscript is very fragmentary

lez p[ar]cell' del h[er]noys deliu[er]tz p[ar] Steph' Freth' a Joh[a]n Torre iij pair' h[er]noise p[u]r jambez enbordurez de lato[u]n iij marc' ix pair' h[er]noys p[u]r jambez pleins dont j sanz Quysshewe xxx s vj pair' sabatons [...] j pair' poleins de laton j pair' poleins noirs ij quysshews ou poleins de laton' j peir' splentes de iij peces p[u]r jambez xviij pair' gauntz del ou[er]aigne de loundres p[ri]s ch[asc]un pair' [...] xxxv pair' gauntz de flaundres p[ri]s le peir' vj d ij palrons bordurez de lato[u]n [...] xij peir' vambras xiij peir' rerebras p[ri]s de ch[asc]un vauntbras oue rerbras v s xvij vauntbras xv rerebras de flaundres p[ri]s le vauntbras ou le rerebras xiij s j bacynet de melayn ou le veser & le Coler h[er]nois dargent j bacynet de loundres ou le veser v bacynetz de flaundres de haut tour p[ri]s le pece [...] iij bacynetz p[u]r ioustes de guerr' [...] xj helmes p[ri]s ch[asc]un iij s iiij d xlj vailles rounde bacynetz [...] v blanc paletz de flaundres j palet noir ij ketelhattes [...] iiij Chenebawdes pris ch[asc]u' xij d j auentaill' dacer de lumbardye [...] j auentaill' dacer de Westfale [...] xxiiij auentaill' de fer' pris le pece ij s vj d vj auentailles vailles & febles p[ri]s le pece vj d vij pauncez & j brace p[ri]s le pece [...] dont j paunce p[u]r le bordre dun pair' [...] vj pesinz pris le pece xij d xxx petitz peces de maile a guyse de voiders vj d lxiiij hab[er]iones p[ri]s le pece vj s viij d j trappur' de maill' [...] ij pair' plates cou[er]e de drape lez bokeles garnys dargent & endorre [...] j pair' plates febles j pair' plates blankes feblez [...] xij brestplates de loundres p[ri]s ch[asc]u' vj s viij d iiij brestplates p[u]r t[u]rnementz [...] xvj brestplates de flaundres pris le pece [...] xj vauntplates x grates vj coronalx p[ri]s entout [...] ij mayn de fers [...] j escut' dac' j chaunfreyn blanc dac' p[u]r le teste dun chiual [...] ij testes p[u]r launcegayes [...] iij fers p[u]r launcez [...] xviij jakes de soy & Fustiane p[ri]s le pece iij s iiij d j sell' p[u]r j bastard [*sic*] oue j bride & peytrell' enbordurez oue les armes darundell' iiij sell' p[u]r t[ur]nementz dont iij enbroudez & le quarte peintez p[ri]s entout [...] v pair' de trepes iiij peytrell' xij pair' espors endorrez j terget iij escutez [...] vj espeys gr[a]unt & petitz p[ri]s de ch[asc]un iiij s j peir' de cutell' de birell' & h[er]noises

dargent endorrez [...] j pair' de cutelx de yuoir garnisez oue lez armez darundell'
[...] j dagg' enamels [...] j dagg' de maser' h[er]neises dargent & endorrez [...] j
dagg' de noir h[er]noises & endorres [...] xvij estuffes p[u]r bacynetz [...] iiij pecez
dun trappur' batuz [...] vj skochons [...] lxx testz p[u]r dartes [...] j pair' de cutelx
dyuory garnisez dargent [...]

the parcels of harness delivered by Stephen atte Fryth to John Torre: three pairs of
legharness bordered with latten three marks, nine pairs of plain legharness one of
which lacks a cuisse 30s. each, six pairs of sabatons [...] one pair of latten poleyns
[...] one pair of black (unpolished steel) poleyns [...] two cuisses with latten poleyns
[...] one pair of leg splints of three pieces [...] 18 pairs of gauntlets of London work
each pair [...] 35 pairs of gauntlets of Flanders work 6d. a pair [...] two pauldrons
bordered with latten [...] 12 pairs of vambrace, 13 pairs of rerebrace, each vambrace
with rerebrace 5s., 17 vambrace, 15 rerebrace of Flanders each vambrace with the
rerebrace 13s., one bacinet of Milan with visor and collar harnessed with silver, one
basinet with visor of London work, five basinets of Flanders with high tops [...]
three basinets for jousts of war [...] 11 helms 3s. 4d. each, 41 old round basinets [...]
five white (polished steel) pallets of Flanders, one black pallet, two kettlehats [...]
four schynbalds 12d. each, one steel aventail of Lombardy [...] one aventail of steel
of Westphalia [...] 24 iron aventails 2s. 6d. each, six old and worn out aventails 6d.
each, seven paunces and one (mail) sleeve [...] one of these paunces is for bordering
a pair of (prob. plates), six pisans 12d. each, 30 little pieces of mail in the form of
voiders 6d., 64 haubergeons 6s. 8d. each, one trapper of mail [...] two pairs of plates
covered with cloth the buckles garnished with silver and gilded [...] one worn out
pair of plates [...] one worn out white pair of plates [...] 12 breastplates of London
6s. 8d. each, four breastplates for tournaments [...] 16 breastplates of Flanders
[...] 11 vamplates, ten grapers, six coronals [...] two manifers [...] one shield of
steel [...] one white shaffron for a horse's head [...] two heads for lancegays [...]
three lanceheads [...] 18 jacks of silk and fustian (strong fabric made from any two
of cotton, flax, or wool) 3s. 4d. each, one bastard saddle with one bit and peytral
embroidered with the arms of Arundel [...] four saddles for tournaments three of
which are embroidered and the fourth painted [...] five pairs of trappers [...] four
peytrals [...] 12 pairs of gilt spurs [...] one targe [...] three shields [...] six large
and small swords 4s. each, one pair of knives of beryl (crystal) and harnessed with
silver-gilt [...] one pair of knives of ivory garnished with the arms of Arundel [...]
one enamelled dagger [...] one dagger of maple harnessed with silver and gilt [...]
one black dagger harnessed and gilt [...] 17 basinet linings [...] three pieces of a
decorated trapper [...] six escutcheons [...] 70 heads for darts [...] one pair of ivory
knives garnished with silver [...]

144

Kew, National Archives, E 136/77/4
Inventory of the Arms and Armour of Thomas, Duke of Gloucester,
Pleshey Castle, Essex, 1397

Lez p[ar]celles de armur' quex Stephan' atte Freth armurer mons' le Roy ad deliure
a Joh[an]e Torre' [...] ij bassnettes oue visers & ij auentaill' iiij li ij ketelhattes lun
blanc oue j bordur' dargent endorrez lautr' oue j auentail cou[er]ez de russet veluet x
s iij habergeou[n]s dou[n]t deux de petit maille de lumbardye lx s j brestplate oue j
paunsse dasser xx s ij paunsses & j braieux dasser p[u]r plates oue j peir' bras xxxiij s
iiij d j peir' chaussou[n]s de maille x s j pallet de lumbardy oue j viser xx s ij basnets
p[u]r ioustes de guerre oue peses de healmes xl s j court auentaill' & j peir' gussets
j petit braieux & iij peir voidours xiij s iiij d iij healmes p[u]r ioustes de pees oue
ij vmbrers xxxiij s iiij d j peir' briganters cou[er]ez de rouge veluet garnisez darg'
endorrez oue j peir' maunches de plate lxvj s viij d j peir' briganters cou[er]ez de blu
baudekyn garnisez darg' oue les manches sanz plate' lxvj s viij d j peir' briganters
cou[er]ez de rouge veluet garnisez de cupr' enorrez ouesq[ue] j coler dasser p[u]r
ioustes de guerre xl s j peir' plates cou[er]ez de blu veluet p[u]r ioustes de guerre xl
s ij peir' plates cou[er]ez de noir veluet lxxiij s iiij d j peir' de plates p[u]r ioustes de
pees cou[er]ez de rouge veluet xl s j peir' de plates enorrez p[u]r ioustes de pees oue
vantbras & rerebras j gaunt & j maindeferr' c s j peir' plates de blu baudekyn q[ue]
fuist iadys a Roy Edward x s j peir' briganters dou[n]t le pys & le dos blanc & le bas
cou[er]ez de blu veluet xxvj s viij d ij peir' legherneys appellez forherneys xiij s iiij d
iij peir' legherneys entiers xx s ij peir' rerebras iiij peir' vantbras & j peir' sabatou[n]
s xxiij s iiij d iiij peir' gantz de plates dou[n]t ij garnisez de lato[u]n enorrez xiij s iiij
d iij peir' rerebras iiij vambras iiij mandeferr & ij gantz p[u]r io[uste]s de pees xxx s
j maindeferr' & j vantbras j rerebras p[u]r ioustes de pees ij s vj d viij basnettes sanz
aventaill' oue iij visers xxiiij s iij brestplates iij s ij peir' vantbras j peir' rerebras xij s
iij peir' legherneis entiers & ij peir' sabatou[n]s xvj s viij d iiij hab[er]geou[n]s veil'
de ferr' & v auentaill' fiebl' xiij s iiij d vn beal espe de burdeux oue le gayne de veluet
rouge & le pomel hilte & le ceintur bien garnisez dargent enorrez lx s j espe descoce
herneis de cupre enorrez vj s viij d j espe de burdeux herneis dargent enorrez oue le
gayne de noir veluet xiij s iiij d j veil' espe oue le gayne h[er]neis de cupr' enorrez iij
s iiij d j court espe de guerr' le pomel hilte & gayne h[er]neis darg' enorrez vj s viij
d j veil' espe dou[n]t le hilte & pomel h[er]neis dargent enorrez xiij s iiij d j longe
espe de burdeux oue le hilt' & pomel herneis dargent enorrez x s iiij courtes espes de
guerre sanz herneis darg' xxx s x aut[re]s espes plus longes ascuns fortz ascuns t[re]
nchantz xx s j espe de guerr' oue ij vantplates p[u]r les lystes vj s viij d j nouel baslard
de bordeux oue mazerhaste & le gayne leg[er]ement h[er]neis dargent enorrez x s iiij
veil' baslardes & fauchou[n]s v s j large teste de bordeux herneis darg' endorrez vj s
viij d v petitz testes p[u]r launces iij s iiij d x testes p[u]r launces gra[un]tz & petitz
xiij s iiij d vij courtes daggers herneis dargent endorrez vn cotel cort dirland oue la
maunche dun teste gayne herneis darg' endorrez [...] j dagger p[u]r les lystes oue ij

vantplates [...] x larges testes de guerr' p[u]r launces dou[n]t j p[u]r le sengle j large teste de bordeux herneis darg' endorrez [...] v petitz testes p[u]r launces [...] x testes p[u]r launces g[r]a[u]nt & petitz [...] j bastard sadell' app[ar]aillez p[u]r ioustes de guerr' oue les armes du ducs de Glouc' enorrez xiij s iiij d

The parcels of armour that Stephen atte Frythe, King's Armourer has delivered to John Torre' [...] two basinets with visors and two aventails £4, two kettlehats one of which is white (polished steel) with a border of silver gilt the other has one aventail covered with russet velvet 10s., three haubergeons two of which are of small mail (links) of Lombardy (make) 60s., one breastplate with one steel paunce 20s., two paunces and one brayer of steel for pairs of plates with one pair of (mail) sleeves 33s. 4d., one pair of mail chausses 10s., one pallet of Lombardy with one visor 20s., two basinets for jousts of war with *pièces* (reinforcing plates) for helms 40s., one short aventail, one pair of gussets, one little brayer, and three pairs of voiders 13s. 4d., three helms for jousts of peace with two umbrers 33s. 4d., one pair of brigandines covered with red velvet garnished with silver gilt with one pair of plate sleeves 66s. 8d., one pair of brigandines covered with blue baldachin (exotic silk woven with silver thread) garnished with silver with sleeves without plates 66s. 8d., one pair of brigandines covered with red velvet garnished with gilded copper with one steel collar for jousts of war 40s., one pair of plates covered with blue velvet for jousts of war 40s., two pairs of plates covered with black velvet 73s. 4d., one pair of plates for jousts of peace covered with red velvet 40s., one gilt pair of plates for jousts of peace with vambrace and rerebrace, one gauntlet, and one manifer 100s., one pair of plates of blue baldachin which once belonged to King Edward 10s., one pair of brigandines the chest and the back of which are white (polished steel) and the lower (part) covered with blue velvet 26s. 8d., two pairs of legharness called 'foreharness' 13s. 4d., three pairs of complete legharness 20s., two pairs of rerebrace, three pairs of vambrace, and one pair of sabatons 23s. 4d., four pairs of plate gauntlets two of which are garnished with gilt latten 13s. 4d., three pairs of rerebrace, three vambrace, three manifers, and three gauntlets for jousts of peace 30s., one manifer, one vambrace, and one rerebrace for jousts of peace 2s. 6d., eight basinets without aventails with three visors 24s., three breastplates 3s., three pairs of vambrace, one pair of rerebrace 12s., three pairs of complete legharness and two pairs of sabatons 16s. 8d., four old iron haubergeons and five worn out aventails 13s. 4d., one *fine* sword of Bordeaux (make) with the grip of red velvet and the pommel, hilt, and belt well garnished with silver gilt 60s., one sword of Scotland harnessed with gilt copper 6s. 8d., one sword of Bordeaux harnessed with silver gilt with the grip of black velvet 13s. 4d., one old sword with the grip harnessed with gilt copper 3s. 4d., one short war sword the pommel, hilt, and grip harnessed with silver gilt 6s. 8d., one old sword the hilt and pommel of which is harnessed with silver gilt 13s. 4d., one longsword of Bordeaux with the hilt and pommel harnessed with silver gilt 10s., four short war swords not harnessed with silver 30s., ten other longer swords, some for thrusting, others with sharpened edges (for cutting) 20s., one war sword with two vamplates (rondels) for (single combat) in the lists 6s. 8d., one new baselard of Bordeaux with a maple grip – this grip is lightly harnessed with silver gilt 10s., four old baselards and falchions 5s., one large lancehead of Bordeaux harnessed with silver gilt 6s. 8d., five small lanceheads 3s. 4d., ten lance-heads both large and small 13s. 4d., seven short daggers harnessed with silver gilt […] a short knife of Ireland with the sheath (in the shape) of a head – the grip harnessed with silver gilt […] one dagger for the lists with two vamplates (rondels) […] ten large lanceheads for war one of which is for boar hunting […] one large lancehead of Bordeaux harnessed with silver gilt […] five little lanceheads […] ten large and small lanceheads […] one gilt bastard saddle equipped for jousts of war with the arms of the Dukes of Gloucester 13s. 4d.

145

Kew, National Archives, C 145/266/11
Inventory of the Effects of Thomas, Earl of Warwick, Warwick Castle, Warwickshire, 18 July 1397

Ric' Groue [and others provide valuation for] j loricam acer' xxvj s. viij d. iiij Basenett' cu' auentayls liij s. iiij d. j sculls de Basenett' j loricam & j basenet' xvj s. viij d.

Richard Grove [armourer of London and others provide valuation for] one steel hauberk 26s. 8d., four basinets with aventails 53s. 4d., one basinet skull, one hauberk, and one basinet 16s. 8d.

146

Chroniques de Froissart, ed. J. A. Buchon, 15 vols (Paris, 1826), III, p. 317
A Chronicler describes the Preparations made by Thomas, the Earl Marshal, and Henry, Earl of Derby, for a Judicial Duel to be fought at Coventry, Warwickshire, September 1398

Et se pourvéirent ces deux seigneurs grandement de tout ce que pour le champ appartenoit. Et envoya le comte Derby grands messages en Lombardie devers le duc de Milan, pour avoir armures à son point et à sa volonté. Le dit duc descendit moult liement à la prière du comte Derby, et mit à choix un chevalier qui se nommoit messire François, que le comte Derby avoit là envoyé, de toutes ses armures pour servir le dit comte. Avec tout ce, quand le dit chevalier dessus nommé eut avisé et choisi toutes les armures, tant de plates que de mailles du seigneur de Milan, le dit seigneur de Milan d'abondance, et pour faire plaisir et amour au comte Derby, ordonna quatre les meilleurs ouvriers armoyers qui fussent en Lombardie aller en Angleterre avecques le dit chevalier pour entendre à armer à son point le comte Derby. Le comte Maréchal, d'autre part, envoya aussi en Allemagne, et là où il pensoit à recouvrer et être aidé de ses amis, et se pourvéit aussi moult grandement pour tenir la journée.

And so it was that these two great lords extensively provided themselves with all that was necessary for the field (of combat). Thus the Earl of Derby sent word to the Duke of Milan in Lombardy to have armour that fitted him and was to his liking. The Duke was much taken by the Earl's plea, and gave a knight called Sir François – whom the Earl of Derby had sent there – the pick of all his armours for the Earl's use. With all this, when the aforesaid knight had appraised and selected from all the Lord of Milan's armour – both plate and mail, the Lord of Milan – going beyond – and for the affection and love he had for the Earl of Derby, commanded four of the best craftsman armourers in Lombardy to go to England with this knight to ensure the fit of the Earl of Derby's armour. Meanwhile, the Earl Marshal sent to Germany where he thought to obtain (good armour) and was assisted by his friends; for he too thoroughly prepared himself for the day of battle.

147

Household Account of Louis, Duke of Orléans, Paris, 3 December 1397–9 May 1400
Glasgow Museums, R. L. Scott Library, MS E.1939.65.1174, fol. 29r [3 December 1397]

noz amez & feaulx ch[eva]ll[ie]rs & chambellans mess' Regnault guilliam de Barbasan & mess' guill[aum]e de Coleuille quatre Cens frans Cest ass' a chascu' deux cens frans pour leur aidier a supporter les fraiz missions & despens que leur couuendra faire tant a auoir armeures abillem[en]s & choses neccessair' a eulx pour faire c[er]taines armes que a laide de dieu Ilz doiuent p[ro]che[ne]ment faire alencontre daucu[n]s arragonnois

our beloved and loyal knights and chamberlains Sir Regnault Guillaume de Barbazan and Sir Guillaume de Coleville 400 francs – that being 200 francs to each to assist and defray the expenses that they shall accrue to have armours, habiliments, and necessities to perform certain feats of arms which (with God's aid) they must soon do against certain Aragonese (knights)

London, British Library, Additional Charter 2585 [25 July 1398]

Bonifface de morez escuier de corps de mon s' le Duc dorliens dix escuz dor la quelle Jauoye prestre baill' & deliuree a vn heaumier de par' pour cause dunes plates par lui f' pour ycelluj seign[eu]r

Boniface de Morez, personal squire to my Lord the Duke of Orléans ten gold *écus* which I have immediately granted and delivered to a heaumer (plate armourer) of Paris for a pair of plates made by him for this Lord

London, British Library, Additional Charter 2588 [9 May 1400]

This manuscript is very fragmentary

Colart de laon paintre et varlet de Chambre de mon s' le duc dorleans Cinquante
& huit frans pour et a cause dun harnoys de Joustes fait pour le duc en la mani[er]
e quil sensuit Cest assauoir selle pissi[er]e chanfraing & escu dorez dor et semiz de
porc espy de paniture Et pardessus toutes ces choses ont este couu[er]s f' en mani[er]
e de haubregie ou dor gippe Et sur le heaume vn timbre de pl' leue au Ront yssant
dun Rosier Et sur la croupe du ch[ev]al vn porcespy [...] au long et p[ar] dessus la
maille dessus d[i]te tout seme de grans fueilles dorees [...] celleme[n]t la croupi[er]e
du dit ch[ev]al fa[it]e a maille lesquelles choses dessus d[i]ts ont es[t par] moy fa[it]
es pour iiij xx fr'

Colart de Laon, painter and *valet de chambre* to my Lord the Duke of Orléans 58
francs for, and because of, a jousting harness made for the Duke in the following
manner – that is to say: saddle, peytral, shaffron, and shield gilded with gold and
strewn with painted porcupines. Above all these things, it was covered in the manner
of hauberger's craft (mail) with gilt gypsum. And a crest of plumes raised around
issuing from a rosebush on the helm, a porcupine on the crupper of my Lord's horse
[...] along and above this mail completely strewn with large gilt leaves [...] only the
crupper of this horse made of mail. These things aforesaid have been made by me for
four score francs

London, British Library, Additional Charter 2589 [c. 1400]

toutes les pieces darmeure Lesquelles mon s' auoit [...] a Milan

all the pieces of armour which my Lord has (had imported) from Milan

148

London, British Library, Additional Manuscript 21357, fol. 4r
Reply from Sir John Cornwall and Janico Dartasso, Squire, to a Challenge from Household Knights and Squires of Louis, Duke of Orléans,
written at the English Royal Court, c. 1399–1400

Tres honn[er]e sires nous auons veues et lires vos honn[or]e li[ttr]es et p[ar] ycelles
auons entendu que vous portez vn gartier et vne chaine p[ar] telle condit[i]on que
quiconq[ue]s vous electa lun ou laut' il vous doit acomplir c[er]tain' armes a pie [et]
a cheual Cest assauoir dix caulz de lanche assiz sur sell' de coursierz basses deuant
& derriere et targes sans fer et achier les deux bras mis de harnas & bachinet sans
visiere ne bauiere lanches de mesme [apres] la Jouste combatre a cheual xx colz despee
sans Reprinse a selles basses deuant et derriere et en haubregon estui puis ap[re]
s deschendre a pie et combatre xx cops de dague sans Reprinse en haubregon estui

sans aucune m' de harnas mais que tout ainsy quil destenderoit de dessus les cheualx
et puis a piez x cops de hache sans Reprinse en tel harnas co[m]me cascun [...] mais
vne chose nous veous en vos li[ttr]e' a la Jouste de cheual vous deuisez les deux bras
mis et le bachinet sans visiere et au combatre des espees et dagues vous ne faites point
ment[i]on se le bachinet ara visiere ou non ne se les bras seront armez ou non pour
quoy nous vous prions que p[ar] le porteur de ces p[rese]ntes nous voeull' c[er]tefier
se les bras seront mis ou armez et se le bachinet aura visiere ou non Et aussy a la
Jouste en quelle maniere le corps sera armez ou de plates ou de haubregon Car tout
en telle maniere co[m]me vous voudrez vos armes & harnais ordener & deuiser en
telle maniere nous so[m]mes prest et app[ar]eill' de faire & acomplir ainsy sans delay
Sur quoy pour le grant honneur et proesche darmes qui est en vous nous auons grant
volente daprendre encelly mest aueucques nous et a layde de dieu & de saint Jorge
nous vous serons aise des dis gartiers chaines En ault' en vos dictes l[ect]res deuises
auoir seelles espees et dagues p[ar]eilles et aut[re]s choses pour quoy nous pour p[ri]
ons que vous faichiez ordonner deux paires de harnas entiers dont nous cens vous lun
et vous laut' ou nous en ordonnerons deux qui seront p[ar]eil desquelz vous coisuez
ad fin quil ny ait point de tardement Et se ainsy ne vous plaist ordonnez pour vous et
nous ordenerons pour nous Et ainsy ny ara il point de delay En nous faisant scauoir
sil vous plaist le Jour que vous vo[u]dres est' prest & app[ar]eill' au quel nous y serons
aussy prest et ordonnez mais quil ny ait trop loing t[er]me co[m]me quil nous samble
et est aduis que le iiije Jour de mois de may est temps et Jour assez couuenable
Jehan Cornuaille ch[eua]l[ie]r [...]attaise escuier

Most honourable Sirs,
We have seen and read your honourable letters. By these, we have thus understood
that you sport a garter and chain. Whomsoever either of you elect to this (chivalric)
order must accomplish certain feats of arms both on foot and on horseback – that
is to say: ten lance-strokes mounted in saddles for coursers (these saddles being low
in front and behind) with targes without iron or steel, both arms without harness,
basinet without visor or bevor, and lances of the same length. Then, after the joust,
to fight 20 sword-strokes without reprise from horseback in saddles that are low in
front and behind and (armed) in standard haubergeons; thereafter to dismount to
fight 20 dagger-strokes on foot without reprise in a standard haubergeon without
any other type of harness. But then, as soon as they shall have dismounted from
horseback, ten axe-strokes shall be fought on foot without reprise in such harness as
each sees fit. However, we have noticed one discrepancy in your letters: in the joust
on horseback you have stated that the arms are to be left unarmed and the basinet
have not a visor. Yet, for the combat with swords and daggers you make no mention
of whether the basinet shall have a visor or not; nor if the arms shall be armed or
not. To wit, we pray that by sending these present letters we might agree if the arms
shall be left unarmed or armed and if the basinet have visor or not. Also, in what
manner shall the body be armed in the joust? Be it with either pairs of plates or with
a haubergeon? For as you desire all your arms and harness to be agreed and chosen in
such manner we are thus ready and equipped to do and achieve these feats of arms

without delay. Thereupon for the great honour and prowess of arms which is in you, we have a great desire to discover it within ourselves and (with God's aid and that of Saint George) we shall relieve you of these garter chains so that you may accomplish all the aforementioned feats of arms. Furthermore, because in your letters you have stated that we must use similar saddles, swords, daggers, and other things, we pray that you command two pairs of complete harness be made that you shall send both of us. We shall also command two pairs of complete harness be made which shall be the same as yours – you will have the choice of these in order that there be no delay. And so, may it please you to ready yourselves – and for us to ready ourselves – so that there be no delay. If it please you, let it be made known to us the day you wish to be ready and equipped so that we may also be ready and in order. Let it not, however, be in the too distant future. It seems to us that we are of the opinion that 4 May is the most suitable time and day.

John Cornwall, Knight

[Janico] Dartasso, Squire

149

Kew, National Archives, C 145/278/37

Inventory of the Effects of John, Earl of Huntingdon, Dartington, Devon, 21 February 1399/1400

Joh[ann]is Grou' [and others account for] ij justynsad' cu' ij testeres p[ro] equis ij helmes vj maynfers & iij p[ar]ia cirothec' de plate vij vaumbraces & ij p[ar]ia rerbraces & vnu' par de polies [*sic*] & xvij vamplates j pollax de cupro

John Grove [armourer of London and others account for] two jousting saddles with two testers for horses, two helms, six manifers, three pairs of plate gauntlets, seven vambrace and two pairs of rerebrace, one pair of poleyns, 17 vamplates, and one copper pollaxe

150

York, Borthwick Institute, Abp Reg 16: Richard Scrope (1398–1405), fol. 134v

Will of Sir Philip Darcy, Guisborough, Yorkshire, 16 April 1399

philippo filio meo vna' lorica' de milayne

my son Philip a hauberk of Milan (make)

151

Lambeth Palace Library, Register of Archbishop Arundel, fol. 163r–fol. 163v

Will of Eleanor, Duchess of Gloucester, Pleshey Castle, Essex, 9 August 1399

vn habergeon' oue vn Crois de laton m[er]chie sur le pis encontre le cuer quele feust a mon s[eigneu]r son piere

[to my son] one haubergeon marked on the chest with a cross of latten surrounding the heart which belonged to my Lord his father

Part III

Illustrated Glossary

A

Ailettes (**3**, **15**, **18**, **94**)

from the Fr. for little wing, a decorative piece of rigid leather or textile worn at the shoulder; most often of rectangular form. They display the wearer's heraldic blazon referred to as a man's 'arms' (see Figure 1 and Figure 19). In the documents they are often paired with the coat armour – a fabric over-garment for displaying these arms: whence 'coat of arms'. There is no evidence for ailettes or coat armours serving any defensive purpose.

Aketon (**3–115**)

from Arabic *alqūtn*: cotton, a well-padded all-fabric torso defence, usually with sleeves. There are two instances of sleeves reinforced with whale baleen (**9**, **15**). Documents (**28**, **79**) provide detail of materials and construction. It was an essential foundation for the hauberk, haubergeon, and other mail defences (e.g. **22**). That the aketon could also be for men of means or serve as a livery is evidenced by reference to those emblazoned with a red lion with forked tail (**34**) and to the heraldic arms of the Despensers (**35**). They could be upcycled from other defences, as one was made from a gambeson (**9**). The 'white' aketon (**28**, **34**, **39**) possibly had a good-quality linen facing and was thus superior to the standard type.

Anelace (**12**)

a thrusting dagger – the name derived from awl: a stout, cylindrical, sharp-pointed tool for making holes in wood, leather, and other materials.[1]

Arm defences: see *Besagews, Bracer, Couter, Cuir bouilli, Gusset, Manifer, Pauldron, Rerebrace, Sleeves, Spaudlers, Vambrace.*

Arming doublet: see *Doublet.*

Arming sword: see *Sword.*

Armour

coverings: these can be divided into two categories – the first, coverings that are integral to a defence in its construction, such as the facing riveted to the pair of plates or brigandine. The

---

[1]   *Middle English Dictionary*, ed. R. E. Lewis and others (Ann Arbor, MI, 1952–2001), in *Middle English Compendium*, ed. F. McSparran and others (Ann Arbor, MI, 2000–18), online edn.

Figure 1. Detail of an ivory diptych, Parisian, early-fourteenth century.

second are of removable type or easily detached by cutting thread stitching (see Figure 2). They come in a range of materials of varying quality and cost depending on the depth of the buyer's pockets.

linen: see *Linen*.

linings: the regulations of the armourers of London and Paris provide great detail as to materials and construction. See *Pourpoint*. Lining of armour for single combat (**14, 128**), of basinets (**79, 143**), of various defences (**81, 138**), of pallets (**94**), eaten by rats (**101**), insides of armour parts lined with satin (**136**) (see Figure 2 and Figure 3).

packing and carriage of: there are leather bags (**9, 22, 31, 124**) and coffers (**9, 30, 35, 36, 61, 92**) for this purpose. The coffers are mostly made of cuir bouilli.

white (**34, 81, 131, 138, 143, 144**): this means pieces of plate armour that are of polished steel. From this derived the fifteenth-century term 'white harness'/'*harnois blanc*' for a complete harness.

Armourer, linen (**28**)

one who makes textile body defences such as aketons, as well as helmet linings.

Armourer, plate: see *Heaumer*.

Armourers

regulations: of Paris (**1, 16, 79**), of London (**28, 66**), regarding hire of London Armourers' wares for tournaments (**40**).

tools (**140**): this source lists hammers, anvils, bicorns (a common type of anvil), stakes (specially-shaped anvils for shaping armour), tongs, and shears; for sledgehammers see (**104**).

Armpit defences: see *Besagews, Gusset, Voiders*.

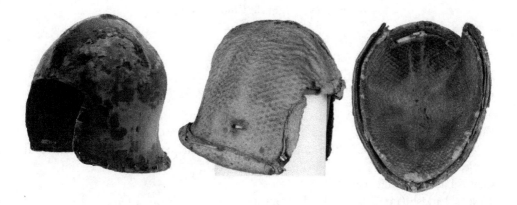

Figure 2. Venetian Sallet or barbute with original lining, Italian, c. 1450.

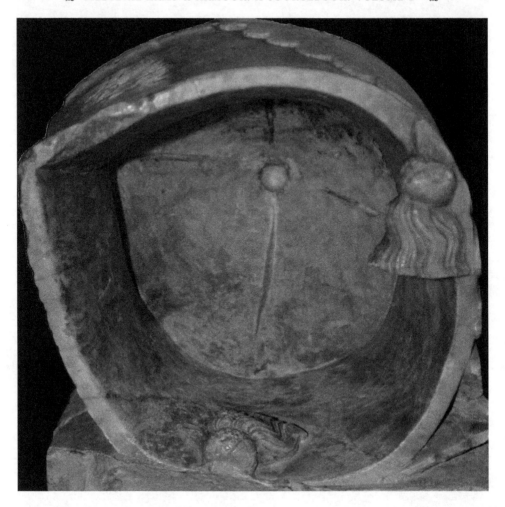

Figure 3. Detail of the carving of the helm lining on the tomb effigy of Sir John Marmion (d. 1387), West Tanfield Church, Yorkshire.

Arrow (see Figure 4)

barbed (**19, 62**).

feathers for: see *Fletching*.

fire-arrows (**125**).

Saracen (**27, 62**): probably trophies brought back from a crusade. The designation 'Saracen' is a medieval shorthand for non-Christian peoples of the Middle and Near East.

shaft: of ash, of birch (**19**).

Turkey, Turkish (**131**): also probably trophies.

other types: barbed, cloth, dog, Scottish, Welsh (**19**). Other than providing some

Figure 4. Arrowhead, fourteenth century.

measurements, there is no more information provided to help identify these various types. See also *Fletcher, Fletching, Proofing, Quiver*, and *Sheaf.*

Assaying, of armour: see *Proofing.*

Aventail (4–145)

from Fr. *aventer* – to exhale. A circular-cone-shaped neck defence of mail attached to the lower edge of the basinet. A leather tab is affixed to the aventail's top edge. The placement of holes in this tab corresponds to the staples riveted around the base of the basinet skull. In current scholarship (following Blair) these are referred to as *vervelles.*[2] However, 'estaples' is employed in a source from England (**105**). A cord is passed through these staples to firmly affix the aventail to the basinet. It can be easily detached by drawing the cord back through the staples (see Figure 9). To better preserve the mail there is reference to latten-coated links (e.g. **81**) as well as fabric aventail-covers (e.g. **35**, **127**). For aventail-covers see also *Hourson.*

Axe

battle axe (**71**, **127**).
of Bordeaux (**105**): possibly refers to the quality of manufacture (see the discussion in the introduction).
Danish (**35**): a long-hafted axe of Norse origin.
furnished and equipped (**124**).
Irish sparth (**27**): another long-hafted axe of distinctive design.[3]
Norse axe (*securis norreise*) (**85**): a long-hafted axe of Norse origin.

---

[2]   C. Blair, *European Armour, circa 1066 to circa 1700* (London, 1958), p. 68.
[3]   For the Irish sparth, see Moffat, 'A Sign of Victory?', pp. 122–43.

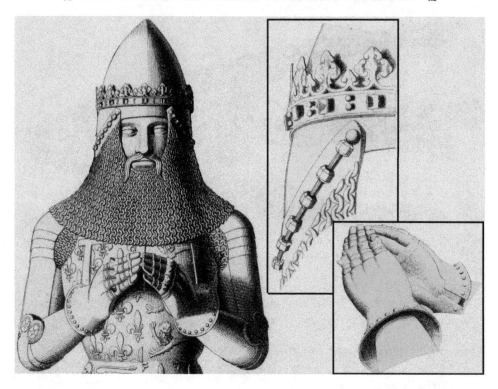

Figure 5. Details of an etching of the tomb effigy of Edward, the Black Prince (d. 1376), Canterbury Cathedral, Kent.

pollaxe (see *Pollaxe*).
Scottish (**131**): a long-hafted axe of distinctive design.[4]
silvered (**108**): inlaid or applied decoration.
with a thrusting spike (**2**).
Turkey, little axe of (**131**): probably a trophy brought back from a crusade.
for war (**72**): probably just an alternative name for battle axe.
wyex (**71**): an Old Eng. name for battle axe.

B

Baldric (7–142)

a stout leather belt fitted with a hook for spanning a crossbow, using the strength of
the body only.

---

4   For the Scottish axe, see Moffat, 'A Sign of Victory?', pp. 122–43.

Baleen

the large keratinous plates from the mouths of baleen whales: filter feeders such as the bowhead and right whale. The substance is used to make cuisses, greaves, gauntlets, spaudlers, reinforced aketon sleeves, and crossbows – as part of the construction of a composite bow-stave. The manner of its use in the construction of defences is found in the Paris Armourers' regulations of 1296 and 1364 (**1** and **79**). In this century baleen gauntlets are a ubiquitous soldier's hand defence.[5]

Barber (**52, 70, 138**)

from Fr. *barbe* (beard): a reinforcing plate strapped over the front of a helmet in Eng. sources; usually for use in the joust (see Figure 6 and Figure 30). It should not be confused with the Fr. *barbière*: bevor – a mail chin and neck defence.

Barbière (**24–128**)

Fr. name for a mail chin and neck defence – see *Bevor*.

Barbuta (**49, 81**)

derived from the Italian for beard: *barba*, it is explicitly a mail defence for the chin and throat. It should not be confused with the fifteenth-century helmet of the same name.

Baselard (**70, 108, 113, 144**)

a dagger with a distinctive H-shaped hilt, named for the town of Basel (see Figure 7).[6] Of Bordeaux (**144**) – of good-quality manufacture from this town.

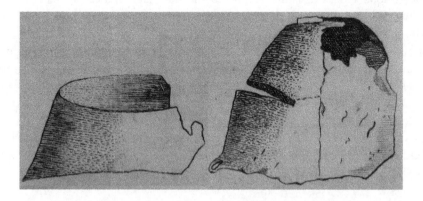

Figure 6. Etching of a (now-lost) early-fourteenth-century helm with barber (plate reinforce), Scottish, 1793.

---

5   Moffat and Spriggs, 'The Use of Baleen for Arms', pp. 211–12.
6   C. Blair, 'The Word "Baselard"', *Journal of the Arms & Armour Society* 11 (1984), pp. 193–206.

Figure 7. Baselard, fourteenth century.

Basinet (2–148)

by far the most ubiquitous helmet type in the sources, its name derives from the Fr. *bacinet*: small basin. It takes many forms, from close-fitting hemispherical to high-peaked conical. Shaped to protect the cheeks, ears, and nape of the neck, the attachment of the aventail provides mail protection for the rest of the neck. It is customary in Anglophone arms and armour scholarship to follow the spellings set out by Blair.[7] I diverge here in order to better reflect the Eng. diminutive of basin.

arming (**85, 88, 115**): a shorthand for its being fully equipped with lining and aventail.

beaten white (**52**): of polished steel hammered from scratch.

black-beaten (**45, 52**): meaning the metal has been left black from the hammer – it has not been planished or polished to a fine finish.

cases ('bacinie[re]s') made for (**124**).

Chiaramonte (poss. Clermont) type (**81**): this is unexplained

coffers for (**92**).

dog, in the manner of a (**81**): *possibly* refers to the visor shape.

of Flanders make (**122, 143**): almost certainly marked in the same way as those of London make.

footsoldiers' (**81**): possibly of a poorer quality and lacking a visor.

high 'bretesque' (**22**): this is unclear, *possibly* in the shape of a castle's battlement.

high, low, old round, round: refers to the roundness of shape and apex height of the helmet.

hounskull: this is an erroneous name for a basinet fitted with a visor with a pointed snout. It is some kind of mail defence for the head and neck of unknown form.[8]

iron parts of (**28**): i.e. the metal parts yet to be lined, fitted with straps, and/or covered with fabric or leather.

letter describing the shape of (**123**).

of London make (**122, 143**): each London craftsman had their own mark. The Wardens of the Craft also had a mark to prove the product was of suitable quality (**66**).

---

[7] Blair, *European Armour*, pp. 51–2.

[8] C. Retsch, 'Warum die Hundsgugel im Spätmittelalter kein Helm war (und was die englische Haube für ein Helm gewesen sein könnte)', *Hieb- und Stichfest. Waffenkunde und Living History. Festschrift für Dr. Alfred Geibig. Jahrbuch der Coburger Landesstiftung* (Petersberg, 2020), pp. 190–215; R. Moffat, 'A word "I was delighted to meet": why we must now bid Auf Wiedersehen to *Hounskull* as the name for the "pig-faced" basinet', *Arms and Armour: Journal of the Royal Armouries* (forthcoming).

Figure 8. Basinet, c. 1350.

with nasal (**70, 81**): a section of metal attached (or integral) to the brow of the helmet, descending over the centre of the face to protect against horizontal blade strokes.

perforations for lining (**1, 79, 81**).

for performing feats of arms (**81**): probably of different construction to those used in war.

Piedmont, made in (**81**).

pouch ('fonceau') made for (**79**).

two pivots at the sides (**81**): the parts by which a visor is raised and lowered.

proofed, half-proofed: see *Proofing*.

skull (**81, 101, 145**): the main bowl of the helmet. Chiaramonte (poss. Clermont) type (**81**): this is unexplained.

with surcils 'eyebrows' (**18**): a unique usage, possibly an applied decoration replicating the effect of these facial features.

template for craftsmen (**81**).

tinned: see *Tin*.

type: Avignon, Liège, London, Lyon, Milan, Paris, Toulouse (**81**). Unfortunately, the shape and style of the variety of distinct types mentioned is not here elucidated.

with umbrer (**35, 45, 86, 144**): a peak of some sort – from Fr. *umbre* and Lat. *umbra* shade.

visor (**9–148**): of various shapes and number of breath and sight apertures (now known as 'breaths' and 'sights') (see Figure 9, Figure 26, and Figure 43). Of Toulouse (**81**), it is not clear if this is made there or is of a distinct style.

Figure 9. The Lyle Bacinet, probably Milanese, late-fourteenth century.

Baton (**4**)

a short club.

Baviera: see *Bevor*.

Besagews (**27, 138**)

plates affixed to protect the armpits; commonly disc-shaped in the fourteenth century. Possibly named for the Fr. for saddlebag (*besage*) as they hang from both shoulders in the manner of a beast of burden. A similar-sounding Fr. word – *besaiguë*: double-headed axe – is more dramatically martial but less convincing in relation to a disc-shaped plate.

Bevor (**22–148**)

from Fr. for bib, derived from the verb *baver*: to dribble, slaver from the mouth. A mail defence that fits closely to the chin and throat. It should not be confused with the piece of plate armour of the same name and function developed in the fifteenth century. Sources in Fr. use the word *barbière* – from *barbe* (beard) for a mail chin and throat defence. This causes some confusion as in Eng. sources a barber (also from Fr.

Figure 10. Etching of a tomb brass of Sir John D'Aubernoun (d. 1339–50),
Stoke D'Abernon Church, Surrey.

barbe) is a reinforcing plate strapped over the front of a helmet. A probable example of betacism – interchangeability of the letters *b* with *v* in both speech and writing – this linguistic quirk is responsible for some interpretative difficulty. The basinet with *baviera* (**81**) might *possibly* have been some sort of integrated solid 'chin plate'.[9]

Biddow (**35, 74, 99**)

a type of dagger. Possibly an Eng. corruption of Bordelais: Bordeaux and its hinterland which was then part of English-controlled Gascony. Long Gascon (**35**) – of the type made or used in the region.

Bohemia: see *Sword,* Bohemia.

Bolt, for crossbow: see *Quarrel.*

Boot, feathered with iron (**27**)

made from overlapping metal scales.

Bordeaux, axe (**105**), sword (**120, 124, 144**), lancehead (**105, 144**)

the sources do not give any indication as to whether these weapons are of a distinct form or simply of good-quality manufacture from this town. The armourer Stephen atte Fryth (**144**) and chronicler Jehan Froissart (**120**) both describe Bordeaux swords as 'fine' (see the discussion in the introduction).

Bow, hand bow

meaning spanned by hand, later known as a longbow – for hunting (**92** and **131**), 'called Turkish' (**19**), of Turkey (**76, 131**), Saracen (**27**). There is one 'called Turkish made of Spanish yew' (**19**). This suggests the designation 'Turkish/Turkey' to have assumed a meaning relating to type and size. This bow is recorded as being 1½ ells long whilst the others are two ells or longer.

Bow-stave, for hand-spanned bow (i.e. longbow) (**92**)

the type of wood (or other material) is sometimes recorded: baleen (**15**), elm (**10, 19**), wood from Ireland (**92**), Irish yew and Spanish yew (**19**). This is presumably due to some noteworthy quality. Some are stated to be white (**92**) or painted (**94**): perhaps for decorative or preservation purposes – or both.

Bowstring (**94, 127**)

no information is provided as to the materials from which they were made.

---

[9] See T. Capwell, *Armour of the English Knight, 1400–1450* (London, 2015), p. 86, for the introduction of this 'chin plate' in the early-fifteenth century.

Figure 11. Detail of an etching of the tomb of Sir Oliver Ingham (d. 1344), Ingham Church, Norfolk.

Bracer (**8–105**)

from Fr. for arm (*bras*) + derivational suffix *-ière*: i.e. 'for the' arm. The word has different meanings. At the very start of the century, a sleeve reinforced with baleen (**8, 9**), then an upper-arm defence (**15, 27, 43**). In the second half of the century a distinction is made between mail sleeves and bracers made of solid plates (**75**), (**84**), pairs of complete (**102**), iron (**105**). It is also found in the form 'braces' (**72**). This type from the second half of the century may be a forerunner of the arm harness comprising vambrace, couter, and rerebrace but possibly of a simpler design and, perhaps, defended the outside of the arm only (see Figure 10). In Fr. sources it seems to mean a solid defence for the upper arm – equivalent to the vambrace in Eng. sources (**22, 49**) – in the latter sources it is for both the outside and inside of the arm, see also (**101**). There is no evidence to suggest that any of these sources refer to an archer's bracer.

Brayer (**14, 22, 144**)

mail defence shaped in the same way as the fabric undergarment for the loins. The 'brayer for the seat of the paunce' (**22**) means that the fabric or leather was affixed to line the mail. Other examples of fabric brayers are (**79, 128**).

Brayette (**128**)

the addition of the *-ette* suffix makes it a diminutive of mail brayer – groin defence.

Breastplate

a solid plate defence for the front of the thorax. It first appears in the documents as the Fr. for breast: *poitrine* (**52**), followed by the Eng. word (**76**). This form is, as yet, unknown. The fact that it is often paired with the pair of plates is indicative of an initial function as a secondary reinforce. A late-fourteenth-century breastplate from the castle armoury of Churburg in the South Tyrol is comprised of a main front plate with additional side sections; the whole being cross-strapped at the rear.[10] There is no mention of the backplate in the Fr. and Eng. documents, nor of the cuirass – the term for the breast- and backplate combined – in common use in the fifteenth century.[11] The breastplate is often noted as being for jousting use. It is quite possible that the addition of thicker, heavier, and more rigid plate defences was not such an impediment to the jouster in the lists as to the warrior on the battlefield. 'Red' (**105**) – this is unexplained. Pair of vices for (**70**) – this is *possibly* a means of affixing them to the pair of plates beneath for extra protection in the joust.[12]

Brigandine, pair of brigandines (**138, 144**)

a torso defence constructed of metal plates riveted to a foundation of strong leather or canvas. For the wealthy, it is usually faced with a luxurious fabric and external silvered or gilt rivet-heads creating a decorative pattern. Its name derives from Italian *corazzine brigantine*: lit. 'brigands' small cuirasses': a torso defence named for the mercenaries who plagued the Italian peninsula. In 1367 'chorazine brighantine' are recorded in the accounts of an Avignon-based Tuscan arms dealer.[13] See also (**81**) for other pieces of armour named for these men. It differs from the pair of plates in that it allows greater freedom of movement. By using many more plates of a smaller size, armourers produced a very flexible defence.[14]

Buckler (**29**)

a small round shield of wood and metal (or all-metal) construction, wielded in

---

[10] O. Trapp, *The Armoury of the Castle of Churburg*, trans. J. G. Mann, 2 vols (London, 1929), II, plates X, XI, and XIIb.

[11] Blair, *European Armour*, p. 38 and p. 61; Capwell, *Armour of the English Knight*, pp. 116–22.

[12] See Moffat, '*Alle myne harneys for the justes*', p. 83.

[13] R. Brun, 'Notes sur le commerce des armes à Avignon au XIVe siècle', *Bibliothèque de l'École des chartes* 109 (1951), pp. 209–31 (at p. 220).

[14] See I. Eaves, 'On the Remains of a Jack of Plate excavated from Beeston Castle in Cheshire', *Journal of the Arms & Armour Society* 13 (1989), pp. 81–154 for more detail.

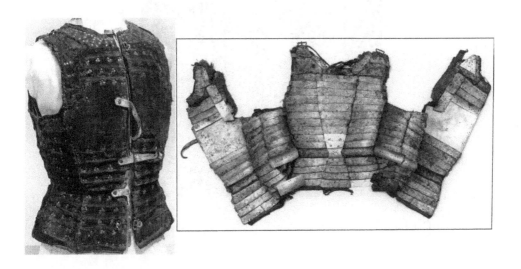

Figure 12. Velvet-covered brigandine, Italian, 1470.

Figure 13. Miniature from the Sherborne Missal, English, 1396–1407.

Figure 14. Detail of the painting on a wooden chest, the 'Bury Chest', English, 1337–40.

conjunction with an arming sword. Sometimes fitted with a sharp central boss, it can be used to attack as well as defend (see Figure 13 and Figure 14).[15] See also *Parma*.

Bullets: see *Gun*.

C

Caltrap (**76, 86, 92, 94**)

a device made of several metal spikes, one of which will remain in an upright position when thrown on the ground. Deployed in large numbers, they are designed to catch in horses' hooves to disrupt a cavalry charge.

Camail (**4–136**)

Fr. for aventail: a mail neck defence attached to the basinet. The Fr. name is probably a borrowing from the Italian *camaglio*: a portmanteau of cape and mail. For the purposes of our study I have translated this into Eng. aventail.

Camisia de Chartres: see *Chemise de Chartres*.

---

[15] For details, see I. Edwards and C. Blair, 'Welsh Bucklers', *Antiquaries Journal* 62 (1982), pp. 74–115, and H. Schmidt, *The Book of the Buckler* (Quidenham, 2015).

Cannon (125)

for shooting garrots (80): large darts, see *Gun*.

Capelline (81)

Italian and Fr. for little cap: a close-fitting hemispherical helmet. An English indenture for service in France of 1431 stipulates that the archers must have 'a capelyn or a palet'.[16] Types: Avignon, English, new, made of scales (81). The nature of these various types is, as yet, unknown. See also *Pallet*.

Casside (9)

a helmet of some sort. Drawing from Classical Lat. literature, only Hugh Bungay (9, 33) employs this word. It is not clear how it differs from other helmet types. In an English Assize of Arms of 1181 both 'cassidem' and 'galeam' are employed to mean helmet.[17]

Catapult: see *Siege engines*.

Cervelière (2–128)

in Eng. and Fr. sources a helmet lining. Italian *cervelliera* (81) is a metal skullcap.

Chambly, mail of (24, 31, 121)

a town north of Paris. Nearby Puiseux-le-Hauberger (lit. Hauberger Mill Lade) preserves in its name the memory of the mail-maker's craft. The product must have been of some quality to be worthy of note in these documents.

Chapeau de Montauban (4, 5, 22, 31, 81)

a helmet most probably named after the town of Montauban near Toulouse. The documents do not confirm if they were produced there or were, perhaps, made in the shape of a distinctive fashion of hat sported by the Montalbanais. It might have been similar in shape and function to the chapel de fer. An anonymous Frenchman writing of the armour borne in his day (1446) tells us that:

chapeaux de Montauban are round on the head with a two-inch-high crest in the middle as long as the top (i.e. a medial keel running from front to rear). And right around is a brim four or five inches wide in the shape and manner of a chapeau (hat).

les chappeaulx de montaulban sont Rons en teste a vne creste ou meilleu qui vait tout du long de la haulteur de deux doiz Et tout autour y a vng auantal de quatre ou de cinq doiz de large en forme et maniere dun chapeau.[18]

---

[16] Carlisle Archives, DLONS/L/5/1/50/12. Thanks are due to Ms Louise Smith for her kind assistance with locating this document.

[17] *Select Charters and other Illustrations of English Constitutional History* [...], ed. W. Stubbs, 8th edn (Oxford, 1870), pp. 154–5.

[18] Paris, Bibliothèque nationale de France, MS fr. 1997, fol. 65r.

Chapel de fer (4–141)

Fr. for iron hat – the helmet skull of single-piece or segmented construction with a wide brim. Beaten white (52): of polished steel hammered from scratch. With visor, round, Milan type, with rivets around the skull, made to bear a plume, in the style of a small basket (Italian *cabasette*) (81) – the sources provide no information as to the nature of these different types. Leather coffers for (36).

Chapel of sinew (12–86)

presumably a helmet of the same shape as the chapel de fer but constructed of animal sinew.

Chausses (4–144)

leg defences constructed of mail links in the form of fabric hose. Of silver (42), of latten (49) – reveals the use of precious-metal-covered, and copper-alloy, wire for decorative purposes. For the tourney (74) almost certainly constructed of larger mail links – see *Mail*. There is a single instance of plate chausses (61).

Figure 15. Detail of an etching of the tomb of Aymer de Valence (d. 1324), Westminster Abbey.

Chemise de Chartres/ Camisia de Chartres (**2, 14, 22, 27, 31**)

'A garment in the shape of, and that had come into contact with, the *Sancta Camisia* of Chartres cathedral'.[19] The *Camisia* was held to have been worn by the Virgin Mary as she gave birth to the Christ Child. It offers the warrior sacred protection should all his worldly defences be penetrated.

Ciroteca: see *Gauntlet.*

Coat armour (**3, 18, 23, 109, 128**)

a fabric over-garment for the body worn over armour. It displays a heraldic blazon referred to as a man's 'arms': whence 'coat of arms'. Currently, it is often incorrectly referred to as a surcoat. Usually tailored from a sumptuous textile, there is no evidence in the documents for it having any defensive properties (see Figure 16, Figure 17, Figure 26, and Figure 43).

Coat of mail, of iron, of steel

an alternative name for the haubergeon usually found in Fr. documents in the form *cote de fer* (**110, 125, 126, 136**) or *cote d'acier* (**124**).

Coat of plates

a modern name applied to the pair of plates. The term is nowhere used in the documents. See *Pair of Plates.*

Coif (**7–80**)

a mail head defence of balaclava form, named for a type of close-fitting headwear common in medieval Europe (see Figure 16 and Figure 45).[20] Of the old type (**74**) – *possibly* with a flat top as seen in tomb effigies of previous centuries. With latten fleur-de-lys (**74**) – a decoration produced by incorporating copper-alloy wire links into the mail (see Figure 16). The Lat. form *tena* is found in (**7**).

Coif, of Chartres

a singular occurrence (**2**), most probably a slight misunderstanding of the Chemise de Chartres by an English religious writer.[21]

Collar

neck defence, for crossbowmen (**20**), of linen (**14, 23**): made of tough fabric, of plate

19 Moffat, '*The Manner of Arming Knights for the Tourney*', p. 10.
20 See the entry in *The Encyclopedia of Medieval Dress and Textiles of the British Isles, c. 450–1450*, ed. G. Owen-Crocker, E. Coatsworth, and M. Hayward (Leiden, 2012).
21 Moffat, '*The Manner of Arming Knights for the Tourney*', pp. 8–11.

Figure 16. Tomb effigy, Spanish, early-fourteenth century.

(**57, 138**): meaning of solid plates or pair-of-plates construction (see Figure 15). For 'pair-of-plates construction' see *Pair of Plates*.

Cologne: see *Sword*.

Construction, 'pair-of-plates' type: see *Pair of Plates*.

Coppegorge

a knife of some unknown sort – lit. cutthroat in Fr. – a unique usage (**99**).

Coronal (**27–143**)

lit. 'little crown': a jousting lancehead comprised of prongs designed to catch in an opponent's armour, causing the lance-shaft to shatter. Employed in the joust of peace rather than for war (see Figure 17).

Corset (**4–79**)

of fabric, mail, steel, iron, plate. Diminutive of Fr. *cors* (body), this torso defence probably reflects the small shape and close fit of the fabric garment of the same name of everyday wear.

Cote-pointe, coustepoint (**56, 79, 85**)

Fr. for a pourpointed coat – see *Pourpoint*.

Couter (**4–92**)

from Fr. for elbow (*coude*) + derivational suffix *-ière*: i.e. 'for the' elbow. A shaped defensive plate secured by means of a strap and buckle. Some have an extending 'wing' providing protection for the crook. When combined with the rest of the arm defences (vambrace and rerebrace) it is sometimes referred to – usually in Fr. sources – as arm harness.

Figure 17. Miniature from the Sherborne Missal, English, 1396–1407.

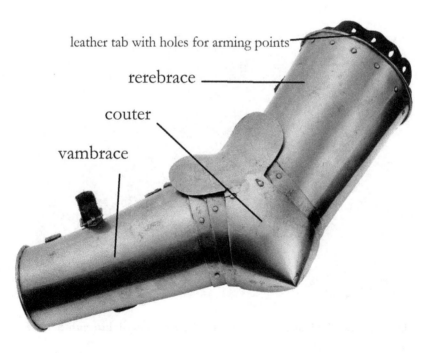

Figure 18. Plate arm defence from the 'Avant' harness, Milanese, 1438–40.

Cover, for horse: see *Horse cover*.

Cressets, of iron for shooting fire (**94**)

clearly a projectile of some sort.

Crests (**9–147**)

a decoration affixed to a helmet often displaying heraldic arms (see Figure 30 and Figure 17). There are a wide variety of forms and materials: gilt copper, and gilt nails, parchment, peacock feathers, pearls (**9, 33**), plume (**147**), for chapel de fer (**81**), plume/crest holder (**81**) (see Figure 28), of the leopard for the Black Prince's tomb effigy (**100**).

Crossbow (**4–142**)

a predominantly hand-held missile weapon deployed in large numbers in this period. It varied in size as is evidenced by the categorization 'one foot' or 'two foot': this deriving from the length of the bow-stave.[22] One is recorded as being of six feet in length (**94**). The stock – called the tiller – is usually of wood. Two different types are mentioned in the documents: wood and horn. This indicates the manner of construction of the bow-stave – the first being only wood. Species are sometimes specified, for instance: elm, holly, and yew. The second, horn, is a shorthand for

Figure 19. Detail of an ivory mirror case, Parisian, early-fourteenth century.

---

[22] M. Loades, *The Crossbow* (Oxford, 2018), p. 35; T. Richardson, 'Springald Sizes in 14th-Century England', *ICOMAM 50: Papers on Arms and Military History, 1957–2007*, ed. R. D. Smith (Leeds, 2007), pp. 326–31.

Figure 20. Wooden crossbow. The bow-stave is fourteenth century,

Figure 21. Composite crossbow, fifteenth century.

what are now referred to as composite crossbows.[23] The stave is constructed of a wooden core wrapped in several layers of horn, and/or baleen, and sinew – the baleen 'bellies' (**11**) and 'ribs' (**57**) almost certainly refer to these components (see Figure 21). Called 'savage' (**94**): this is not clear – perhaps a moniker for an individual piece. This name is also applied to a springald (**92**): a large base-set torsion weapon of similar design implying a degree of interchangeability between the two. Called 'pee' (**92**): possibly a Fr. variant of *pied*: foot – meaning set on a base. There are two examples of the place of origin or type – Genoa (**4**) and Turkey (**131**). None of the documents give information as to the materials used to make the cords. Tools for constructing (**27**) – unfortunately these are not individually described. Trigger nut – a component of the release mechanism often made of stag antler.

Crossbow spanning devices

the way a crossbow is spanned depends on the draw weight. A hook set on a belt (baldric) can be used for some. A crossbowman places his foot in a stirrup set at the front of the tiller and uses the force of his body to span. More powerful crossbows require a mechanical device of some sort. Thus we find the types: torsion – derived from Lat. *tortione*: to twist (e.g. **4**, **10**), as well as those that are spanned with a vice (e.g. **35**).

Crupper (4–147)

a defence for the hindquarters of a horse.

Cuir bouilli

in a literal sense in Fr. 'boiled leather', this is a substance made of animal hide that has been soaked and heat treated to shape and harden it. Mustilers (**2**): lower leg defences. Cuisses (**27**): thigh defences. Couters (**35**), vambrace (**70**): arm defences. Arm, leg, and foot defences for jousting, and pallet: small helmet (**131**). Cuirie for the tourney (**79**). It was certainly a material well suited to the construction of scabbards (**4**) and bespoke cases for the care and transport of metal armour (**9**, **68**).[24]

Cuirie (1–94)

from the Fr. for a large piece of leather – a cuir bouilli (hardened leather) defence for the torso. See (**79**) for constructional detail. It has been relegated from the battlefield to use in the tourney by the time the regulations in (**79**) are promulgated. For the tourney (**92**, **94**).

Cuisse (1–101)

Fr. for thigh – a defence for this part of the body. It can be of a single plate,

[23] A. G. Credland, 'Crossbow Remains (Part 2)', *Journal of the Society of Archer-Antiquaries* 9 (1981), pp. 9–16.
[24] For recently-excavated defences, see M. Rijkelijkhuizen and M. Volken, 'A poor man's armour? Late-medieval leather armour from excavations in the Netherlands', *Leather in Warfare: Attack, Defence and the Unexpected*, ed. Q. Mould (Leeds, 2017), pp. 57–77.

pair-of-plates construction, mail (**57**), cuir bouilli (**43**), padded fabric, or baleen (**31**, **34**). For 'pair-of-plates construction' see *Pair of Plates*. It is affixed by means of straps and buckles. With poleyns attached (**35**) – integrated with knee defences. When incorporated into the complete leg defence with the poleyn and greave it forms the legharness (see Figure 33). Cuisse for destrier – a single occurrence (**65**), this *perhaps* refers to some kind of solid leather or cuir bouilli defence for the warhorse's forelegs.

D

Dagger, for the lists (**144**), rondel

rondels are disc-shaped plates – here comprising a hand guard and pommel. For the difference between a dagger and a knife, see *Knife*. See also *Anelace, Baselard, Biddow, Coppegorge, Misericord*.

Danish axe: see *Axe*.

Dart (**46, 56, 143**), of ash (**80**)

a light casting spear that can be hurled over-arm. It may well be distinguished from the lance by its being fitted with fletchings.

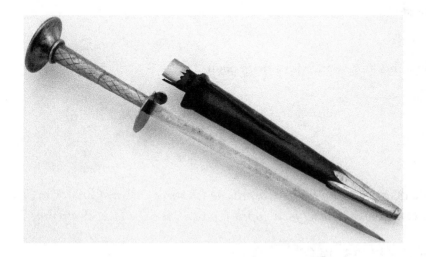

Figure 22. Rondel dagger and sheath, c. 1500.

Doublet (71–128)

as everyday attire: a padded, close-fitted torso garment. In the context of armour: a padded foundation sewn with reinforced holes (eyes). Through the eyes pass the laces (points) to which the steel plates of the harness are attached through pierced leather tabs. It is called an arming doublet at the start of the fifteenth century. The 'doublet for armour' (**131**) is clearly an example. No surviving medieval arming doublets have, as yet, come down to us.[25] See also *Jupon.*

Duel, equipment for (**69, 84, 128, 137, 146**)

harness for single combat such as a judicial duel. Parity of the manufacture and design would have been of paramount importance to the combatants and judges.

E

Ensis, -em

a Lat. word for sword, used interchangeably with *gladius, -um.*

Escutcheon (**4, 35, 74, 80, 85, 143**)

a heraldic device in the shape of a shield.

Espee, Espie

Fr. for sword.

Estoc (**80**)

Fr. for a thrusting sword with a sharp point.

F

Fabric defences: see *Aketon, Chemise de Chartres, Collar, Corset, Cuisse, Fustian, Gambeson, Greave, Jack, Jupel, Jupon, Linen, Paltock, Pourpoint, Trapper.*

Falchion (**27, 35, 144**)

---

[25]   See Moffat, "'Armed & redy to come to the felde'", pp. 121–33, for further detail.

a heavy sword with cleaver-like blade flaring at the tip. A fine example of this weapon is the Conyers Falchion in Durham Cathedral.[26]

False stirrup (54, 93)

possibly some kind of mace of currently-unknown form.

Flail (2)

a close-quarter weapon developed from an agricultural implement.

Flancher (4, 24)

a horse's flank defence.

Fletcher (92)

a man who crafts arrow fletchings. By this period it most likely applies to the maker, or assembler, of the complete arrow.

Fletching (10–129)

a bird's flight feathers (or other materials) set on the shaft of an arrow or quarrel to ensure true flight. The word derives from Fr. *flèche* – arrow – possibly cognate with Eng. 'fledge': to develop flight feathers. It is applied to the shot of hand-spanned bows (i.e. longbows), crossbows, and springalds: the former of goose or peacock (129), the latter two most often of copper, iron, latten, or wood (e.g. 10, 53) (see Figure 42).

Foot defences

see *Cuir bouilli, Jamber, Sabater, Sabaton, Shoes.*

Furbisher (12, 59)

a craftsman who polishes and refits armour and weapons.

Fustian

a strong fabric made from any two of cotton, flax, or wool. Banners of (125), capelline covered in (81), jacks of (99, 113, 143), pair of plates covered in (80).

---

[26] For several examples, see R. W. Jones, '".j. veel feble fauchon dil anxien temps." The Selection of the Falchion as Symbol of Tenure: Form, Function and Symbolism', *The Sword: Form and Thought*, ed. L. Deutscher, M. Kaiser, and S. Wetzler (Woodbridge, 2019), pp. 167–75.

G

Gadelings (69)

knuckleduster-like spikes on a gauntlet, from gad/goad: 'sharp point, spike' + suffix *-lings* meaning small (see Figure 5).

Gaignepain (15, 34, 42)

a type of specialized gauntlet for the right hand for use in the tourney and joust from the late-thirteenth century.[27] The documents provide no evidence for its form or construction.

Galea, -am (2–118)

a Classical Lat. word for helmet, in the practical working sources of our period its specific meaning is helm.

Gambeson (1–79)

a padded torso defence borne on its own or above armour.[28] Details as to the manner of its construction are in (**1**). The noun can be used adjectively as 'gamboised'. There are gamboised leg and horse defences mentioned in the documents (**4, 24, 79**). A possible differentiation between it and the pourpoint is the shape of the padded sections: the former stitched in long parallel tubes or strips – the latter in smaller sections of square or lozenge shape (see Figure 23 and Figure 2). There is an instance of one being made into an aketon (**9**).

Garba: see *Sheaf.*

Garrot (46)

almost certainly Fr. for springald: a large crossbow-type weapon set on a base. It is of the same etymological origin as garrotte, suggesting the build-up of torsional force by twisting ropes. The ammunition is referred to in Fr. as *carreaux à garrot* (garrot quarrels) (**46**). There is one instance of it being ammunition for cannon (**80**). Garrot is also, confusingly, an Eng. name applied to the large quarrels shot by the springald (**35, 39, 41, 62**).

---

[27] Moffat, '*The Manner of Arming Knights for the Tourney*', pp. 15–17.
[28] For the etymology and origin, see the entry in *The Encyclopedia of Medieval Dress and Textiles of the British Isles, c. 450–1450*, ed. G. Owen-Crocker, E. Coatsworth, and M. Hayward (Leiden, 2012).

Figure 23. Etching of the tomb effigy of Sir Robert Shurland, Minster Church, Kent, c. 1325.

Gauntlet (1–149)

an armoured glove. A diminutive of *gaunt* (Fr. glove), they are frequently described as 'of iron' or 'of plate', meaning they are constructed of metal plates riveted to a canvas or leather glove, these plates being either covered with fabric with exposed external rivet-heads, or left uncovered – both being of pair-of-plates construction (see Figure 25).[29] For 'pair-of-plates construction' see *Pair of Plates*. Baleen, as well as iron and steel, was used in their manufacture (**1**), this type being in common use by soldiers.[30] This Parisian source also provides information on how best to protect the metal parts from corrosion. The century saw the introduction of the 'hourglass' form,[31] consisting of a large main section with a flaring cuff narrowing at the wrist then extending over the hand (see Figure 5, Figure 24, Figure 26, and Figure 43). This design allows greater manoeuvrability as well as providing increased protection. The knuckles could be fitted with spikes (see *Gadelings*). Many of our documents' writers employ the Classical Lat. *ciroteca* (e.g. **9**) – itself a borrowing from Ancient Greek.

Gauntlet, of mail (39, 48)

by constructing mail from various sizes of link, intricate shapes were formed – even for each finger (see Figure 16).

Genoa: see *Crossbow* and *Sword*, longsword.

Genuler (2, 7, 25)

a knee defence of some sort. From the Fr. for knee (*genou*) + derivational suffix *-ière*: i.e. 'for the' knee. Probably a forerunner of the poleyn but of a simpler design and likely lacking a side wing. The documents do not state if they are constructed of fabric or solid materials – or both.[32]

Gisarme (35, 80, 85)

a long-bladed staff weapon most often associated with common soldiers.

Gladius, -um (2–142)

a Lat. word for sword, used interchangeably with *ensis, -em*.

Glaive (4, 54, 85, 99, 112, 125)

a long-bladed staff weapon, it most frequently appears in Fr. sources where the word

---

[29] B. Thordeman, *Armour from the Battle of Wisby, 1361*, 2 vols (Copenhagen, 1939), I, pp. 230–44.
[30] Moffat and Spriggs, 'The Use of Baleen for Arms', pp. 211–12.
[31] Thordeman, *Armour from the Battle of Wisby*, I, pp. 234–7; J. G. Mann, 'Two 14th-Century Gauntlets from Ripon Cathedral', *Antiquaries Journal* 22 (1942), pp. 113–22; Blair, *European Armour*, p. 66.
[32] Moffat, '*The Manner of Arming Knights for the Tourney*', p. 8.

Figure 24. Gauntlet, possibly English, c. 1350.

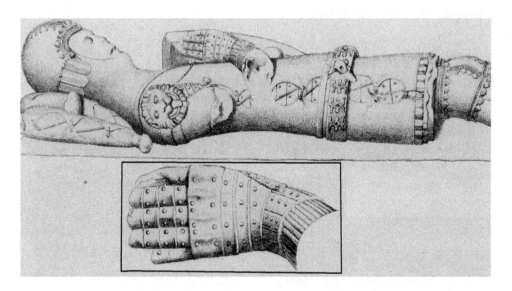

Figure 25. Etching of the tomb effigy of an unknown knight, Ash Church, Kent, early-fourteenth century.

is somewhat nebulous, being used more generally for lancehead and blade (e.g. **54, 85, 112, 125**). Glaive-head (**4, 24, 74**).

Godendag (**80, 85**)

Dutch for 'good day': a wooden club with metal spikes.

Gorget (**1–141**)

derived from Fr. for throat (*gorge*): a mail neck defence lined and covered with fabric. 'High' (**22, 24**) refers to it providing more protection to the throat and chin, 'double' (**24, 27, 31, 57, 61**) to it incorporating two layers of mail.

Grapper (**27–138**)

from Fr. *aggrape* (grip, seize, clutch), a fitted section behind the grip of the lance to engage in the lance-rest. This is a metal bracket attached to the top right of the breastplate, which takes its name from Fr. *arrêt*: stop – as this is its function. When the grapper engages the lance-rest, the wielder's lance does not shoot backwards on impact. Moreover, the full force of man and horse is directed through the lancehead. This system was used in both war and the joust.

Great sword: see *Sword*, longsword.

Greave (**2–137**)

lower leg defence (see Figure 33). Of unclear etymology, it comprises two shaped, hinged metal plates strapped and buckled together to encase the shin and calf. 'Closed' (**4**) means fully-encompassing. A demi-greave (**4**) protects the front of the leg only (see Figure 10 and Figure 15). There is one instance of their being of padded fabric (pourpointed) (**8**). They can also be of baleen (**34**) or leather (**92, 94**). When combined with the rest of the leg defences (poleyn and cuisse) it is called the legharness (see Figure 33).

Groin defences: see *Brayer, Brayette, Gusset, Paunce.*

Guige (**5, 9**)

shield strap (see Figure 23 and Figure 45).

Gun

we find artillery pieces of various types: of latten (**53**), with three chambers, large iron (**92**), rybaude (**92**): a field piece comprised of multiple guns mounted on a carriage. Payment was made for helving guns – fitting them with wooden stocks (**92**) – *possibly* suggesting hand-held weapons. Those at Durham Priory might also be handguns (**127**). Pellets of lead for (**92**) – an early name for bullet.

Gunpowder, materials for

saltpetre, quick sulphur, willow faggots (**92**) and (**94**).

Gusset (**4–144**)

a section of mail fitted to the arming doublet at the armpit, elbow crook, or groin – acts as a voider.

H

Hand defences: see *Baleen, Dagger* with rondel, *Gadelings, Gaignepain, Gauntlet, Sword,* with vamplates.

Harness (**9–148**)

the origins of this word are obscure. By the time of our sources it is a well-established term for the complete assemblage of defences for the body. As the horse is strapped and buckled into its harness so the man is into his. The term is also applied to the combined plate defences for the leg: legharness (e.g. **78**) and, often in Fr. documents, arm harness (e.g. **58**). The word in past-participle form is also employed for 'decorated' or 'equipped' – often in relation to sword fittings (e.g. **144**).

Harness, of mail (**49, 58, 70**)

the meaning here being that the entire body is protected by a combination of the various separate body defences of mail, such as paunces and sleeves.

Hasegay: see *Lancegay.*

Haubergeon (**4–151**)

a mail body defence of a shorter form than the hauberk, its name being a diminutive thereof. It serves as one of the most common armour-types in our period. The sources record a variety of types and forms: light (**70**), standard (**148**), of large mail links for the tourney (**61**), of Chambly make (**121**) (see Figure 27).

Hauberger (**9–147**)

lit. 'one who crafts hauberks': a mail-maker.

Figure 26. Detail of a carved and gilded altarpiece produced for Champmol Monastery, Burgundy, in the 1390s.

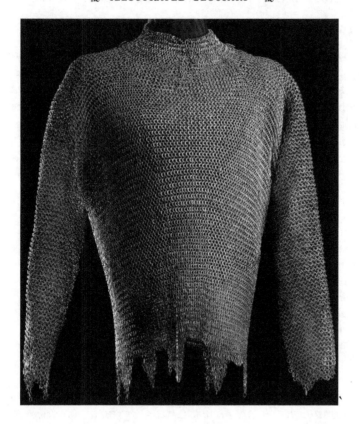

Figure 27. Haubergeon, fourteenth century, with fifteenth-century modifications at the neck.

Hauberk (2–145)

a long mail body defence. The etymology has been traced back to Old Norse *hals* (neck) + *bergan* (to protect) and adopted by various European languages.[33] By our period the appellation is firmly established as being for this long mail defence. For tourneying: a heavier defence constructed of larger links.[34] Of Chambly make (**31**). Standards for: separate mail neck defences – see *Standard*. For the Lat. word for hauberk see *Lorica*.

Heaumer (28–147)

lit. 'one who crafts helms'. By the fourteenth century it was a catch-all name for plate armourer or – as the Londoners in 1347 put it – those who make armour 'forged with the hammer'.

---

[33] For example: *The Oxford English Dictionary*, ed. J. Simpson (Oxford, 2004), online edn.
[34] See Moffat, '*The Manner of Arming Knights for the Tourney*', pp. 14–15.

Helm (2–149)

a helmet of large form enclosing the entire head (see Figure 17, Figure 19, Figure 28, Figure 29, and Figure 30). It consists of several plates riveted together, having apertures for vision and perforations for ventilation (now known as 'sights' and 'breaths'). It is currently categorized in the scholarship as a 'great helm' to distinguish it from other types.[35] This term does not appear in the sources. Its diminutive – helmet – is a word that makes its first appearance in fifteenth-century Eng. sources. The Classical Lat. word *galea, -am*, used by many of our writers, is a specific designation for helm by this century.

> black-beaten (**45**): meaning the metal has been left black from the hammer – it has not been planished or polished to a fine finish.
> gilded, gilt (**3**, **34**, **61**)
> for the joust (e.g. **43**): by this century a heavier, better-reinforced piece of equipment designed to reduce the chance of injury from an opponent's lance. The front can also be fitted with a reinforcing barber or *pièce* (see Figure 6 and Figure 30).
> for the tourney (**27**, **34**, **61**): of an, as yet, unknown form. Gilt (**43**).
> types: Catalan, Catalan crested, Chambéry – unfortunately, the shape and style of the variety of distinct types mentioned (**81**) is not here revealed.
> for war: this adjective is used to differentiate it from those for jousting and tourneying (e.g. **27**).

Helmets: see *Basinet, Capelline, Casside, Cervelière (cervelliera), Chapeau de Montauban, Chapel de fer, Chapel of sinew, Crests, Galea, Helm, Hounskull, Kettlehat, Pallet, Skull, Skullcap, Vetta.*

Hide, animal: see *Leather.*

Horse armour: see *Crupper, Cuisse* for destrier, *Flancher, Gambeson, Horse cover, Jazerant, Peytral, Shaffron, Tester, Trapper.*

Horse cover (4–70)

a mail defence protecting most of the horse – from Fr. *couverture,* from Lat. *coopertura.* There are a few references to 'gamboised' (i.e. padded fabric) horse covers (see *Gambeson*) and one of plate (**65**): this most likely means of pair-of-plates construction. For 'pair-of-plates construction' see *Pair of Plates.* The cover could also be crafted in the manner of the lavish jazerant. That it is in the main a mail defence is clearly evidenced by various summons to provide military service in English dominions from the 1270s. Men of high status were obliged to serve with an expensive *equus coopertus* whilst those lower down had to provide a simple

---

35 Blair, *European Armour*, p. 37 and p. 40.

Figure 28. Crown-plate of a helm, the 'Braidwood Gill helm', fitted with a crest holder, early-fourteenth century.

Figure 29. Helm from the tomb of Sir Richard Pembridge (d. 1375), Hereford Cathedral.

Figure 30. Stained glass panel, German, late-fourteenth century.

equus discopertus.[36] The executors of the Bishop of London in 1303 (**7**) make a very clear distinction between iron (mail) horse covers and horse trappers.

Hounskull: see *Basinet.*

Hourson (**79, 101, 126, 128, 136**)

a fabric aventail-cover – almost certainly cognate with the 'vrysoun ouer þe auentayle' described in the arming of the Green Knight of the popular English romance.[37] Eaten by rats (**101**).

Huce (**24, 32**)

a shield cover.

I

Indies, shield of, jazerant of (**24**)

exotic imports to Christendom.

J

Jack (**34–143**)

sharing its name with the short, close-fitting jacket of everyday attire, the fighting version was (almost certainly) better stuffed for protection. Of all-textile construction, some were made of fustian: a strong fabric made from any two of cotton, flax, or wool (**99, 113, 143**). An example – possibly from our period – is the Rothwell jack from a church in West Yorkshire.[38] They were faced with luxurious fabrics for those with the necessary means (e.g. **99**) and came in a variety of types: e.g. light jack (**34**) and jack of defence (**78**).

---

[36] *Parliamentary Writs and Writs of Military Summons*, ed. F. Palgrave, 2 vols (London, 1827–34), I, pp. 201, 231, and 238.

[37] See Capwell, *Armour of the English Knight*, pp. 72–3.

[38] See the entry in *The Encyclopedia of Medieval Dress and Textiles of the British Isles, c. 450–1450*, ed. G. Owen-Crocker, E. Coatsworth and M. Hayward (Leiden, 2012).

Jamber (**6–140**)

a leg defence of unknown form, most likely of pair-of-plates construction. For 'pair-of-plates construction' see *Pair of Plates*. Its name derives from Fr. leg (*jambe*) + derivational suffix *-ière*: i.e. 'for the' leg. Jambers with the vamps (feet) (**6**): also providing defence for the foot. Burnished (**33**): polished-steel finish, meaning the plates remain uncovered. With poleyns (**33**): these solid knee defences could certainly be integrated into the pair-of-plates construction of the entire piece. Cuisses with jambers of cuir bouilli also confirm the possibility of this integration (**45**).

Jazerant (**4–136**)

a mail hauberk covered with rough silk-waste and inserted into a beautifully-made garment of luxurious textiles.[39] A French source describes the manner of their construction (**79**). Other sections of mail – sleeves, paunces, and even horse covers (**24, 35**) – were also made in this lavish style. Of the Indies (**24**) – one from the East (see Figure 31).

Joust of peace, armour for (**65, 131, 138, 144**)

by this century heavier, better-reinforced pieces of equipment to reduce chances of injury from an incoming lance.

Joust of war, armour for (**137, 143, 144**)

this is not completely clear from these sources; perhaps it apes the style of war harness but is of thicker and heavier pieces. It was most probably employed in single combat, often between men from warring kingdoms such as Scotland and England. We should be *very* wary of making a definite distinction at this time. Henry, earl of Derby, had a pair of plates (torso defence) 'both for peace and for war' (**138**).

Jousting armour – complete harness for (**124**): see *Barber, Breastplate, Gaignepain, Grapper, Helm, Lance-rest, Manifer, Pair of Plates, Pièce, Vambrace* with wing.

Jousting lance and fittings: see *Coronal, Grapper, Lance, Lance-rest, Vamplate.*

Jupel (**57**)

referred to as 'armour of linen', this is a fabric torso defence or foundation for metal armour of some kind, perhaps an Anglo-Norman variation of Fr. *jupon.*

---

[39]   For its etymology and introduction to Christendom from the East, see the entry in *The Encyclopedia of Medieval Dress and Textiles of the British Isles, c. 450–1450*, ed. G. Owen-Crocker, E. Coatsworth and M. Hayward (Leiden, 2012).

Figure 31. Jazerant, South Asian, post-medieval.

Jupon

a close-fitting garment. It appears only once in a Fr. source (**79**) and is not used to describe a garment displaying heraldic arms – see *Coat armour*. In another Fr. source the jupon is evidently an arming doublet. Sir Philippe de Mézières recounts a tale of Godfrey of Bouillon being 'en so[n] Juppon darmer en vng petit paueillon' ('in his arming jupon in a little pavilion'). Emissaries sent from the Sultan do not realize that he is the commander of the crusader army as he is not in fine robes or armour but simply 'en son Juppon'.[40]

K

Kettlehat (**70**, **95**, **111**, **129**, **131**, **143**, **144**)

an Eng. (and Scots) nickname for the chapel de fer, due to its similarity to the domestic utensil (see Figure 15, Figure 32, and Figure 49). The British Museum holds an example excavated in London that has been converted into a kettle.

[40]   Paris, Bibliothèque nationale de France, MS NAF 25164, fol. 133v.

Figure 32. Chapel de fer or kettlehat, late-fifteenth century.

Knife

a knife differs from a dagger in that its blade always has a cutting edge (or edges) and is also for everyday non-martial use. A dagger is for thrusting at an opponent and does not necessarily have a cutting edge. A variety of knife-types are recorded: Irish (**19**, **144**), Welsh (**35**, **36**), Gascon (**80**): these might have seemed somewhat exotic to an Englishman. Hunting (**35**): comprised of one large knife with a set of by-knives in its sheath (now categorized as a trousse) used in the unmaking of quarry.

L

Lance

a staff weapon of a type that had been wielded by warriors for centuries. Ranging in length from roughly nine to fourteen feet, one source records some as 'long' (**94**). Those for jousts were openly measured (**135**). The separation of the use of the word lance for mounted combat and spear for foot – now commonly employed – is not a contemporary one.[41] Red lance with Bordeaux head (**105**) – this is unexplained. See also *Spear*.

Lancegay, also as hasegay (**131, 142, 143**)

a casting spear of unknown form. The name, originating in the Berber language, belies its origin in North Africa and use in Southern Spain by light horsemen.[42]

Lance-rest

from Fr. *arrêt de lance*: lit. 'lance stop' – a hinged bracket affixed to the top right of the breastplate. A lance fitted with a grapper behind the hand grip engages in the lance-rest so preventing its shooting backwards on impact. Moreover, the full force of man and horse is directed through the lancehead. This system was used in both war and the joust (see Figure 26).

Lance-stave (**27, 35**)

the wooden shaft of the lance. It is sometimes purchased separately from the metal head. Without vamplates (**92, 94**) – see *Vamplate*.

Latten

an alloy chiefly comprised of copper and tin but also containing lead and zinc.[43] Used for both decoration and preservation of metal surfaces, it also provides an effective base layer for the application of gilt and silver gilt. We find gilt-latten borders on the steel plates of the harness and gauntlets with gilt knuckles (**92**) (see Figure 43). Gun of – see *Gun*.

Leather

in a strict sense it is an animal's hide that has been stripped of the fur and flesh and treated with chemicals (tanned). However, variations of the word are used as a shorthand for the de-furred skins of a range of different mammals.[44] Buckskin (**22, 30**), white and red buckskin (**30**), white for a sword belt (**35**), white, azure, and rose for aventail-covers (**81**). Goatskin or doeskin (**5**). Cow (**22, 57, 61, 124**). Red goatskin (**9, 35**). Roe hide to affix an aventail to a basinet (**92**). Prohibition of the use of *mégis*: poor-quality goat or sheepskin (**1**) and black sheepskin (**16**). Red sheepskin (**61, 92**). See the discussion in the introduction. Hardened leather – see *Cuir bouilli*.

---

[41] C. Blair, *European and American Arms, c. 1100–1850* (London, 1962), pp. 26–7.
[42] D. Scott-Macnab, 'The Treatment of *Assegai* and *Zagaie* by the *OED*, and of *Assegai* by the *Dictionary of South African English*', *Neophilologus* 96 (2012), pp. 151–63.
[43] C. Blair and J. Blair, 'Copper Alloys', *English Medieval Industries: Craftsmen, Techniques, Products*, ed. J. Blair and N. Ramsay (London, 1991), pp. 81–106.
[44] J. Cherry, 'Leather', *English Medieval Industries: Craftsmen, Techniques, Products*, ed. J. Blair and N. Ramsay (London, 1991), pp. 295–318.

Leathers

the name used then and now for strips of leather riveted to the inside of plate armour for the purposes of articulation. The process of fitting these is called leathering (e.g. **30**).

Leg defences: see *Chausses, Cuisse, Genuler, Greave, Jamber, Legharness, Mustilers, Poleyn, Schynbald, Splints, Voiders*.

Legharness (**78**)

the Eng. name for the combined components of plate cuisses, poleyns, and greaves (see Figure 33). Foreharness (**144**) – probably a description of a set of plates that provides protection to the front of the leg only (see Figure 1, Figure 10, and Figure 15). Equipped with mail at the back (**126**) – see *Voiders*.

Linen, armour, harness (**9, 57, 40**)

a shorthand for fabric padded defences and foundations such as the aketon and gambeson. These being essential for affixing mail and plate armour.

Linen armourer: see *Armourer, linen*.

Longbow: see *Bow*.

Longsword: see *Sword*.

Lorica (**2–150**)

hauberk – a long mail body defence. The word, originating in Classical Lat., has undergone many permutations. Deriving from the solid leather 'six pack' body-hugging torso defences of Roman emperors it was subsequently adopted by auxiliary troops to denote mail shirts. By the early-fourteenth century the word is the *specific* designation for hauberk.[45] Of Milan make (**150**).

Loricarius (**9**)

Lat. for mail-maker – see *Hauberger*.

Loricarum

Lat. term used for coifs 'of mail' ('coifes loricar[um]') (**27**).

---

[45] Moffat, '*The Manner of Arming Knights for the Tourney*', p. 13.

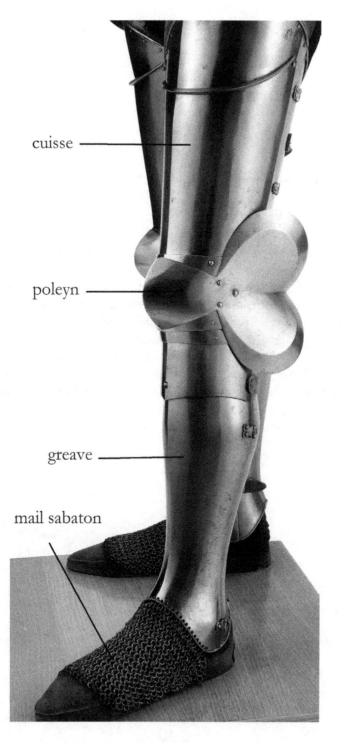

cuisse

poleyn

greave

mail sabaton

Figure 33. Plate legharness from the 'Avant' harness, Milanese, 1438–40.

M

Mace (4–35)

a percussive weapon for close-quarter fighting. It has a head fitted with flanges (see Figure 34).

Mail

from Lat. *macula* (mesh) to Fr. *maille* to Eng. In use for centuries before (and after) our period, the word is the *specific* designation for interlinked wire rings of varying size and shape forming a flexible defence. In order to be effective mail must be borne over padded textile defences such as the aketon. Blair has provided a thorough academic demolition of the postulated concept of the existence of various types – 'chain', 'ring', 'banded', etc.[46] In the sources mail defences of all-riveted links are singled out as being of better quality and value (e.g. **35, 106**). This manner of construction clearly provided better protection than those made of a combination of solid and riveted links. The section of the wire – round or flat – is also sometimes noted (e.g. **24, 97**) as is the substance: steel or iron (see Figure 35 and Figure 36). Latten and silver-coated wire are used for both decorative and conservational

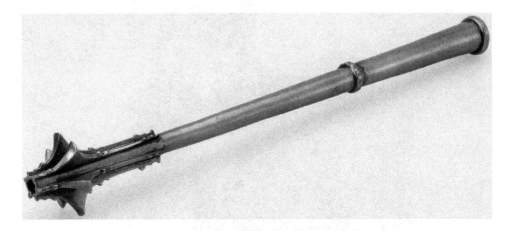

Figure 34. Mace, c. 1450.

[46] Blair, *European Armour*, pp. 20–3 and pp. 35–6; C. Blair, 'The Conington Effigy: 14th-Century Knights at Conington, Dodford and Tollard Royal', *Church Monuments* 6 (1991), pp. 3–20 (at pp. 11–12).

purposes (see Figure 16 and Figure 27).[47] Defences for the tourney are constructed of larger links (**4, 61, 74**). Separate defences of – see *Aventail, Barbière, Basinet* (Hounskull), *Bevor, Brayer, Chausses, Coif, Gauntlet, Gorget, Gusset, Haubergeon, Hauberk, Horse cover, Jazerant, Lorica, Musekins, Paunce, Pisan, Sleeves, Standard, Voiders.* Barrel for scouring (**59, 62, 92, 94, 101**).

Makers' marks (**66**)

aventail links, (**81**), aventail by Simone Corrente (**81**), haubergeon with all the links marked (**97**). On basinets of Flanders and London make (**122**). Wardens' inspection (**66**).

Manifer (**52, 63, 138, 143, 144, 149**)

a bridle-hand and arm defence for jousting. From Fr. for iron hand, none survive from the century. Those of a later date are a thick, solid plate defence (see Figure 37).

Mantlet (**92**)

a type of shield or defensive structure for a field gun.

Marks, makers', wardens': see *Makers' marks.*

Misericord (**4, 12, 24**)

from Lat. for mercy. 'Its precise meaning is unclear,' Blair informs us, 'the most probable interpretation is that it was a general term for a "knightly" dagger.'[48] Of Verzy, near Reims (**24**) – probably refers to its manufacture in this town.

Musekins (**35–75**)

an, as yet, undescribed mail arm defence.[49]

Mustilers (**2, 42**)

lower leg defences of unknown form only in use in the first half of the century.[50]

---

[47] For constructional details, see W. Reid and E. M. Burgess, 'A Habergeon of Westwale', *Antiquaries Journal* 40 (1960), pp. 46–57.

[48] Blair, *European and American Arms*, p. 16. I am grateful to Mr R. C. Woosnam-Savage for raising this point.

[49] Mr Keith Dowen has generously relayed the information that there is work underway to identify the defence. A. C. Oliveira, '*Musekins/Musekyns* or *Mosequinés* in Iberian Sources', *Arms and Armour: Journal of the Royal Armouries* (forthcoming 2022). I hope to include this in the subsequent volume.

[50] Moffat, '*The Manner of Arming Knights for the Tourney*', pp. 7–8.

Figure 35. Detail of the mail links of a haubergeon, fourteenth century.

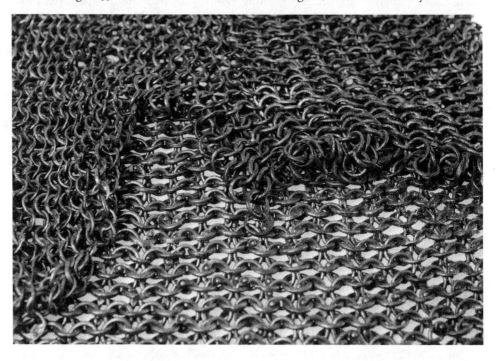
Figure 36. Detail of the links of a mail sleeve, 1500s.

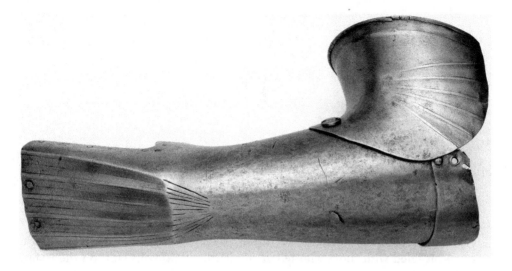

Figure 37. Manifer, Flemish, c. 1500.

N

Neck defences: see *Aventail, Barbière, Barbuta, Baviera, Bevor, Camail, Collar, Gorget, Pisan, Standard.*

Norse axe: see *Axe.*

O

Osmund (**92, 104**)

a billet of good-quality iron from Scandinavia or the Baltic.

P

Pair of Plates

often simply referred to as 'plates' (**2–148**), it is a torso defence constructed of metal plates riveted to a foundation of strong leather or canvas (see Figure 25). The number of plates employed is only mentioned in one document: one pair is made from seven pieces of steel for the Count of Savoy in 1327 (**97**). The remains of a number of these defences have been excavated from a grave-pit filled with those who fell at the Battle of Visby in 1361, on the Island of Gotland, Sweden. The archaeologists' reconstructions demonstrate a wide variety of shapes and sizes of plates.[51] In the vast majority of the sources they are described as being covered with fabric, the rivet-heads appearing on the outside in a pattern determined by the placement of each plate. They might also be left uncovered (**51**) or have removable covers (**18**). 'Pair-of-plates construction' is the term I use to categorize defences for other parts of the body such as sleeves, departing from Thordeman and Blair's term 'coat of plates'.[52] For jousting (**70, 136, 144**): almost certainly of thicker and heavier construction – perhaps with larger plates at the front. With three chains on the breast (**80**) – refers to chains affixed to prevent the loss of helm, sword, and dagger. German (**2, 56, 132**) – of high-quality German steel. With the *pièce* (**2**) – most likely having a frontal reinforcing metal plate.[53]

Paletot (79)

Fr. form of paltok – a fabric torso defence of unknown form.

Pallet (34–144)

probably cognate with 'pate': crown of the head, suggesting a rounded, skullcap-like helmet. One is fitted with an aventail (mail neck defence) presumably in the same way as is fitted to a basinet (**96**), another is of cuir bouilli (**131**). An English indenture for service in France of 1431 stipulates that the archers must have 'a capelyn or a palet'.[54] See also *Capelline*.

---

[51] Thordeman, *Armour from the Battle of Wisby*, I, pp. 210–25.
[52] Thordeman, *Armour from the Battle of Wisby*, I, p. 211; Blair, *European Armour*, pp. 40–3.
[53] Moffat, 'The Manner of Arming Knights for the Tourney', p. 18.
[54] Carlisle Archives, DLONS/L/5/1/50/12. Thanks are due to Ms Louise Smith for her kind assistance with locating this document.

Paltock (**83, 88, 108**)

of uncertain etymology – a fabric torso defence of some kind, probably similar to the jack.

Panzeria (**49**)

an Italian name for a mail shirt.

Parma (**72**)

a Classical Lat. word for a small, round, hand-held shield. Here it most probably means buckler or targe.

Pauldron (**143**)

plate shoulder defence. Derived from Fr. for shoulder blade (*paleron*), it is comprised of lames (metal plates) articulated by internal leathers and rivets all shaped to encompass the shoulder whilst, at the same time, ensuring good manoeuvrability.

Paunce, pair of paunces (**14–144**)

a mail skirt – from paunch (stomach), suggesting it was borne high on the waist towards the bottom of the rib cage covering the belly and extending downwards to protect the groin, hips, and buttocks. The designation 'pair' implies it was a defence with two parallel vertical edges that could be strapped and buckled at the side or rear. Just such an arrangement is illustrated in Honoré Bonet's *Tree of Battles*, French c. 1400 (London, British Library, MS Royal 20 C.viii, fol. 2v) where one soldier's paunce is secured with five buckles at the rear.

Pavise (**41–131**)

named after the City of Pavia, this large shield can be propped up to shelter a cross-bowman whilst he spans (**41**). It is constructed of wood and leather. Of spruce (**74**): conifer wood from Prussia and the Baltic. Emblazoned with a heraldic coat of arms (**105**) (see Figure 38 and Figure 39).[55]

Peytral (**27–147**)

a solid defence for the horse's breast, from Fr. *poitrail*, from Lat. *pectorale*: breast cover. Of white leather (**131**).

Pièce

a word employed for two different pieces of plate armour, both of which act as reinforces. In these sources (**2, 124**) it is a frontal plate for torso defences such as

---

[55] K. DeVries, 'The Introduction and Use of the Pavise in the Hundred Years War', *Arms & Armour* 4 (2007), pp. 93–100.

Figure 38. Detail of an illustration from the Beauchamp Pageant, English, fifteenth century.

Figure 39. Pavise, Bohemian, c. 1450.

pairs of plates. In (**80**, **138**) it is used for a secondary defence for the front of a jousting helm (see Figure 6 and Figure 30).

Pisan (4–129)

a mail collar named after the City of Pisa. The reason for the appellation has not been found in these sources. That it originated as 'a joke casting aspersions on the safety of that city' is wild speculation.[56] That it was closely fitted to the neck is attested by the fact it could be borne beneath a basinet's aventail, thus providing a second layer of defence (e.g. **75**) (see Figure 40). Furthermore, it is twice referred to as a 'colerete' (**24**) and (**68**). The *-ette* suffix acts as a diminutive of collar. Blair's interpretation of its being shaped at the neck by a 'thickening of the rings so that the mesh became semi-rigid' is a most plausible one.[57] Covers for (**35**, **45**, **57**). With cape (**12**).

Plate armour

the term used for defences constructed of metal plates.

Plate sleeves: see *Sleeves*.

Figure 40. Detail of the fifteenth-century neck modifications to a fourteenth-century habergeon.

---

[56] R. Moffat, 'Arms and Armour', *A Companion to Chivalry*, ed. R. W. Jones and P. Coss (Woodbridge, 2019), pp. 159–85 (at p. 170).
[57] Blair, *European Armour*, p. 47.

Plates, pair of: see *Pair of Plates*.

Points

laces for securing the plates of the harness to the arming doublet. See *Doublet*.

Poitrine (**52**)

the Fr. word for breast – an early form of breastplate (of unknown form) probably borne as a secondary defence over the pair of plates. See *Breastplate*.

Pole-arms: see Staff weapons.

Poleyn (**6–149**)

a plate defence shaped to protect the knee secured by means of a strap and buckle (see Figure 33). The word comes to Eng. through Fr., ultimately deriving from Lat. *patella*: kneecap. Most have a side wing extending from the main plate to offer some protection to the outside of the knee and the hamstring behind. There are rare examples of a poleyn with two wings (see Figure 43). With its integration into the other leg defences – cuisses and greaves – it forms the legharness.

Pollaxe (**21, 131, 142**), of copper (**149**)

axe with the Eng. prefix poll (head). This medium-length staff weapon might also have a fluke (curved spike), a hammer with textured face like that of a meat tenderiser, a thrusting spike, and yet another spike at the haft-end: the queue (tail). All these in addition to the main axe blade (see Figure 41).

Pommel (**14–144**)

an often elaborately-shaped piece of metal (extremely rarely crystal or stone) fitted to the end of a sword hilt acting as a counterbalance to the blade. Of crystal (**4**), enamelled (**24**), of red stone (**74**), of silver (**4, 35**), 'shaped like an extended hand' – a description of the lobated type (**141**). The distinctive Scottish type is of a teardrop shape and hollow construction.[58] Oakeshott's comprehensive study describes the wide variety of shapes and sizes.[59]

Pourpoint (**1–132**)

a textile body defence. The name comes to Eng. through Fr., originating in the Lat. verb *perpungere* – to prick through, describing its construction of sewn padded sections (see Figure 2).[60] The noun can be used adjectively: thus we find

---

[58] Moffat, 'A Sign of Victory?', pp. 122–43.
[59] E. Oakeshott, *The Sword in the Age of Chivalry* (Woodbridge, 1994), pp. 80–111.
[60] See the entry in *The Encyclopedia of Medieval Dress and Textiles of the British Isles, c. 450–1450*, ed. G. Owen-Crocker, E. Coatsworth and M. Hayward (Leiden, 2012).

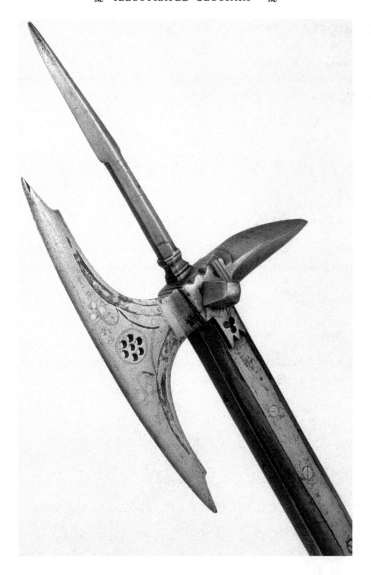

Figure 41. Pollaxe, mid-fifteenth century.

'pointed' and 'pourpointed' defences such as greaves and cuisses (e.g. **8**). A possible differentiation between it and the gambeson is the shape of the padded sections: the former stitched in small sections of square or lozenge shape, the latter in long parallel tubes or strips. Pourpoint-maker (**58**), of Paris (**125**).

Proofing, of armour (**56, 60, 81, 103**)

the sources show that there were two levels of proof: half and full. The meaning, as fifteenth-century sources attest,[61] is the power of the weapon used to shoot an arrow or quarrel at close range at each piece. Thus harness is 'half-proofed' with a hand-spanned bow (i.e. longbow) or crossbow and 'fully proofed' with a powerful crossbow spanned with a mechanical device. One Eng. source employs the word 'assay' (**52**), almost certainly alluding to this same process.

Q

Quarrel (7–94)

a crossbow bolt. From Fr. *carreau*: four-cornered, the name is descriptive of the head's rectangular cuboid shape with a square-pyramidal tip (see Figure 42).

Quarterstaff: see *Staff*.

Quiver (36, 86)

a pouch for arrows or crossbow quarrels usually slung from a waist belt. Of Saracen work (**36**), of Turkey (**86**) – this refers to exotic foreign craftsmanship.

R

Reinforcing plate: see *Barber*, *Breastplate*, *Pièce*, and *Poitrine*.

Rerebrace (50–149)

from Fr. *arrière-bras* – rear of the, or upper, arm – as distinct from *avant-bras*: forearm. A plate defence for this part of the body. With the rest of the arm defences: the vambrace and couter, it is referred to (usually in Fr. sources) as the arm harness (e.g. **58**) (see Figure 18). Of those 'of the new manner' (**52**), regrettably, no more

Figure 42. Crossbow quarrel, c. 1500.

61   Moffat, 'The Importance of Being Harnest', pp. 10–12.

detail is provided as to the meaning. For the vocabulary of the fourteenth-century arm harness, I depart from Blair and do not 'follow the modern practice, based partly on 16th- and 17th-century usage, of referring to the parts above and below the couter as the upper and lower cannons of the vambrace respectively'.[62]

Rivet

in the sources there is no distinction made between it and the nail. In fifteenth-century sources they are referred to as 'arming nails'. The precious metal *rivets* in Parisian armourers' regulations of 1312 (**16**) are to be placed beneath the nail-heads used to construct a gauntlet. They are, therefore, most likely washers. Riveting of mail – see *Mail*. For a sword (**138**).

Rondel: see *Dagger*.

Rybaude: see *Gun*.

S

Sabater (**9**)

Fr. for shoe (*sabot*) + derivational suffix -*ière*: i.e. 'for the'. The Fr. version of sabaton in Eng.

Sabaton (**35–144**)

from Fr. for shoe (*sabot*) + derivational suffix -*ion*: a foot defence constructed of lames (metal plates) articulated by means of internal leathers and rivets (see Figure 10, Figure 26, and Figure 43). In Fr. sources variants of the word *soleret* are used (**58**, **74**, **124**, **128**).

Saddle

bastard (**138**, **143**, **144**): the meaning is not clear. It could be interpreted as referring to a type somewhere between those for war or jousting – neither one nor the other. It is possibly synonymous with the 'low saddles' ('bases selles') mentioned in documents (**67**) and (**148**).
for jousting (**63**, **95**, **136**, **147**, **149**): also referred to as a 'high' saddle (**135**, **138**), the shape and fit encloses the jouster and raises him higher on the horse's back

---

[62] Blair, *European Armour*, pp. 44–5.

Figure 43. Stained glass panel, English, late-fourteenth century.

allowing the legs to straighten into the stirrups. He has reduced manoeuvrability but a slimmer chance of injury on impact with his opponent's lance (see Figure 17).

for tourneying (**31, 143**): none from our period survive. It can be assumed that they were of a specific construction for participation in these events.

for war (**4, 93**): recorded as such to differentiate it from those for the joust and tourney. It has a low pommel and cantle to increase manoeuvrability in combat.

Scabbard

a sheath for a sword, dagger, or knife constructed of wood and leather (see Figure 45). The metal fittings: chape at the tip and locket at the mouth complete its construction. They seem to be only worthy of note when decorated with precious metals and fine leather or fabrics (e.g. **9, 124**).

Schynbald (**24–143**)

a solid shin defence. Its form is not described in the documents. Pieces of iron formed for (**39**), of plate (**50**): confirm it is made of metal.[63]

Shaffron (**27–147**)

a solid defence for the horse's head (see Figure 44). The word appears as *chamfrain* in the Fr. documents and in Eng. as 'chanfreyn'. Shaffron is the spelling used in Eng. sources from the fifteenth century.

Sheaf (**26, 127, 142**)

drawing on the image of the wheat sheaf in agriculture, it refers to the arrangement of arrows in the quiver or set in the ground before an archer. Archers serving in the Scottish host were legally obliged to provide 24 (**26**). The Lat. word *garba* is often employed (e.g. **92**).

Shield (**2–147**)

in armour scholarship this type is categorized as 'heater-shaped' due to its resemblance to the old-fashioned clothes iron or heater (see Figure 10, Figure 19, Figure 23, Figure 45, and Figure 46).[64] In the documents the word is the default for this common type. Horn, plated with steel, newly-horned for jousting (**70**). The face inlaid with plaques of metal or animal horn – this can be seen in existing jousting shields of fifteenth-century date. See also *Buckler, Escutcheon, Guige, Indies, Parma, Pavise, Targe.*

---

[63] See R. Firth Green and R. Moffat, 'Schynbalds in *The Awntyrs off Arthure* (l. 395): Two Notes', *Notes & Queries*, unnumbered (2020), pp. 1–6.

[64] Blair, *European Armour*, p. 131. See also H. Nickel, 'Der mittelalterliche Reiterschild des Abendlandes' (Doctoral Dissertation, Freie Universität Berlin, 1958). Nickel's comprehensive study is yet to be translated for a wider readership.

Figure 44. The 'Warwick Shaffron', 1400.

Shoes, plate (**27**, **29**, **31**)

this designation suggests they were of pair-of-plates construction and were, most probably, a forerunner of the sabaton. For 'pair-of-plates construction' see *Pair of Plates*.

Short sword: see *Sword*.

Siege engines

Edward of Caernarfon's (**9**). At Beaumaris (**10**, **13**). Timbers for (**17**). Ladders (**110**). Large (**39**). Tools/implements for: regrettably, these are not listed in detail (**76**, **86**). Stones for (**13**, **92**, **94**). The form of the catapult at Durham Priory (**127**) is not described. See also *Springald*, *Trebuchet*, and *Vetta* (helmet) for wall-scaling at sieges.

Sinew

animal tendons – part of the construction of a composite crossbow-stave (see Figure 21), chapels of – see *Chapel of sinew*.

Figure 45. Etching of the tomb effigy of Robert, Earl of Oxford (d. 1221), Hatfield Broad
Oak Church, Essex. The effigy was erected in the fourteenth century.

Figure 46. Drawing in the margin of the Herdmanston Breviary, Scottish, c. 1360.

Skirt, mail: see *Paunce*.

Skull

the main bowl of a helmet. It is usually applied to the basinet – see *Basinet*.

Skullcap

a close-fitting metal cap. The form of the different types in (**81**) – brigands', Florentine, Gascon, Milan, reinforced with little wings, for shipboard crossbowmen, with ventilations, for marine fighting – is, disappointingly, not revealed.

Sleeves

of mail (**4–144**): short sleeves (**70**). Mail arm defences shaped like those of everyday fabric clothing (see Figure 47). Sleeves of plate (**27, 35, 131, 144**): of pair-of-plates

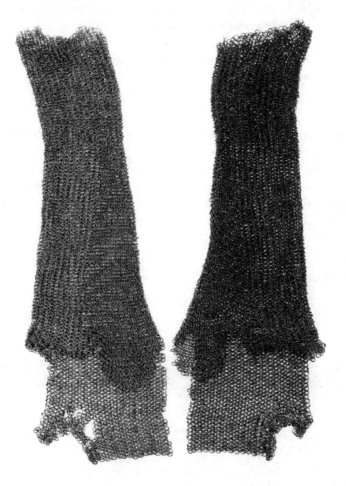

Figure 47. Mail sleeves, 1500s.

construction. For 'pair-of-plates construction' see *Pair of Plates*. Reinforced with baleen plates for an aketon (**9, 15**). Of cuir bouilli (hardened leather) (**45**).

Soleret: see *Sabaton*.

Sparth: see *Axe*.

Spatam (**80**)

this is most likely a Lat. word for longsword.

Spaudlers (**4, 34, 43, 61, 79**)

a shoulder defence – from Fr. *épaule* + derivational suffix *-ière*: i.e. 'for the' shoulder. In the early part of the century they were made of leather and baleen and used for tourneying.[65] Later, their form is that of a forerunner of the pauldron but of a simpler and closer-fitting construction comprising a hemispherical cap and overlapping lames (metal plates) articulated by internal leathers and rivets (see Figure 5). This latter meaning is the one most commonly employed in the scholarship.[66]

Spear

a staff weapon, comprising a sharpened metal head set on a wooden shaft, of a type wielded by warriors for centuries (see Figure 1, Figure 19, Figure 23, Figure 43, and Figure 48). The separation of the use of the word lance for mounted combat and spear for foot – now commonly employed – is not a contemporary one.[67] Boar spear (**144**) – a type fitted with a crossbar at the base of the head to prevent the enraged creature forcing itself up the shaft to injure the hunter.

Spikes

affixed to the body or the horse (**14**). See also *Axe, Gadelings, Godendag*.

Figure 48. Spearhead, medieval.

[65] Moffat and Spriggs, 'The Use of Baleen for Arms', pp. 209–11; Moffat, '*The Manner of Arming Knights for the Tourney*', pp. 16–17 and p. 22.
[66] For example Blair, *European Armour*, p. 45; Capwell, *Armour of the English Knight*, pp. 134–7.
[67] Blair, *European and American Arms*, pp. 26–7.

Splints (94)

for the shins (92), leg splints of three pieces (143)
limb armour constructed of vertical metal strips – probably externally riveted to a
leather or canvas base to create a design.

Springald (7–94)

in essence a large crossbow set on a base and spanned by the torsional force of twisted
ropes (see Figure 49). The word's root is the same as 'spring' in the sense of 'to
fly out suddenly or violently'.[68] Of varying size (62, 76), ash for the bow-staves is
recorded (53), and ropes made of canvas or horsehair (10, 13). Ammunition for: see
Garrot and *Quarrel*. Of horn (92): meaning a bow-stave of composite construction
– see *Crossbow*. Green and savage (92): these are unexplained. False cord (46, 53):
a system of spanning using an extra cord.[69]

Staff

a wooden stave wielded in both hands for close combat. The appellation 'Kentish' is

Figure 49. Drawing of a detail of the Carlisle Charter of 1315, English.

---

68 *The Oxford English Dictionary*, ed. J Simpson (Oxford, 2004), online edn.
69 M. Loades, *The Crossbow* (Oxford, 2018), p. 6.

unexplained (**19**). It is also known as a quarterstaff (**4, 80**). One is fitted with silver ferrules with four nails (**80**).

Staff weapons: see *Dart, Gisarme, Glaive, Godendag, Lance, Lancegay, Pollaxe, Spear, Staff.*

Standard

a close-fitting collar of thick mail links, usually associated with fifteenth-century harness.[70] Its lower edge can either spread over, or fit beneath, the neck opening of the breastplate. Here, they are for hauberks (**92**) suggesting a mail neck defence of a different form to the pisan collar.

Surcoat

an erroneous name currently in use for the coat armour.

Sword

arming (see Figure 10, Figure 14, and Figure 45): a sword of medium length (70–80cm) usually wielded in one hand, it is habitually slung at the hip of the knight, squire, and man-at-arms.[71]

Avignon (**74**): either made in, or exported from, this town.

Bohemia (**80**): probably made somewhere in this kingdom.

Bordeaux (**120, 124, 144**): a designation that most likely refers to the quality of metals and skill of manufacture.[72]

Bray, near Rouen (**24**): either made in, or exported from, this town.

Castile (**124**): either made in, or exported from, this kingdom.

Cologne (**19**): this being of quality German manufacture prized throughout Christendom;[73] 'of Cologne work' (**80**).

curved (**87**): a sword with a curved blade.

Genoa (**4, 141**): either made in, or exported from, this city.

Langres (**124**): either made in, or exported from, this city.

Lombardy: work marked with the sign of the scorpion (**80**).

longsword (**84, 144**): a large sword (110–125cm) wielded in one or two hands (see Figure 51 and Figure 52).[74] The Duke of Burgundy's 'grant espee' (**124**) is a Fr. name for this type.

marked with the sign of the scorpion (**80**): this means the blade is marked with an individual craftsman's makers' mark. See the discussion in the introduction.

---

[70] Blair, *European Armour*, p. 78; Capwell, *Armour of the English Knight*, p. 307.
[71] Oakeshott, *The Sword in the Age of Chivalry*, pp. 44–7.
[72] See Moffat, 'A Sign of Victory?', pp. 124–5. See also the discussion in the introduction.
[73] See Moffat, 'Arms and Armour', pp. 159–61.
[74] Oakeshott, *The Sword in the Age of Chivalry*, pp. 42–7.

Figure 50. Longsword, early-fourteenth century.

Figure 51. Longsword, possibly Italian, c. 1370.

Passau (**131, 138**): this being of quality German manufacture prized throughout Christendom.[75]

riding: this type is unexplained (**35**).

Saracen (**32, 141**): this designation is a medieval shorthand for non-Christian peoples of the Middle and Near East.

Scottish (**35, 131, 144**): of a distinctive type from this realm.[76]

shortsword (**84, 114**): a name employed to distinguish it from the longsword and arming sword.

Toulouse (**24**): either made in, or exported from, this city.

for the tourney (**34, 42, 74**): most likely a sword with rebated (blunted) blade.

of Turkey (**131**): very probably a trophy brought back from a crusade.

with vamplates for the lists: i.e. single combat (**144**). This refers to a hilt fitted with a circular hand defence and pommel – referred to now as rondels (see Figure 22).

Verzy, near Reims (**24**): either made in, or exported from, this town.

T

Targe (**4–148**)

a round shield of metal and wood (or horn) construction, larger than the buckler. Of Lombardy (**35**) – made in that region. Of the arms of Saint George, arms of England (**57, 92**) – emblazoned with heraldic arms. Round, small, of horn (**92**) – reveals a range of different types. Target for jousts of war (**131**). How this differs from the standard type is not explained. See also *Parma*.

Tena

Lat. for coif (see *Coif*).

Tester (**4–149**)

a horse's head defence. It is probably a variant form of the shaffron. From Fr. *teste* (head) + derivational suffix *-ière*: i.e. 'for the' head.

Textile defences: see Fabric defences.

Thigh defences: see *Cuisse*.

---

[75] See Moffat, 'A Sign of Victory?', pp. 124–5; Moffat, 'Arms and Armour', pp. 159–61.
[76] See Moffat, 'A Sign of Victory?', 122–43.

Tin

this metal is used as a coating to prevent iron and steel armour corroding (**1**, **16**, **76**, **86**).

Tools, armourers: see *Armourers*, tools: for constructing crossbows – see *Crossbow*.

Torso defences: see *Aketon, Breastplate, Brigandine, Corset, Cuirie, Doublet, Gambeson, Haubergeon, Hauberk, Jack, Lorica, Musekins, Pair of Plates, Paltock, Pièce, Pourpoint*.

Tourneying

armour and equipment, basinet, chausse, cuirie forged or of cuir bouilli (**79**), haubergeon, of large mail (links), hauberk, peytral, spaudlers, tourney saddle. None of this equipment survives from our period. The use of leather and cuir bouilli, along with mail with larger links, is clear evidence of the development of specialized kit.[77]

Trapper (**7–143**)

a fabric horse cover, its name is derived from Fr. *drapeur*: drapery. Although there is one reference to 'pourpointed horse trappers' (**8**) and one of mail (**144**), on the whole they were principally for the purposes of heraldic display rather than defence (see Figure 1, Figure 17, and Figure 19). See also *Horse cover*.

Trebuchet (**10**)

a machine often used in siege warfare. It hurls stones and other projectiles by the force of a sling on the end of a counterweighted beam (see Figure 49). Stones for (**92**).

Tunic, of mail

used only in two Lat. documents (**80**, **85**).

Turkey, Turkish

see *Arrow, Axe, Bow, Crossbow*, and *Sword*.

U

Umbrer: see *Basinet*.

---

[77] Moffat, '*The Manner of Arming Knights for the Tourney*', pp. 5–29.

V

Vambrace (43–149)

from Fr. *avant-bras*: forearm – it is usually constructed of two hinged plates, secured by straps and buckles, that are shaped to encase this part of the limb. When borne with the other arm defences – couter and rerebrace – Fr. sources often call it arm harness (see Figure 18). With wing (**138**) – the same defence with a section extending to provide protection for the crook of the left elbow during the joust.[78] Of those 'of the new manner' (**52**), regrettably, no more detail is provided as to the meaning. For the vocabulary of the fourteenth-century arm harness, I depart from Blair and do not 'follow the modern practice, based partly on 16th- and 17th-century usage, of referring to the parts above and below the couter as the upper and lower cannons of the vambrace respectively'.[79]

Vamplate (27–149)

a strong metal plate fitted over, and nailed to, the war and jousting lance to provide protection to the wielder's right-hand side (see Figure 52). From Fr. *avant-plate*: fore-plate, their early form was of a flat disk: thus 'of the old type' (**74**). A conical, and – latterly – curved-cone, shape followed.

Varnish (1–94)

there are ubiquitous instances of its use to preserve both metal armour, shields, and crossbows. See the discussion in the introduction.

Vervelles (128), Italian *varvela* (81)

a series of staples riveted around the base of the basinet for affixing the aventail. See *Aventail*.

Vetta

a small, close-fitting helmet only found in (**81**). With little ears, Milan, brigands', secret, for wall-scaling men (i.e. sieges), English, footsoldiers' – the shape and style of the variety of distinct types is not described.

Vices, for breastplate: see *Breastplate*: for spanning crossbows – see *Crossbow spanning devices*.

---

[78] See Moffat, '*Alle myne harneys for the justes*', pp. 85–7.
[79] Blair, *European Armour*, pp. 44–5.

Figure 52. Vamplate, German, mid-sixteenth century

Vireton (**56, 103, 125**)

a Fr. word for crossbow quarrel.

Visor (**9–148**)

for basinets, helms, chapel de fers, half visor: these face defences come in a very wide variety of forms (see Figure 1, Figure 9, Figure 26, Figure 43, and Figure 46).

Voiders

small sections of mail attached to the pertinent areas on the arming doublet and hose to fill the gaps – voids – left unprotected by the metal plates of the harness. Thirty little pieces of mail 'in the form of voiders' are accounted for (**143**). For legharness (**105**) purposefully shaped for use at the back of the thigh and knee. The legharness 'equipped with mail at the back' (**126**) suggests such pieces could be integrated into the articulated plates of the legharness rather than laced to the arming hose beneath (see Figure 26 and Figure 43).

W

Wyex: see *Axe*.

Bibliography

Unpublished Primary Sources

Berkeley Castle Archives, Muniment D1/1/30
Besançon, Bibliothèque municipale, MS 865
Caen, Archives du Calvados, G/279/1
Cambridge, Corpus Christi College Library, MS 174
Cambridge, Gonville and Caius College Library, MS 424/448
Carlisle Archives, DLONS/L/5/1/50/12, and DRC/1/2, Bishops' Registers
Chaumont, Archives départementales de la Haute-Marne, 2 G 115
Chippenham, Wiltshire and Swindon Archives, Bishops' Registers
Durham Cathedral Archives, Durham Priory Accounts
Edinburgh, National Library of Scotland, Adv. MSS
Edinburgh, National Records of Scotland, GD 150/62
Edinburgh University Library, MS 183
Glasgow Museums, Object File E.1939.65.e, and R. L. Scott Library, MS E.1939.65.1174
Grenoble, Archives départementales de l'Isère, FR.AD38–9B2
Kew, National Archives, C 66, C 81, C 145, DL 25, DL 28, DURH 3, E 36, E 41, E 101, E 136, E 154, E 159, E 163, E 352, E 361, KB 27, SC 1, SC 8
Lambeth Palace Library, Archbishops' Registers
Leeds, Royal Armouries Library, MS RAR.0035(I.35)
Lille, Archives départementales du Nord, B450/4401
London, British Library, Additional Charters, Additional Manuscripts, MS Cotton Vespasian F. VII, Sloane Charter XXXI 2, Stowe Charter 622
London, Library of the Society of Antiquaries of London, MS SAL/MS/541
London, London Guildhall Library, CLC/L/BF/A/021/MS05440
London, London Metropolitan Archives, Court of Husting Rolls, DL/A/J/001/ MS25176, London Letter-Books, Liber Albus, Plea and Memoranda Rolls
Los Angeles, J. P. Getty Museum, MS Ludvig XV 13
Mons, Archives de l'État, Chartrier des archives de la ville, no. 146
Montauban, Archives départementales de Tarn-et-Garonne, registre G372
Nantes, Bibliothèque municipale, Fonds Bizeul, MS 1701

New York, Pierpont Morgan Library, MS M775
Norwich, Norfolk Record Office, NCR 5C-6, 7, 9
Nottingham University Library, Middleton MS
Oxford, Bodleian Library, MS Ashmole 856, MS Eng. hist. b. 229, MS Tanner 13
Paris, Archives de la Préfecture de Police, cote AD 4, Collection Lamoignon
Paris, Bibliothèque nationale, MSS fr., MS NAF 25164
Rouen, Bibliothèque municipale, MS U28 (1147)
Truro, Cornwall Record Office, Arundell Family of Lanherne and Trerice AR/15/2
Westminster Abbey, Abbey Muniments
Winchester, Hampshire Record Office, Bishops' Registers
York, Borthwick Institute, Archbishops' Registers

Published Primary Sources

Ainsworth P., and G. Croenen, eds, *HRI Online Froissart* (Sheffield, 2013)

Arnould, E. J., ed., *Le Livre de Seyntz Medicines: The Devotional Treatise of Henry of Lancaster* (Oxford, 1940)

Ascham, R., *Toxophilus, the Schole, or Partitions, of Shooting* (London, 1545)

Bain, J., and others, eds, *Calendar of Documents Relating to Scotland, AD 1108–1516*, 5 vols (Edinburgh, 1886)

Brewer, J. S., ed., *Letters and Papers, Foreign and Domestic, Henry VIII, vol. 1, 1509–1514* (London, 1920)

Bromyard, J., *Summa Prædicantium*, 2 vols (Venice, 1586)

Buchon, J. A., ed., *Chroniques de Froissart*, 15 vols (Paris, 1826)

Burnett, G., ed., *Rotuli scaccarii regum Scotorum: The Exchequer Rolls of Scotland, Vol. III, A.D. 1379–1406* (Edinburgh, 1880)

Ceruti, A., ed., Galvaneo Flamma, *Chronicon extravagans de antiquitatibus Mediolani* (Turin, 1869)

Coopland, G. W., ed., Philippe de Mézières, *Le Songe du Vieil Pelerin*, 2 vols (Cambridge, 1969)

Dehaisnes, C., *Documents et extraits divers concernant l'histoire de l'art dans la Flandre, l'Artois & le Hainaut avant le XVe siècle*, 2 vols (Lille, 1886)

Déslisle, L., ed., *Actes normands de la chambre des comptes sous Philippe de Valois (1328–50)* (Rouen, 1871)

Devillers, L., ed., *Cartulaire des Comtes de Hainaut, de l'avènement de Guillaume II à la mort de Jacqueline de Bavière (1337–1436)*, 6 vols (Brussels, 1883–96)

Douët d'Arcq, L., ed., *Nouveau recueil de comptes de l'argenterie des rois de France* (Paris, 1874)

Duarte, *Livro da ensinança de bem cavalgar*, n. ed. (Lisbon, 1843)

Duncan, A. A. M., ed., *Barbour's Bruce* (Edinburgh, 1997)

Fallows, N., ed. and trans., L. Zapata de Chaves, *Del Justador*, Madrid, Biblioteca Nacional MS 2790, *Jousting in Medieval & Renaissance Iberia* (Woodbridge, 2010)

Fallows, N., ed., A. de Cartagena, *Tratados militares* (Madrid, 2006)

Giraud, J. B., *Documents pour servir à l'histoire de l'armement au Moyen Âge et à la Renaissance*, 2 vols (Lyon, 1895–1904)

Lalande, D., ed., *Le Livre des fais du bon messire Jehan le Maingre, dit Bouciquaut, mareschal de France* (Geneva: Droz, 1985)

Macpherson, D., and others, eds, *Rotuli Scotiae in Turri Londinensi* [...], 2 vols (London, 1814–19)

Merlin-Chazelas, A., ed., *Documents relatifs au clos des galées de Rouen et aux armées de mer du roi de France de 1293 à 1418*, 2 vols (Paris, 1977–78)

Michaud, J. F., and J. J. F. Poujoulat, eds, Jean Juvénal des Ursins, *Histoire de Charles VI, roy de France*, *Mémoires pour servir à l'Histoire de France* (Paris, 1836)

Monte, P., *Exercitiorum atque artis militaris collectanea in tris libros distincta* (Milan, 1509)

Owen, E., ed., *A Catalogue of the Manuscripts Relating to Wales in the British Museum*, 4 vols (London, 1900–22)

Palgrave, F., ed., *Parliamentary Writs and Writs of Military Summons*, 2 vols (London, 1827–34)

Paviot, J., ed., Sir Roger Stanegrave, *Li Charboclois d'Armes du Conquest Precious de la Terre Sainte*, *Projets de croisade (v. 1290–v. 1330)* (Paris, 2008)

Riley, H. T., ed., Thomas Walsingham, *Historia Anglicana*, 2 vols (London, 1864)

Rothwell, H., ed., *The Chronicle of Walter of Guisborough* (London, 1957)

Skene, F. J. H., ed., *Liber Pluscardensis*, 2 vols (Edinburgh, 1877–80)

Strachey, J., and others, eds, *Rotuli Parliamentorum* [...] *tempore Ricardi R. II*, 4 vols (London, 1767–77)

Stubbs, W., ed., *Select Charters and other Illustrations of English Constitutional History* [...], 8th edn (Oxford, 1870)

Terrier de Loray, H., *Jean de Vienne, Amiral de France, 1341–96* (Paris, 1878)

Thompson, E. M., ed., *Chronicon Galfridi le Baker de Swynebroke* (Oxford, 1889)

Tiñena, J., ed., Ramón de Perellós, *Viatge al Purgatori* (Barcelona, 1988)

Weinbaum, M., ed., *The London Eyre of 1276* (London, 1976)

Reference Works

Du Cange, C. du Fresne, sieur, and others, eds, *Glossarium mediæ et infimæ latinatis* (Niort, 1883–87)

Gamber, O., and others, *Glossarium armorum: Arma defensiva* (Graz, 1972)

Gay, V., *Glossaire archéologique du Moyen Âge et de la Renaissance*, 2 vols (Paris, 1887–1928)

Godefroy, F., *Dictionnaire de l'ancienne langue française*, 10 vols (Paris, 1881–1902)

Latham, R. E., and others, eds, *Dictionary of Medieval Latin from British Sources* (London, 1975–)

Lewis, R. E., and others, eds, *Middle English Dictionary* (Ann Arbor, MI, 1952–2001), in *Middle English Compendium*, ed. F. McSparran and others (Ann Arbor, MI, 2000–18), online edn

Martin, R., and others, eds, *Dictionnaire du moyen français* (Nancy, 1998–), online edn

Owen-Crocker, G., E. Coatsworth and M. Hayward, eds, *The Encyclopedia of Medieval Dress and Textiles of the British Isles, c. 450–1450* (Leiden, 2012)

Simpson, J., ed., *The Oxford English Dictionary* (Oxford, 2004), online edn

Stone, L. W., and W. Rothwell, eds, *The Anglo-Norman Dictionary* (London, 1977–92), online edn

Books and Articles

Anglo, S., *The Martial Arts of Renaissance Europe* (New Haven, CT, 2000)

Beard, C. R., 'Armour and the "New English Dictionary"', *The Connoisseur: An Illustrated Magazine for Collectors*, vol. 81, no. 324 (August 1928), 235–7

Behault de Doron, A., 'Le Tournoi de Mons de 1310', *Annales du Cercle Archéologique de Mons* 38 (1909), 103–256

Blackmore, H. L., *Hunting Weapons: From the Middle Ages to the Twentieth Century* (London, 1971)

Blair, C., *European Armour, circa 1066 to circa 1700* (London, 1958)

— *European and American Arms, c. 1100–1850* (London, 1962)

— 'The Word "Baselard"', *Journal of the Arms & Armour Society* 11 (1984), 193–206

— 'The Conington Effigy: 14th-Century Knights at Conington, Dodford and Tollard Royal', *Church Monuments* 6 (1991), 3–20

— 'Armour and the Study of Brasses', *Monumental Brasses as Art and History*, ed. J. Bertram (Stroud, 1996), 37–40

— 'Hedgehog-Quill Fletchings: A Warning for Future Researchers', *Journal of the Society of Archer-Antiquaries* 46 (2003), 36

Blair, C., and J. Blair, 'Copper Alloys', *English Medieval Industries: Craftsmen, Techniques, Products*, ed. J. Blair and N. Ramsay (London, 1991), 81–106

Boeheim, W., 'Werke Mailänder Waffenschmiede in den Kaiserlichen Sammlungen', *Jahrbuch der Kunsthistorischen Sammlungen des Allerhöchsten Kaiserhauses* 9 (1889), 375–418

Brun, R., 'Notes sur le commerce des armes à Avignon au XIVe siècle', *Bibliothèque de l'École des chartes* 109 (1951), 209–31

Buttin, C., *Notes sur les armures à l'épreuve* (Annecy, 1901)

— *Le Guet de Genève au XVe siècle et l'armement des ses gardes* (Geneva, 1910)

Capwell, T., 'A Depiction of an Italian Arming Doublet, c. 1435–45', *Waffen- und Kostümkunde* 44 (2002), 177–95

— *Armour of the English Knight, 1400–1450* (London, 2015)

Cherry, J., 'Leather', *English Medieval Industries: Craftsmen, Techniques, Products*, ed. J. Blair and N. Ramsay (London, 1991), 295–318

Cowgill, J., M. de Neergaard, and J. Griffiths, *Knives and Scabbards* (Woodbridge, 2008)

Credland, A. G., 'Crossbow Remains (Part 2)', *Journal of the Society of Archer-Antiquaries* 9 (1981), 9–16

Cripps-Day, F. H., 'The Armour at Chartres', *The Connoisseur: An Illustrated Magazine for Collectors*, vol. 110, no. 146 (December 1942), 91–5

— *Fragmenta armamentaria* [...] *Greenwich Armour* (Frome, 1944)

De Cosson, C. A., 'Milanese Armourers' Marks', *Burlington Magazine*, vol. 36 (February 1920), 150–3

DeVries, K., 'The Introduction and Use of the Pavise in the Hundred Years War', *Arms & Armour* 4 (2007), 93–100

Dillon, Viscount, 'On a Ms. Collection of Ordinances of Chivalry of the 15th Century belonging to Lord Hastings', *Archaeologia* 57 (1900), 29–70

Dowen, K., 'The Introduction and Development of Plate Armour in Western Europe, c. 1250–1350', *Fasciculi Archaeologiae Historicae* 30 (2017), 19–28

Eastlake, C. L., *Materials for a History of Oil Painting* (London, 1847)

Eaves, I., 'On the Remains of a Jack of Plate excavated from Beeston Castle in Cheshire', *Journal of the Arms & Armour Society* 13 (1989), 81–154

Edwards, I., and C. Blair, 'Welsh Bucklers', *Antiquaries Journal* 62 (1982), 74–115

Faider, C., *Coutumes du pays et comté de Hainaut*, 4 vols (Brussels, 1871–83)

Fallows, N., *Jousting in Medieval & Renaissance Iberia* (Woodbridge, 2010)

ffoulkes, C. J., 'Italian Armour from Chalcis in the Ethnological Museum, Athens', *Archaeologia* 62 (1911), 381–90

— *Inventory and Survey of the Armouries of the Tower of London*, 2 vols (London, 1916)

Firth Green, R., and R. Moffat, 'Schynbalds in *The Awntyrs off Arthure* (l. 395): Two Notes', *Notes & Queries*, unnumbered (2020), 1–6

Frangioni, L., 'Bacinetti e altre difese della testa nella documentazione di una azienda mercantile, 1366–1410', *Archaeologia medievale* 11 (1984), 507–22

Gelli, J., and G. Moretti, *Gli armaroli Milanese: i Missaglia e la loro casa* (Milan, 1903)

Hartshorne, C. H., 'Caernarvon Castle', *Archaeologia Cambrensis* 1 (1855), 242–6

Hudson, W., 'Norwich Militia in the 14th Century', *Norfolk Archaeology* 14 (1901), 316–20

Hunter, J., 'On Measures [...] for the Apprehension of Sir Thomas de Gournay, one of the Murderers of King Edward II', *Archaeologia* 27 (1838), 274–97

Jones, R. W., *Bloodied Banners: Martial Display on the Medieval Battlefield* (Woodbridge, 2010)

— '".j. veel feble fauchon dil anxien temps." The Selection of the Falchion as Symbol of Tenure: Form, Function and Symbolism', *The Sword: Form and Thought*, ed. L. Deutscher, M. Kaiser and S. Wetzler (Woodbridge, 2019), 167–75

Loades, M., *The Crossbow* (Oxford, 2018)

Lobineau, G. A., *Histoire de Bretagne*, 2 vols (Paris, 1707)

Mann, J. G., 'Armour and the "New English Dictionary"', *The Connoisseur: An Illustrated Magazine for Collectors*, vol. 82, no. 326 (October 1928), 121–2

— Preface to O. Trapp, *The Armoury of the Castle of Churburg*, trans. J. G. Mann, 2 vols (London, 1929), I, v–xviii

— 'The Sanctuary of the Madonna delle Grazie [...] Italian Armour during the 15th Century', *Archaeologia* 80 (1930), 29–54

— 'The Visor of a 14th-Century Bascinet found at Pevensey Castle', *Antiquaries Journal* 16 (1936), 412–19

— 'Two 14th-Century Gauntlets from Ripon Cathedral', *Antiquaries Journal* 22 (1942), 113–22

— 'Three Armours in the Scott Collection', *Scottish Art Review* 6 (1956), 2–17

— 'The Nomenclature of Armour', *Transactions of the Monumental Brass Society* 9 (1961), 414–28

Merrifield, M. P., *Original Treatises [...] on the Arts of Painting [...]*, 2 vols (London, 1849)

Moffat, R., 'The *Manner of Arming Knights for the Tourney*: A Re-Interpretation of an Important Early-14th Century Arming Treatise', *Arms & Armour* 7 (2010), 5–29

— 'Armourers and Armour: Textual Evidence', *The Encyclopedia of Medieval Dress and Textiles of the British Isles, c. 450–1450*, ed. G. Owen-Crocker, E. Coatsworth and M. Hayward (Leiden, 2012), 49–52

— 'The Importance of Being Harnest: Armour, Heraldry and Recognition in the Mêlée', *Battle & Bloodshed: The Medieval World at War*, ed. L. Bleach and K. Borrill (Newcastle, 2013), 5–24

— '"A hard harnest man": The Armour of George Dunbar, 9th Earl of March', *Transactions of the East Lothian Antiquarian and Field Naturalists' Society* 30 (2015), 21–37

— '"Armed & redy to come to the felde": Arming for the Judicial Duel in 15th-Century England', *Courts of Chivalry and Admiralty in Late Medieval Europe*, ed. A. Musson and N. Ramsay (Woodbridge, 2018), 121–33

— 'A Sign of Victory?: "Scottish Swords" and Other Weapons in the Possession of the "Auld Innemie"', *Arms & Armour* 15 (2018), 122–43

— 'Arms and Armour', *A Companion to Chivalry*, ed. R. W. Jones and P. Coss (Woodbridge, 2019), 159–85

— '*Alle myne harneys for the justes*: Documents as a Source for Medieval Jousting Armour', *The Medieval Tournament as Spectacle: Tourneys, Jousts and Pas d'Armes, 1100–1600*, ed. A. V. Murray and K. Watts (Woodbridge, 2020), 77–97

— 'A word "I was delighted to meet": why we must now bid Auf Wiedersehen to *Hounskull* as the name for the "pig-faced" basinet', *Arms and Armour: Journal of the Royal Armouries* (forthcoming)

Moffat, R., and J. Spriggs, 'The Use of Baleen for Arms, Armour and Heraldic Crests in Medieval Britain', *Antiquaries Journal* 88 (2008), 207–15

Oakeshott, E., *The Sword in the Age of Chivalry* (Woodbridge, 1994)

Pyhrr, S. W., 'Armor from the Imperial Ottoman Arsenal', *Metropolitan Museum Journal* 24 (1989), 85–116

Reid, W., and E. M. Burgess, 'A Habergeon of Westwale', *Antiquaries Journal* 40 (1960), 46–57

Retsch, C., 'Warum die Hundsgugel im Spätmittelalter kein Helm war (und was die englische Haube für ein Helm gewesen sein könnte)', *Hieb- und Stichfest. Waffenkunde und Living History. Festschrift für Dr. Alfred Geibig. Jahrbuch der Coburger Landesstiftung* (Petersberg, 2020), 190–215

Richard, J. M., *Une Petite-Nièce de Saint Louis: Mahaut, comtesse d'Artois et de Bourgogne, 1302–1329* (Paris, 1887)

Richardson, T., 'Springald Sizes in 14th-Century England', *ICOMAM 50: Papers on Arms and Military History, 1957–2007*, ed. R. D. Smith (Leeds, 2007), 326–31

— *The Tower Armoury in the Fourteenth Century* (Leeds, 2016)

Rijkelijkhuizen, M., and M. Volken, 'A poor man's armour? Late-medieval leather armour from excavations in the Netherlands', *Leather in Warfare: Attack, Defence and the Unexpected*, ed. Q. Mould (Leeds, 2017), 57–77

Scalini, M., *The Armoury of the Castle of Churburg* (Udine, 1996)

Schmid, W. M., 'Passauer Waffenwesen', *Zeitschrift für Historische Waffenkunde* 8 (1918–20), 317–42

Schmidt, H., *The Book of the Buckler* (Quidenham, 2015)

Scott, J. G., 'Two 14th-Century Helms found in Scotland', *Journal of the Arms & Armour Society* 4 (1962), 68–71

Scott-Macnab, D., 'The Treatment of *Assegai* & *Zagaie* by the *OED*, and of *Assegai* by the *Dictionary of South African English*', *Neophilologus* 96 (2012), 151–63

Stothard, C. A., *The Monumental Effigies of Great Britain* (London, 1876)

Thordeman, B., *Armour from the Battle of Wisby, 1361*, 2 vols (Copenhagen, 1939)

Trapp, O., *The Armoury of the Castle of Churburg*, trans. J. G. Mann, 2 vols (London, 1929)

Ure, D., *The History of Rutherglen and East Kilbride* (Glasgow, 1793)

Wagner, A. R., and J. G. Mann, 'A 15th-Century Description of the Brass of Sir Hugh Hastings at Elsing, Norfolk', *Antiquaries Journal* 19 (1939), 421–8

Ward, M., *The Livery Collar in Late Medieval England and Wales: Politics, Identity and Affinity* (Woodbridge, 2016)

Way, A., 'Accounts of the Constables of the Castle of Dover', *Archaeological Journal* 11 (1854), 381–8

Woosnam-Savage, R. C., 'Robert Lyons Scott 1871–1939: A Biographical Note', F. Joubert, *Catalogue of the Collection of European Arms & Armour formed at Greenock by R. L. Scott*, ed. R. C. Woosnam-Savage and T. Capwell, 2nd edn (Huntingdon, 2006), i–ix

— Woosnam-Savage, R. C., and K. DeVries, 'Battle Trauma in Medieval Warfare', *Wounds and Wound Repair in Medieval Culture*, ed. L. Tracy and K. DeVries (Leiden, 2015), 27–56

Theses and Dissertations

Dupras, N., 'Medieval Armourers and their Workshops' (Ph.D. thesis, University of Leeds, 2012)

Nickel, H. 'Der mittelalterliche Reiterschild des Abendlandes' (Doctoral Dissertation, Freie Universität Berlin, 1958)

Index

References to the illustrations are in **bold**.

Billingsgate, armour shipped from the Tower
  to 157
Black Prince, Edward the,
  armour at seven years old 14, 22, 84
  defeated participant in a duel presented
    to 108
  first battle 14
  funeral procession 169
  gifts from 14
  register of 108
  squire of (Henry Braybrooke) at a joust of
    peace 104
  tomb effigy 29, **224**
  wardrobe account 84
  will 169
Blair, Claude
  on standardized terminology xxxii–xxxiii
  on tomb sculpture 28–9
  on types of mail 264
blazon see under heraldry
boats, for carriage see under ships
Bohemia
  pavise (shield) from **270**
  sword of 126–7, 284
Bohun, family's descent from Godfrey of
    Bouillon 7 see also Hereford, Humphrey
    earl of
Bolingbroke see Derby, Henry, earl of
Bonde, Nicholas, gifted a pair of plates by the
    Black Prince 110
Bonet, Honoré, Tree of Battles 269
Bonis brothers, merchants of Montauban 18,
    98
Bordeaux
  English-controlled 164, 230
  Froissart's opinion of weapons 10
  keeper of, Robert Wykford 164
  Stephen atte Fryth's opinion of swords 10
  swords 284
  quality weapons made in 10
  view mark on weapons 10
Boucicaut, maréschal of France
  exercises of 22, 174–5
  gifted mail armour by Louis, duke of
    Orléans 199
Bouillon, Godfrey of
  antecedent of Bohun family 7
  conquest of Jerusalem 7
  haubergeon of 7, 77
  Sir Philippe de Mézières
    account of his single combat 194–5
    description of in his arming jupon 259
Brabant, county of
  armour for Henry VIII sought in 9
  cloth 203
Braidwood Gill helm xxii, **255**
Brambletye, joust of peace at 204

Bray, sword of 61, 284
Braybrook, Henry
  coat of arms described in a letter of challenge
    to a joust of peace 104
  gifted armour by the Black Prince 110
Bren, Llywelyn, armour 59
British Museum, kettlehat 25
Brittany, arms and armour brought from to the
    Tower 96
Brocas, John, gifted a kettlehat by Edward
    III 86
Brokas, John, bequest to 166
Bromyard, John, preaching of 20, 23, 37
Broomhill Priory, heraldic funeral at 28
Broune, Philip, armourer of London 166
Bruges, Guillaume, armourer of 184
Brun, Robert, study of the Datini archives 19
Brussels
  Edward III gifting armour at 87
  noise of the armourers of xxii
Brut chronicle see under chroniclers
Brutus, King of Albion 104
Bryan, Guy, jousting equipment gifted by
    Edward III 87
Bunbury Church, bequest to 204
Bungay, Hugh, Keeper of Armour to Edward of
    Caernarfon 7, 44–6, 65, 68
Burghersh
  Lord Bartholomew, will 149
  Sir Bartholomew, gifted armour by the Black
    Prince 110–12
Burgos, bishop of see Alonso
Burgundy, Philip duke of 183
Burley, Sir Simon
  inventory 191
  soldiering career xxvi
Bury Chest, painting **234**
Bury Saint Edmunds, Edward III gifting armour
    at 86
Buttord, Sir Baudewyn, gifted armour by the
    Black Prince 110–11
Byker, John, King's Crossbow-Maker in the
    Tower of London 160

Calais
  arrows sent to from the Tower 157
  Black Prince gifting armour at 111
  victualler of, Willam Redness 164
Calveley, Sir Hugh
  receives pavises (shields) from the Tower 164
  will 204
cannon see under guns
Canterbury
  Black Prince's corpse led through 169
  Cathedral 29, 224
care of armour 8, 14–15; wrapping in
    wool 184 see also emery, oil, and rust

Armour and Weapons